SAVE
58% OFF
THE COVER PRICE!
THAT'S LIKE GETTING 7 ISSUES FREE!

THIS MONTHLY MAGAZINE IS INJECTED WITH 6 OF THE ___JO ___M GA R___ OF A___ SE CULTURE, STYLE, & MORE!

☐ I want 12 GIANT issues of *Shojo Beat* for $29.95*!

NAME ....

ADDRESS ....

CITY .... STATE .... ZIP ....

EMAIL ADDRESS ....

DATE OF BIRTH ....

☐ **Yes!** Send me via email information, advertising, offers, and promotions related to VIZ Media, *Shojo Beat*, and/or their business partners.

☐ CHECK ENCLOSED (payable to *Shojo Beat*) ☐ BILL ME LATER

CREDIT CARD: ☐ VISA ☐ MC

ACCOUNT #: ....

EXPIRE DATE: ....

SIGNATURE ....

CLIP & MAIL TO:
SHOJO BEAT SUBSCRIPTIONS SERVICE DEPT.
P.O. BOX 438
MOUNT MORRIS, IL 61054-0438

P9GNC1

* Canada price: $41.95 USD, including GST, HST, and QST. US/CAN orders only.
Allow 6-8 weeks for delivery. *Shojo Beat* is rated T+ for Older Teen and is recommended for ages 16 and up.
HONEY HUNT © Miki Aihara/Shogakukan Inc. KOKO DEBUT © 2003 by Kazune Kawahara/SHUEISHA Inc.
Vampire Knight © Matsuri Hino 2004/HAKUSENSHA, Inc.

ratings.viz.com   www.viz.com

Honey Hunt

story and art by

2 Miki Aihara

CHARACTERS

YURA ONOZUKA ★
The only child of celebrity parents. She is a surprisingly average, ordinary girl, considering her father is a world-famous musician and her mother is an award-winning actress.

KEIICHI MIZOROGI ★
President of the entertainment company Meteorite Productions. He scouted Yura and became her manager.

Q-TA MINAMITANI ★
The singer of popular music group Assha (also known as "h.a."). He likes Yura.

HARUKA ★
A member of the pop idol group KNIGHTS. Q-ta's twin brother and rival.

Honey Hunt 2

STORY

★ When Yura's parents tell her they are getting a divorce, Yura becomes determined to make her own way and become a better actress than her mother. She moves in with her new agent Keiichi and begins her new life.

★ After many failed auditions, Yura finally lands the lead role for the "Noodle Girl" campaign. At her first meeting with the other cast members she realizes that Keiichi didn't give her all the facts about the role, which is actually a big project involving a commercial and a tie-in TV drama. She also learns that Haruka and Q-ta will be working on the project with her and receives congratulatory kisses from both of them.

★ After the kissing incident, Yura can't stop thinking about Q-ta. She tries to focus for her first shoot and is again distracted when she runs into her mother at the studio.

★ Yura's mom tells her that she doesn't have the talent to become an actress and should go to school instead. Haruka thinks it's "not cool" that Yura let her mom talk to her that way, but Yura knows that the only way to get back at her mom is to prove her wrong by succeeding in her acting career.

★ However, Yura's first day on the job is foiled when she arrives at wardrobe and finds a huge stain on the uniform she is supposed to wear for the campaign photo shoot...

Honey Hunt 2

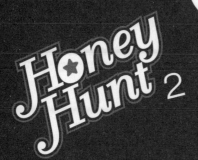

CONTENTS

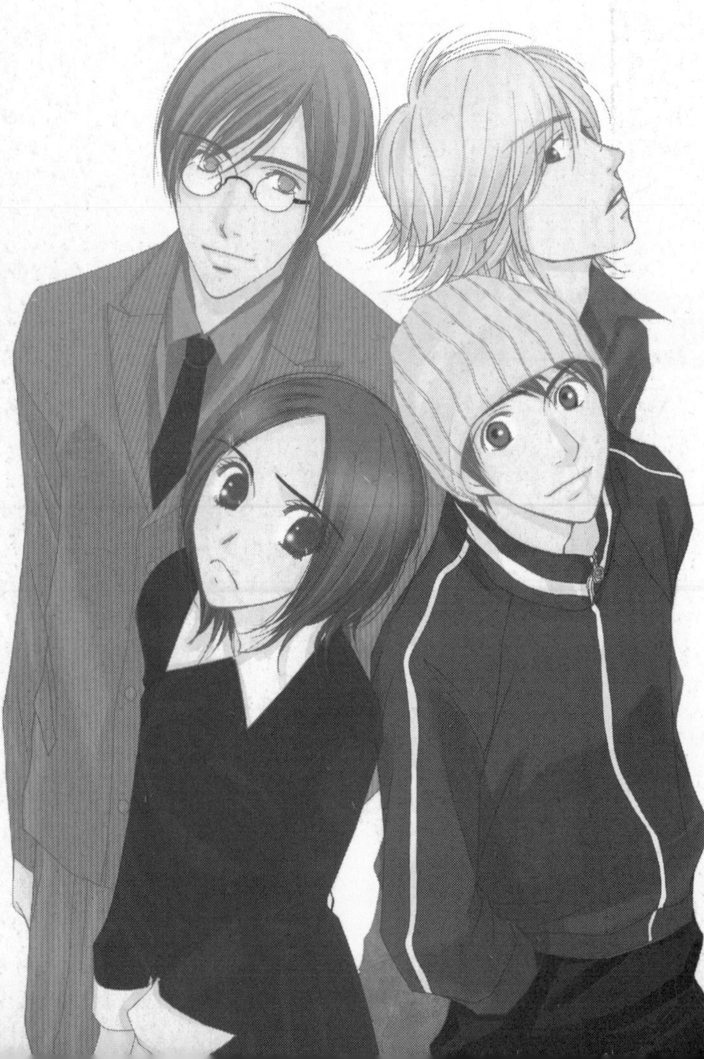

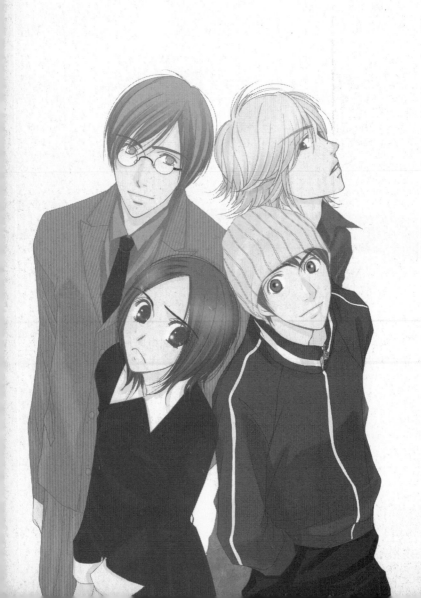

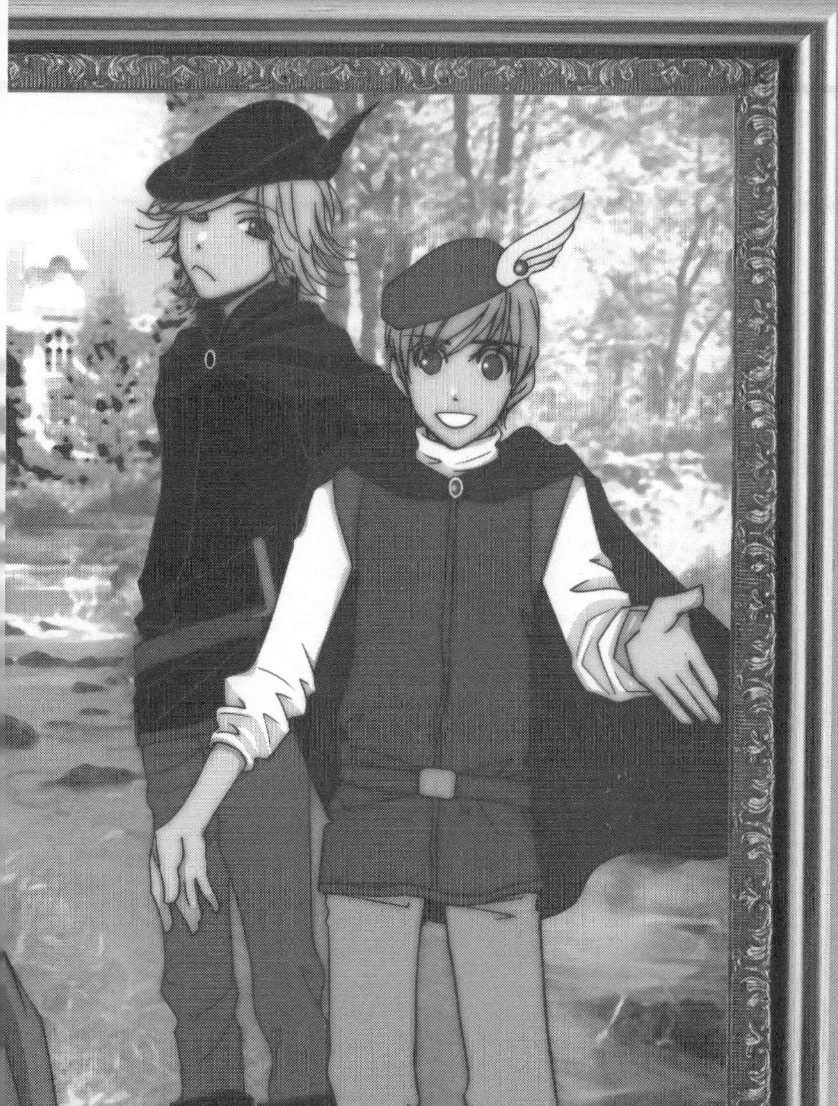

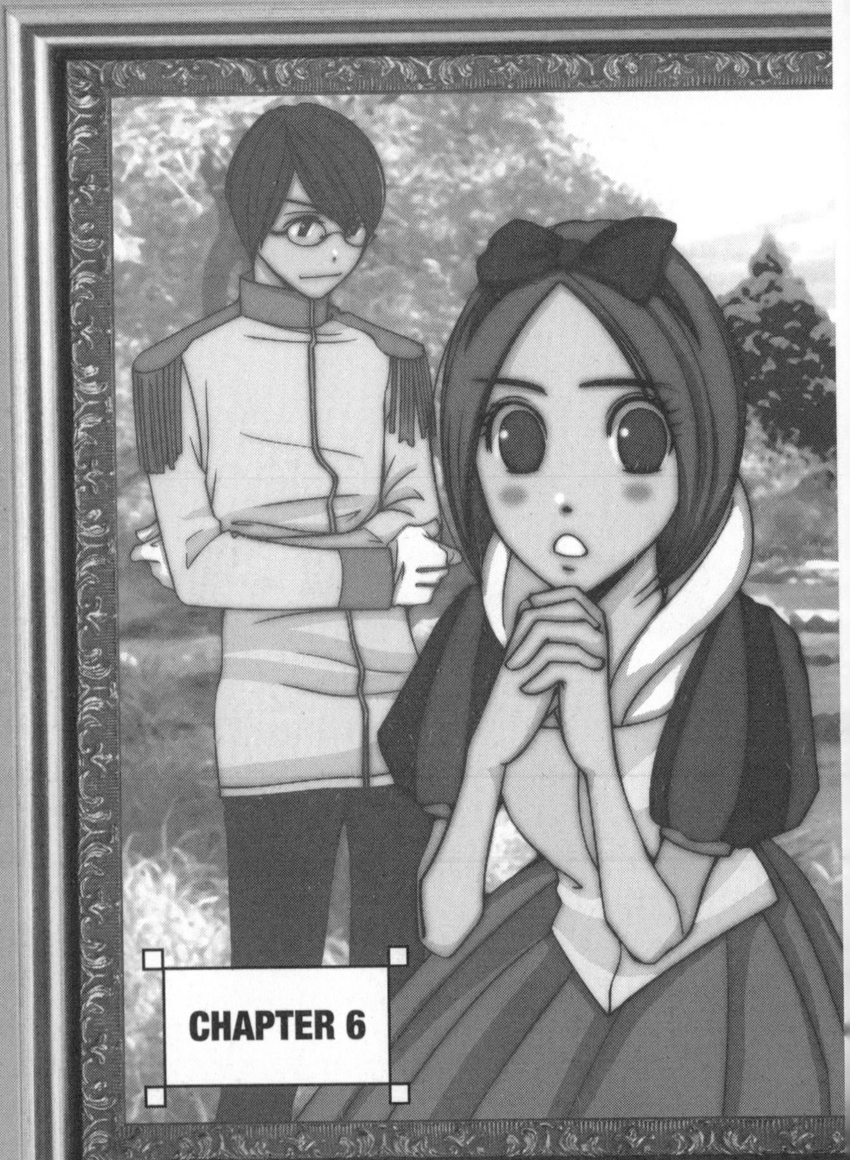
CHAPTER 6

Honey Hunt 02

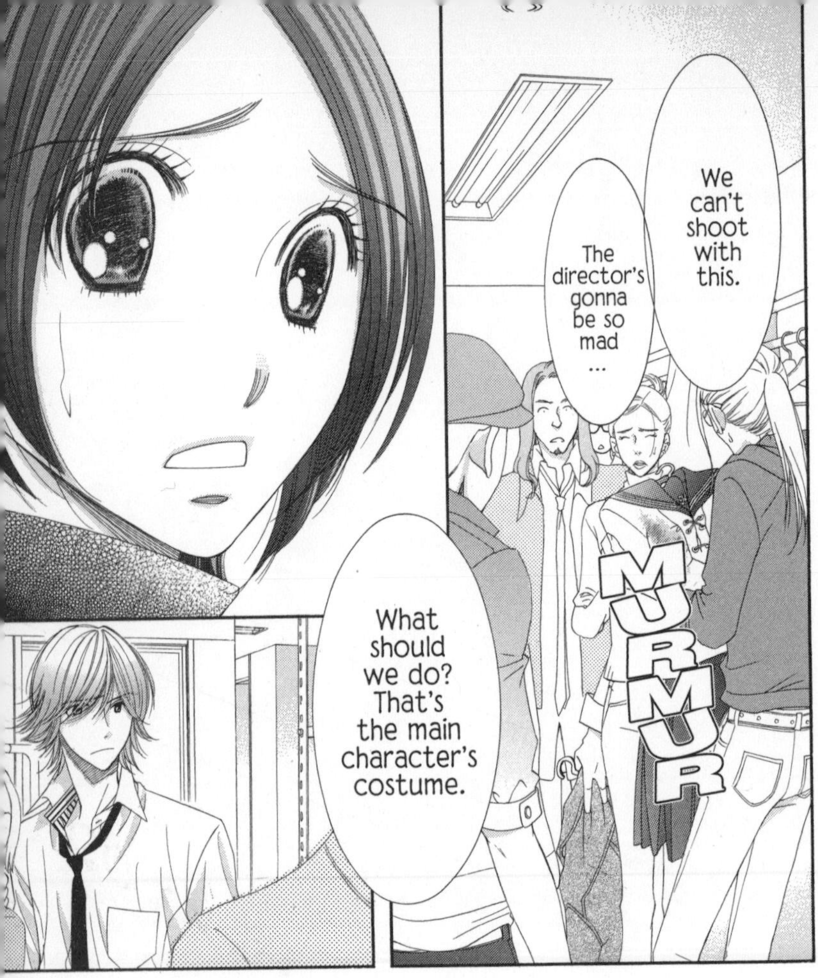
We can't shoot with this.
The director's gonna be so mad ...
MURMUR
What should we do? That's the main character's costume.

Honey Hunt

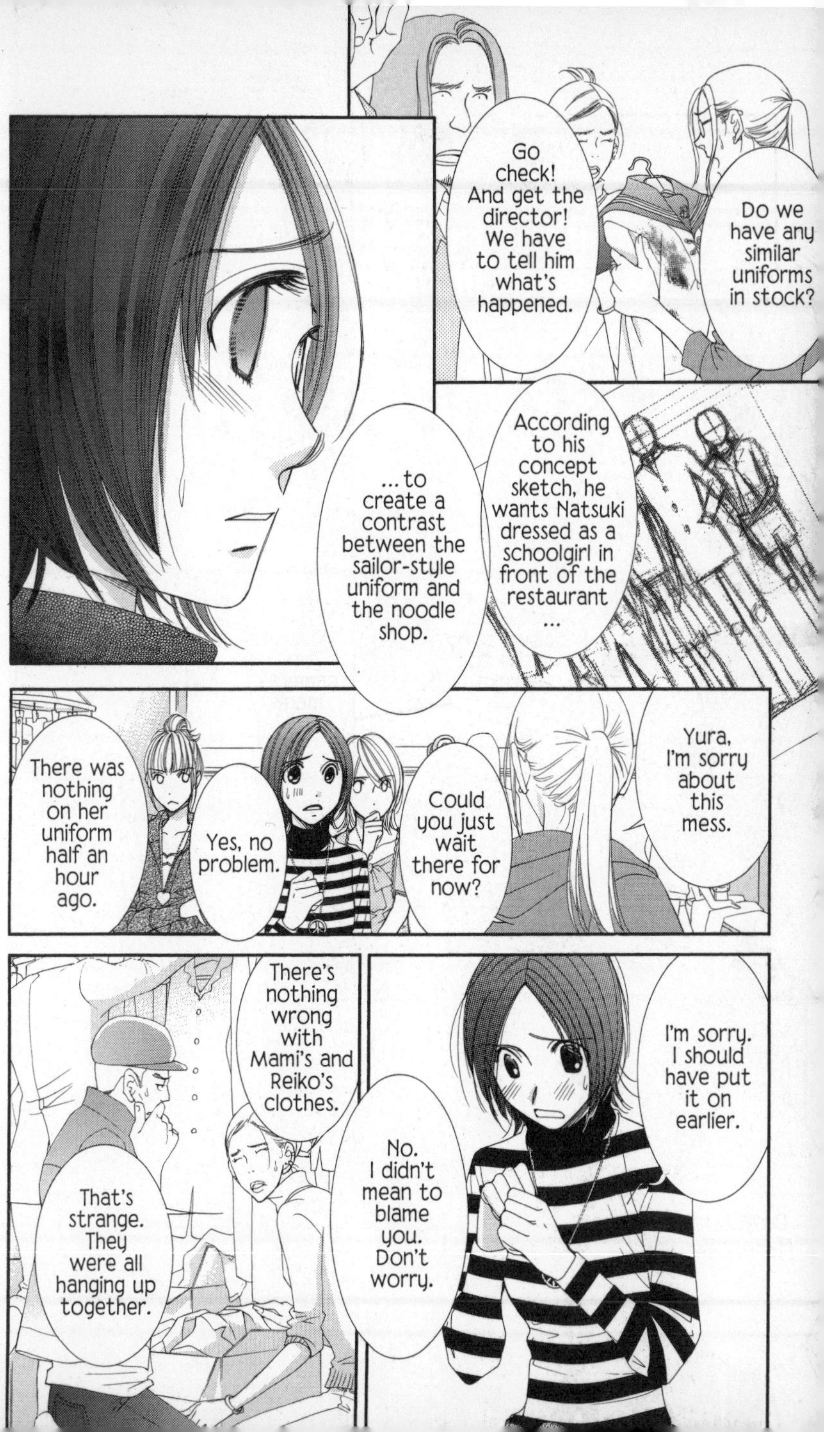
Do we have any similar uniforms in stock?
Go check! And get the director! We have to tell him what's happened.
According to his concept sketch, he wants Natsuki dressed as a schoolgirl in front of the restaurant ...
... to create a contrast between the sailor-style uniform and the noodle shop.
Yura, I'm sorry about this mess.
Could you just wait there for now?
Yes, no problem.
There was nothing on her uniform half an hour ago.
I'm sorry. I should have put it on earlier.
No. I didn't mean to blame you. Don't worry.
There's nothing wrong with Mami's and Reiko's clothes.
That's strange. They were all hanging up together.

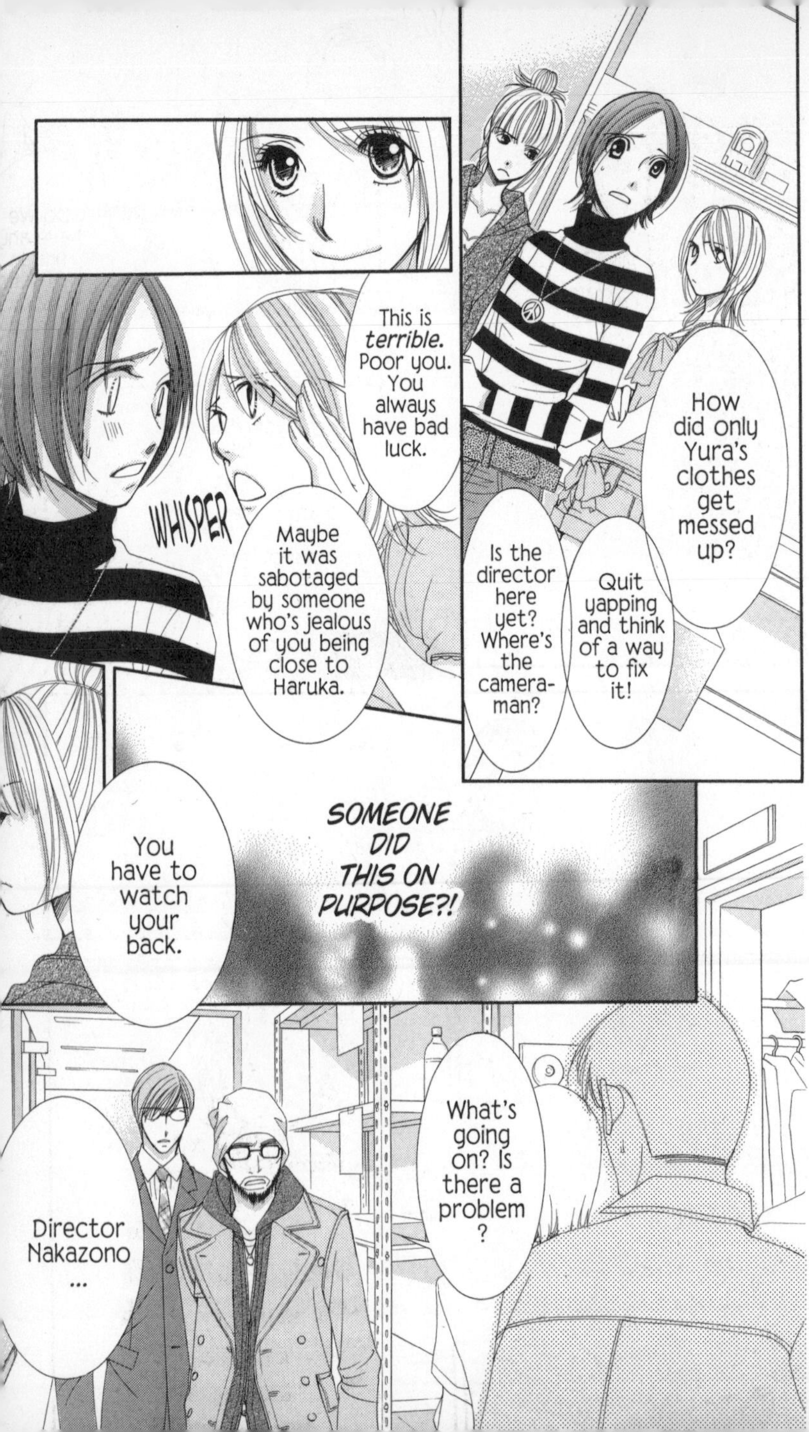
How did only Yura's clothes get messed up?
Quit yapping and think of a way to fix it!
Is the director here yet? Where's the cameraman?
This is *terrible*. Poor you. You always have bad luck.
WHISPER
Maybe it was sabotaged by someone who's jealous of you being close to Haruka.
SOMEONE DID THIS ON PURPOSE?!
You have to watch your back.
What's going on? Is there a problem?
Director Nakazono ...

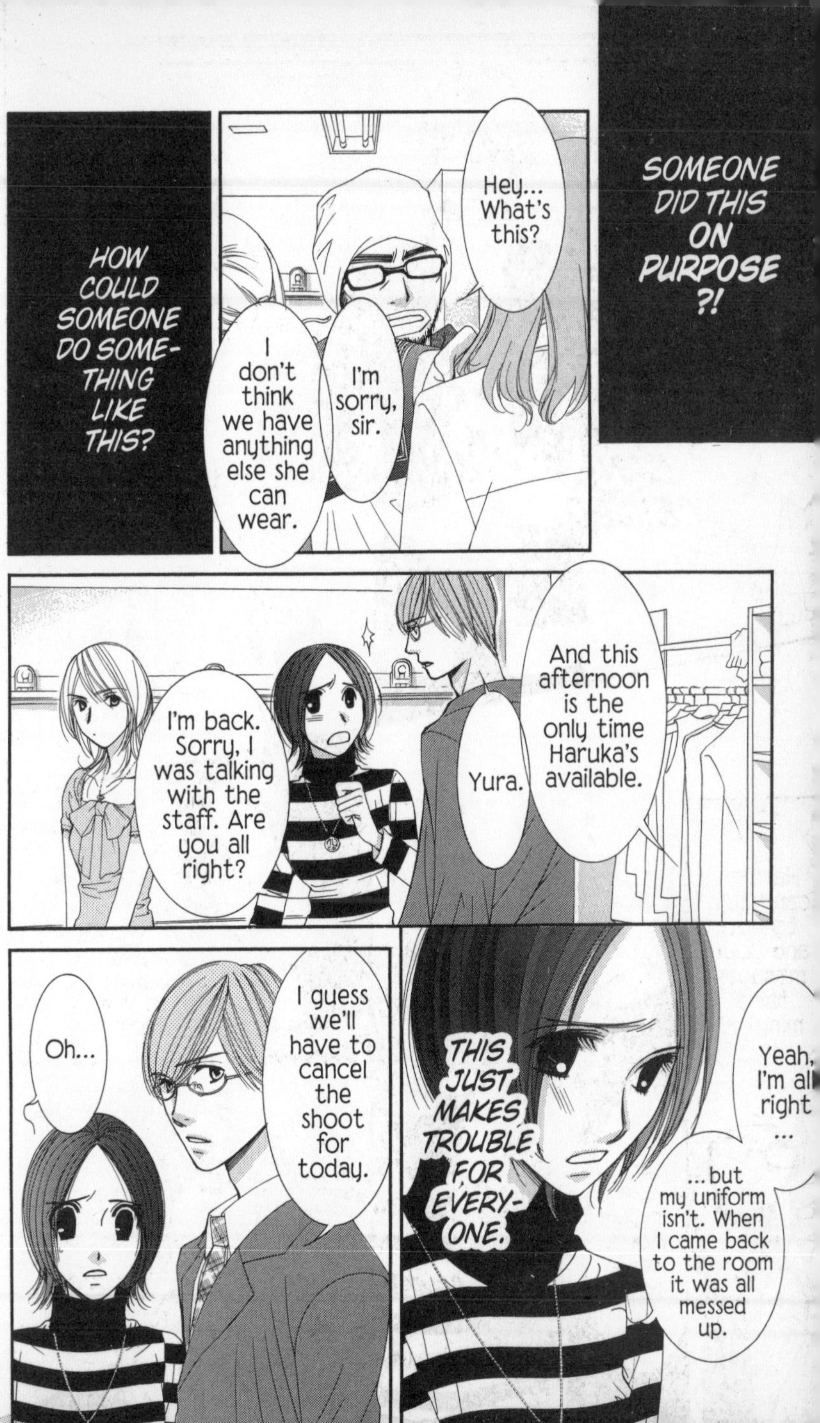
SOMEONE DID THIS ON PURPOSE?!
Hey... What's this?
I'm sorry, sir.
I don't think we have anything else she can wear.
HOW COULD SOMEONE DO SOME-THING LIKE THIS?
And this afternoon is the only time Haruka's available.
Yura.
I'm back. Sorry, I was talking with the staff. Are you all right?
Yeah, I'm all right...
...but my uniform isn't. When I came back to the room it was all messed up.
THIS JUST MAKES TROUBLE FOR EVERY-ONE.
I guess we'll have to cancel the shoot for today.
Oh...

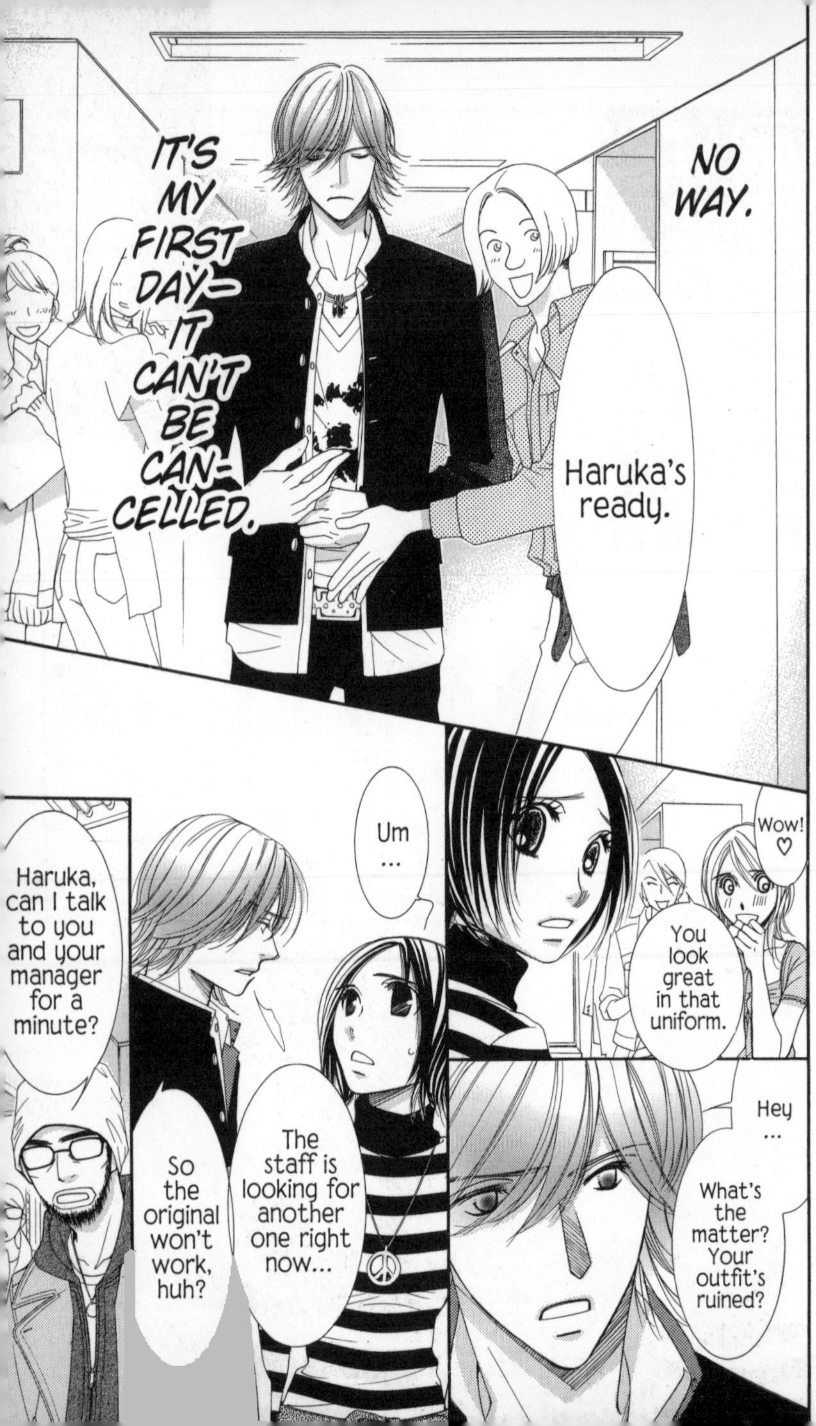
NO WAY.
Haruka's ready.
IT'S MY FIRST DAY—IT CAN'T BE CAN-CELLED.
Wow! ♡
You look great in that uniform.
Hey ...
What's the matter? Your outfit's ruined?
Um ...
The staff is looking for another one right now...
So the original won't work, huh?
Haruka, can I talk to you and your manager for a minute?

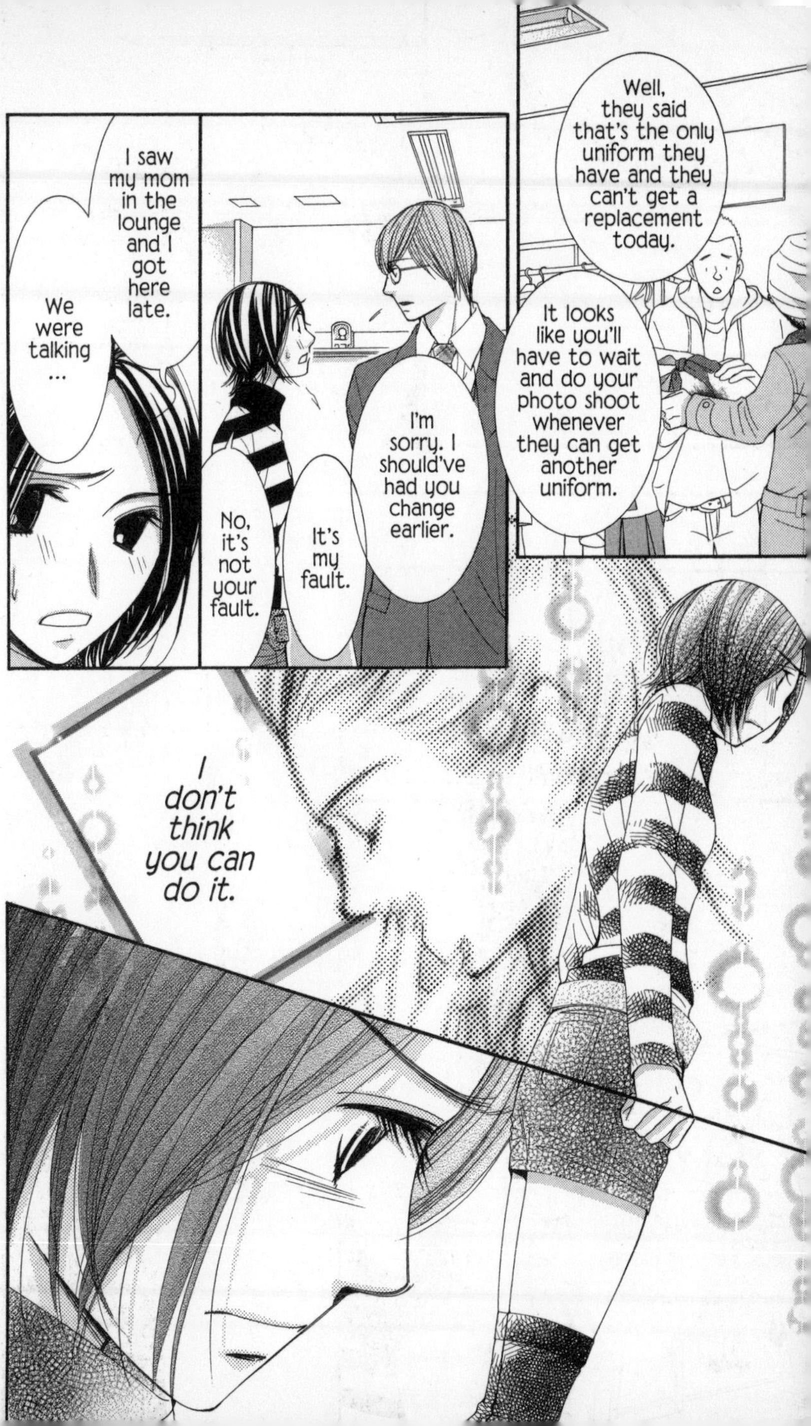
Well, they said that's the only uniform they have and they can't get a replacement today.
It looks like you'll have to wait and do your photo shoot whenever they can get another uniform.
I'm sorry. I should've had you change earlier.
It's my fault.
No, it's not your fault.
I saw my mom in the lounge and I got here late.
We were talking ...
I don't think you can do it.

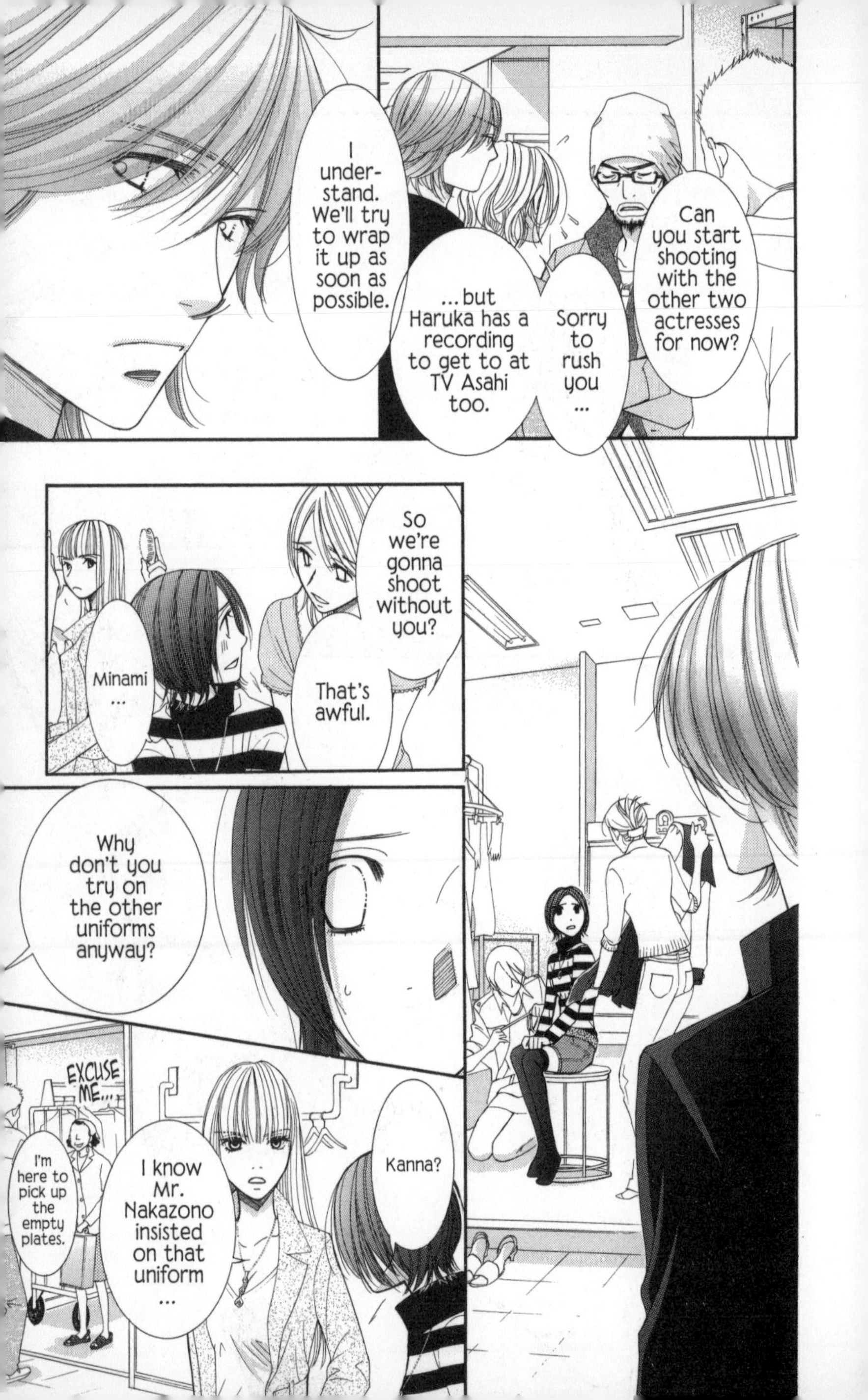
Can you start shooting with the other two actresses for now?
Sorry to rush you ...
...but Haruka has a recording to get to at TV Asahi too.
I under-stand. We'll try to wrap it up as soon as possible.
So we're gonna shoot without you?
That's awful.
Minami ...
Why don't you try on the other uniforms anyway?
Kanna?
I know Mr. Nakazono insisted on that uniform ...
EXCUSE ME...
I'm here to pick up the empty plates.

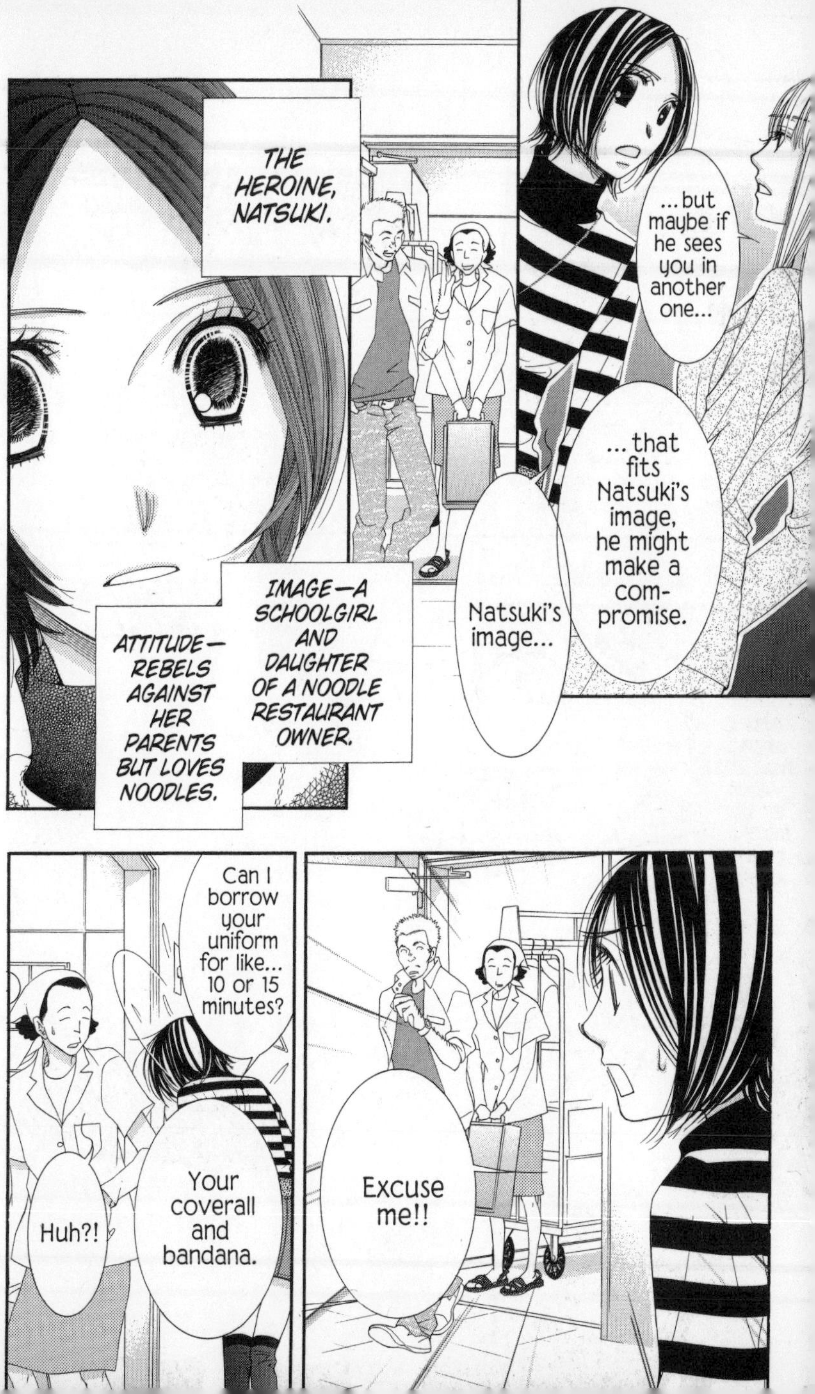
...but maybe if he sees you in another one...
...that fits Natsuki's image, he might make a com-promise.
Natsuki's image...
THE HEROINE, NATSUKI.
IMAGE—A SCHOOLGIRL AND DAUGHTER OF A NOODLE RESTAURANT OWNER.
ATTITUDE—REBELS AGAINST HER PARENTS BUT LOVES NOODLES.
Excuse me!!
Can I borrow your uniform for like... 10 or 15 minutes?
Your coverall and bandana.
Huh?!

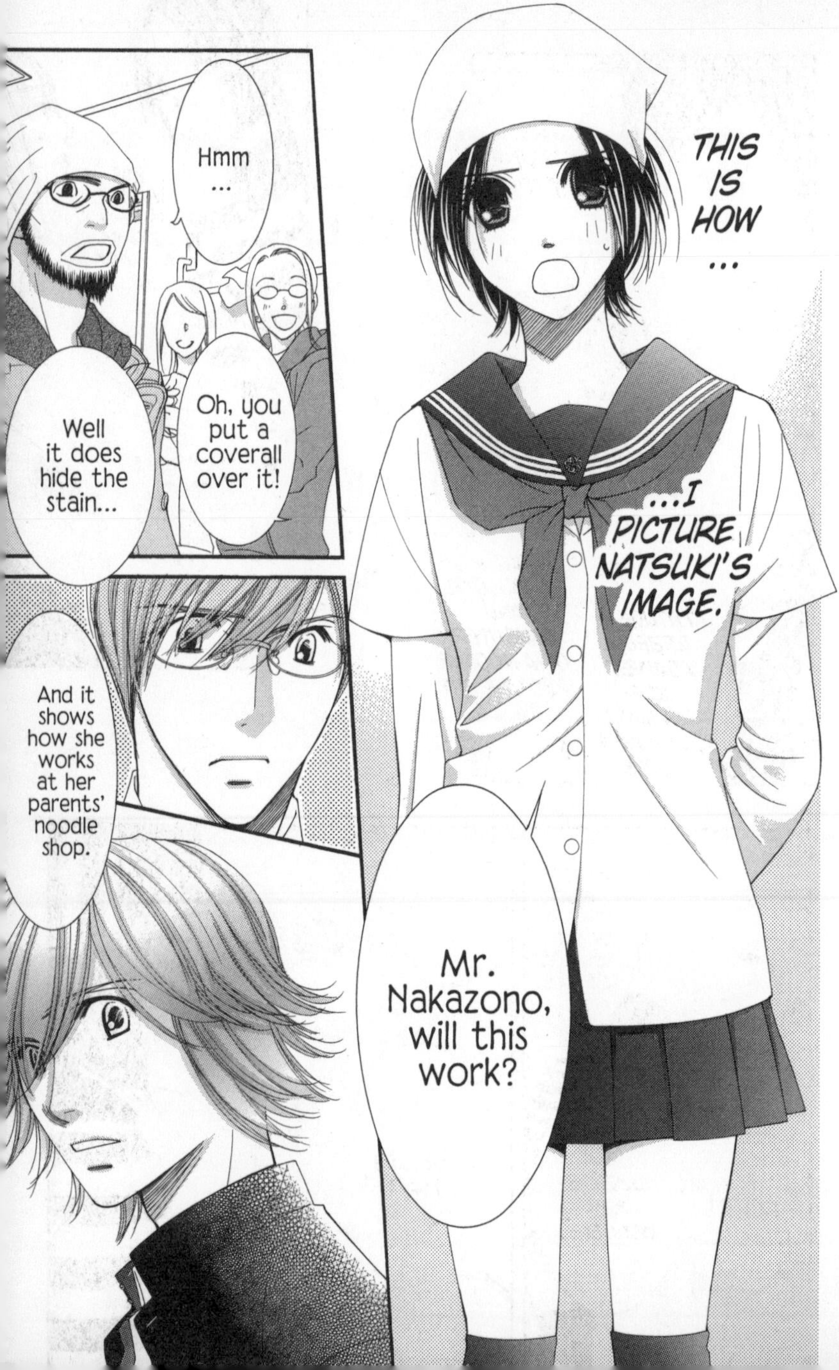
THIS IS HOW ...
...I PICTURE NATSUKI'S IMAGE.
Mr. Nakazono, will this work?
Hmm ...
Oh, you put a coverall over it!
Well it does hide the stain...
And it shows how she works at her parents' noodle shop.

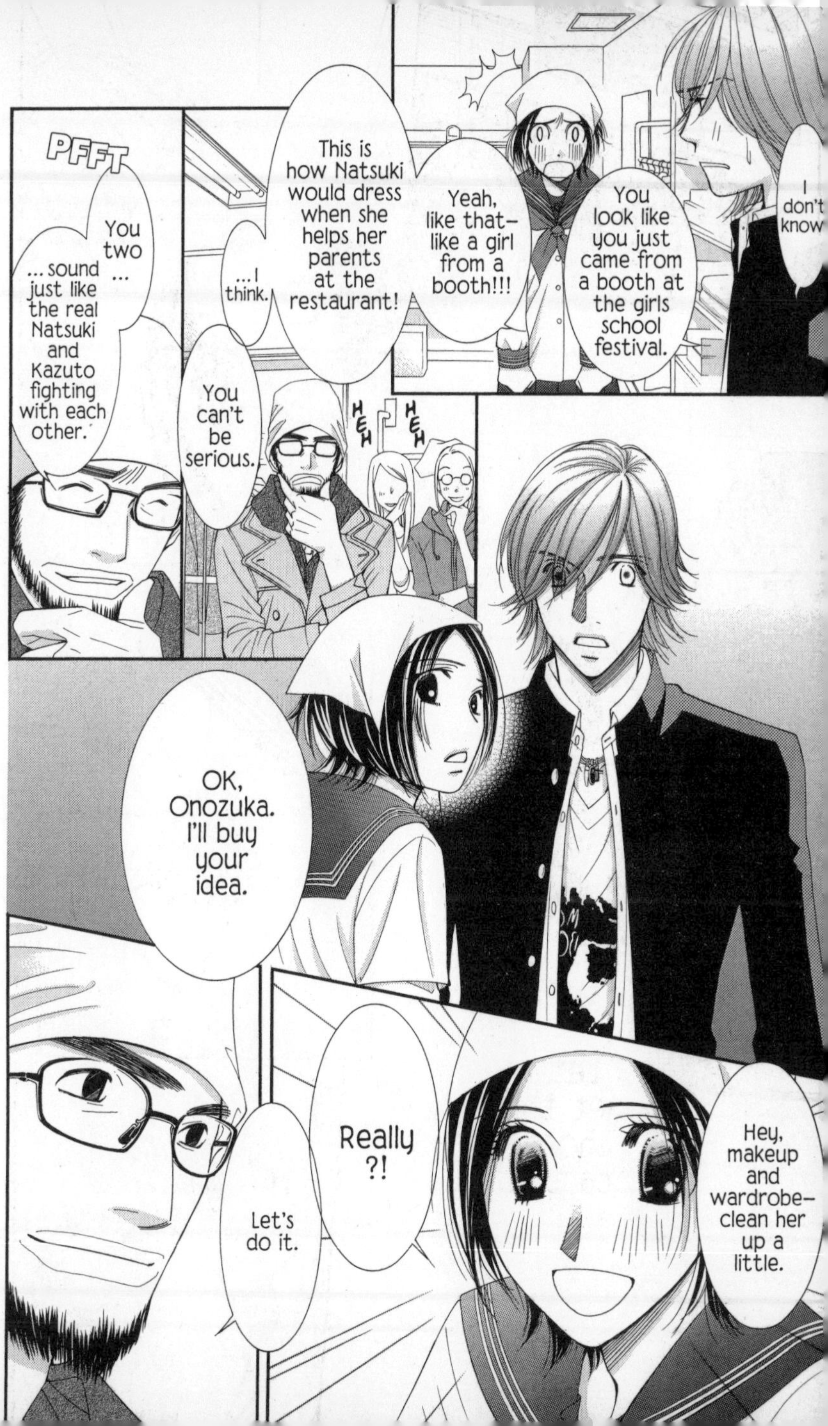
I don't know
You look like you just came from a booth at the girls school festival.
Yeah, like that—like a girl from a booth!!!
This is how Natsuki would dress when she helps her parents at the restaurant!
...I think.
You can't be serious.
HEH HEH
PFFT
You two ...
...sound just like the real Natsuki and Kazuto fighting with each other.
OK, Onozuka. I'll buy your idea.
Hey, makeup and wardrobe—clean her up a little.
Really?!
Let's do it.

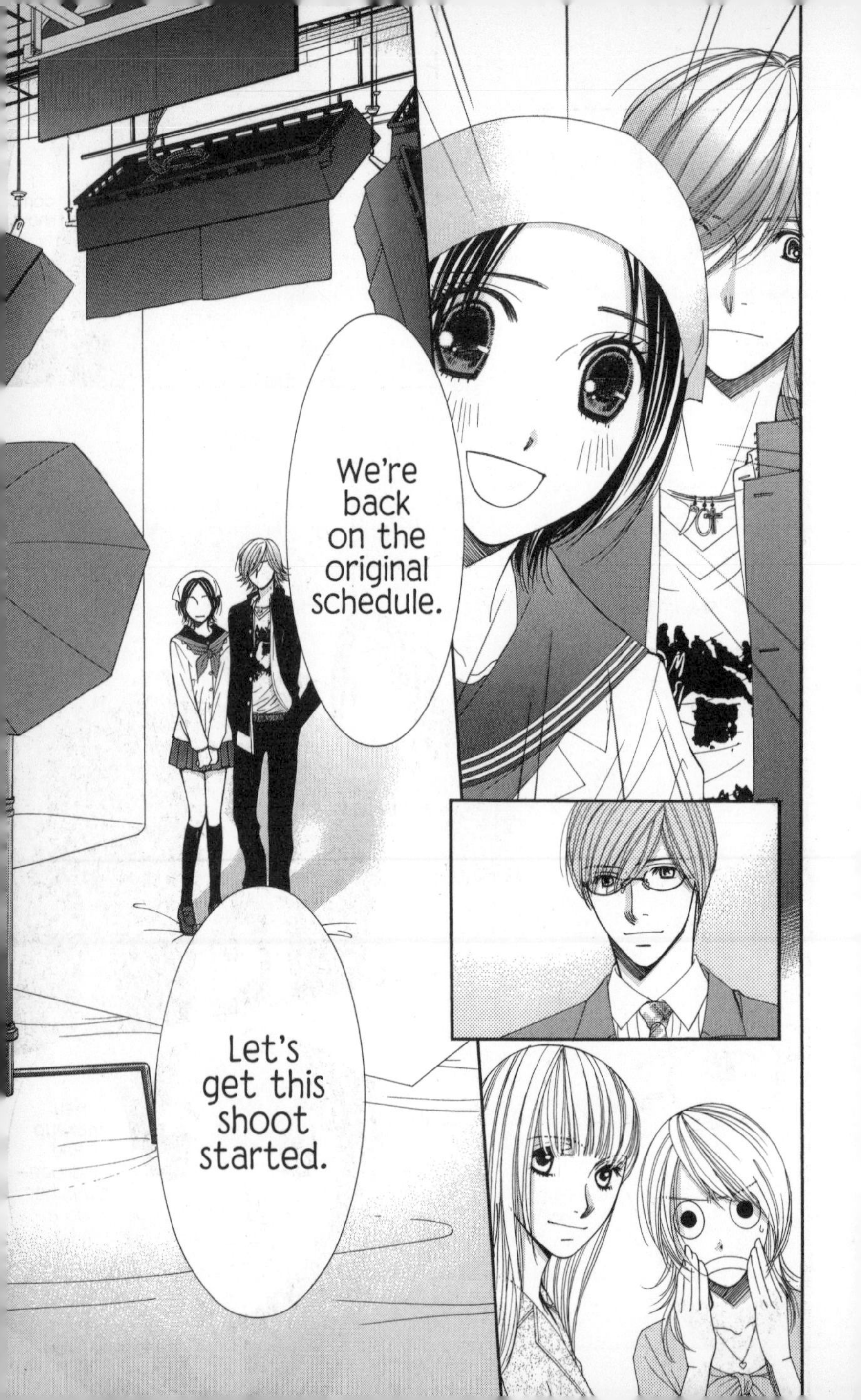
We're back on the original schedule.
Let's get this shoot started.

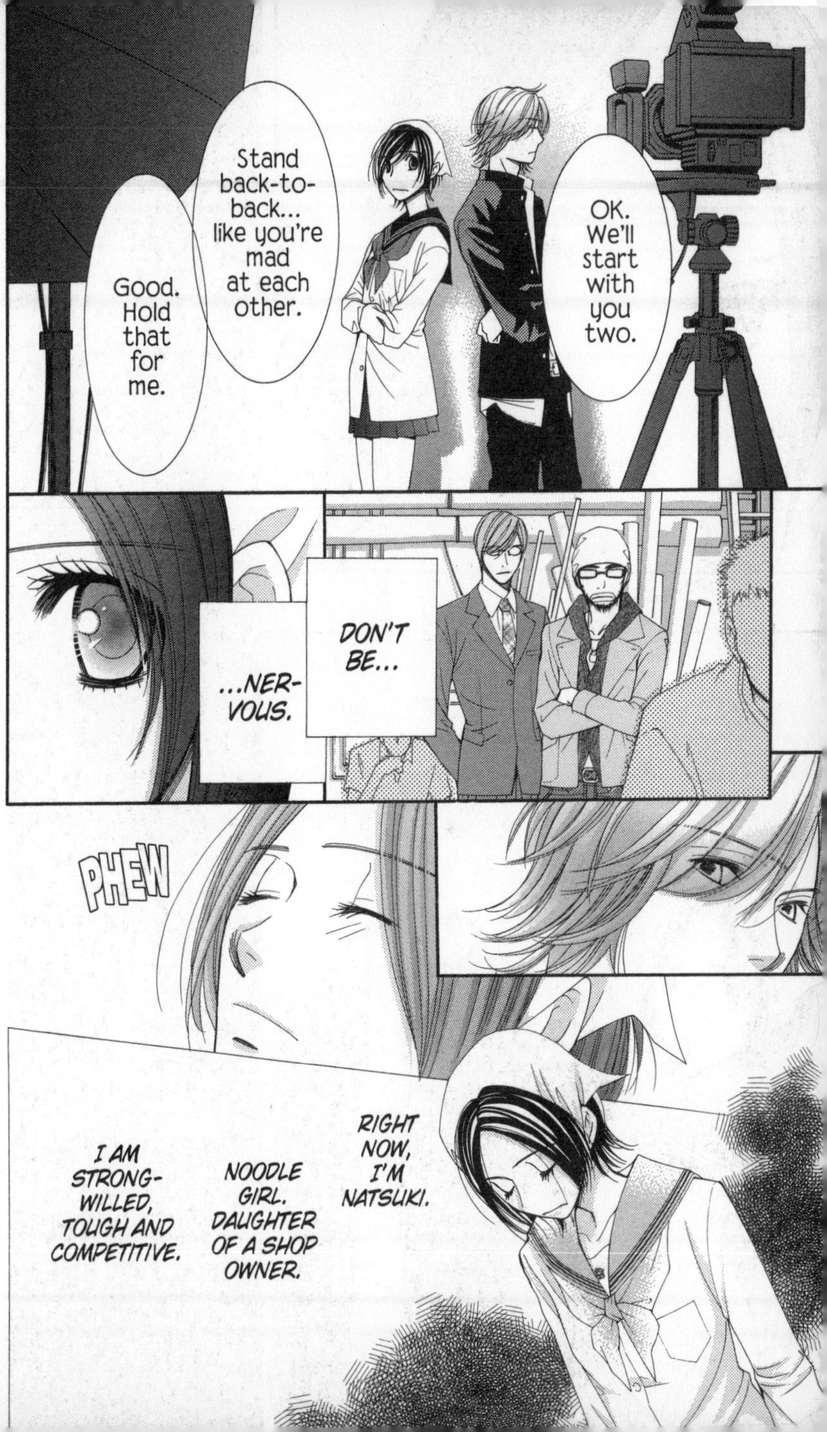
OK. We'll start with you two.
Stand back-to-back... like you're mad at each other.
Good. Hold that for me.
DON'T BE...
...NER-VOUS.
PHEW
RIGHT NOW, I'M NATSUKI.
NOODLE GIRL. DAUGHTER OF A SHOP OWNER.
I AM STRONG-WILLED, TOUGH AND COMPETITIVE.

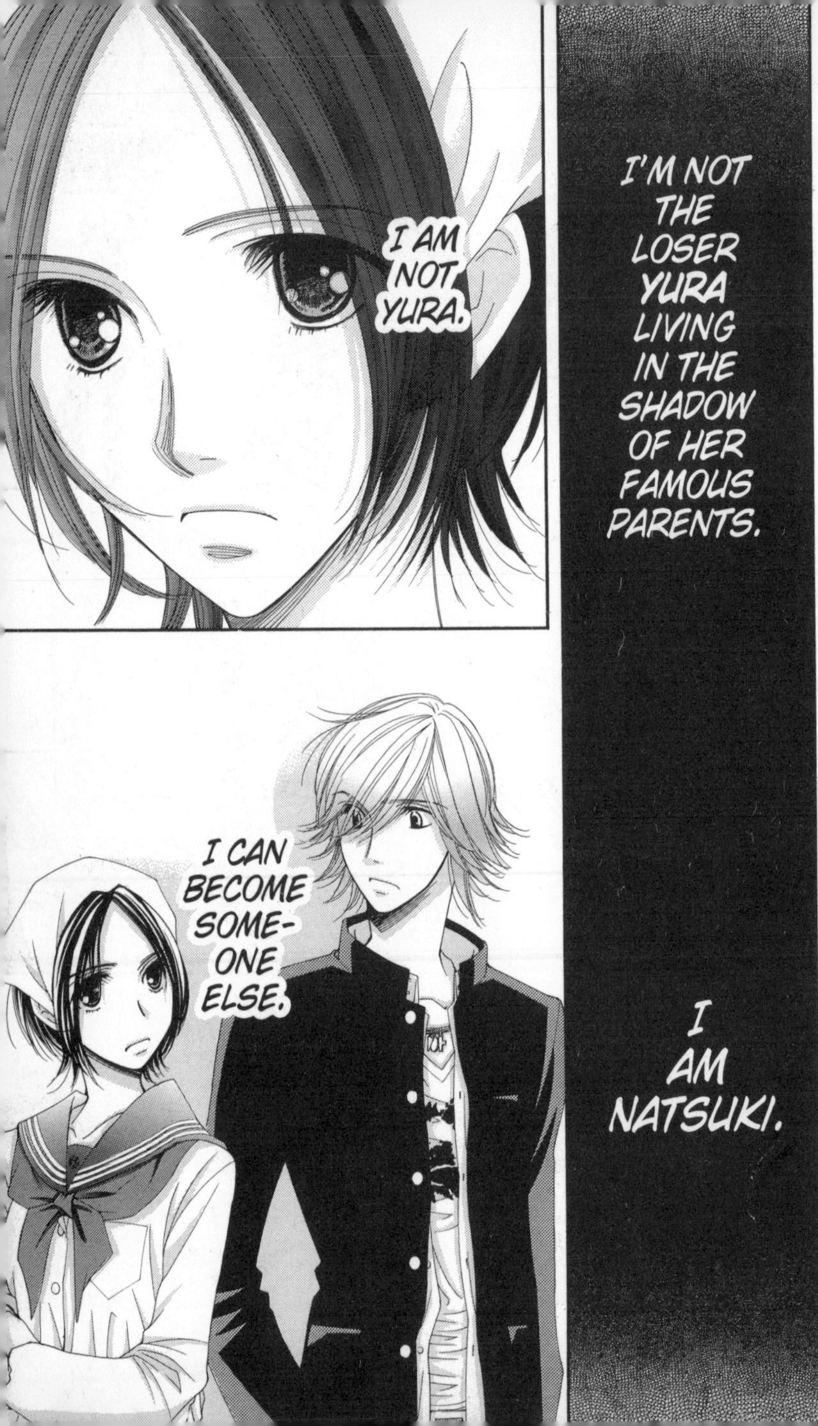
I'M NOT THE LOSER YURA LIVING IN THE SHADOW OF HER FAMOUS PARENTS.
I AM NATSUKI.
I AM NOT YURA.
I CAN BECOME SOME-ONE ELSE.

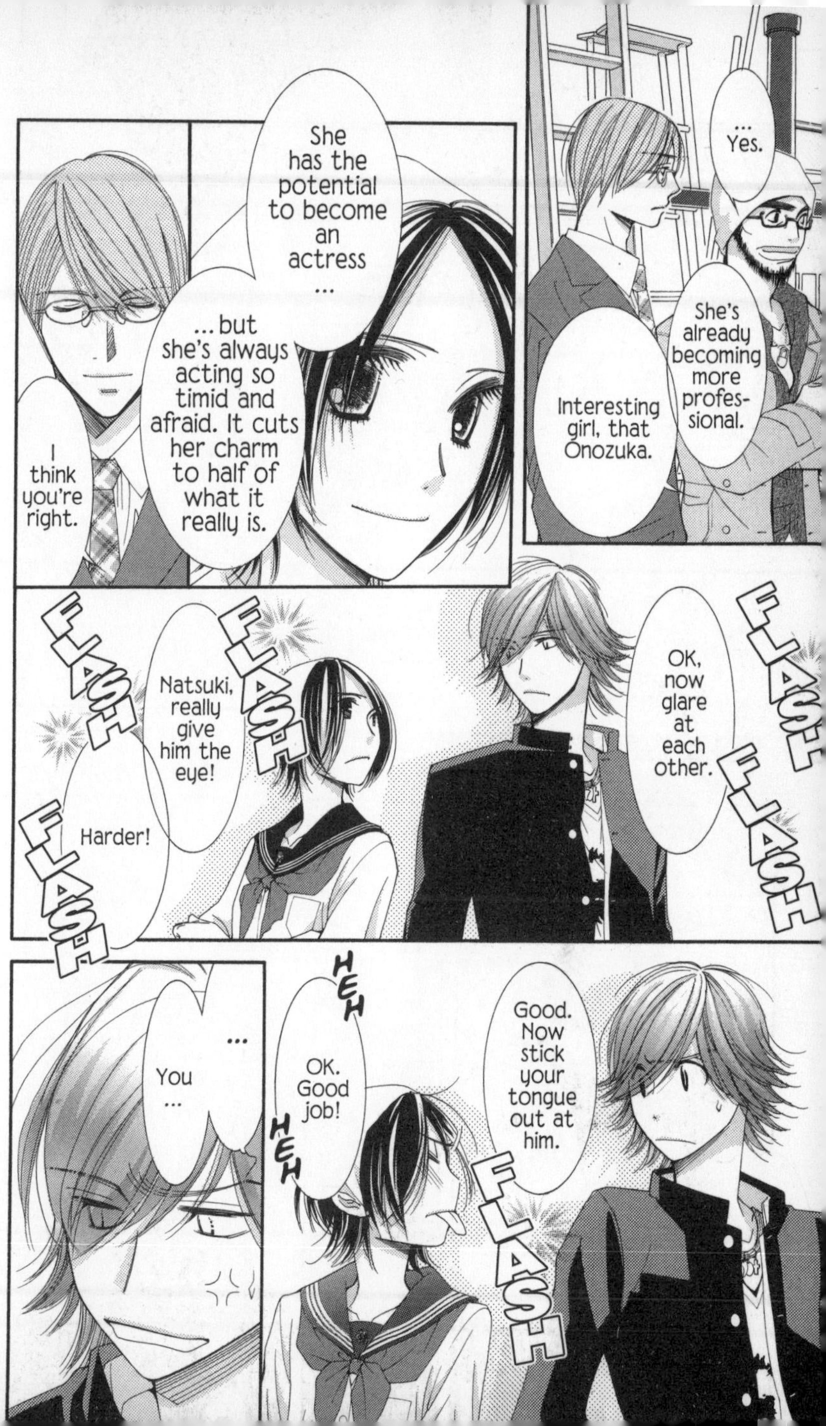
... Yes.
She's already becoming more profes-sional.
Interesting girl, that Onozuka.
She has the potential to become an actress ...
...but she's always acting so timid and afraid. It cuts her charm to half of what it really is.
I think you're right.
FLASH
OK, now glare at each other.
FLASH
FLASH
Natsuki, really give him the eye!
FLASH
Harder!
FLASH
Good. Now stick your tongue out at him.
FLASH
HEH
OK. Good job!
HEH
... You ...

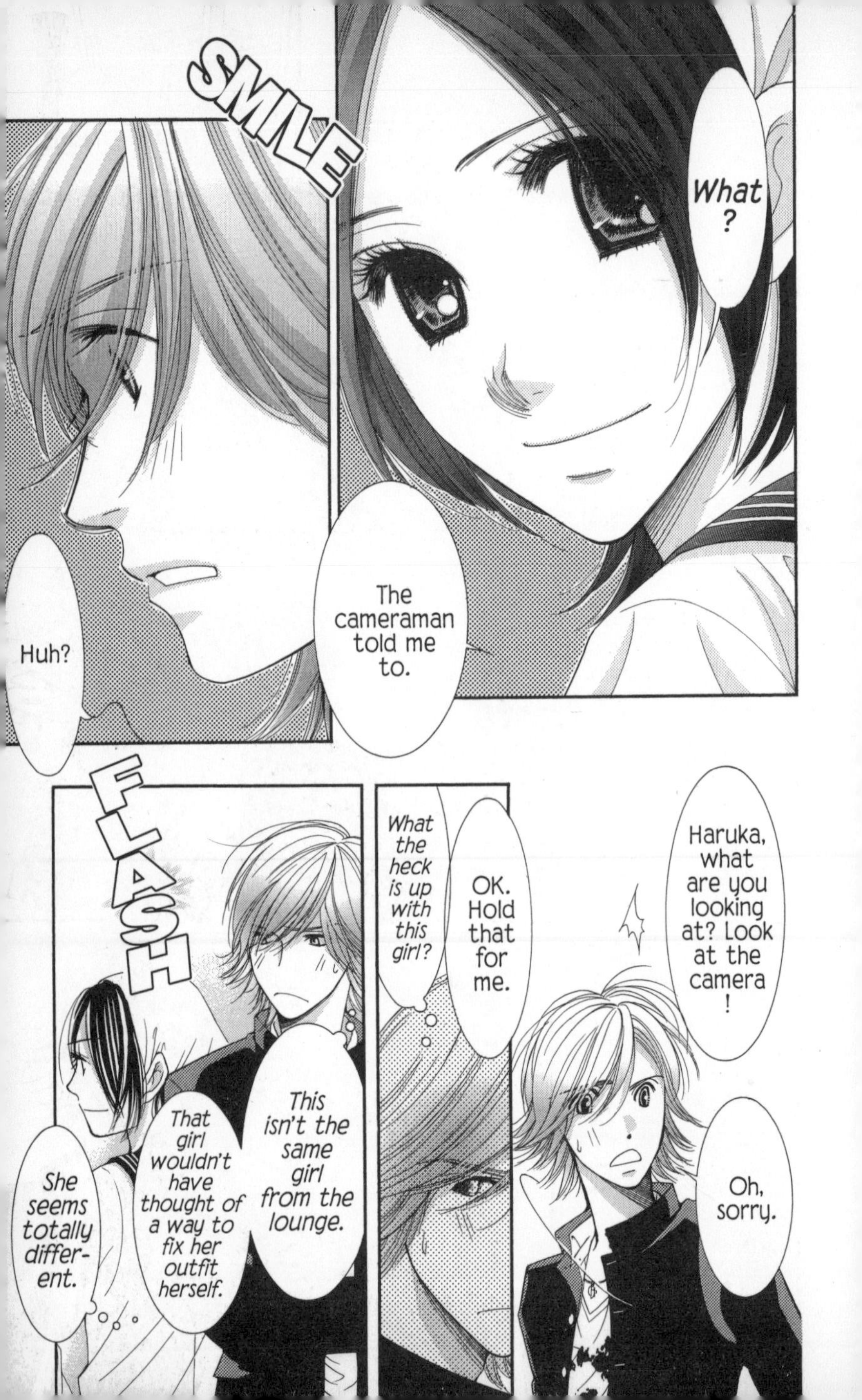
What?
SMILE
The cameraman told me to.
Huh?
Haruka, what are you looking at? Look at the camera!
Oh, sorry.
OK. Hold that for me.
What the heck is up with this girl?
FLASH
This isn't the same girl from the lounge.
That girl wouldn't have thought of a way to fix her outfit herself.
She seems totally different.

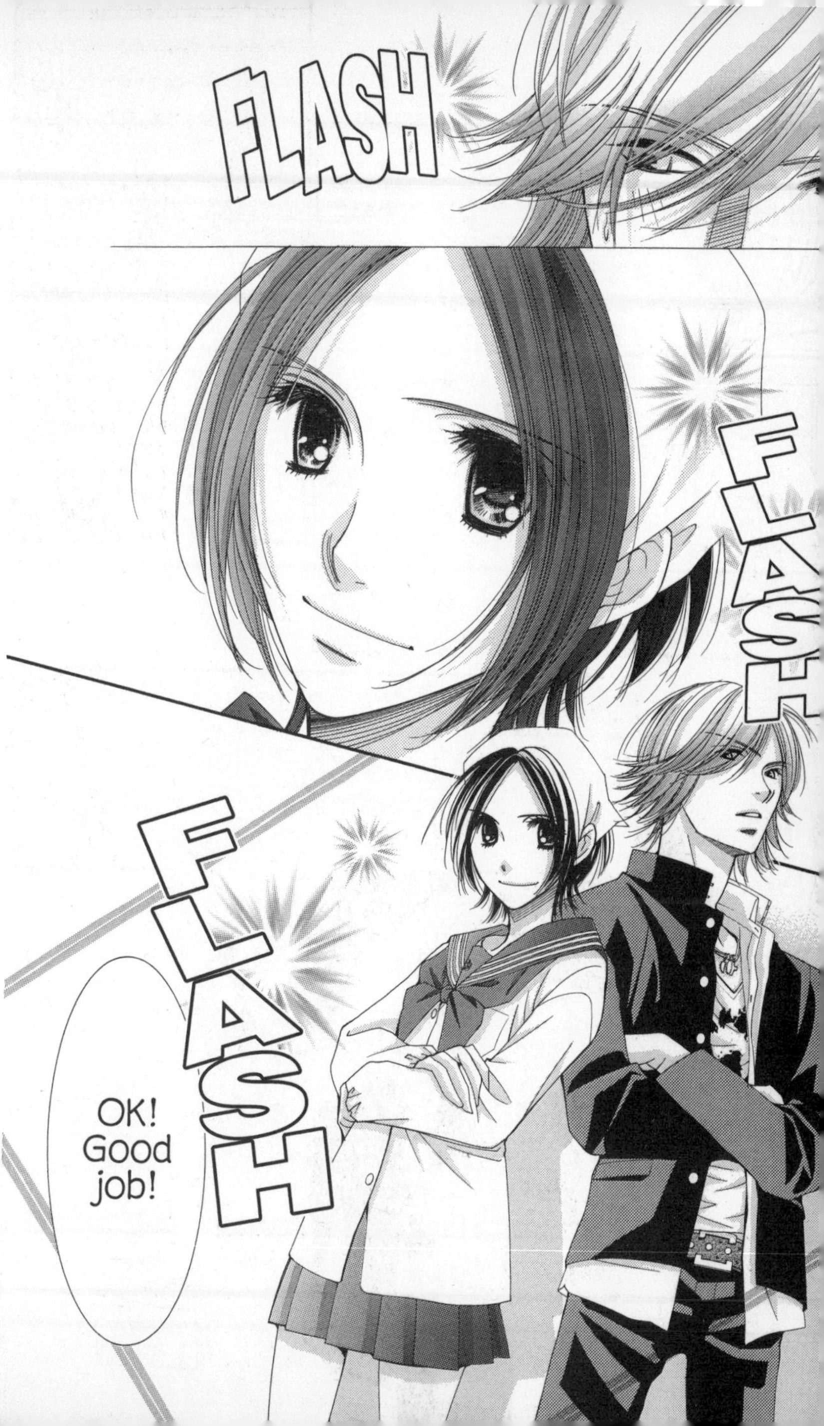
FLASH
FLASH
FLASH
OK! Good job!

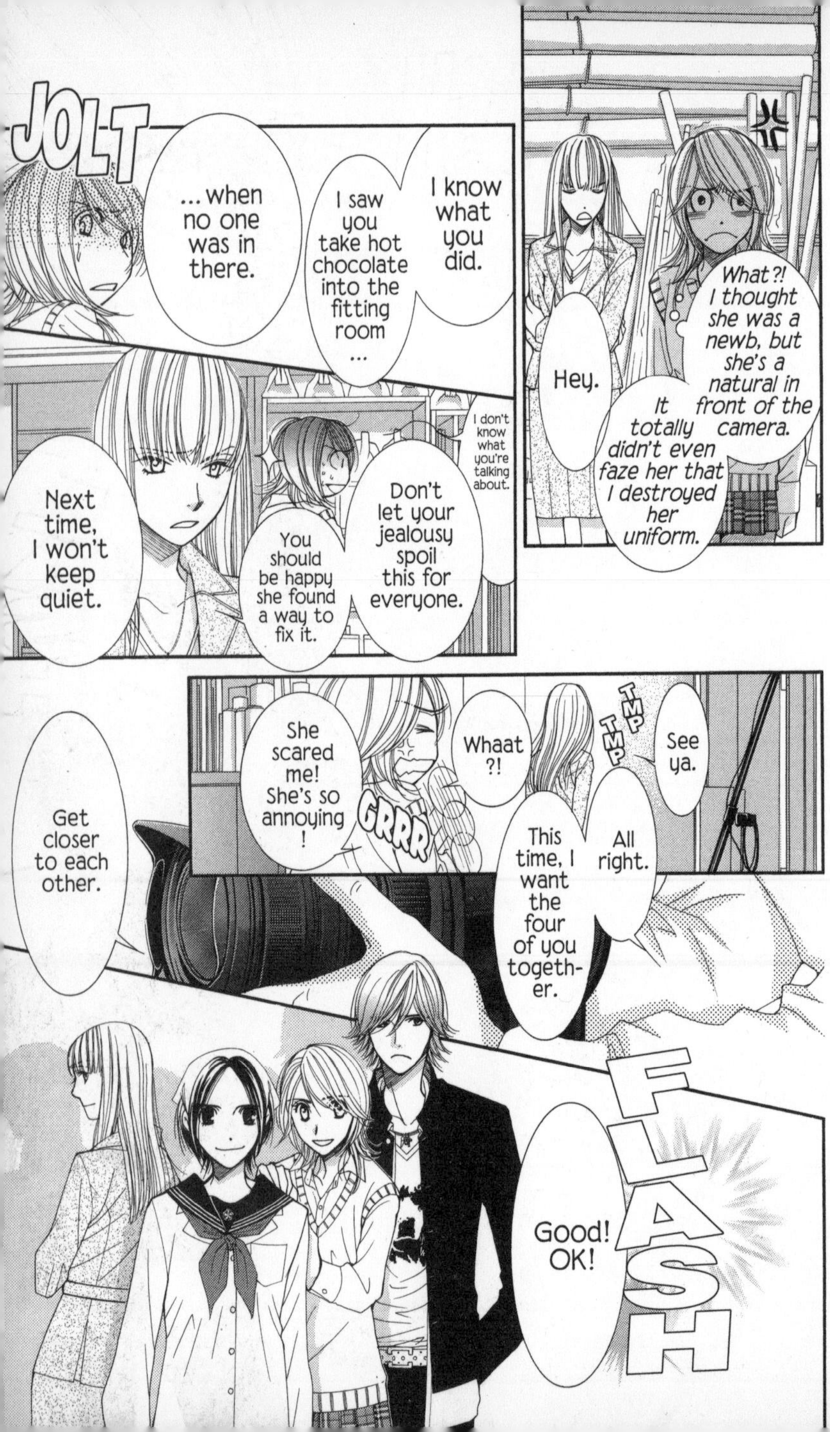
What?! I thought she was a newb, but she's a natural in front of the camera.
It totally didn't even faze her that I destroyed her uniform.
Hey.
I know what you did.
I saw you take hot chocolate into the fitting room...
...when no one was in there.
JOLT
I don't know what you're talking about.
Don't let your jealousy spoil this for everyone.
You should be happy she found a way to fix it.
Next time, I won't keep quiet.
See ya.
TMP TMP
Whaat?!
She scared me! She's so annoying!
GRRR
All right.
This time, I want the four of you together.
Get closer to each other.
FLASH
Good! OK!

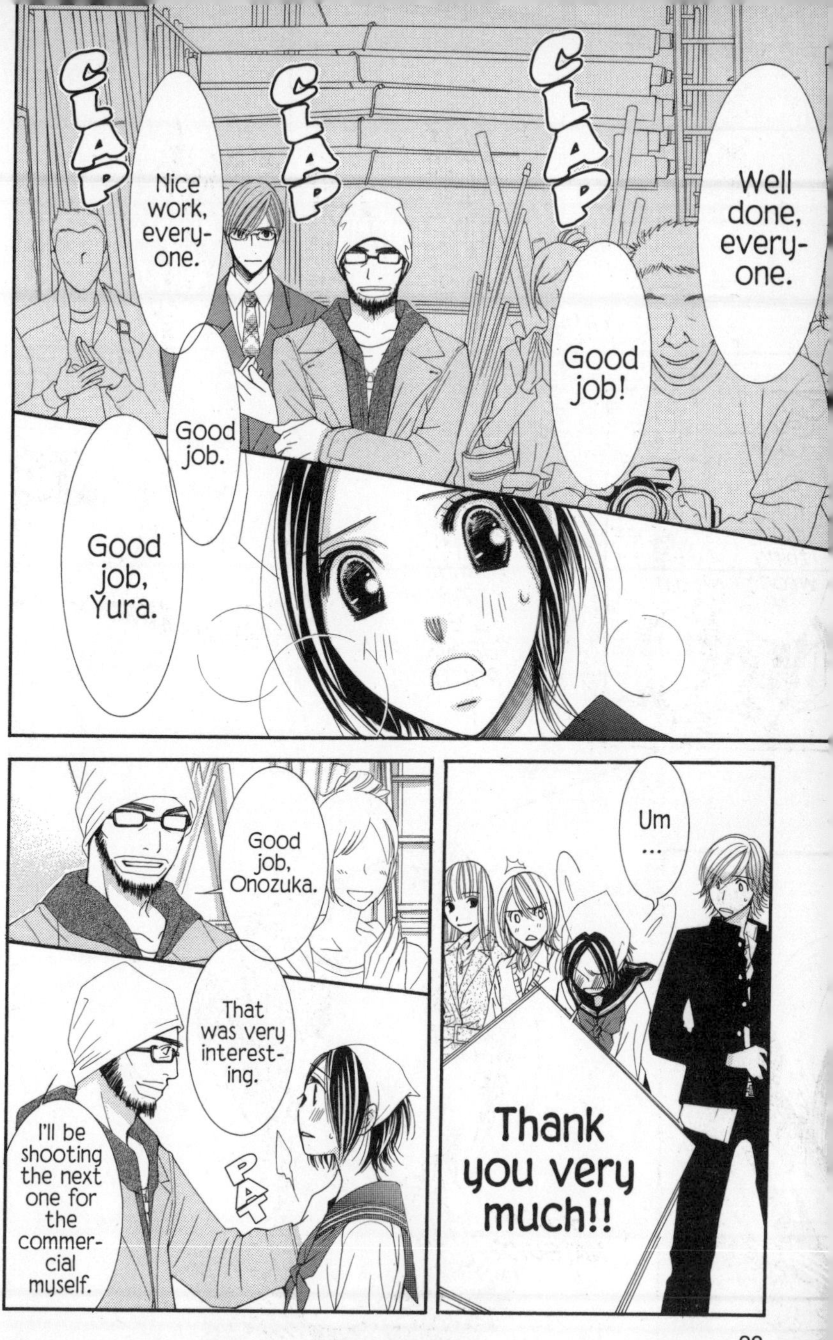
CLAP
Well done, everyone.
Good job!
CLAP
Nice work, everyone.
CLAP
Good job.
Good job, Yura.
Um ...
Thank you very much!!
Good job, Onozuka.
That was very interesting.
PAT
I'll be shooting the next one for the commercial myself.

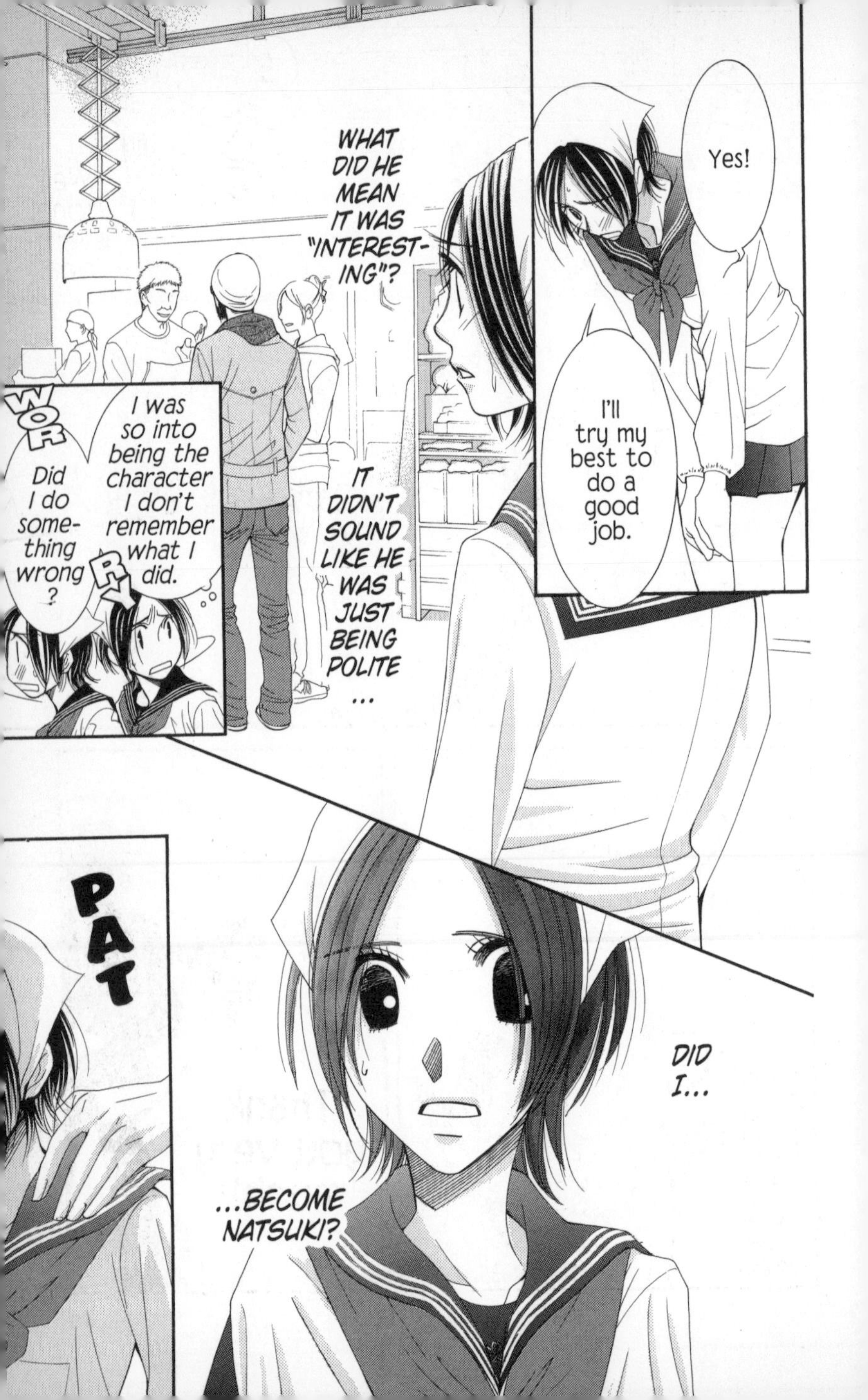
Yes!
I'll try my best to do a good job.
WHAT DID HE MEAN IT WAS "INTEREST-ING"?
IT DIDN'T SOUND LIKE HE WAS JUST BEING POLITE ...
I was so into being the character I don't remember what I did.
WORRY
Did I do some-thing wrong?
DID I...
...BECOME NATSUKI?
PAT

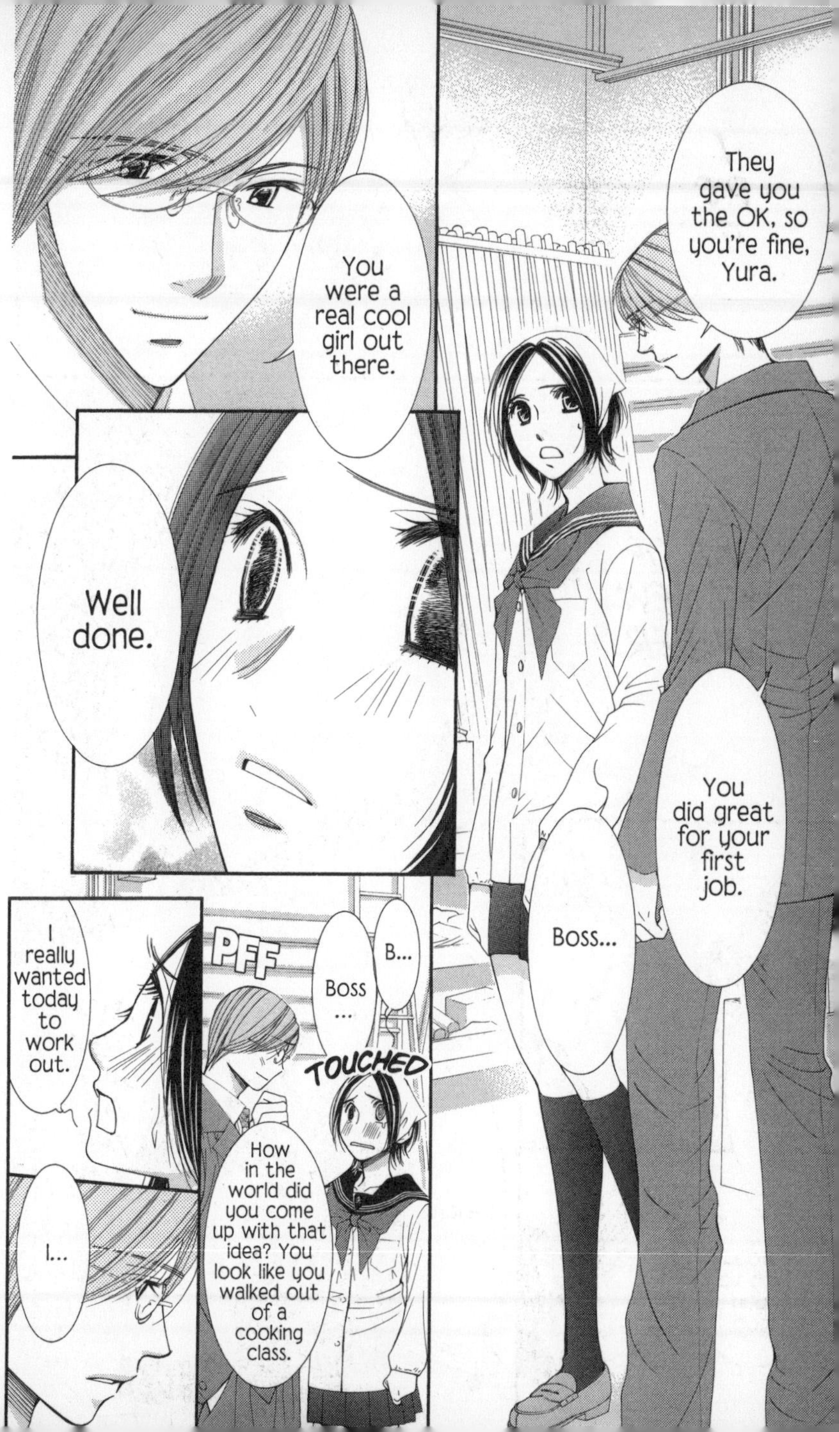
They gave you the OK, so you're fine, Yura.
You did great for your first job.
Boss...
You were a real cool girl out there.
Well done.
B...
Boss ...
PFF
TOUCHED
How in the world did you come up with that idea? You look like you walked out of a cooking class.
I really wanted today to work out.
I...

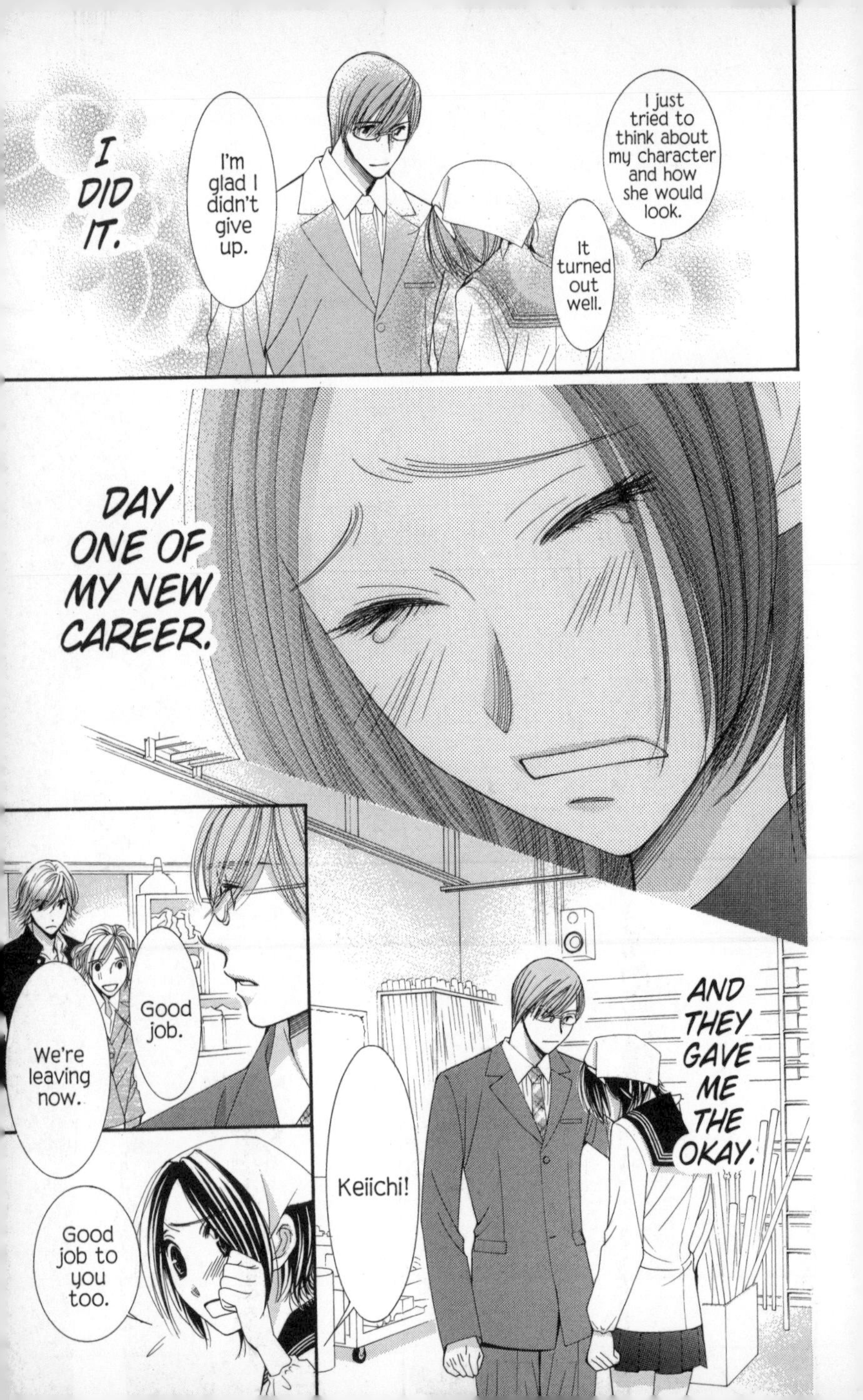
I just tried to think about my character and how she would look.
It turned out well.
I'm glad I didn't give up.
I DID IT.
DAY ONE OF MY NEW CAREER.
AND THEY GAVE ME THE OKAY.
Keiichi!
Good job.
We're leaving now.
Good job to you too.

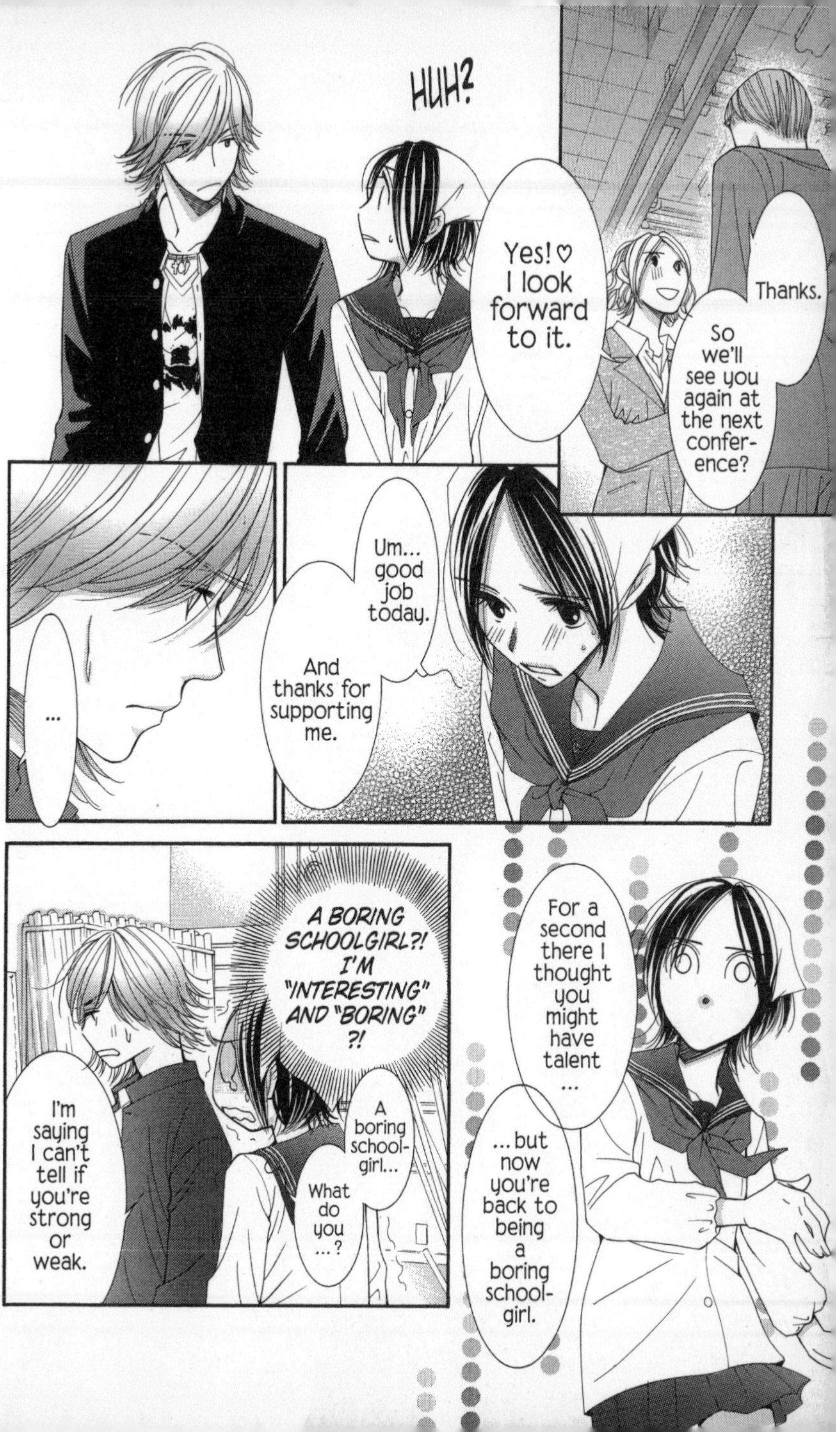
Thanks.
So we'll see you again at the next confer-ence?
Yes! ♡ I look forward to it.
HUH?
...
Um... good job today.
And thanks for supporting me.
...
For a second there I thought you might have talent ...
... but now you're back to being a boring school-girl.
A BORING SCHOOLGIRL?! I'M "INTERESTING" AND "BORING" ?!
A boring school-girl...
What do you ...?
I'm saying I can't tell if you're strong or weak.

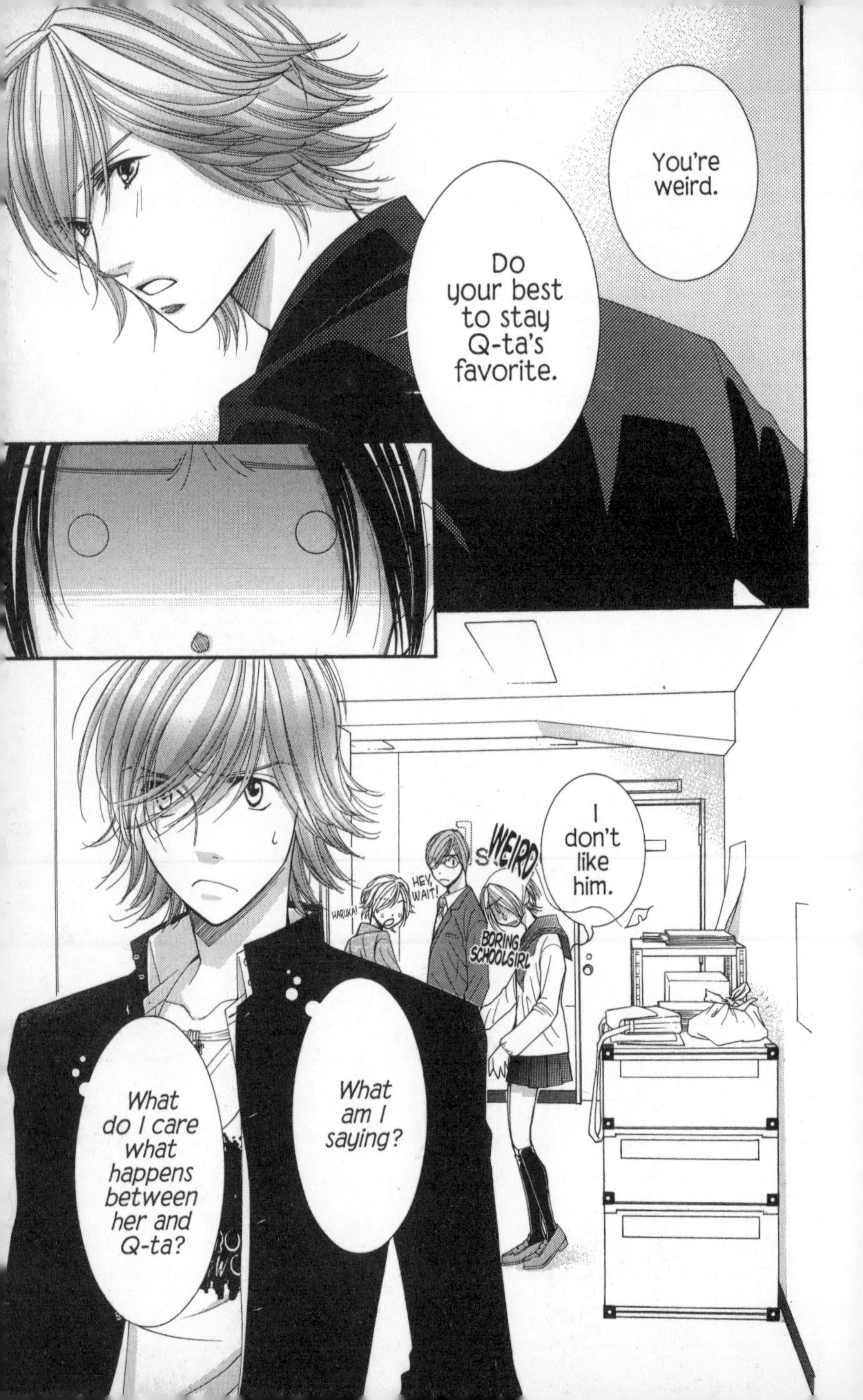
You're weird.
Do your best to stay Q-ta's favorite.
I don't like him.
WEIRD
BORING SCHOOLGIRL
HEY, WAIT!
HARUKA!
What am I saying?
What do I care what happens between her and Q-ta?

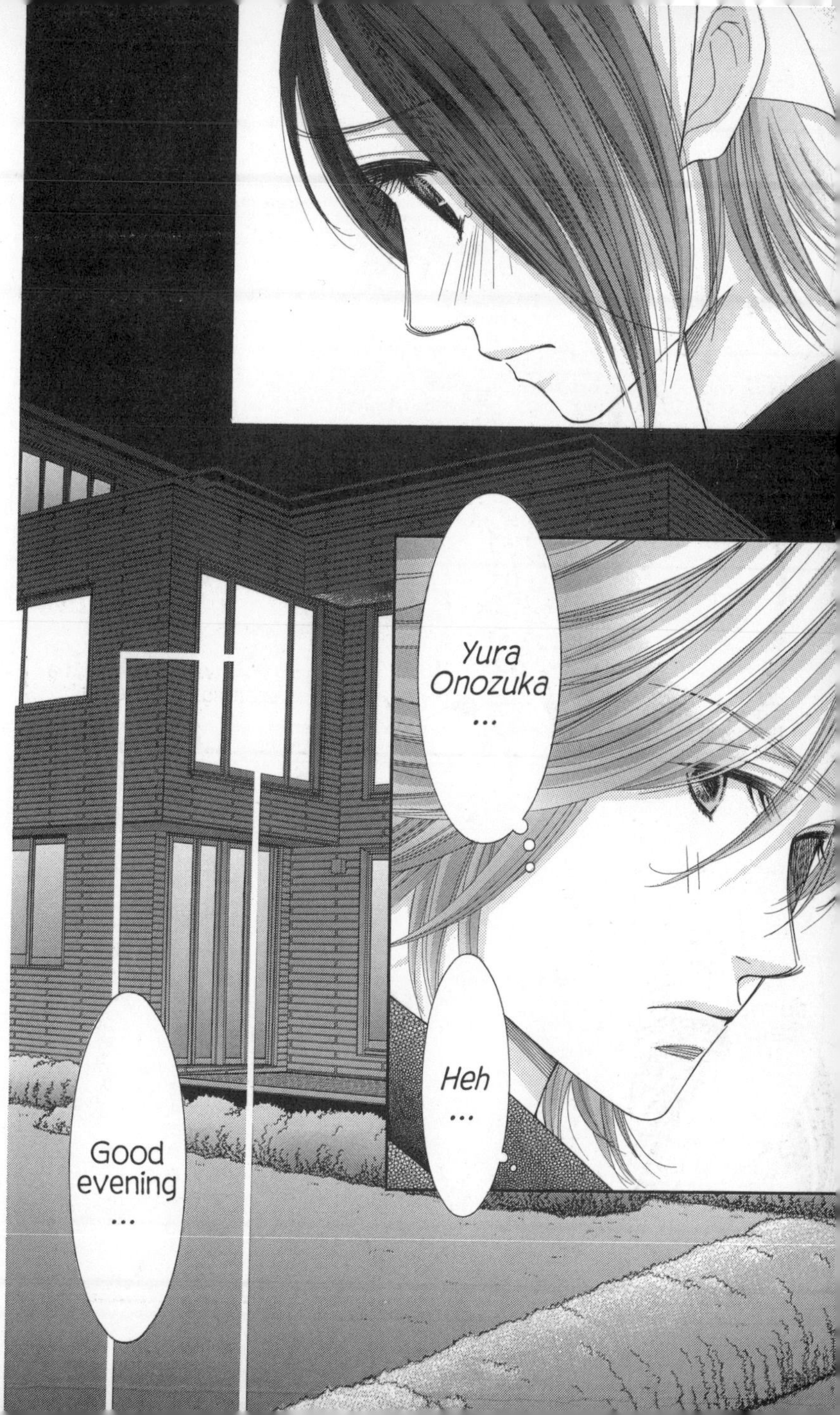
Yura Onozuka ...
Heh ...
Good evening ...

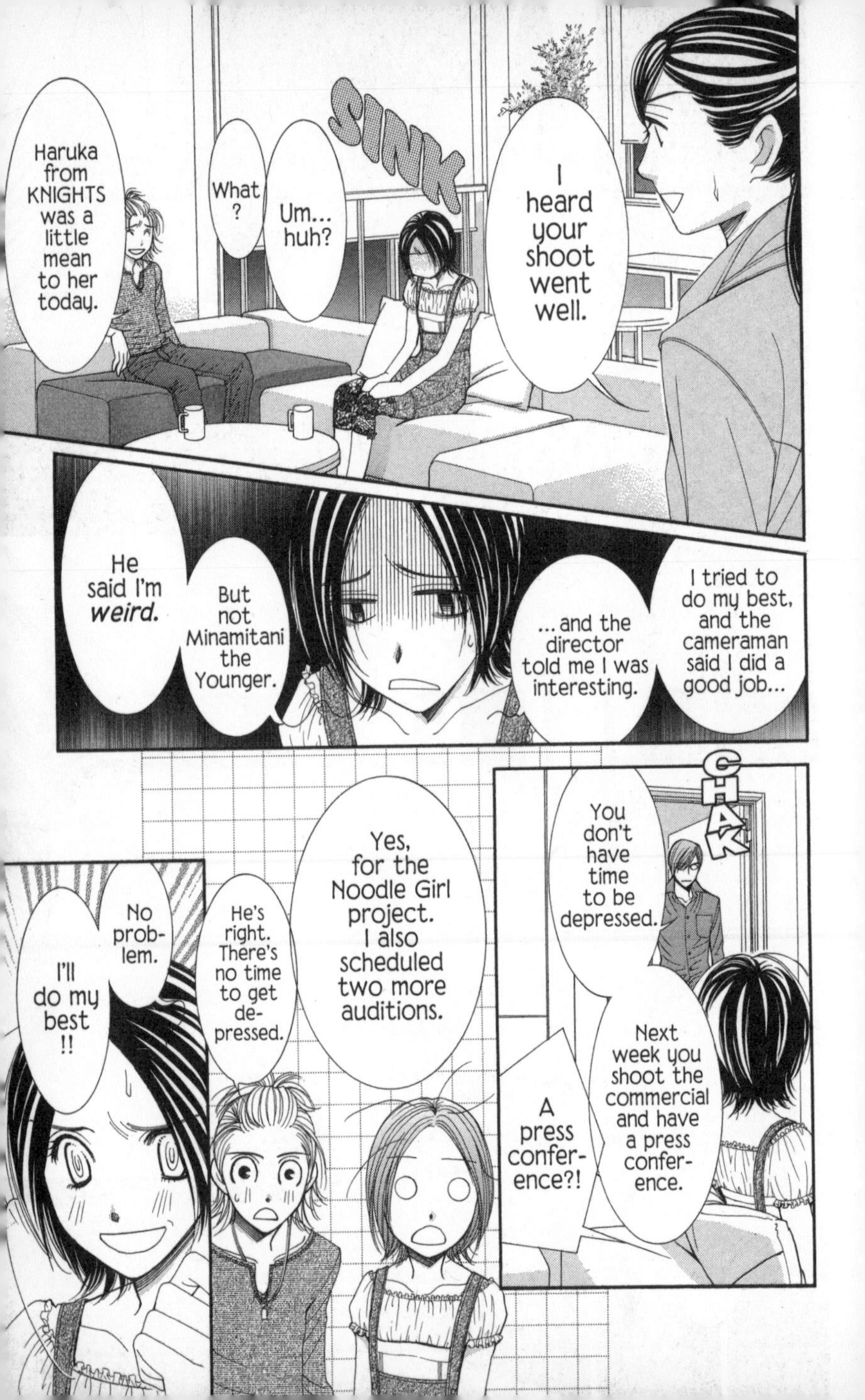
I heard your shoot went well.
SINK
Um... huh?
What?
Haruka from KNIGHTS was a little mean to her today.
I tried to do my best, and the cameraman said I did a good job...
...and the director told me I was interesting.
But not Minamitani the Younger.
He said I'm *weird.*
CHAK
You don't have time to be depressed.
Next week you shoot the commercial and have a press conference.
A press conference?!
Yes, for the Noodle Girl project. I also scheduled two more auditions.
He's right. There's no time to get depressed.
No problem.
I'll do my best!!

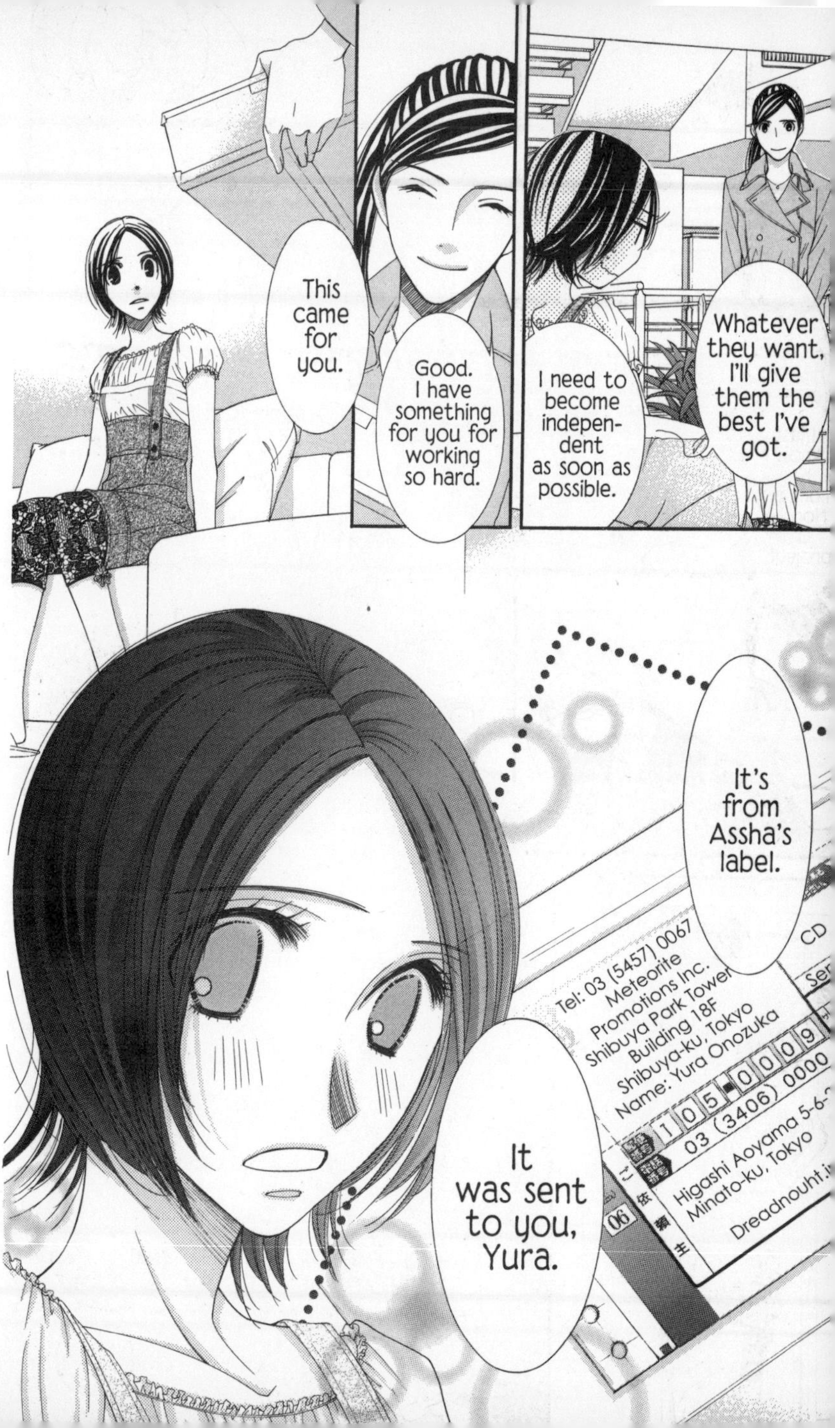
Whatever they want, I'll give them the best I've got.
I need to become independent as soon as possible.
Good. I have something for you for working so hard.
This came for you.
It's from Assha's label.
Tel: 03 (5457) 0067
Meteorite Promotions Inc.
Shibuya Park Tower Building 18F
Shibuya-ku, Tokyo
Name: Yura Onozuka
CD
105-0009
03 (3406) 0000
Higashi Aoyama 5-6-
Minato-ku, Tokyo
Dreadnought
依頼主
06
It was sent to you, Yura.

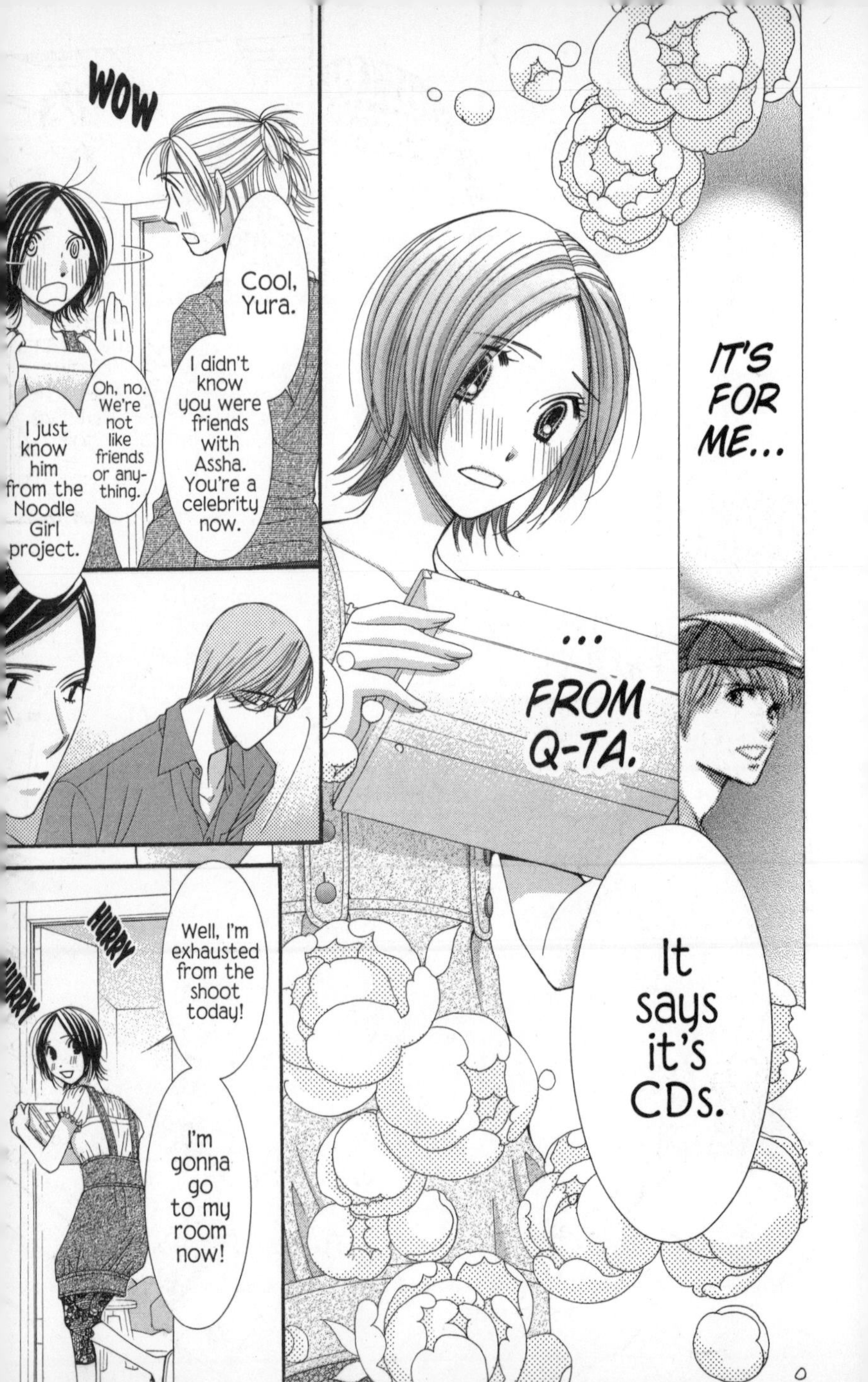
IT'S FOR ME...
... FROM Q-TA.
It says it's CDs.
WOW
Cool, Yura.
I didn't know you were friends with Assha. You're a celebrity now.
Oh, no. We're not like friends or any-thing.
I just know him from the Noodle Girl project.
HURRY
HURRY
Well, I'm exhausted from the shoot today!
I'm gonna go to my room now!

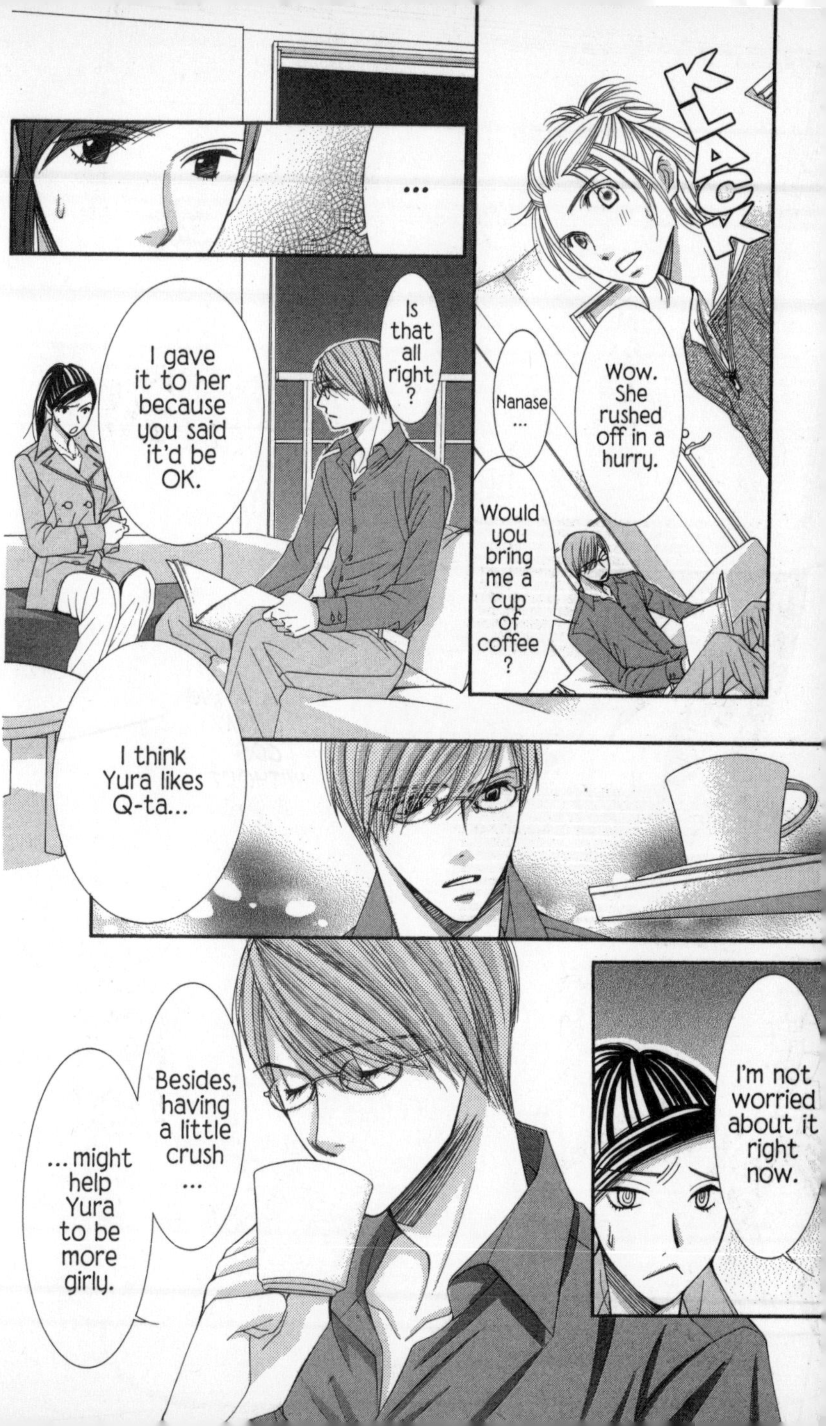
KLACK
Wow. She rushed off in a hurry.
Nanase...
Would you bring me a cup of coffee?
...
Is that all right?
I gave it to her because you said it'd be OK.
I think Yura likes Q-ta...
I'm not worried about it right now.
Besides, having a little crush...
...might help Yura to be more girly.

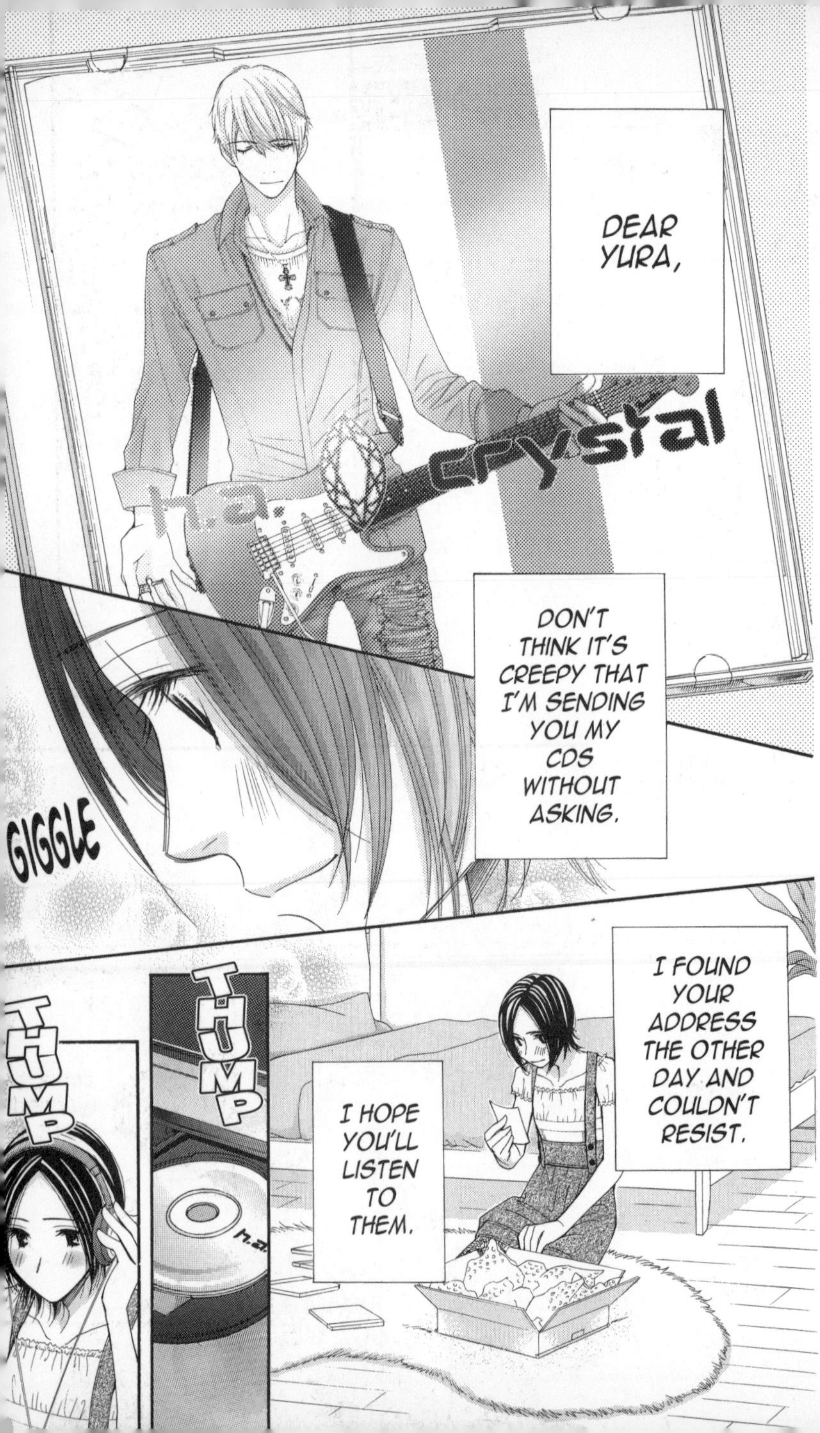
DEAR YURA,
crystal
DON'T THINK IT'S CREEPY THAT I'M SENDING YOU MY CDS WITHOUT ASKING.
GIGGLE
I FOUND YOUR ADDRESS THE OTHER DAY AND COULDN'T RESIST.
I HOPE YOU'LL LISTEN TO THEM.
THUMP
THUMP

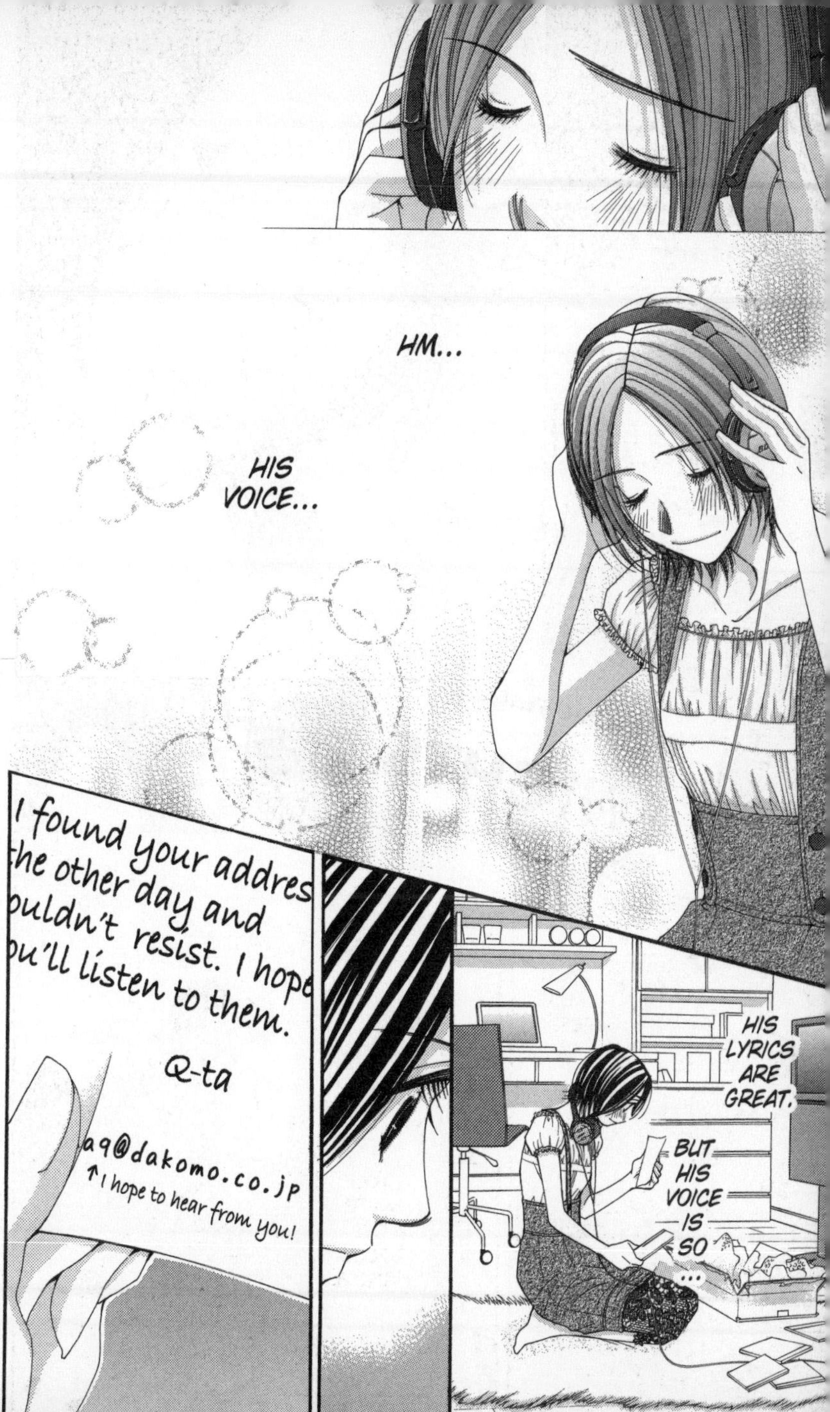
HM...
HIS VOICE...
HIS LYRICS ARE GREAT.
BUT HIS VOICE IS SO ...
I found your addres
the other day and
ouldn't resist. I hope
ou'll listen to them.
Q-ta
aq@dakomo.co.jp
↑I hope to hear from you!

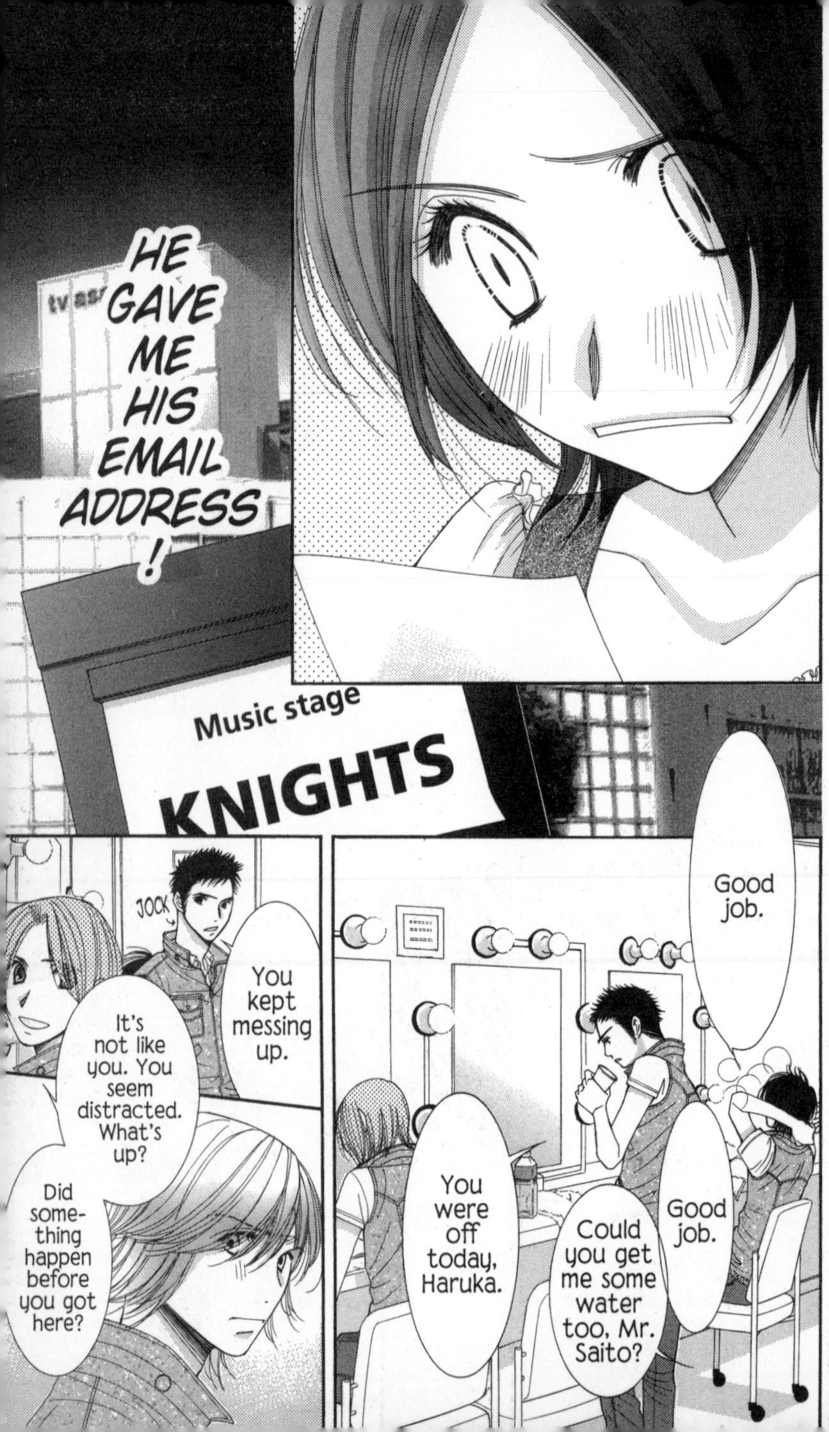
HE GAVE ME HIS EMAIL ADDRESS!
Music stage
KNIGHTS
Good job.
Good job.
Could you get me some water too, Mr. Saito?
You were off today, Haruka.
You kept messing up.
JOCK
It's not like you. You seem distracted. What's up?
Did some-thing happen before you got here?

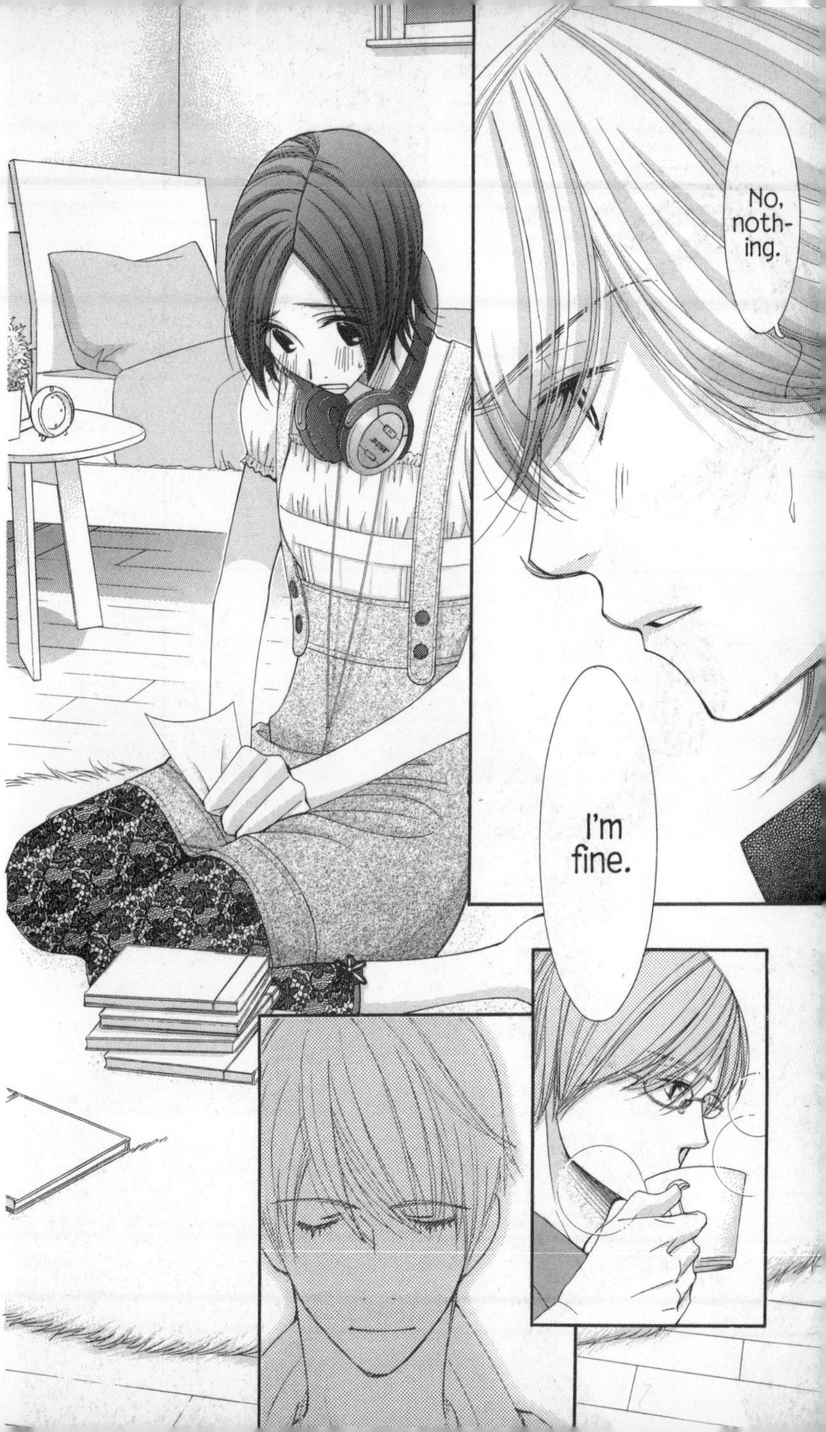
No, nothing.
I'm fine.

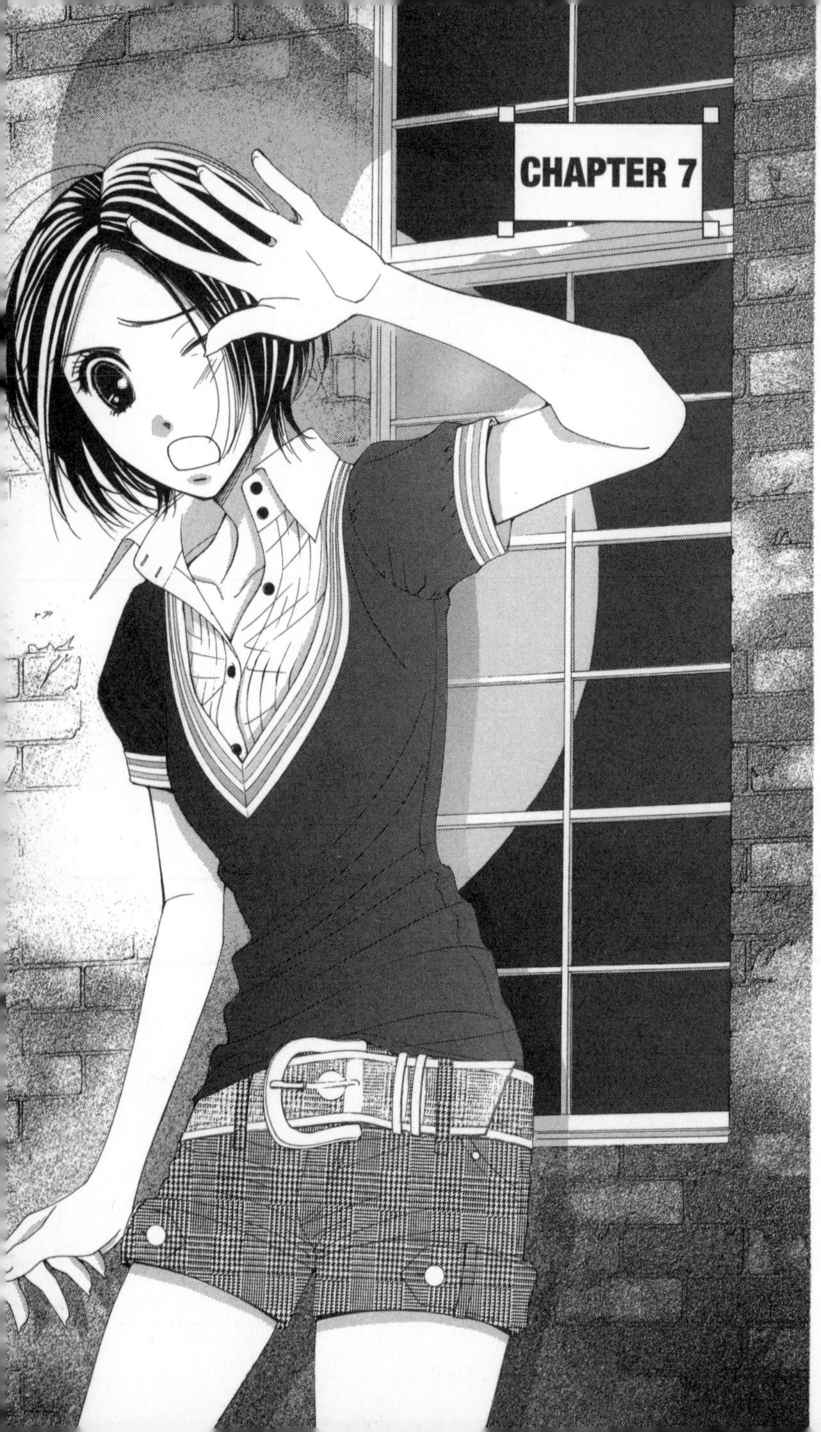
CHAPTER 7

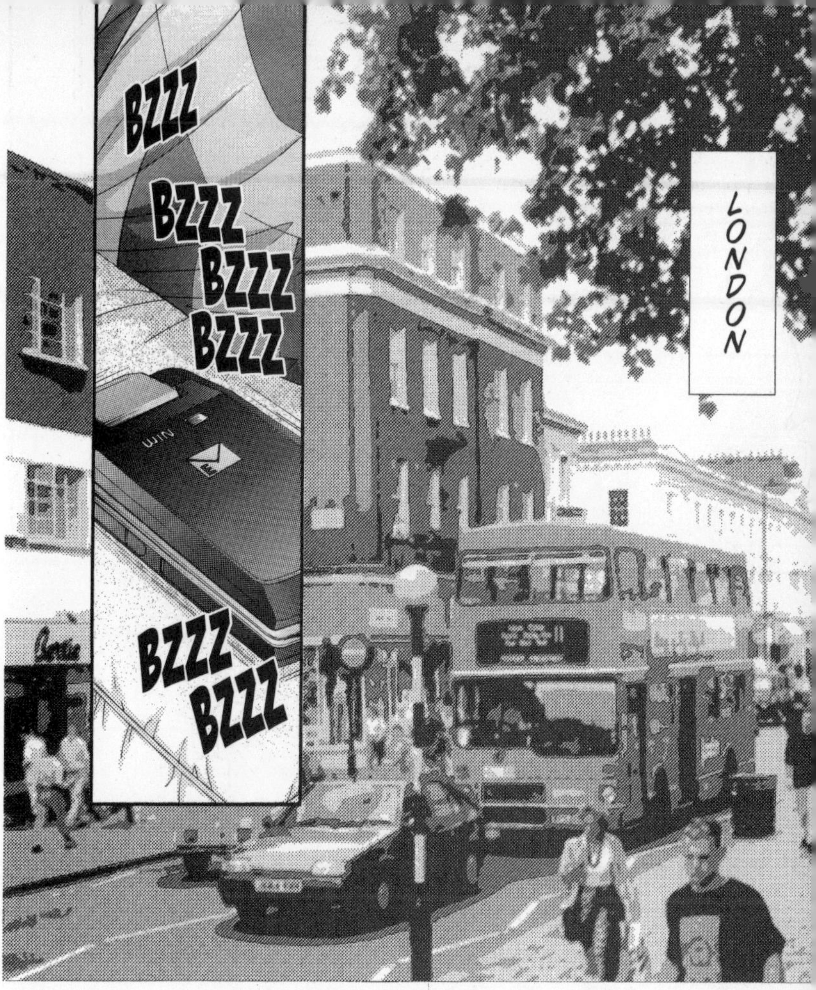
LONDON
BZZZ
BZZZ
BZZZ
BZZZ
BZZZ
BZZZ

Honey Hunt

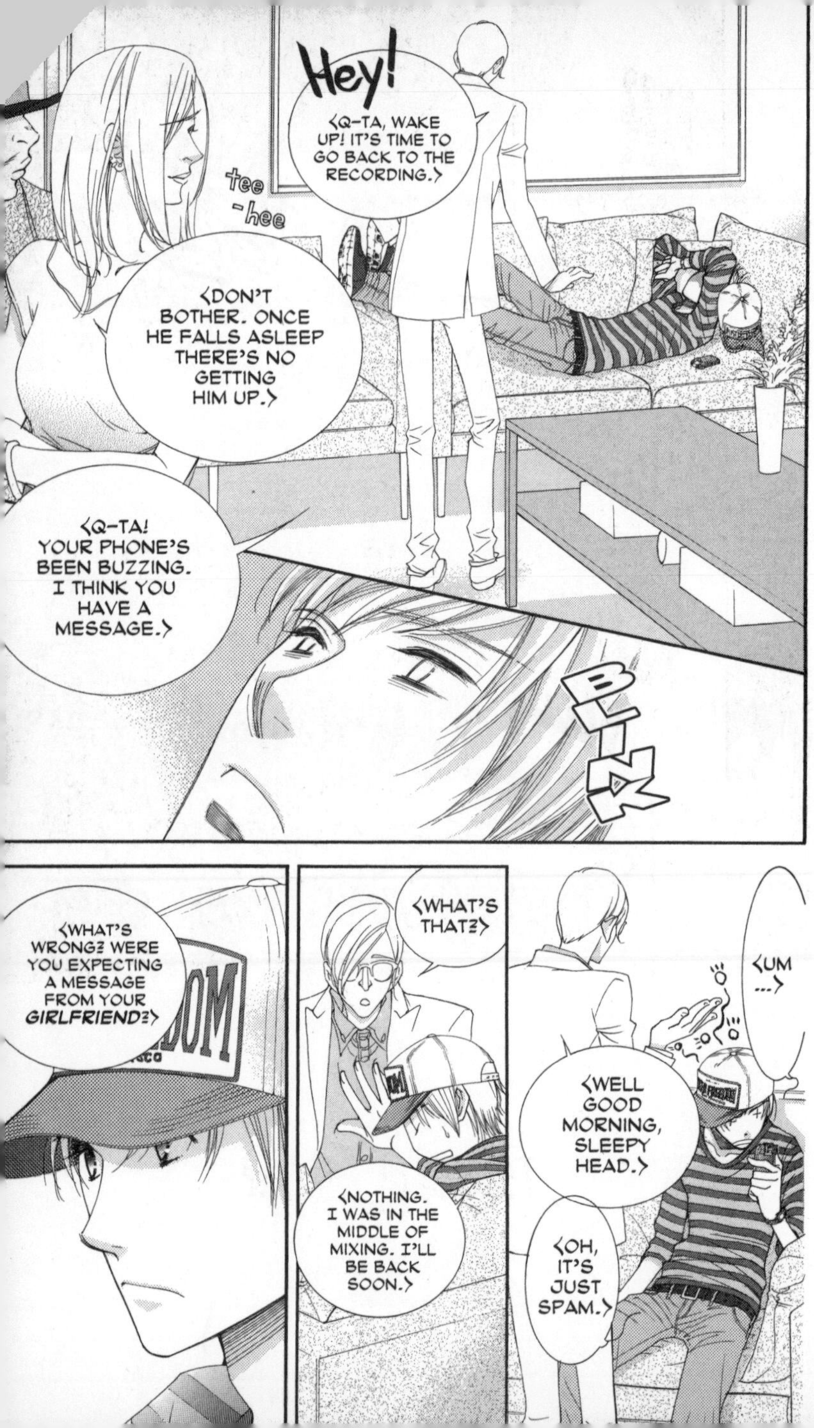
Hey!
<Q-TA, WAKE UP! IT'S TIME TO GO BACK TO THE RECORDING.>
tee -hee
<DON'T BOTHER. ONCE HE FALLS ASLEEP THERE'S NO GETTING HIM UP.>
<Q-TA! YOUR PHONE'S BEEN BUZZING. I THINK YOU HAVE A MESSAGE.>
BLINK
<UM ...>
<WELL GOOD MORNING, SLEEPY HEAD.>
<OH, IT'S JUST SPAM.>
<WHAT'S THAT?>
<NOTHING. I WAS IN THE MIDDLE OF MIXING. I'LL BE BACK SOON.>
<WHAT'S WRONG? WERE YOU EXPECTING A MESSAGE FROM YOUR *GIRLFRIEND*?>

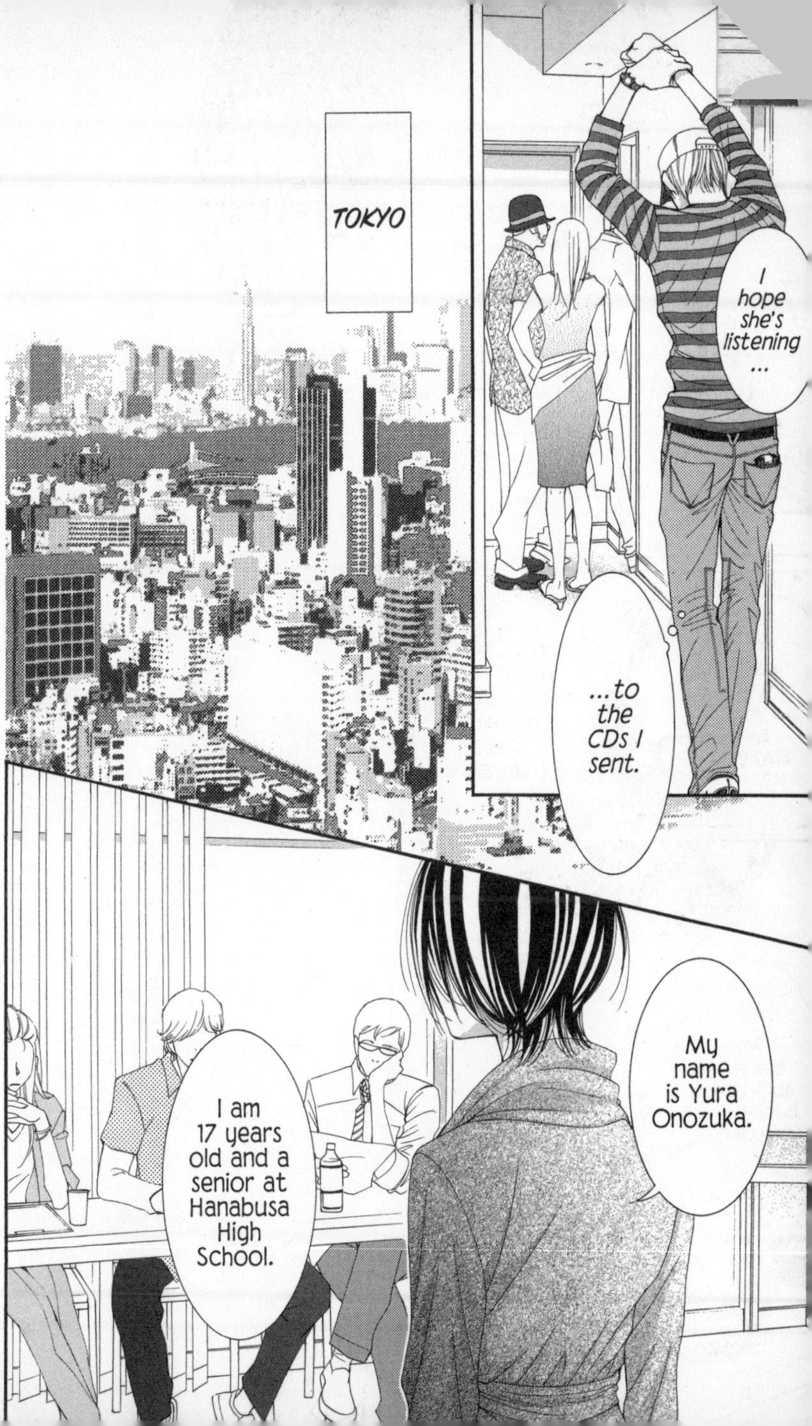
I hope she's listening...
...to the CDs I sent.
TOKYO
My name is Yura Onozuka.
I am 17 years old and a senior at Hanabusa High School.

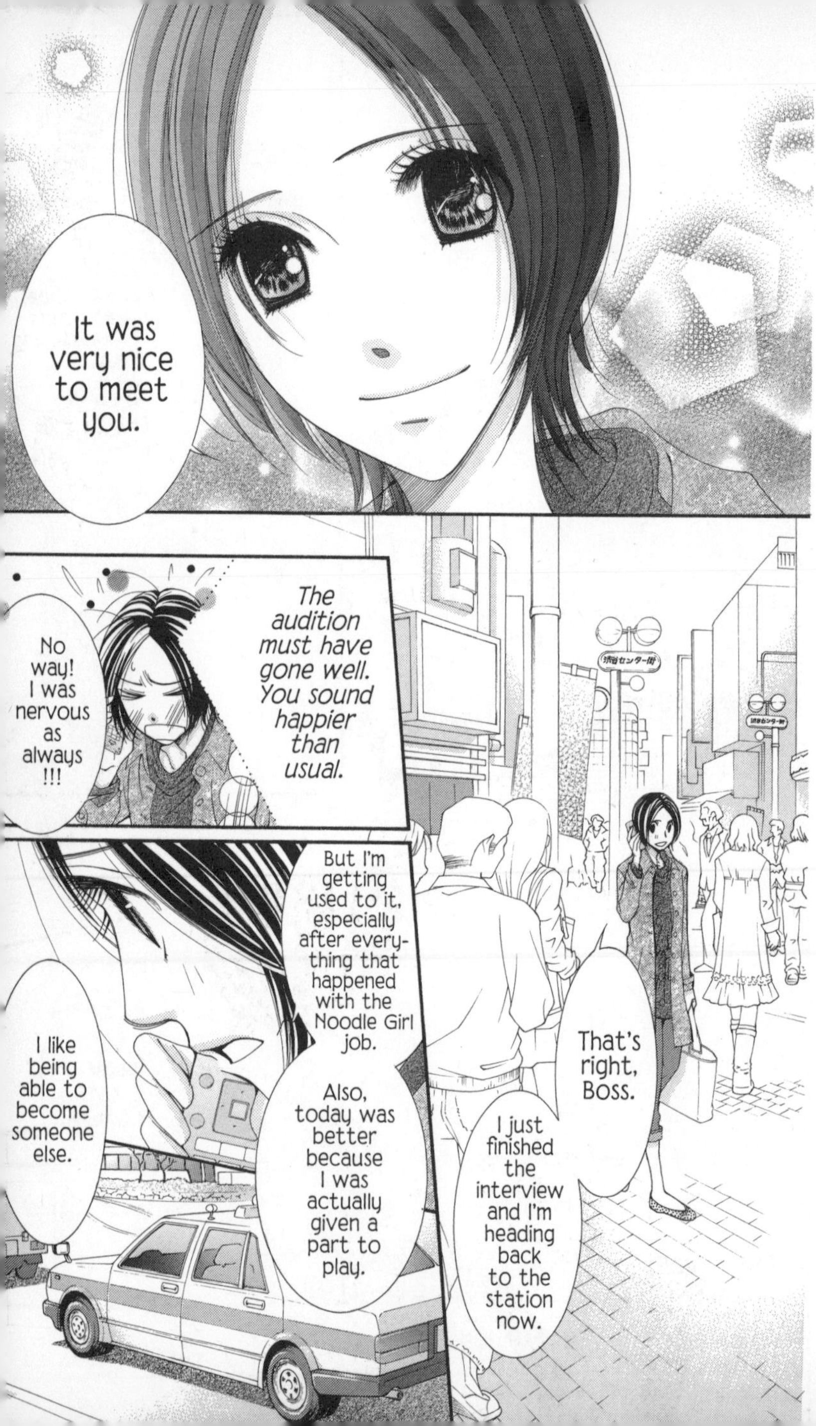
It was very nice to meet you.
That's right, Boss.
I just finished the interview and I'm heading back to the station now.
The audition must have gone well. You sound happier than usual.
No way! I was nervous as always!!!
But I'm getting used to it, especially after everything that happened with the Noodle Girl job.
Also, today was better because I was actually given a part to play.
I like being able to become someone else.

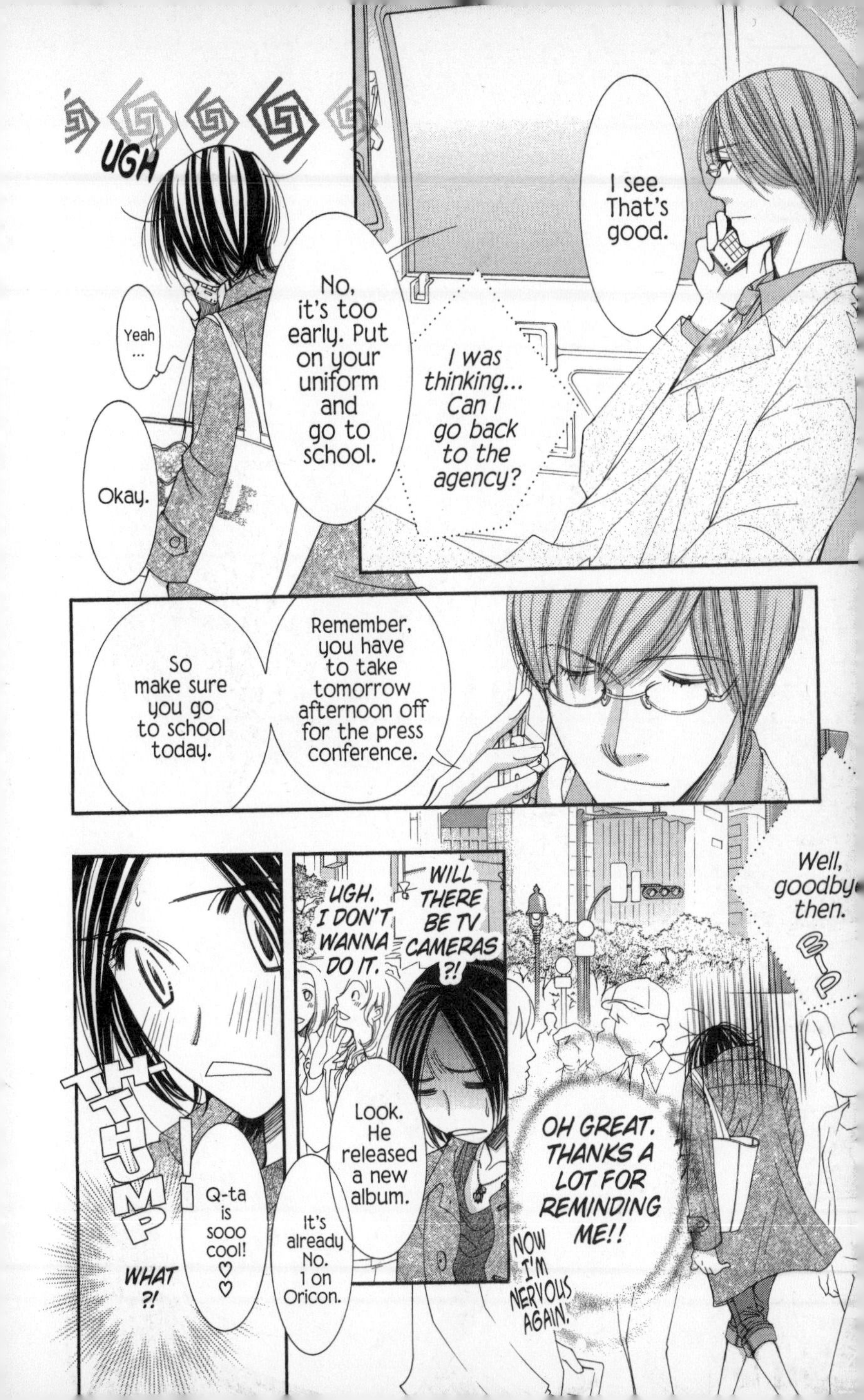
I see. That's good.
I was thinking... Can I go back to the agency?
No, it's too early. Put on your uniform and go to school.
UGH
Yeah...
Okay.
Remember, you have to take tomorrow afternoon off for the press conference.
So make sure you go to school today.
Well, goodbye then.
BIP
OH GREAT. THANKS A LOT FOR REMINDING ME!!
NOW I'M NERVOUS AGAIN!
WILL THERE BE TV CAMERAS?!
UGH. I DON'T WANNA DO IT.
Look. He released a new album.
It's already No. 1 on Oricon.
TH-THUMP
Q-ta is sooo cool! ♡ ♡
WHAT?!

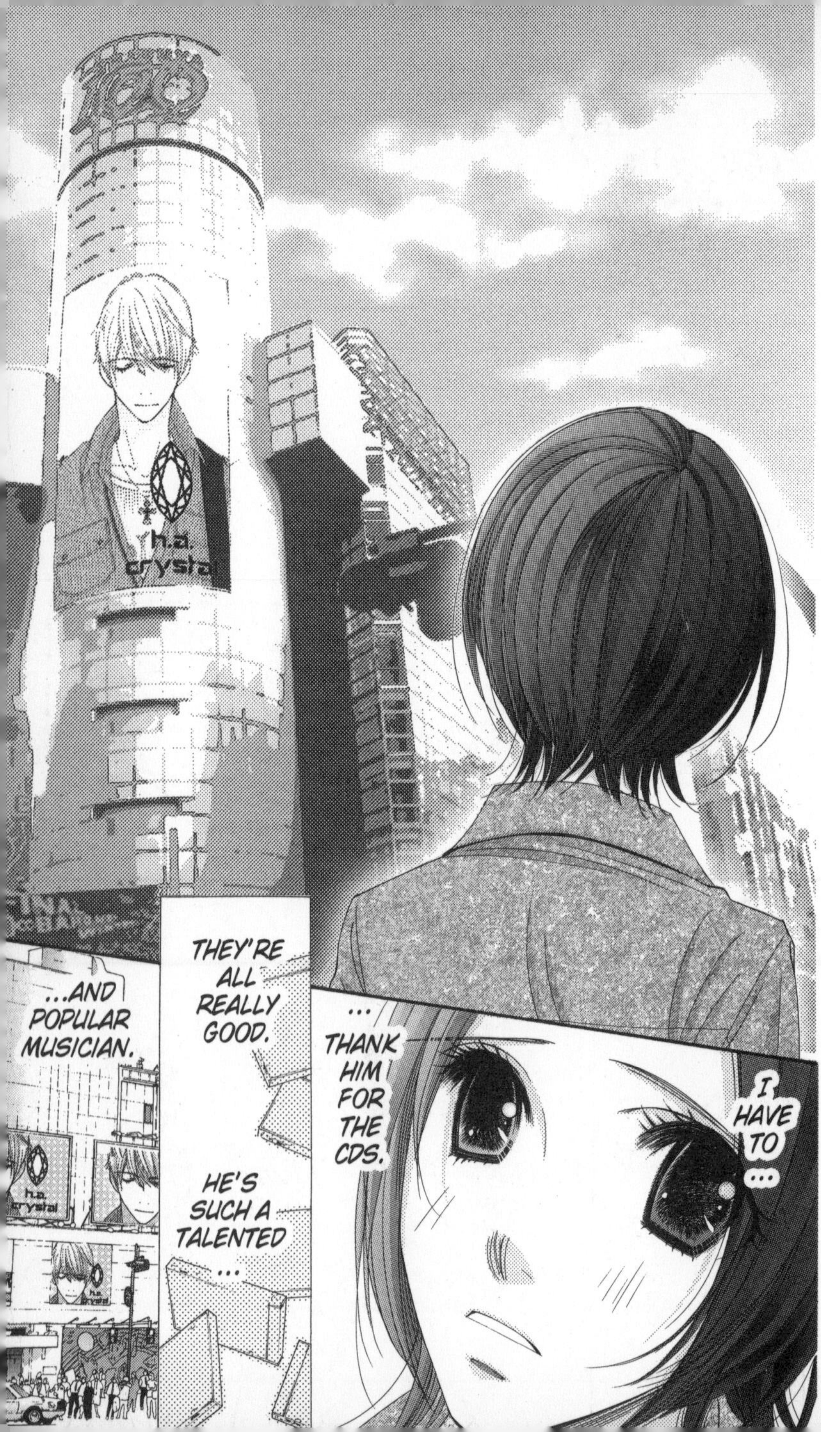
h.a. crystal
I HAVE TO ...
... THANK HIM FOR THE CDS.
THEY'RE ALL REALLY GOOD.
HE'S SUCH A TALENTED ...
...AND POPULAR MUSICIAN.

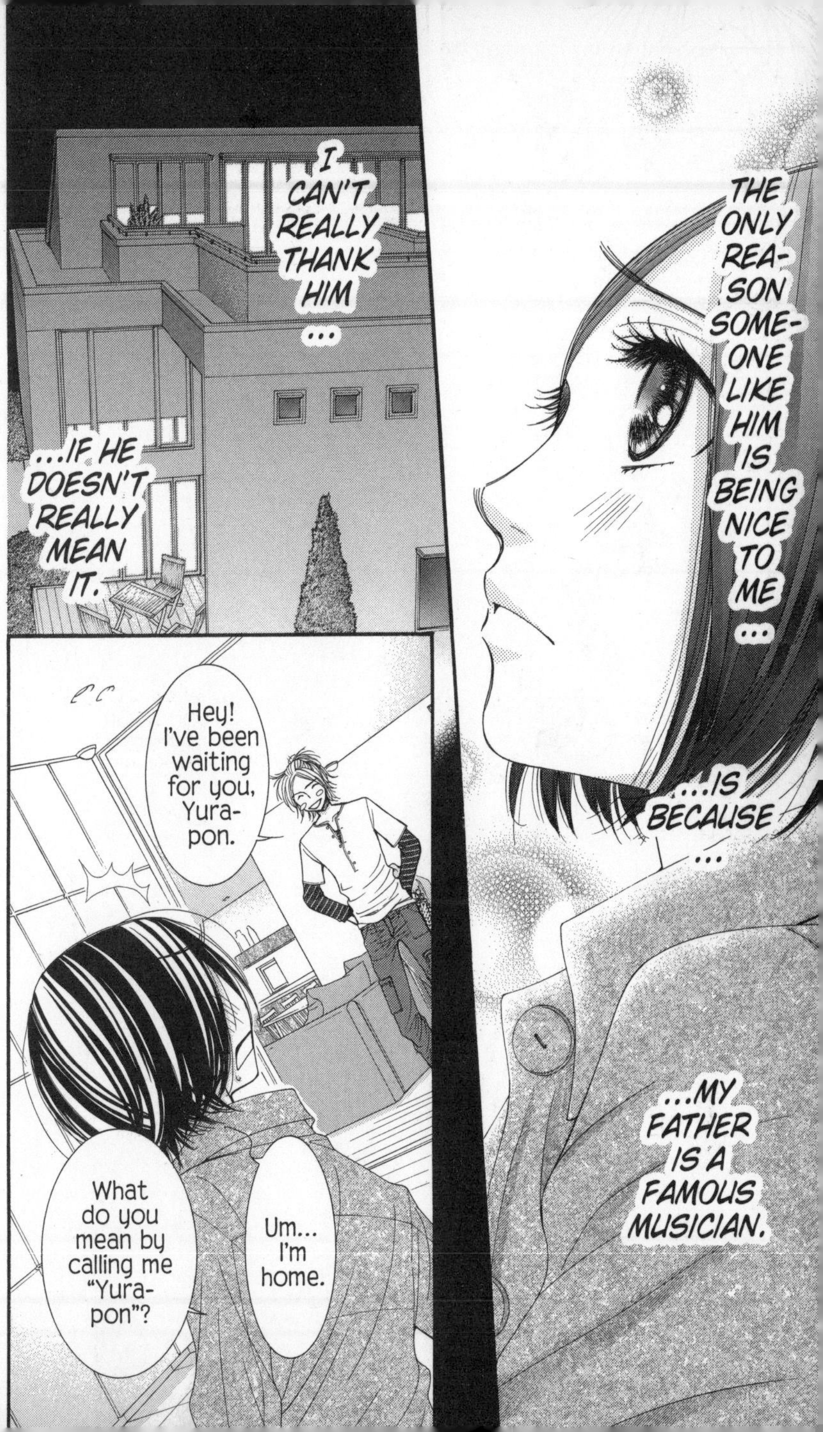
THE ONLY REA-SON SOME-ONE LIKE HIM IS BEING NICE TO ME...
...IS BECAUSE...
...MY FATHER IS A FAMOUS MUSICIAN.
I CAN'T REALLY THANK HIM...
...IF HE DOESN'T REALLY MEAN IT.
Hey! I've been waiting for you, Yura-pon.
Um... I'm home.
What do you mean by calling me "Yura-pon"?

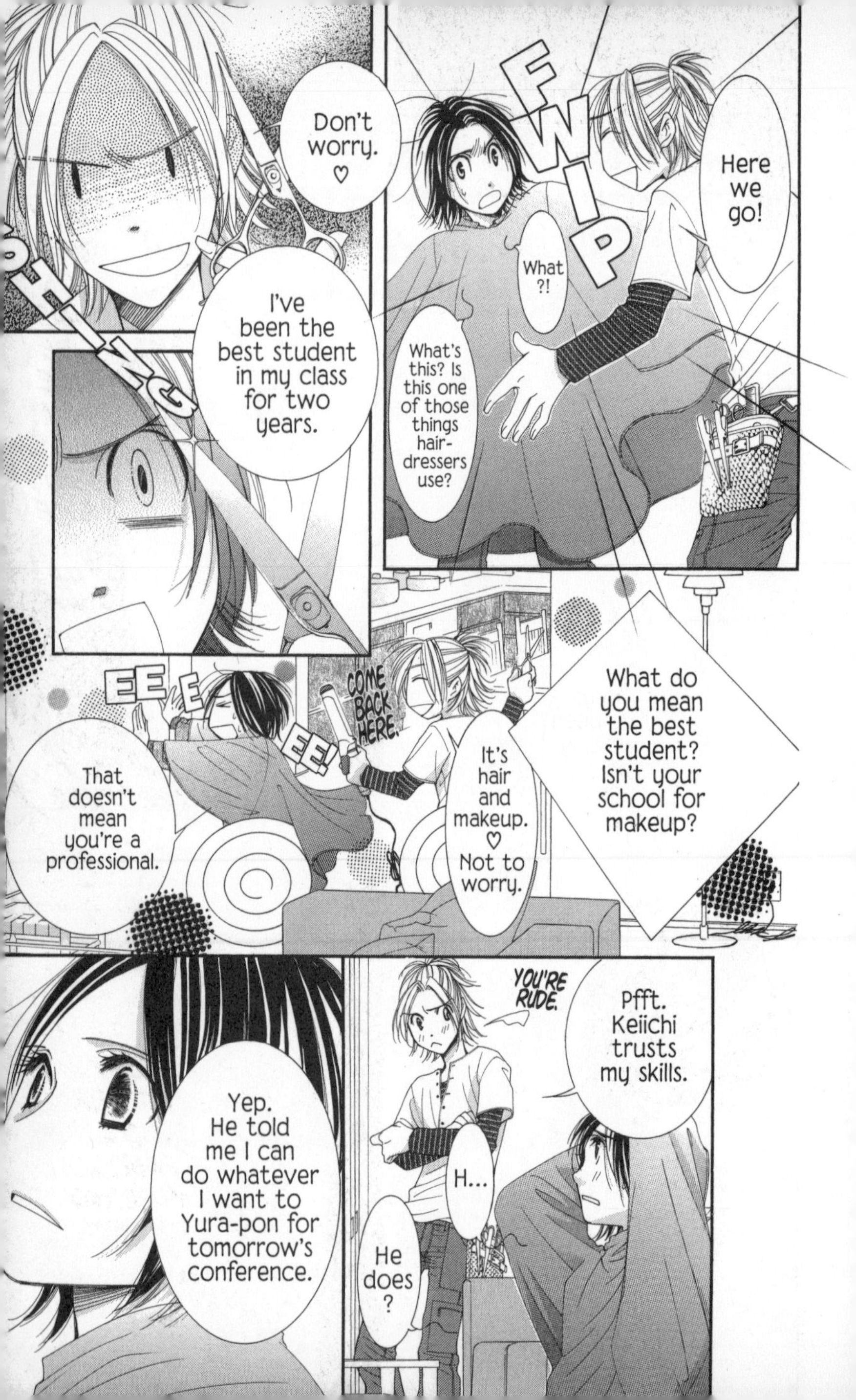
Here we go!
FWIP
What?!
What's this? Is this one of those things hairdressers use?
Don't worry. ♡
I've been the best student in my class for two years.
SHING
What do you mean the best student? Isn't your school for makeup?
It's hair and makeup. ♡ Not to worry.
COME BACK HERE.
EEEEE!
That doesn't mean you're a professional.
Pfft. Keiichi trusts my skills.
YOU'RE RUDE.
H...
He does?
Yep. He told me I can do whatever I want to Yura-pon for tomorrow's conference.

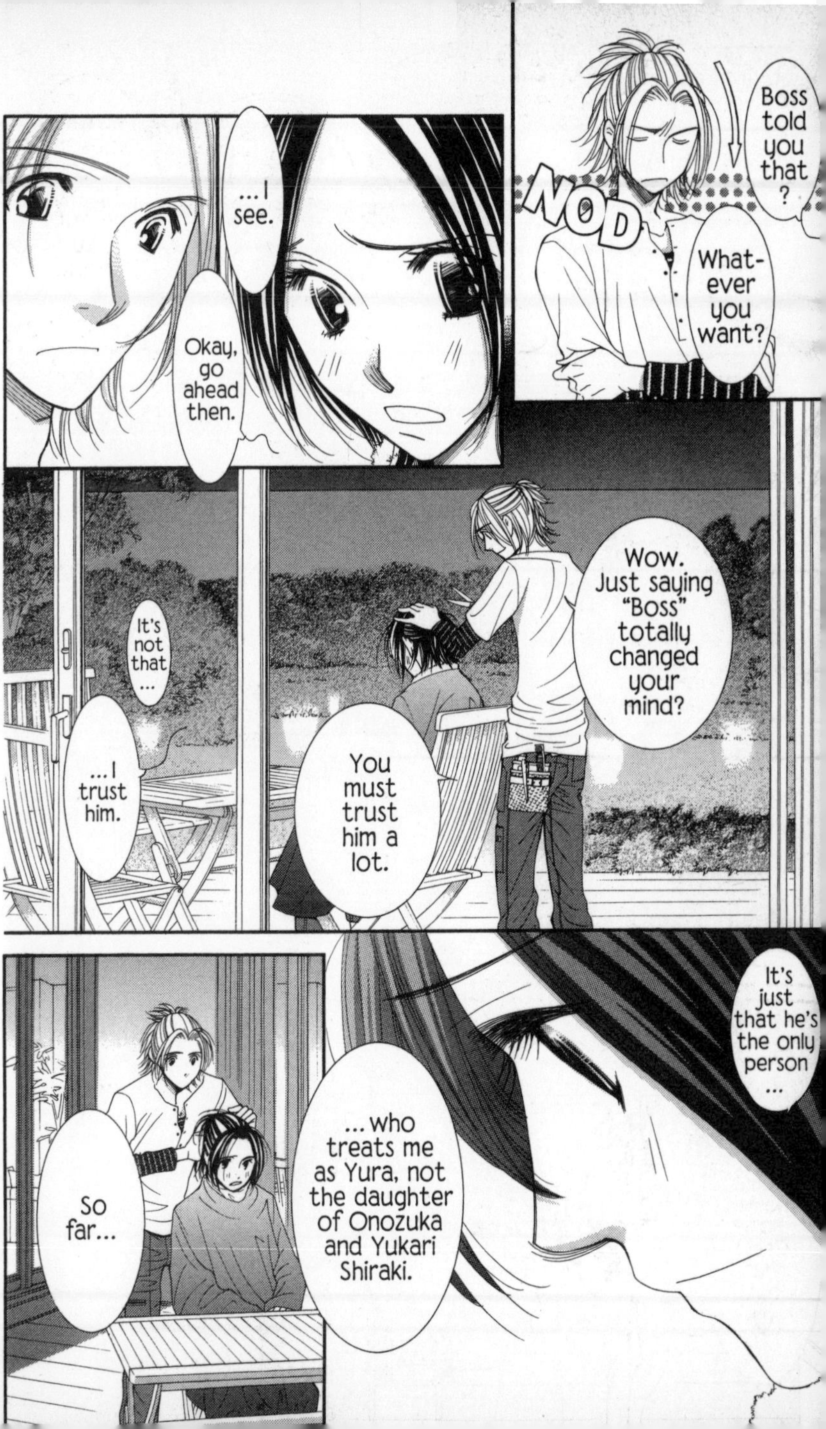
Boss told you that?
NOD
Whatever you want?
...I see.
Okay, go ahead then.
Wow. Just saying "Boss" totally changed your mind?
You must trust him a lot.
It's not that...
...I trust him.
It's just that he's the only person...
...who treats me as Yura, not the daughter of Onozuka and Yukari Shiraki.
So far...

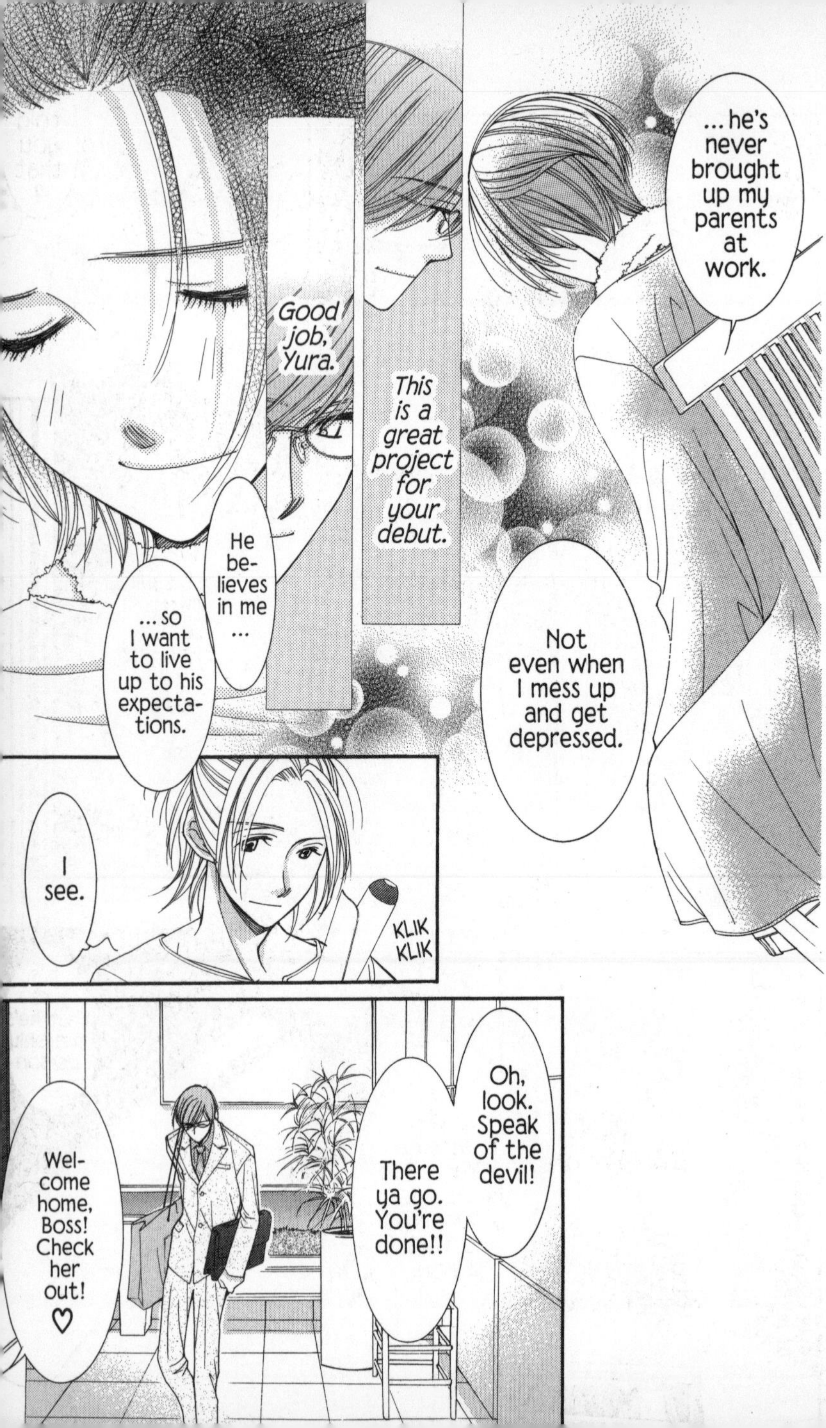
...he's never brought up my parents at work.
Not even when I mess up and get depressed.
This is a great project for your debut.
Good job, Yura.
He believes in me...
...so I want to live up to his expectations.
I see.
KLIK KLIK
Oh, look. Speak of the devil!
There ya go. You're done!!
Welcome home, Boss! Check her out! ♡

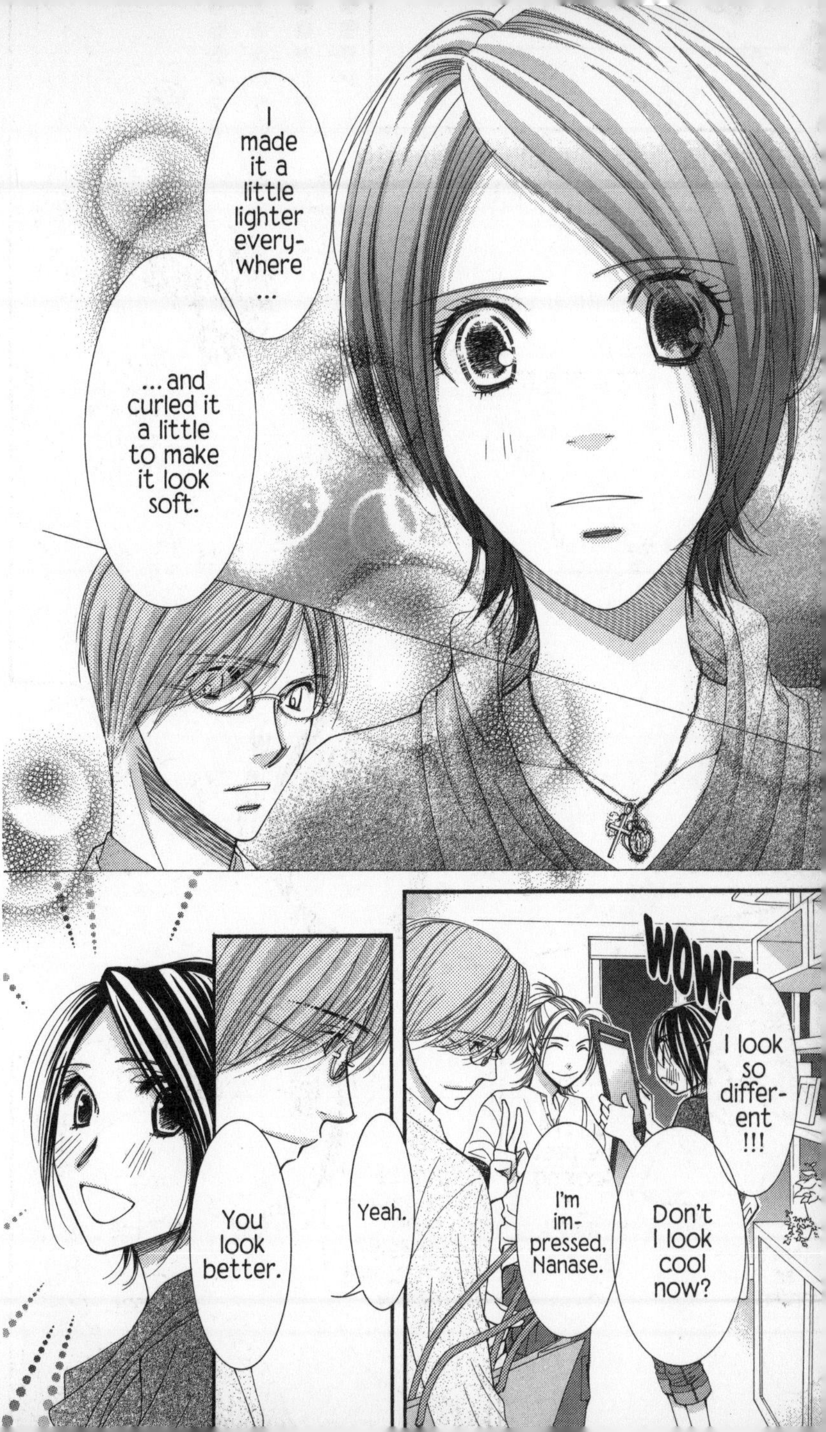
I made it a little lighter every-where...
...and curled it a little to make it look soft.
WOW!
I look so differ-ent!!!
Don't I look cool now?
I'm im-pressed, Nanase.
Yeah.
You look better.

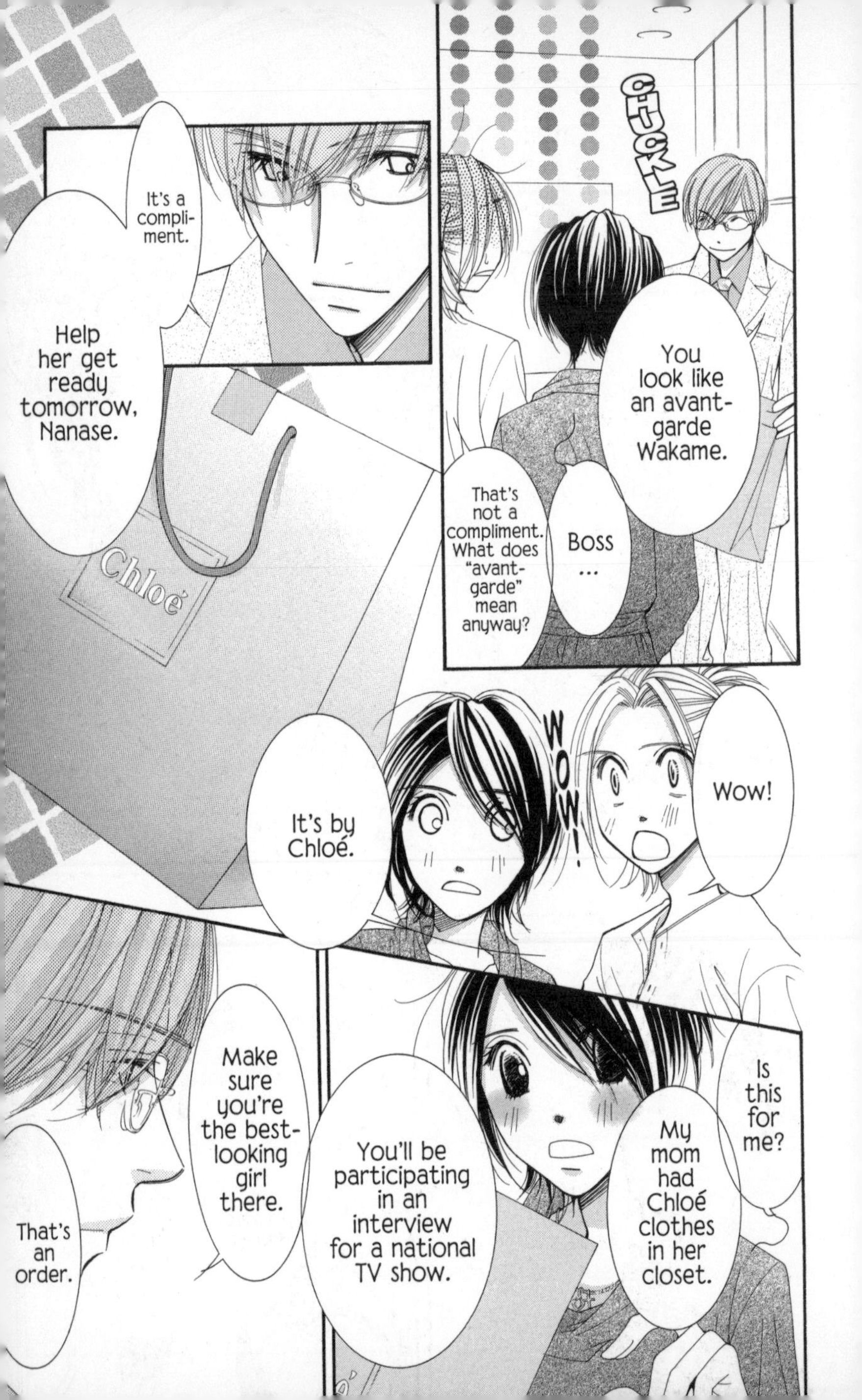
CHUCKLE
You look like an avant-garde Wakame.
Boss...
That's not a compliment. What does "avant-garde" mean anyway?
It's a compliment.
Help her get ready tomorrow, Nanase.
Chloé
Wow!
WOW!
It's by Chloé.
Is this for me?
My mom had Chloé clothes in her closet.
You'll be participating in an interview for a national TV show.
Make sure you're the best-looking girl there.
That's an order.

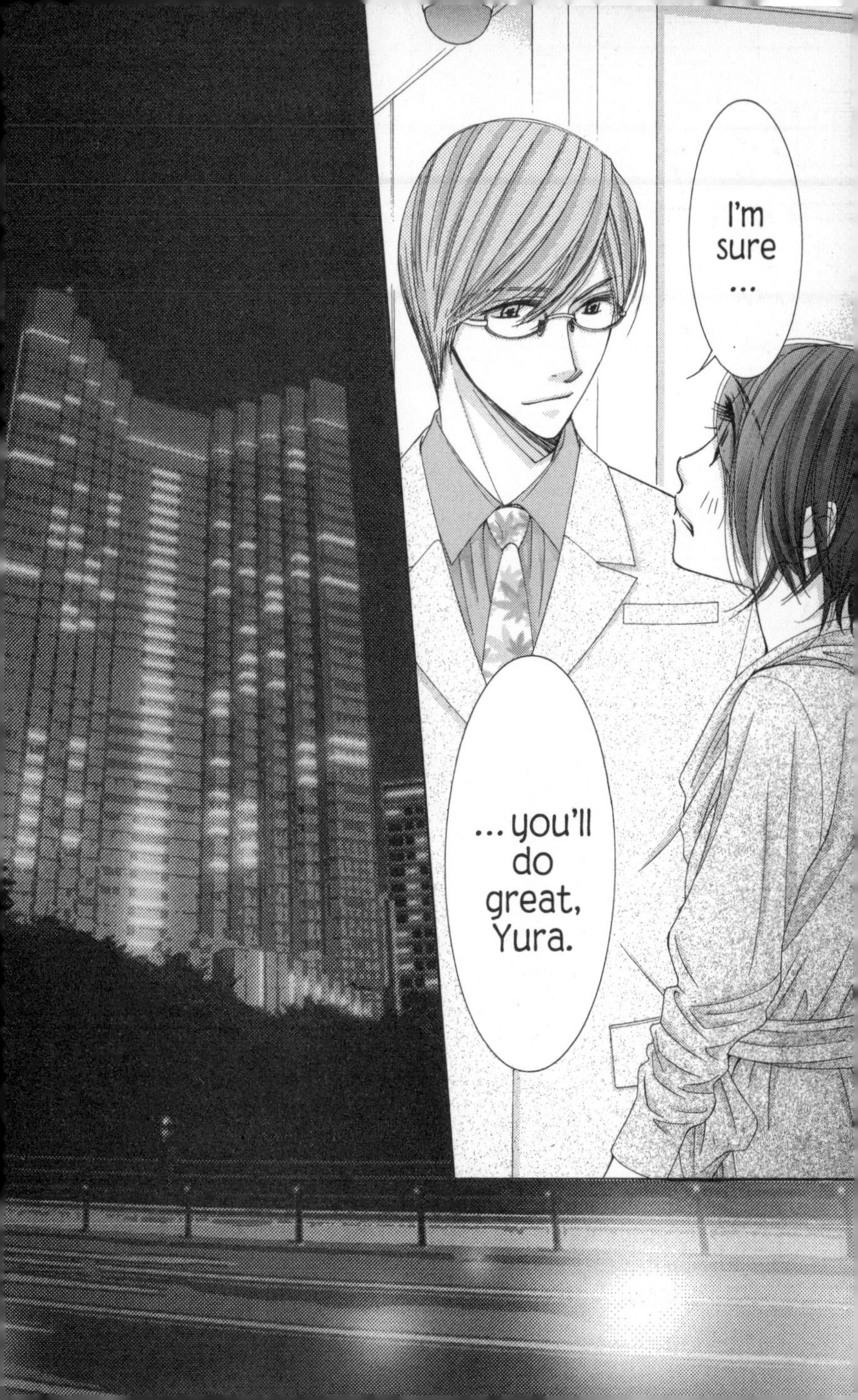
I'm sure ...
... you'll do great, Yura.

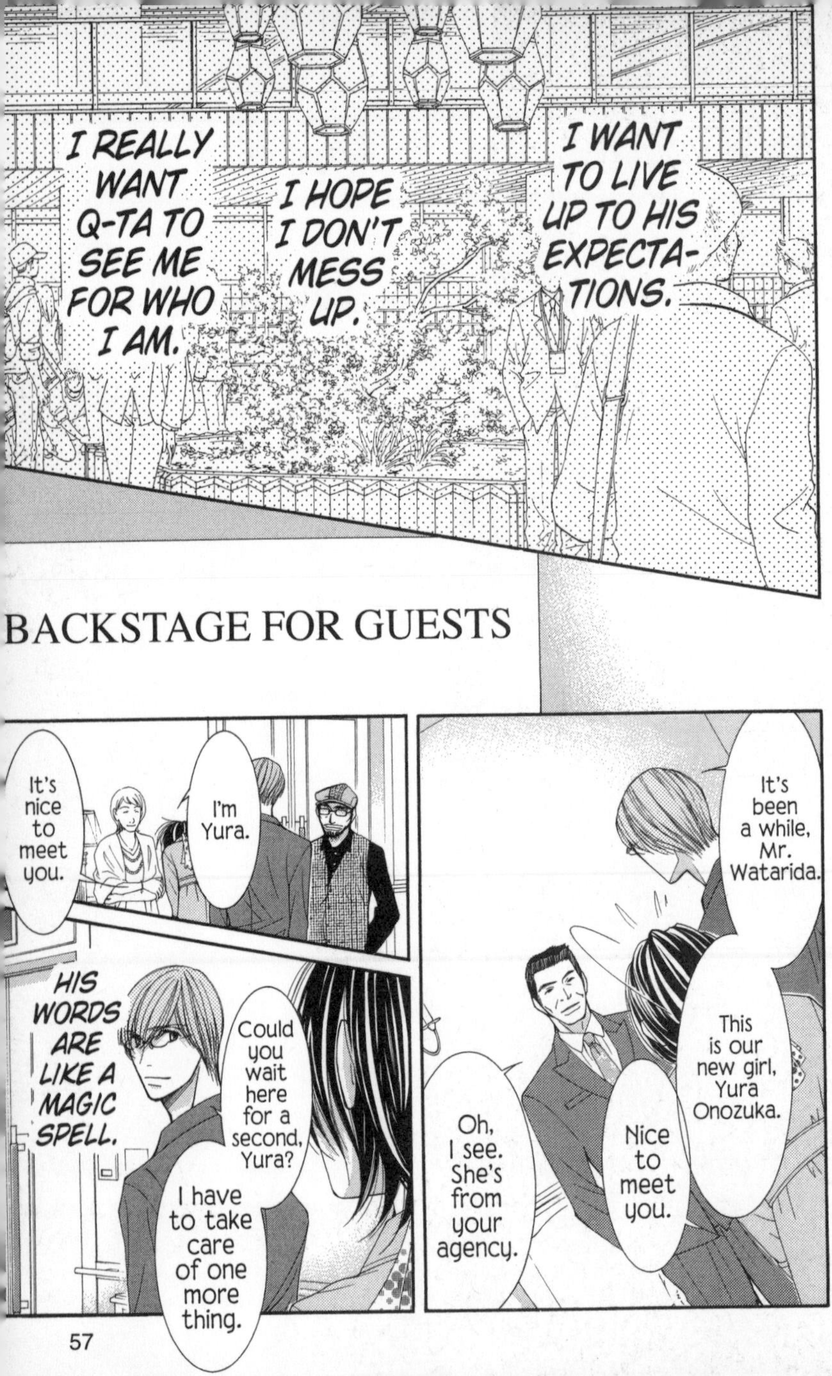
I WANT TO LIVE UP TO HIS EXPECTATIONS.
I HOPE I DON'T MESS UP.
I REALLY WANT Q-TA TO SEE ME FOR WHO I AM.
BACKSTAGE FOR GUESTS
It's been a while, Mr. Watarida.
This is our new girl, Yura Onozuka.
Nice to meet you.
Oh, I see. She's from your agency.
I'm Yura.
It's nice to meet you.
Could you wait here for a second, Yura?
I have to take care of one more thing.
HIS WORDS ARE LIKE A MAGIC SPELL.

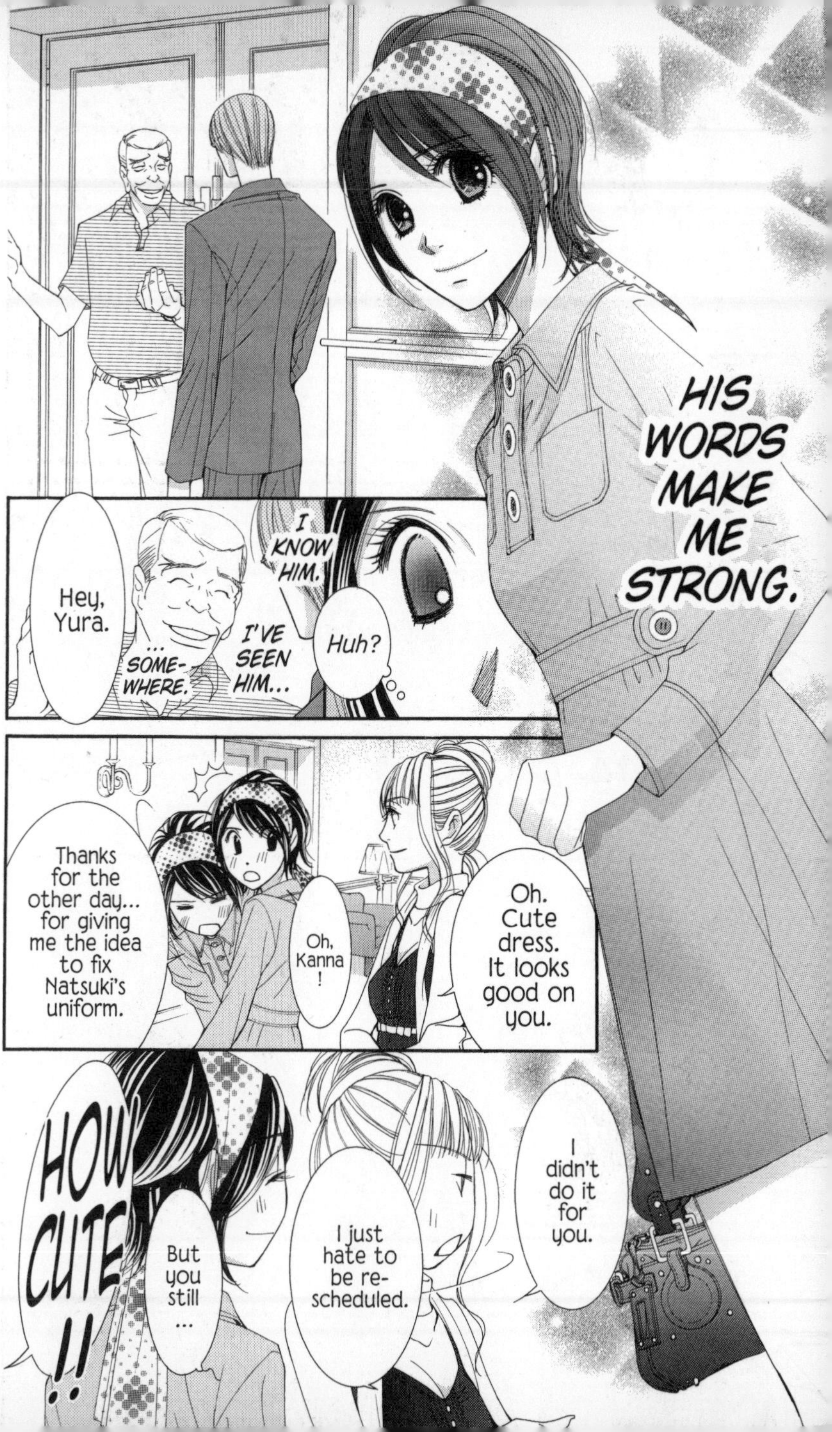
HIS WORDS MAKE ME STRONG.
I KNOW HIM.
Huh?
I'VE SEEN HIM...
...SOMEWHERE.
Hey, Yura.
Oh. Cute dress. It looks good on you.
Oh, Kanna!
Thanks for the other day... for giving me the idea to fix Natsuki's uniform.
I didn't do it for you.
I just hate to be re-scheduled.
But you still ...
HOW CUTE!!

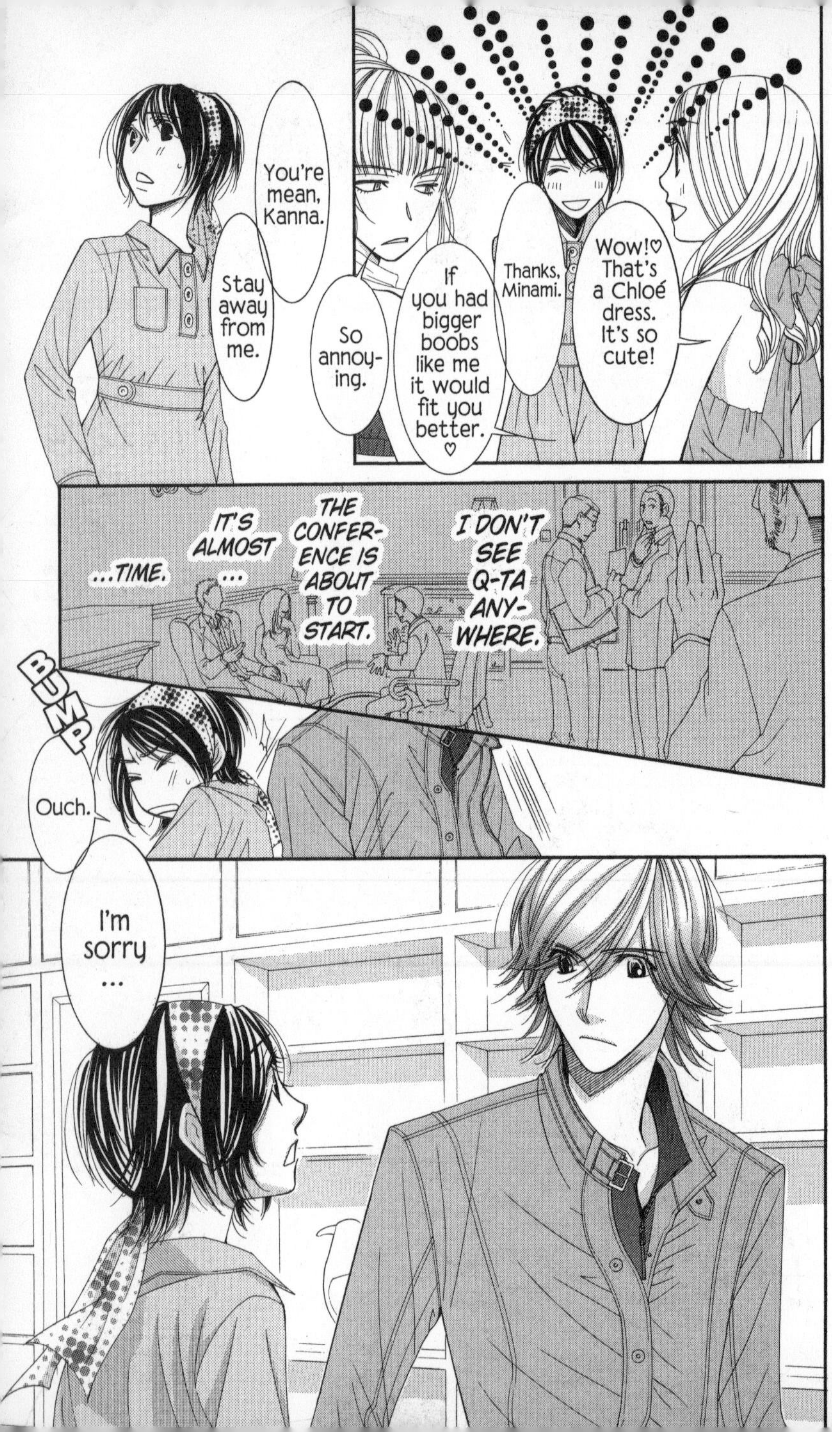
Wow!♡ That's a Chloé dress. It's so cute!
Thanks, Minami.
If you had bigger boobs like me it would fit you better. ♡
So annoy-ing.
You're mean, Kanna.
Stay away from me.
I DON'T SEE Q-TA ANY-WHERE.
THE CONFER-ENCE IS ABOUT TO START.
IT'S ALMOST ...
...TIME.
BUMP
Ouch.
I'm sorry ...

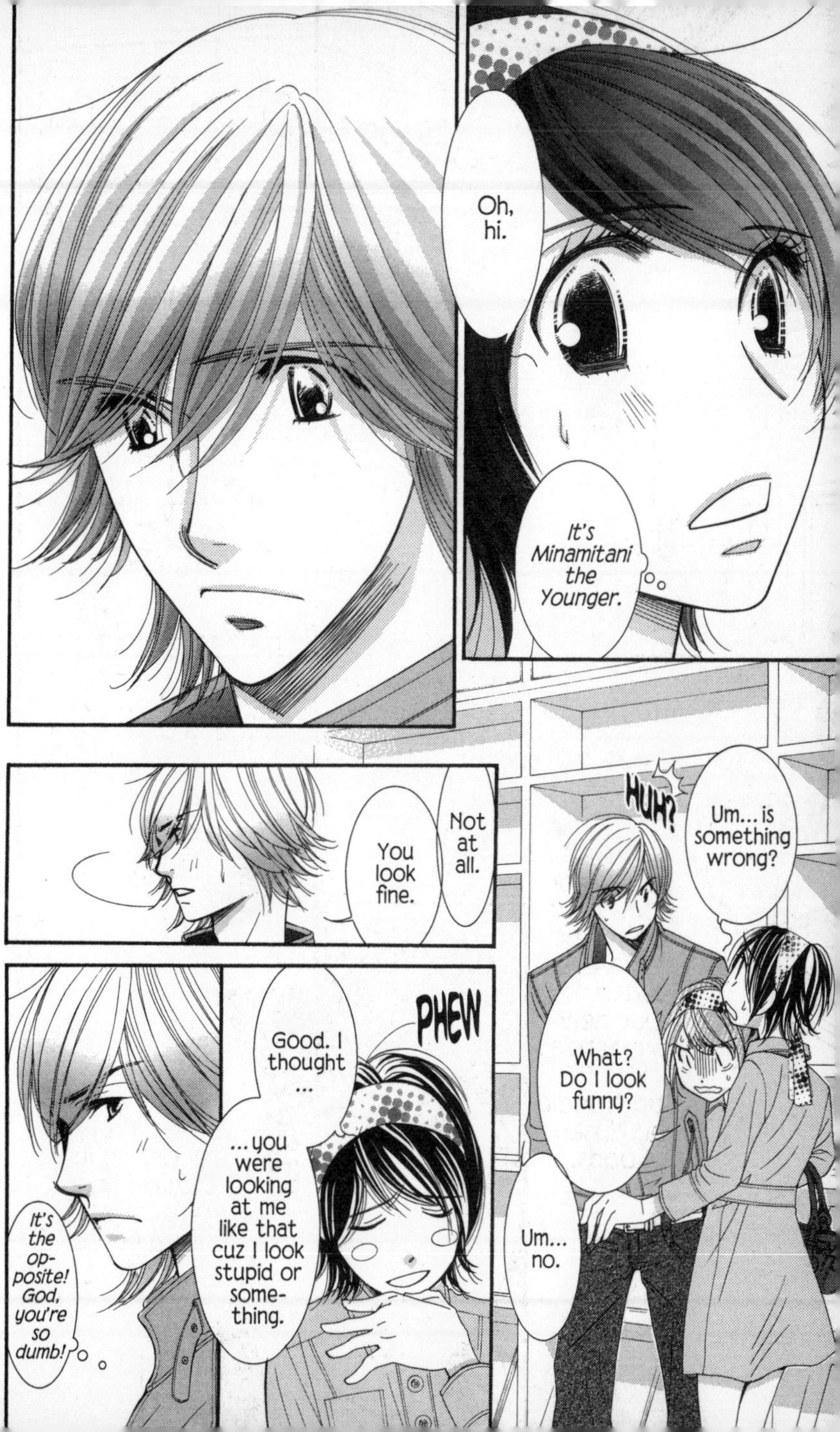
Oh, hi.
It's Minamitani the Younger.
HUH?
Um... is something wrong?
What? Do I look funny?
Um... no.
Not at all.
You look fine.
PHEW
Good. I thought...
...you were looking at me like that cuz I look stupid or something.
It's the opposite! God, you're so dumb!

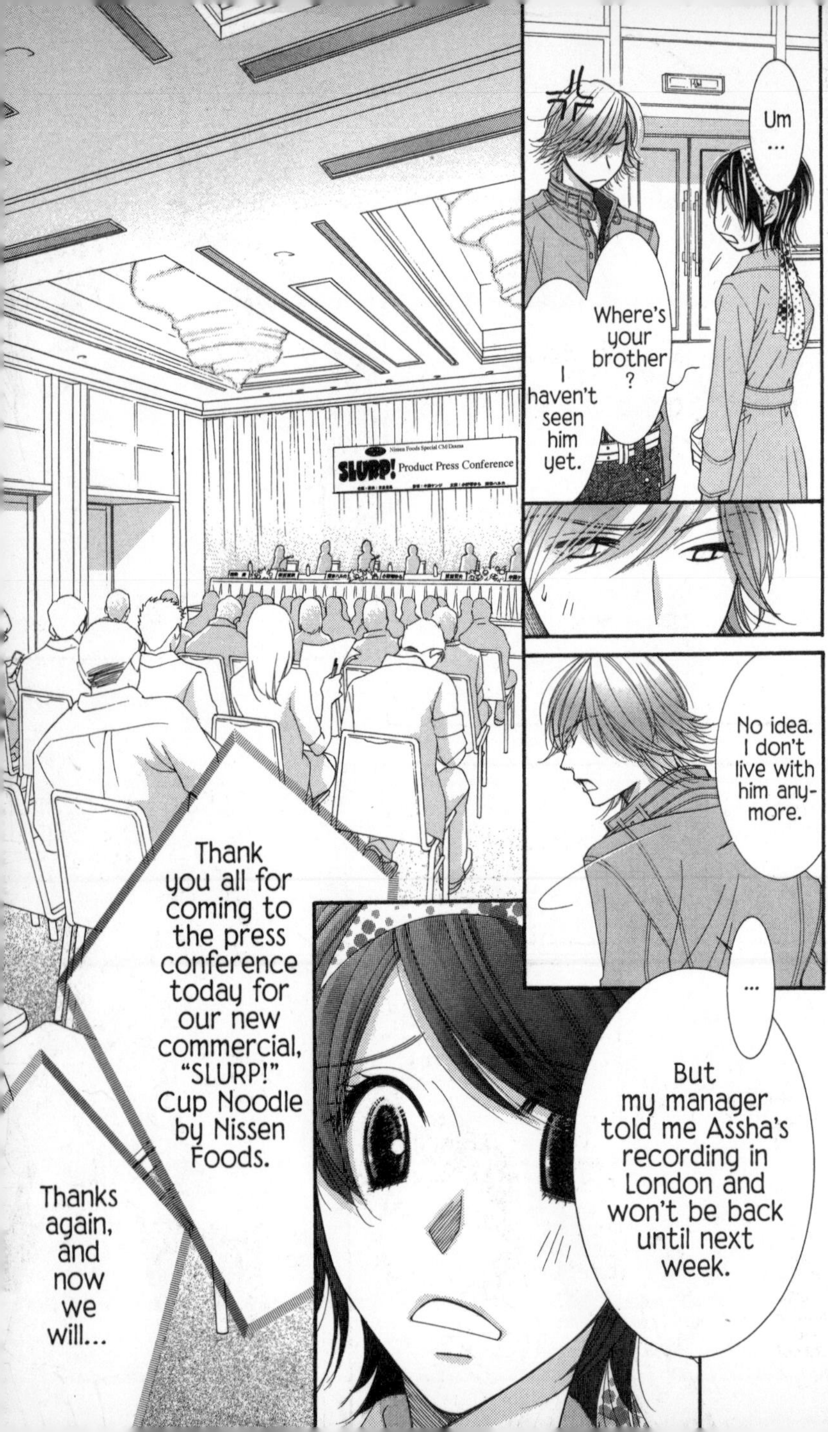
Um...
Where's your brother?
I haven't seen him yet.
No idea. I don't live with him any-more.
...
But my manager told me Assha's recording in London and won't be back until next week.
Nissen Foods Special CM/Drama
SLURP! Product Press Conference
Thank you all for coming to the press conference today for our new commercial, "SLURP!" Cup Noodle by Nissen Foods.
Thanks again, and now we will...

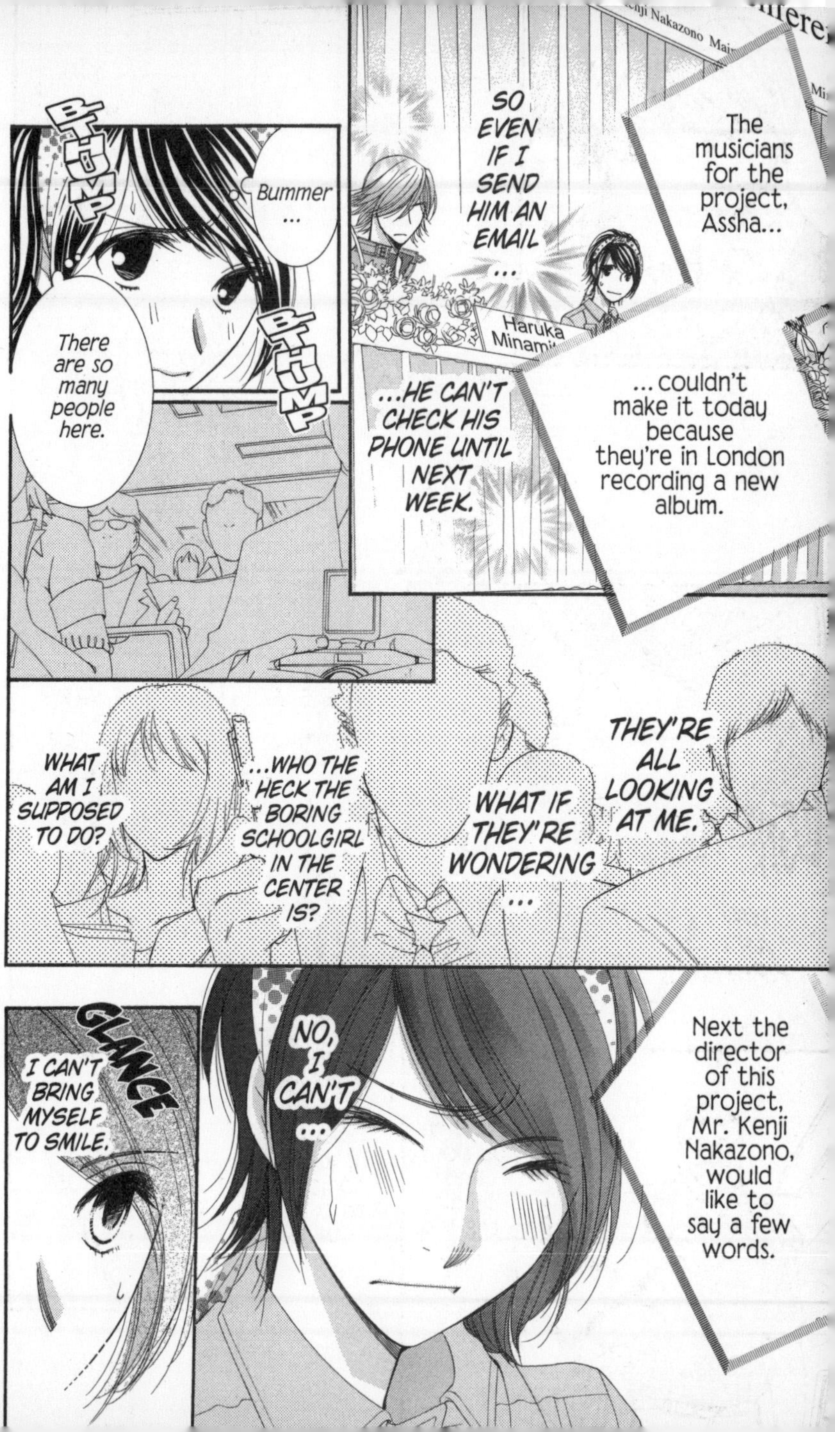

The musicians for the project, Assha...
...couldn't make it today because they're in London recording a new album.
SO EVEN IF I SEND HIM AN EMAIL...
...HE CAN'T CHECK HIS PHONE UNTIL NEXT WEEK.
B-THUMP
B-THUMP
Bummer...
There are so many people here.
THEY'RE ALL LOOKING AT ME.
WHAT IF THEY'RE WONDERING...
...WHO THE HECK THE BORING SCHOOLGIRL IN THE CENTER IS?
WHAT AM I SUPPOSED TO DO?
Next the director of this project, Mr. Kenji Nakazono, would like to say a few words.
NO, I CAN'T...
GLANCE
I CAN'T BRING MYSELF TO SMILE.

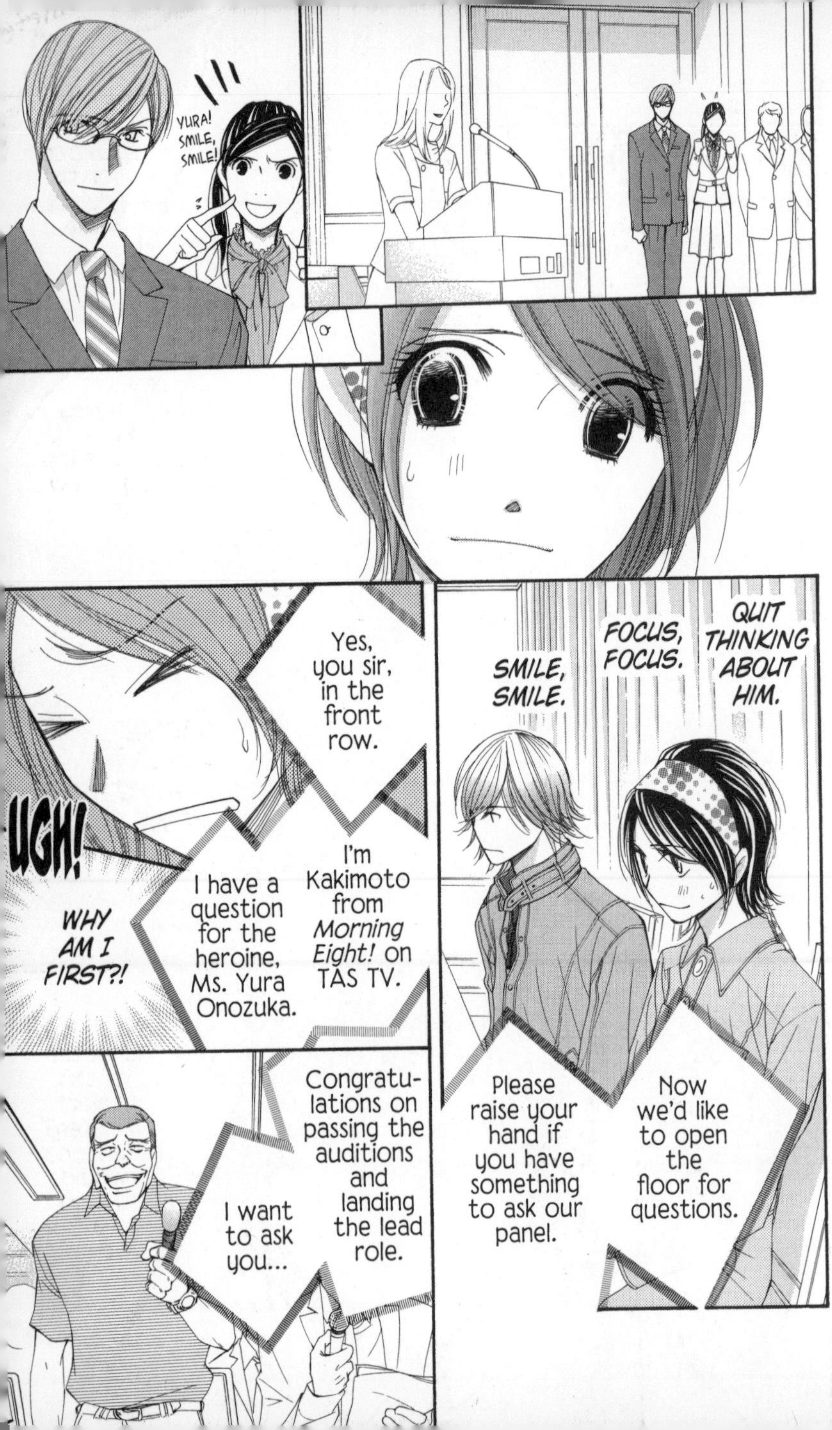
YURA! SMILE, SMILE!
QUIT THINKING ABOUT HIM.
FOCUS, FOCUS.
SMILE, SMILE.
Now we'd like to open the floor for questions.
Please raise your hand if you have something to ask our panel.
Yes, you sir, in the front row.
I'm Kakimoto from *Morning Eight!* on TAS TV.
I have a question for the heroine, Ms. Yura Onozuka.
UGH!
WHY AM I FIRST?!
Congratulations on passing the auditions and landing the lead role.
I want to ask you...

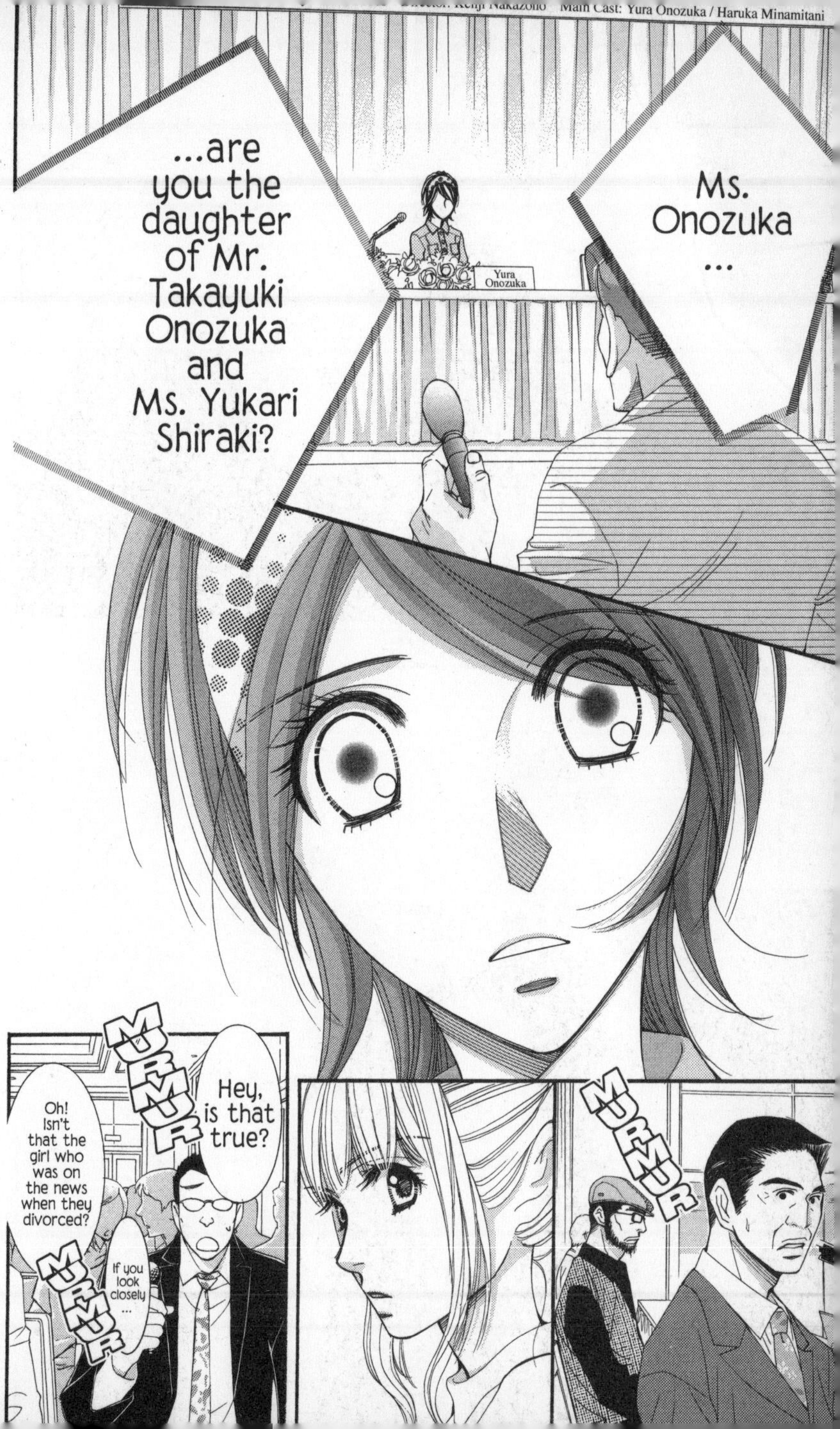

Main Cast: Yura Onozuka / Haruka Minamitani
Ms. Onozuka ...
...are you the daughter of Mr. Takayuki Onozuka and Ms. Yukari Shiraki?
Yura Onozuka
MURMUR
MURMUR
Hey, is that true?
Oh! Isn't that the girl who was on the news when they divorced?
If you look closely ...
MURMUR

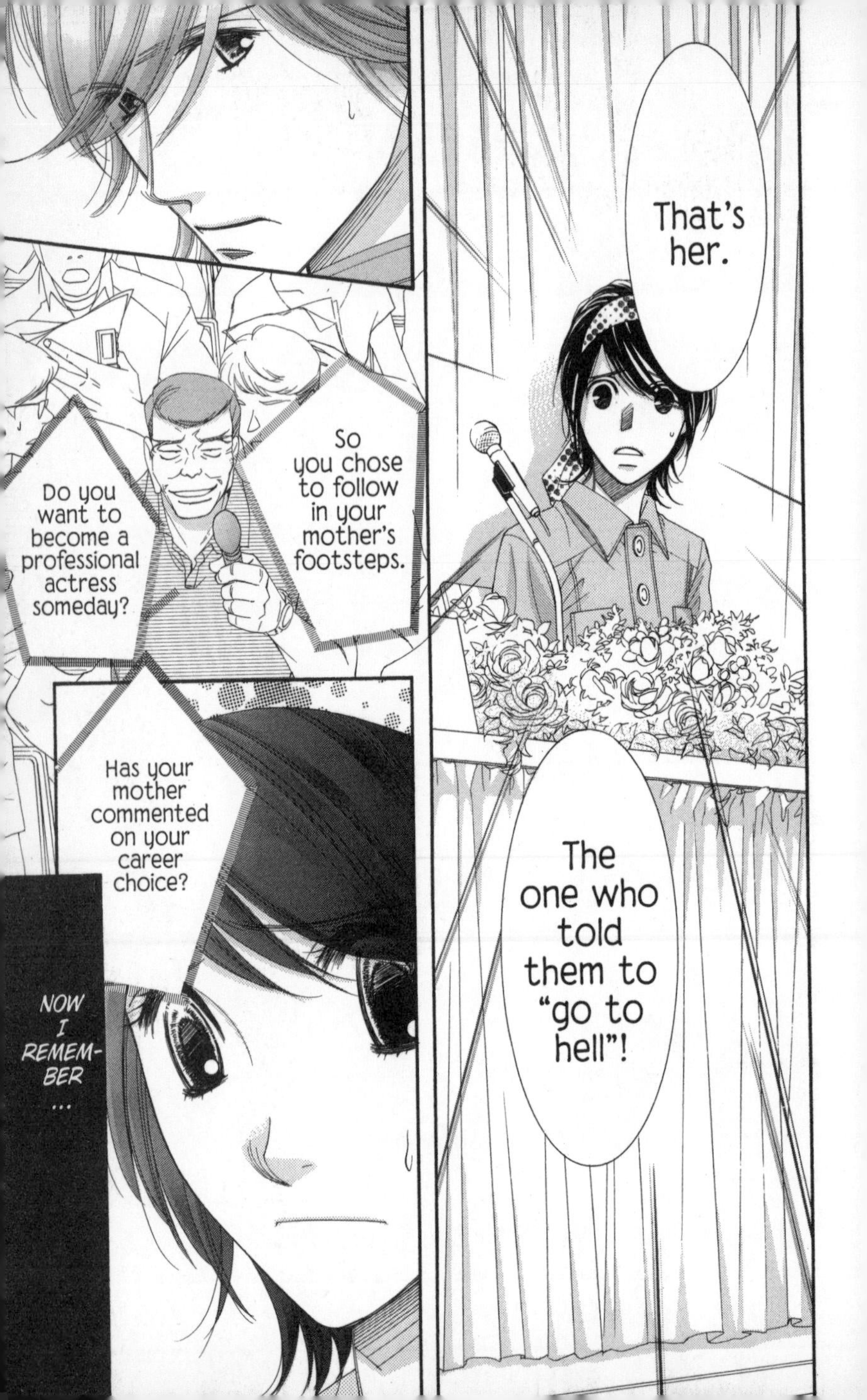
That's her.
The one who told them to "go to hell"!
So you chose to follow in your mother's footsteps.
Do you want to become a professional actress someday?
Has your mother commented on your career choice?
NOW I REMEMBER...

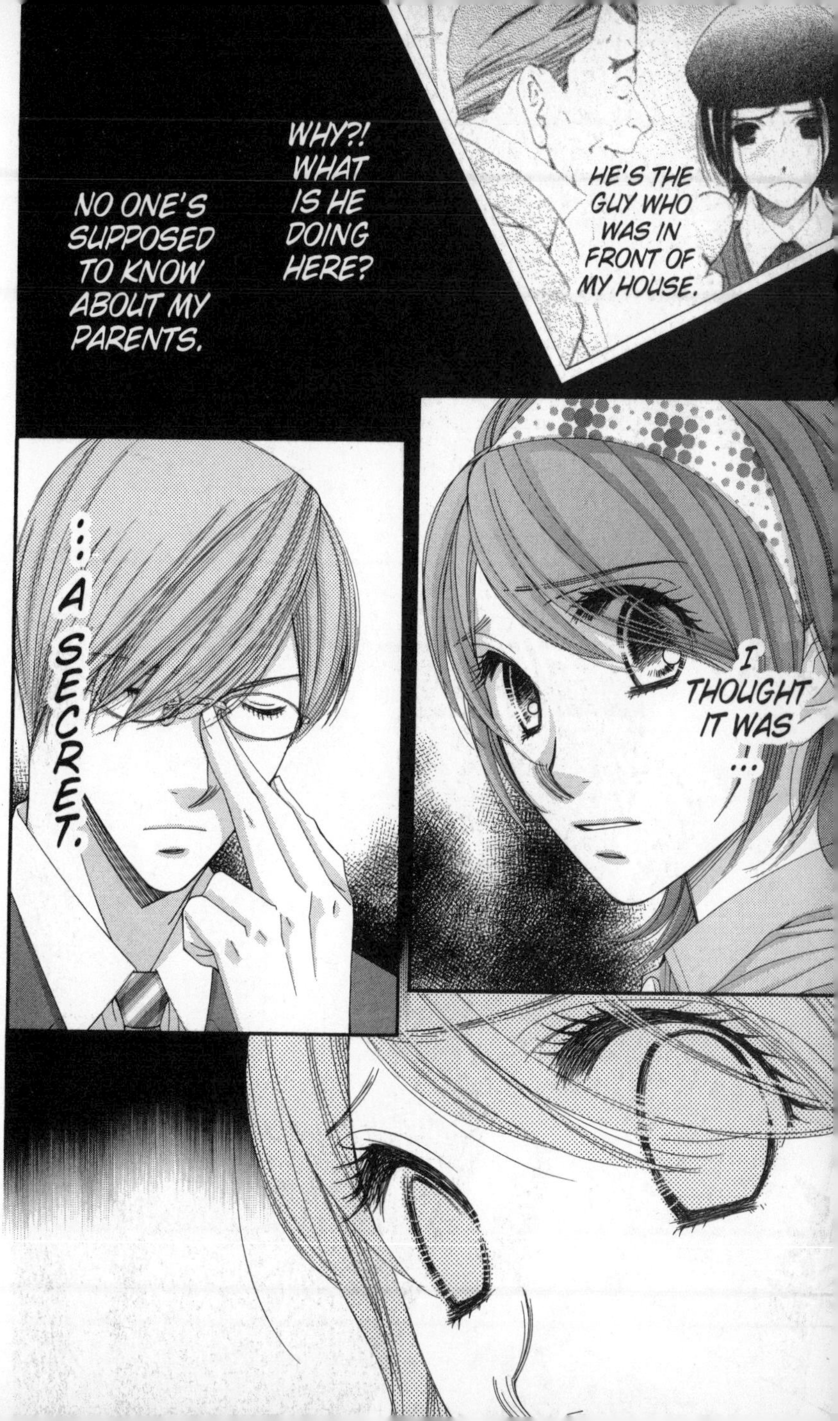
HE'S THE GUY WHO WAS IN FRONT OF MY HOUSE.
WHY?! WHAT IS HE DOING HERE?
NO ONE'S SUPPOSED TO KNOW ABOUT MY PARENTS.
I THOUGHT IT WAS...
...A SECRET.

BOSS?
DID YOU TELL HIM?!
Ms. Onozuka?
Can you answer my question?
FLASH!
FLASH!
FLASH!

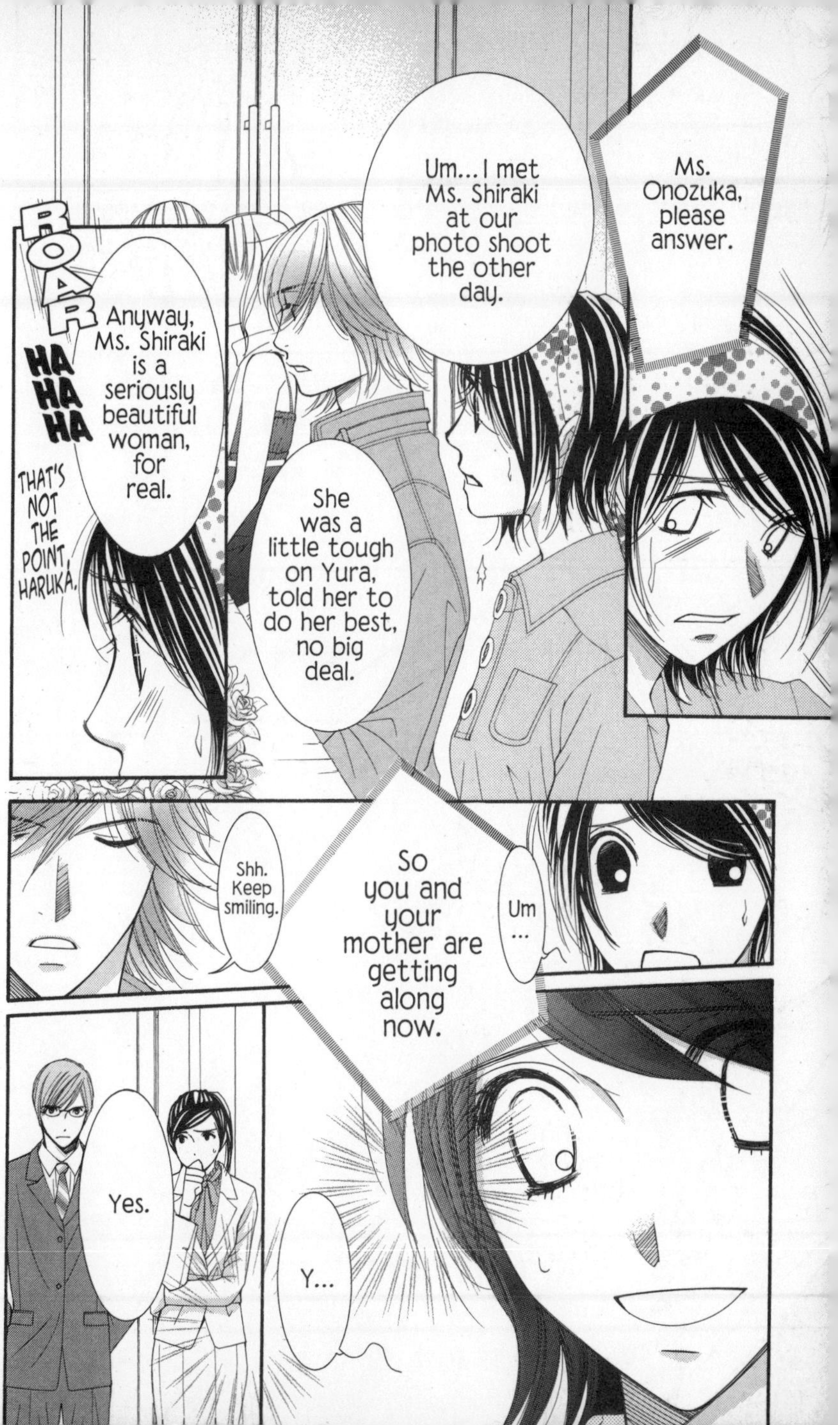
Ms. Onozuka, please answer.
Um...I met Ms. Shiraki at our photo shoot the other day.
She was a little tough on Yura, told her to do her best, no big deal.
ROAR
HA HA HA
Anyway, Ms. Shiraki is a seriously beautiful woman, for real.
THAT'S NOT THE POINT, HARUKA.
Um ...
So you and your mother are getting along now.
Shh. Keep smiling.
Y...
Yes.

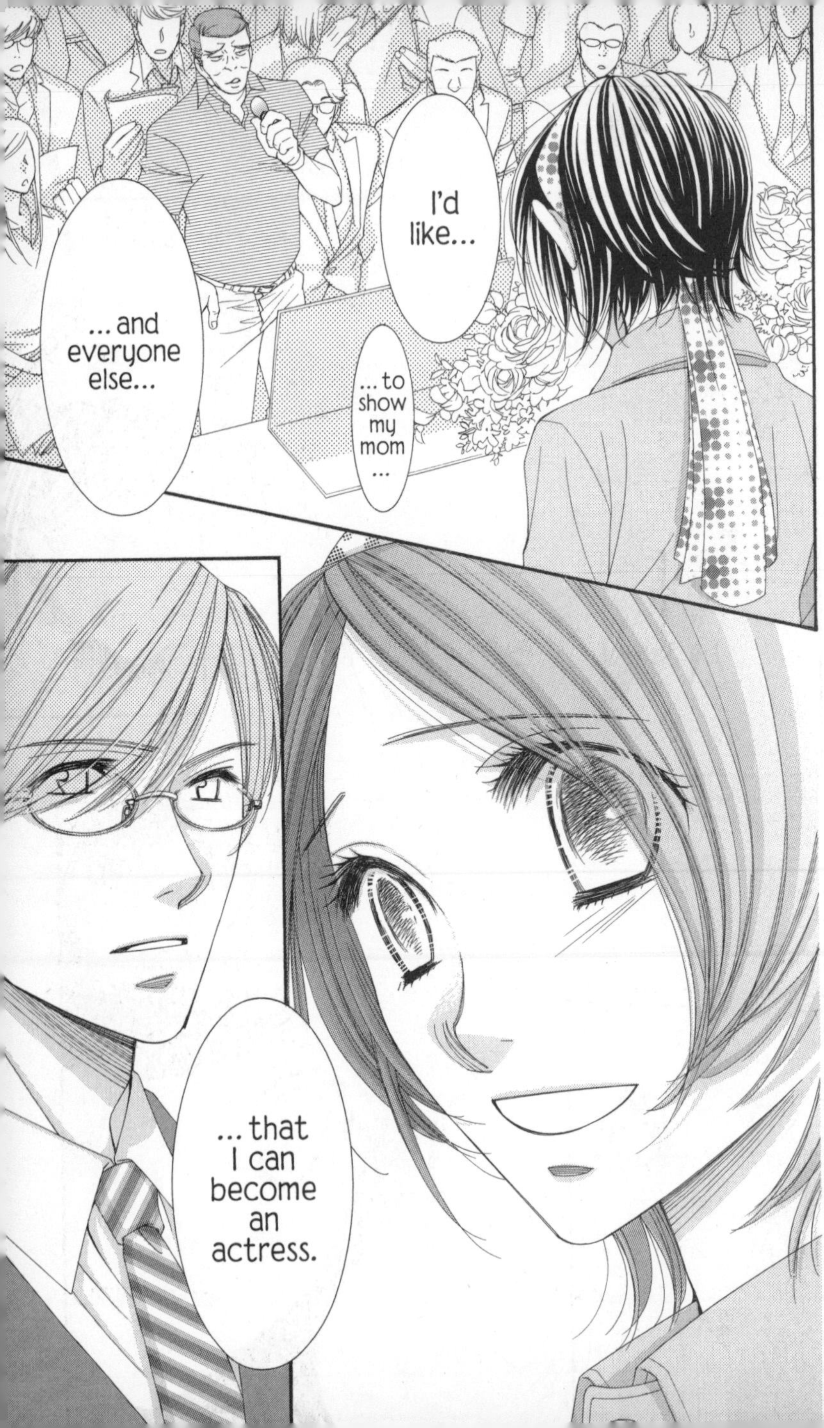
I'd like...
...to show my mom...
...and everyone else...
...that I can become an actress.

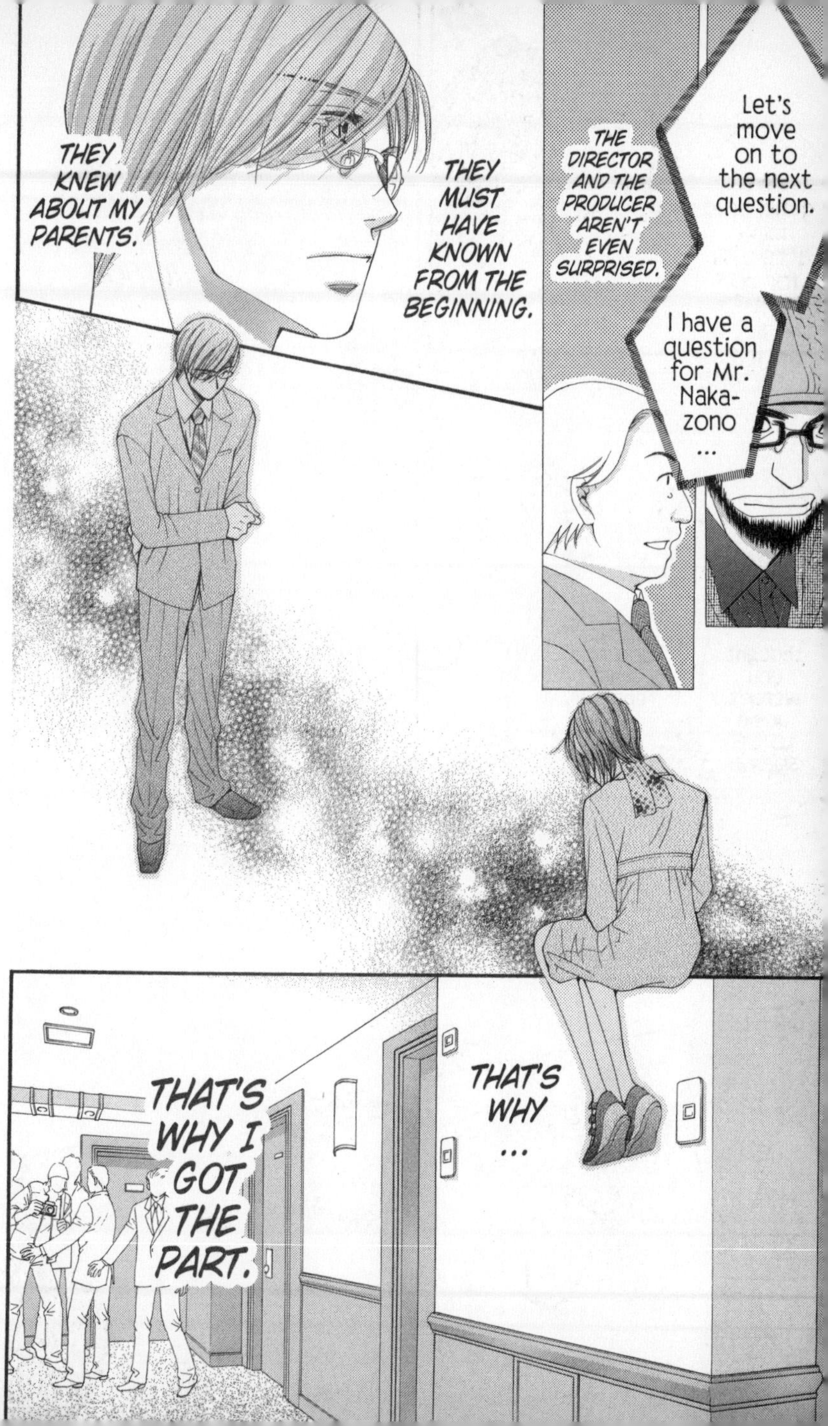
Let's move on to the next question.
I have a question for Mr. Naka-zono ...
THE DIRECTOR AND THE PRODUCER AREN'T EVEN SURPRISED.
THEY MUST HAVE KNOWN FROM THE BEGINNING.
THEY KNEW ABOUT MY PARENTS.
THAT'S WHY ...
THAT'S WHY I GOT THE PART.

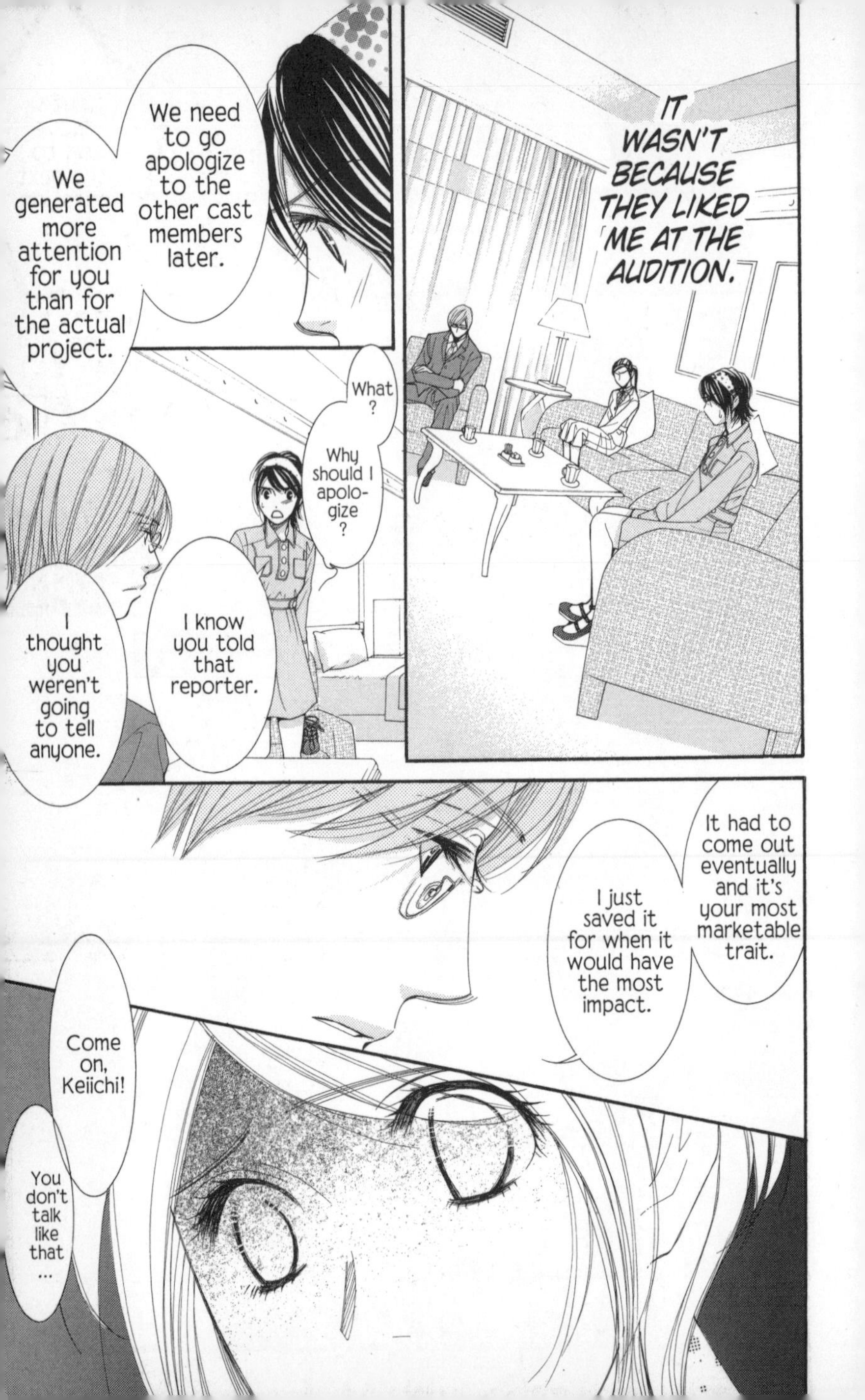
IT WASN'T BECAUSE THEY LIKED ME AT THE AUDITION.
We need to go apologize to the other cast members later.
We generated more attention for you than for the actual project.
What?
Why should I apologize?
I know you told that reporter.
I thought you weren't going to tell anyone.
It had to come out eventually and it's your most marketable trait.
I just saved it for when it would have the most impact.
Come on, Keiichi!
You don't talk like that...

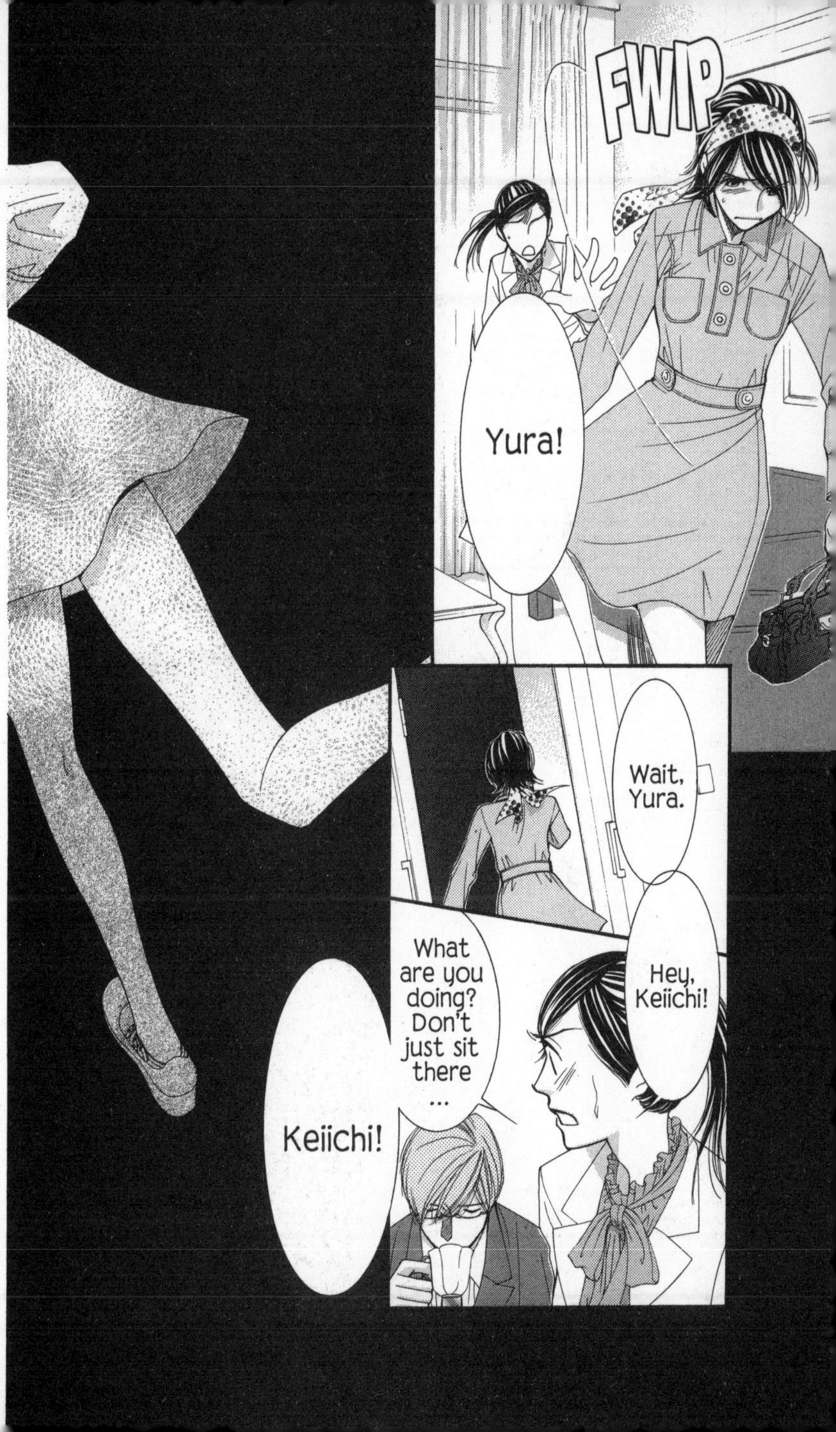
FWIP
Yura!
Wait, Yura.
Hey, Keiichi!
What are you doing? Don't just sit there ...
Keiichi!

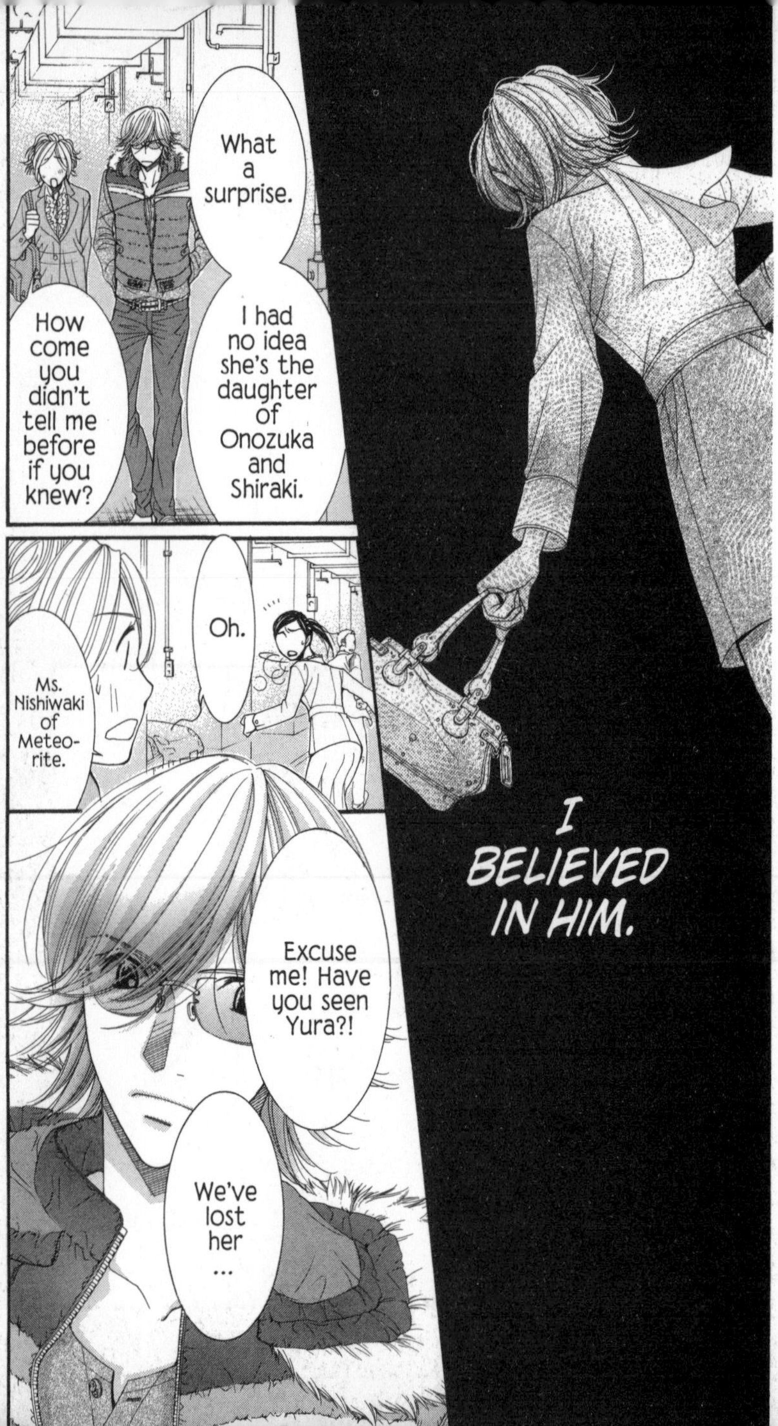
I BELIEVED IN HIM.
What a surprise.
I had no idea she's the daughter of Onozuka and Shiraki.
How come you didn't tell me before if you knew?
Oh.
Ms. Nishiwaki of Meteo-rite.
Excuse me! Have you seen Yura?!
We've lost her ...

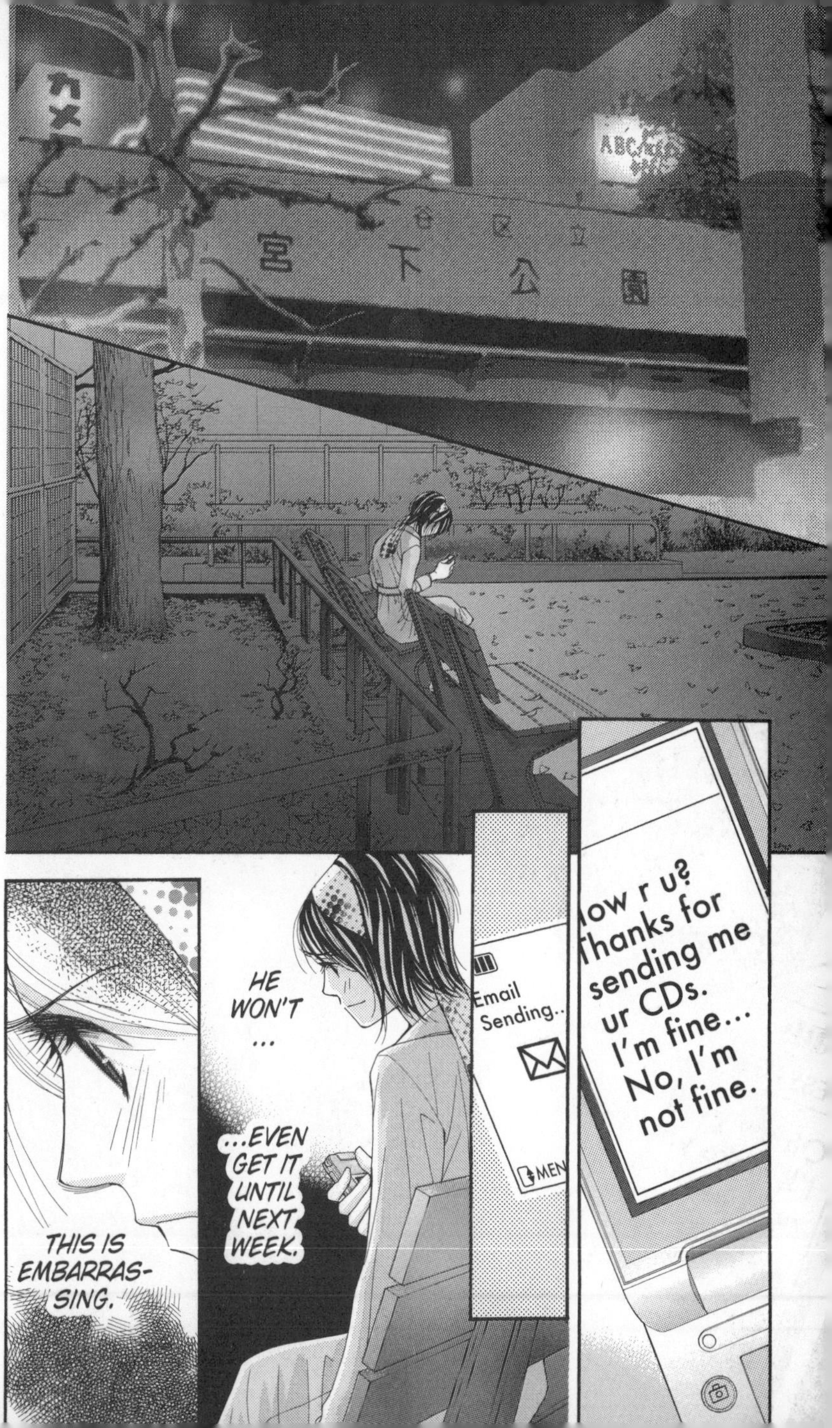
宮下公園
How r u? Thanks for sending me ur CDs. I'm fine... No, I'm not fine.
Email Sending..
MEN
HE WON'T ...
...EVEN GET IT UNTIL NEXT WEEK.
THIS IS EMBARRAS-SING.

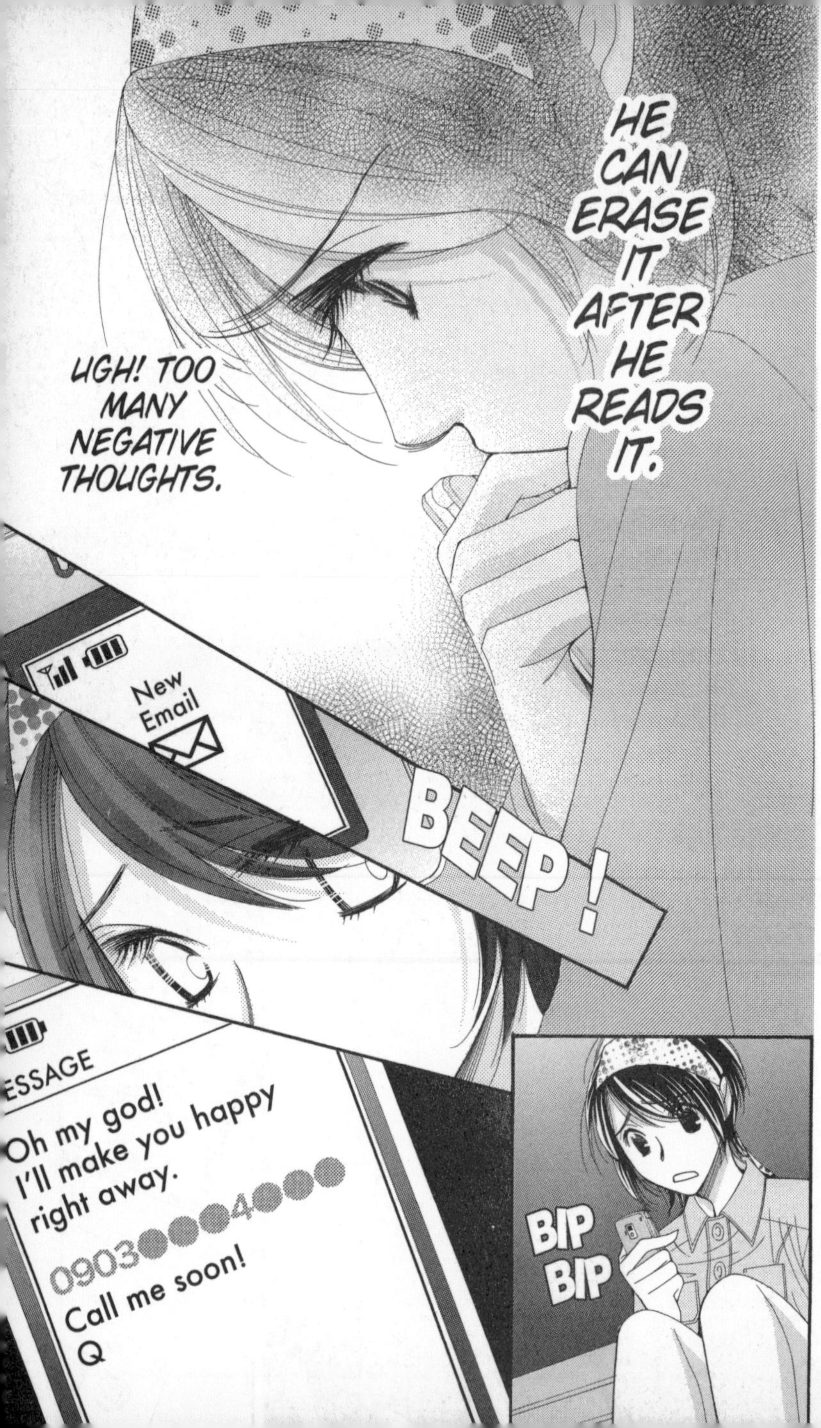
HE CAN ERASE IT AFTER HE READS IT.
UGH! TOO MANY NEGATIVE THOUGHTS.
New Email
BEEP!
BIP BIP
ESSAGE
Oh my god!
I'll make you happy right away.
0903●●●●4●●●●
Call me soon!
Q

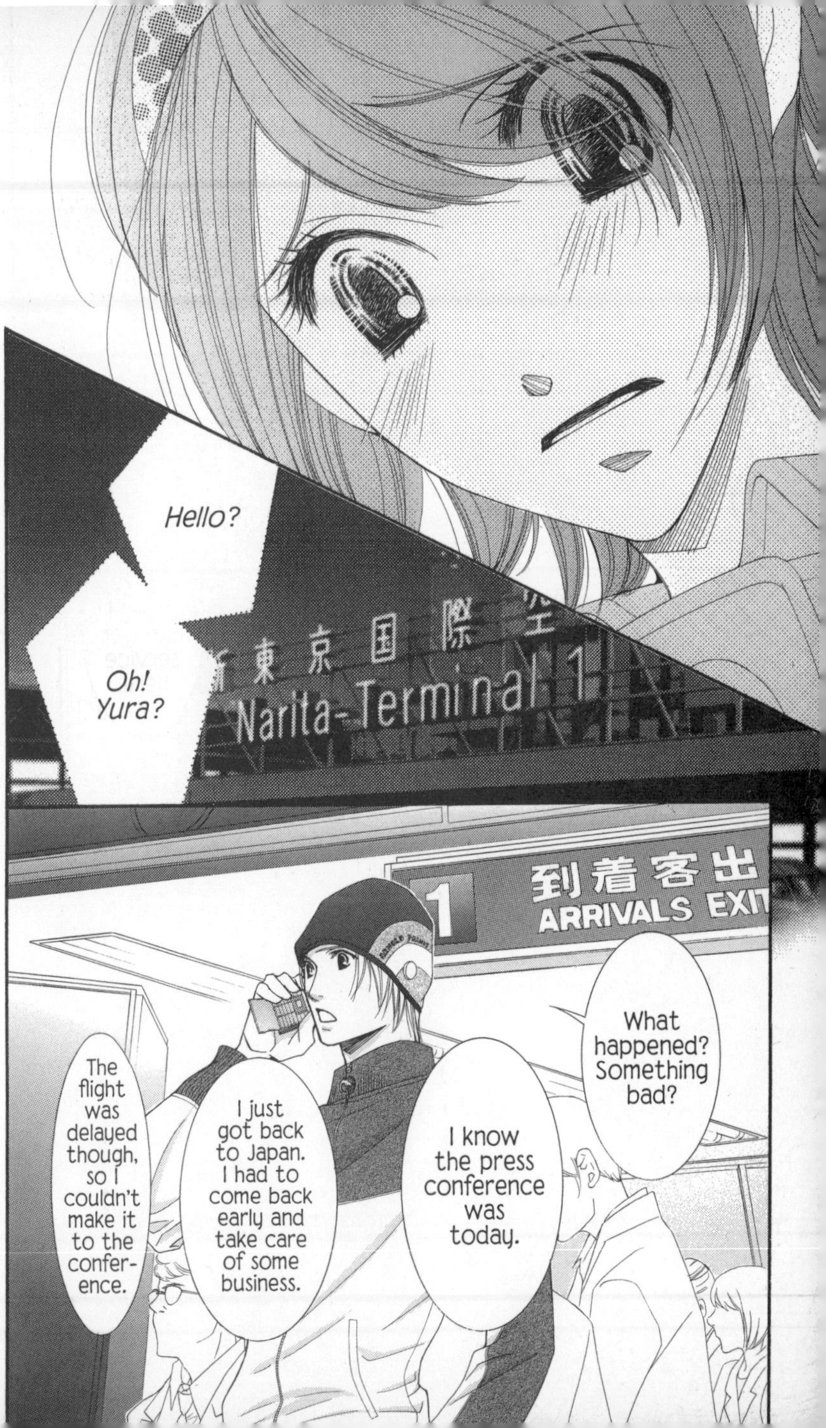
Hello?
Oh! Yura?
東京国際空
Narita-Terminal 1
1
到着客出
ARRIVALS EXI
What happened? Something bad?
I know the press conference was today.
I just got back to Japan. I had to come back early and take care of some business.
The flight was delayed though, so I couldn't make it to the confer-ence.

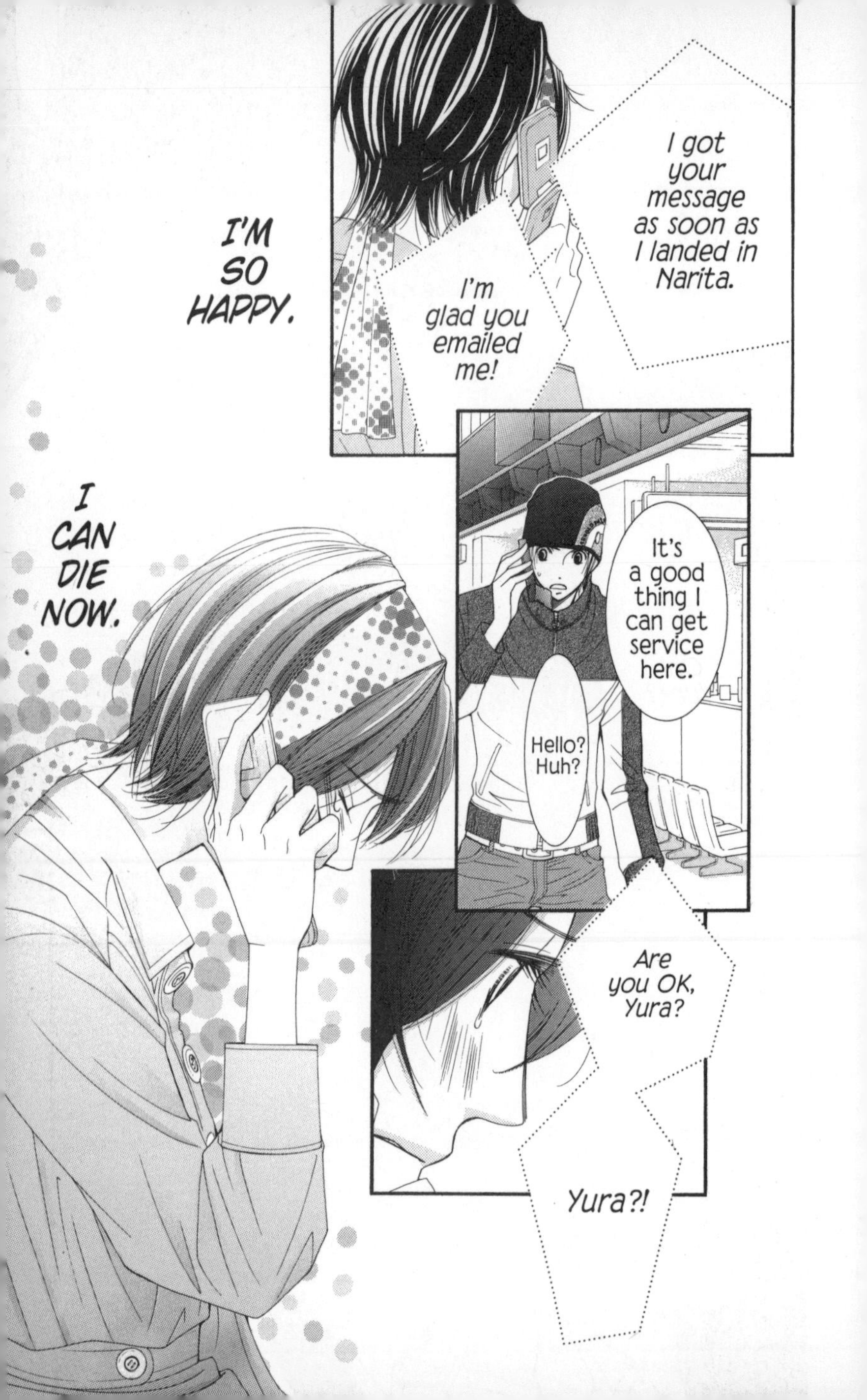
I got your message as soon as I landed in Narita.
I'm glad you emailed me!
I'M SO HAPPY.
It's a good thing I can get service here.
Hello? Huh?
I CAN DIE NOW.
Are you OK, Yura?
Yura?!

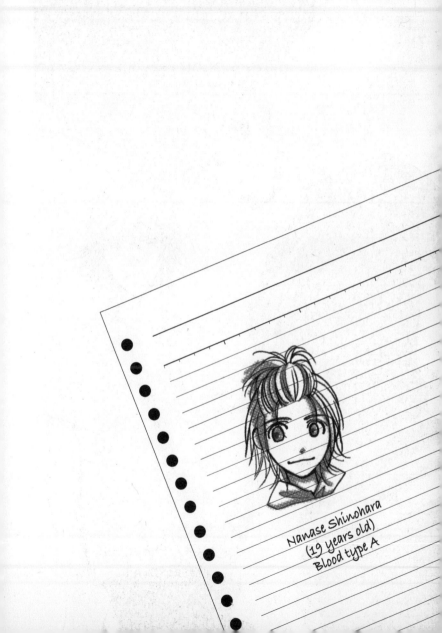

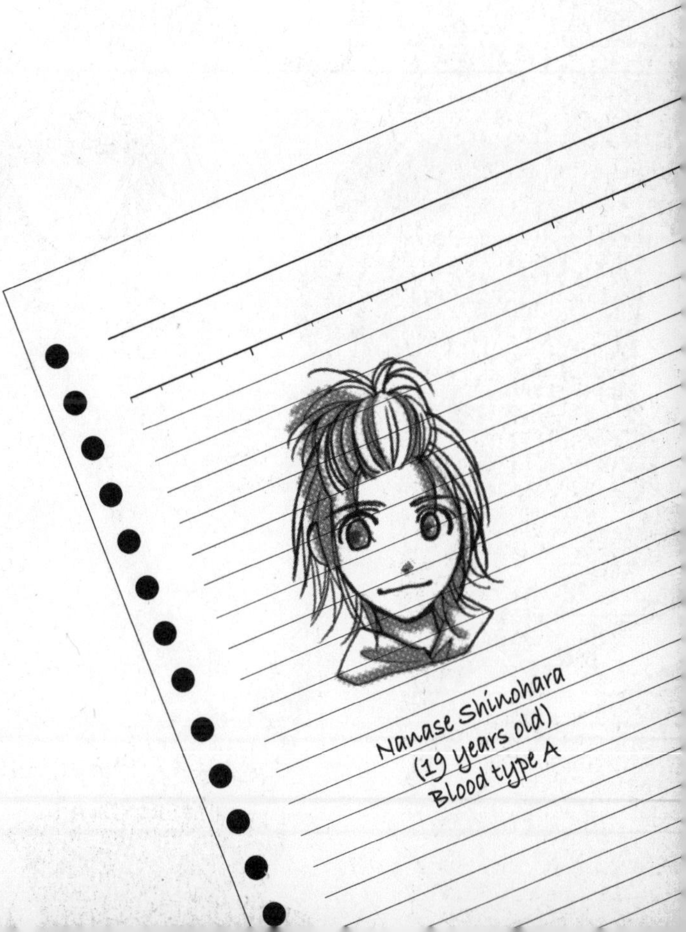
Nanase Shinohara
(19 years old)
Blood type A

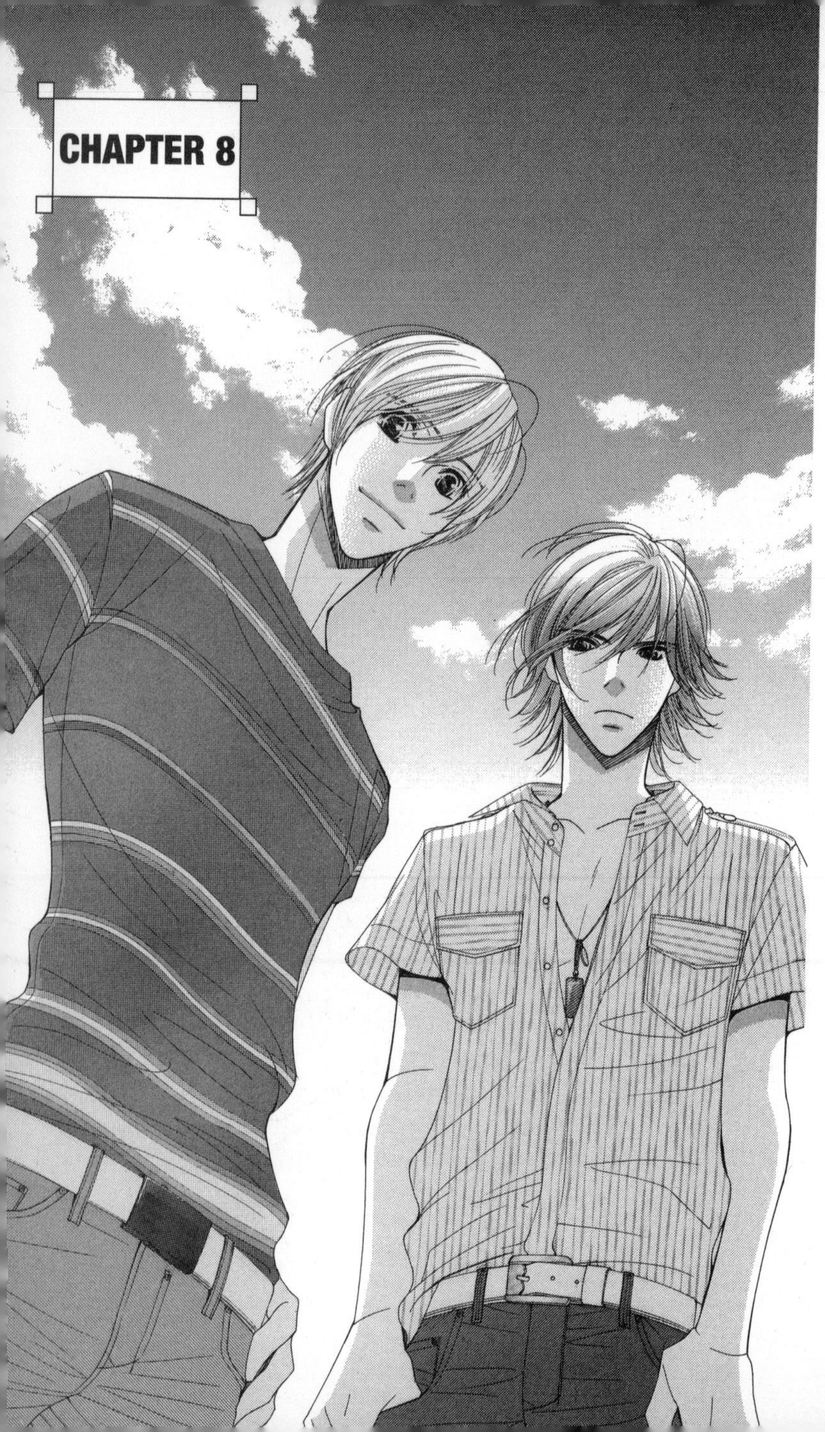
CHAPTER 8

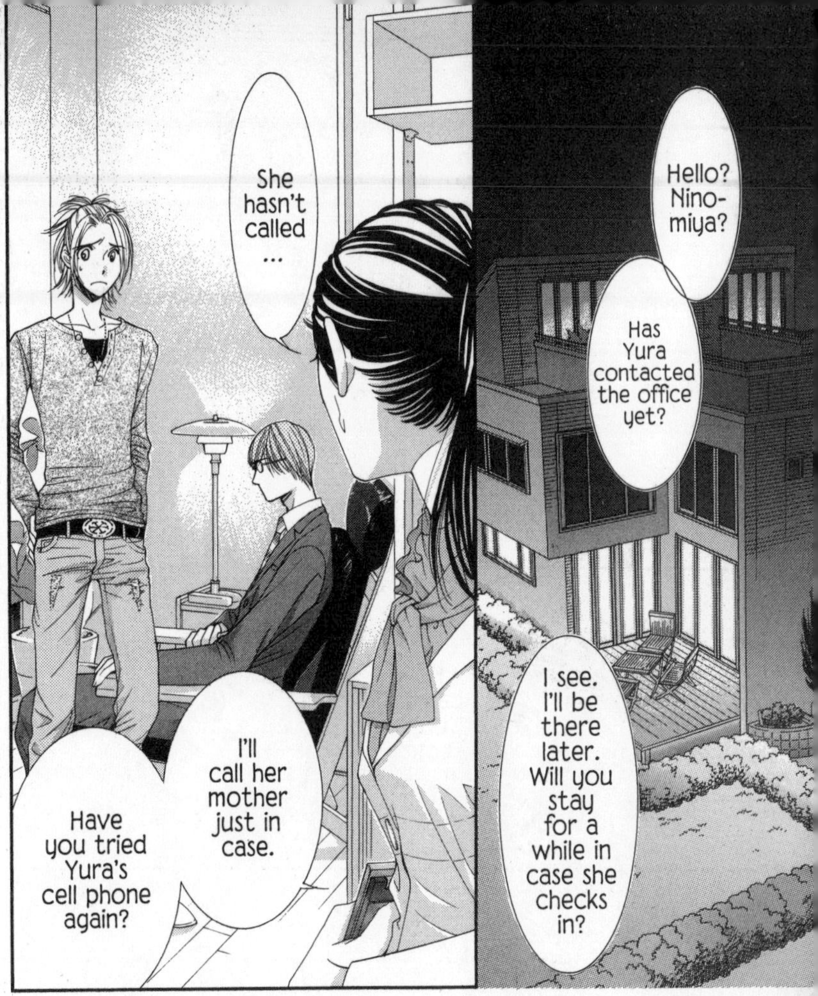

Hello? Nino-miya?
Has Yura contacted the office yet?
I see. I'll be there later. Will you stay for a while in case she checks in?
She hasn't called...
I'll call her mother just in case.
Have you tried Yura's cell phone again?

Honey Hunt

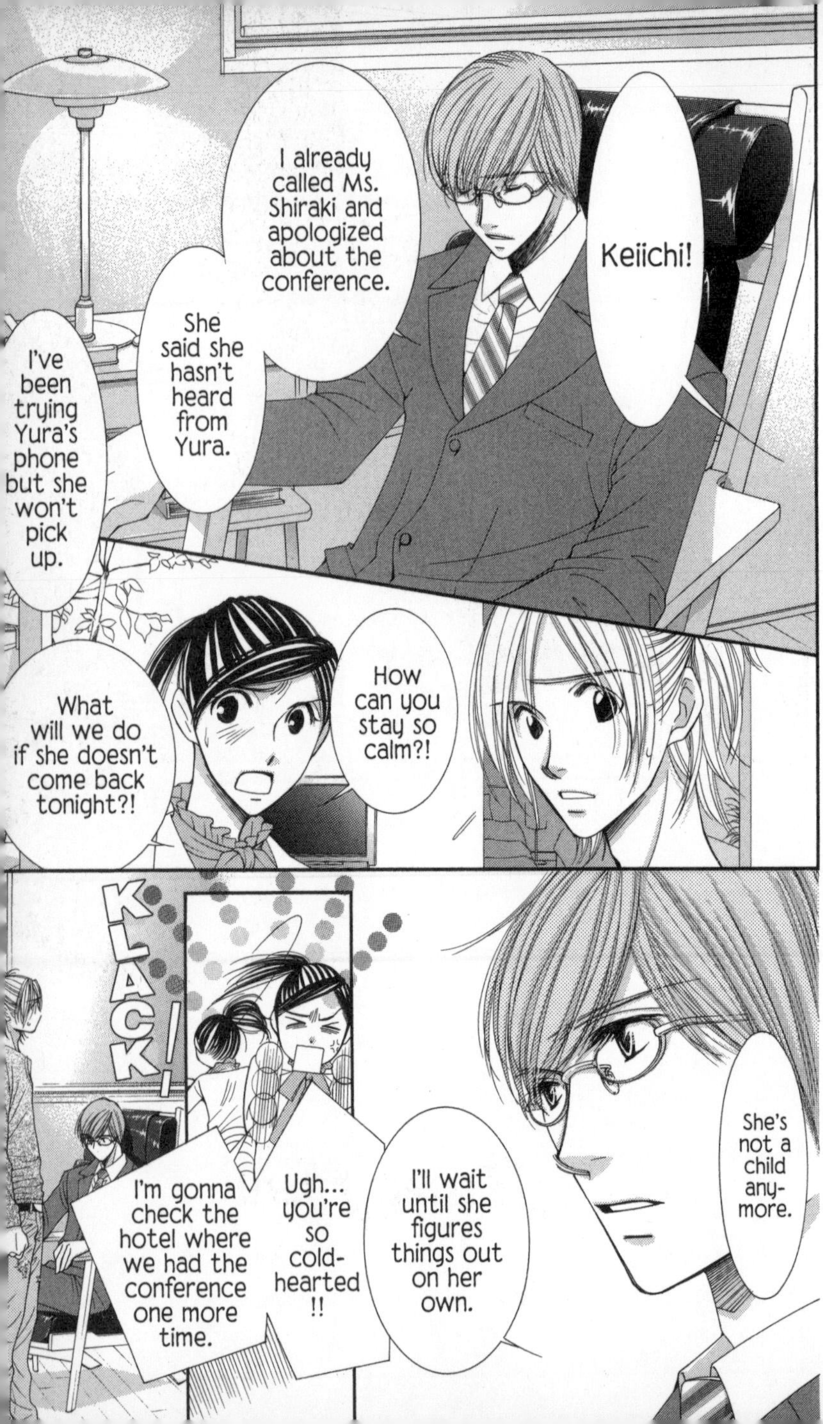
Keiichi!
I already called Ms. Shiraki and apologized about the conference.
She said she hasn't heard from Yura.
I've been trying Yura's phone but she won't pick up.
How can you stay so calm?!
What will we do if she doesn't come back tonight?!
She's not a child anymore.
I'll wait until she figures things out on her own.
Ugh... you're so cold-hearted!!
KLACK!
I'm gonna check the hotel where we had the conference one more time.

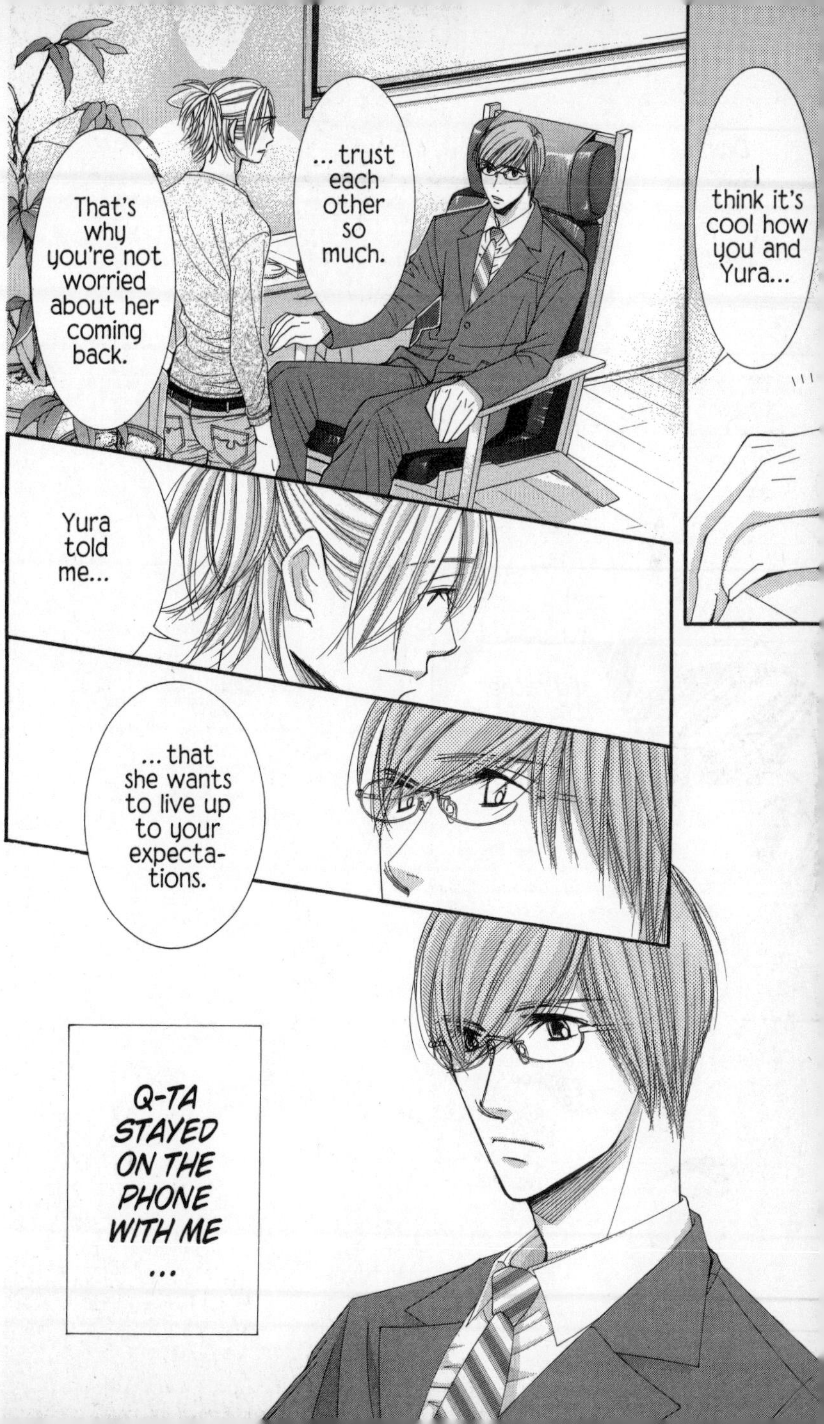
I think it's cool how you and Yura...
...trust each other so much.
That's why you're not worried about her coming back.
Yura told me...
...that she wants to live up to your expectations.
Q-TA STAYED ON THE PHONE WITH ME ...

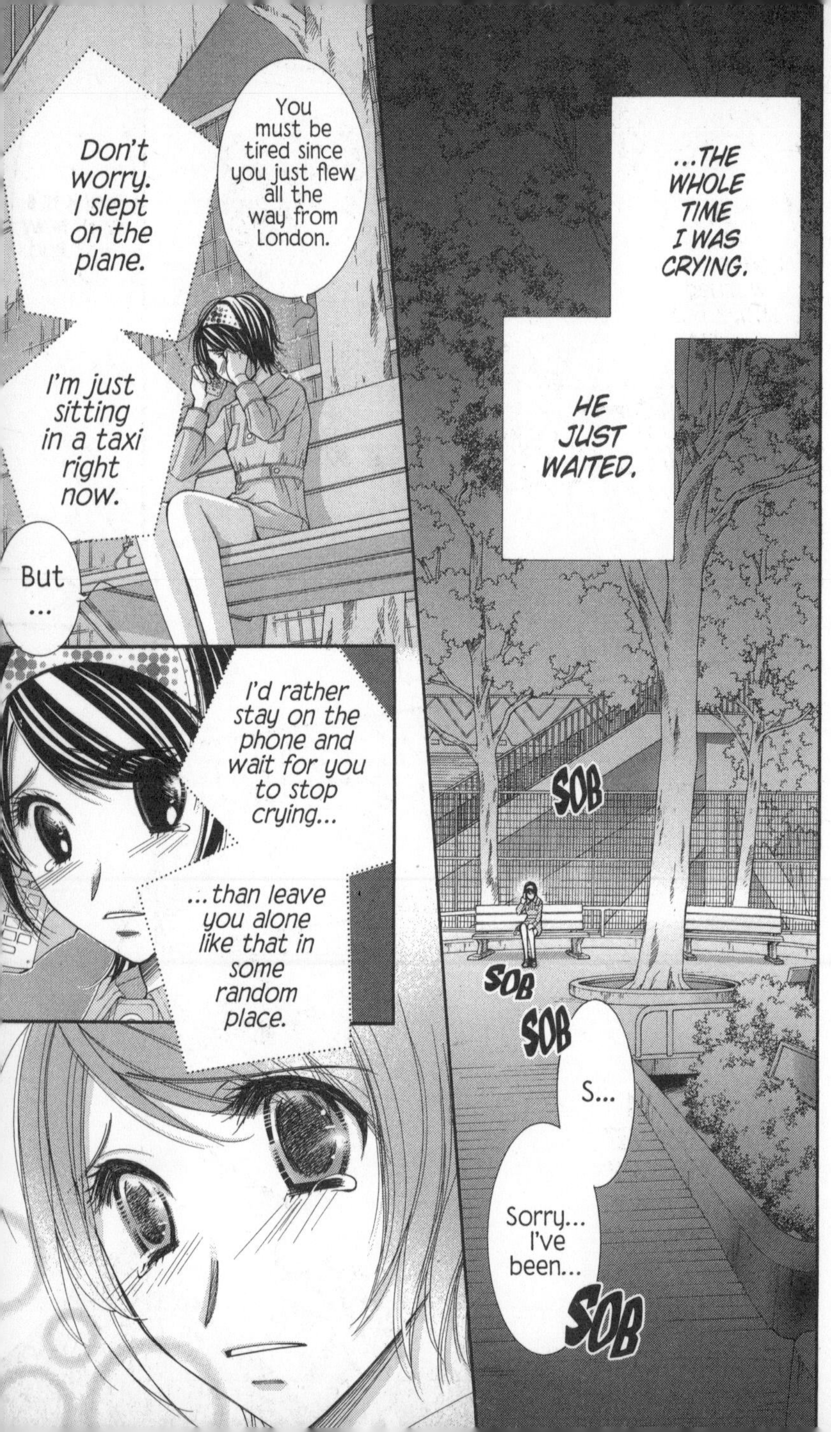
...THE WHOLE TIME I WAS CRYING.
HE JUST WAITED.
SOB
SOB
SOB
S...
Sorry... I've been...
SOB
You must be tired since you just flew all the way from London.
Don't worry. I slept on the plane.
I'm just sitting in a taxi right now.
But ...
I'd rather stay on the phone and wait for you to stop crying...
...than leave you alone like that in some random place.

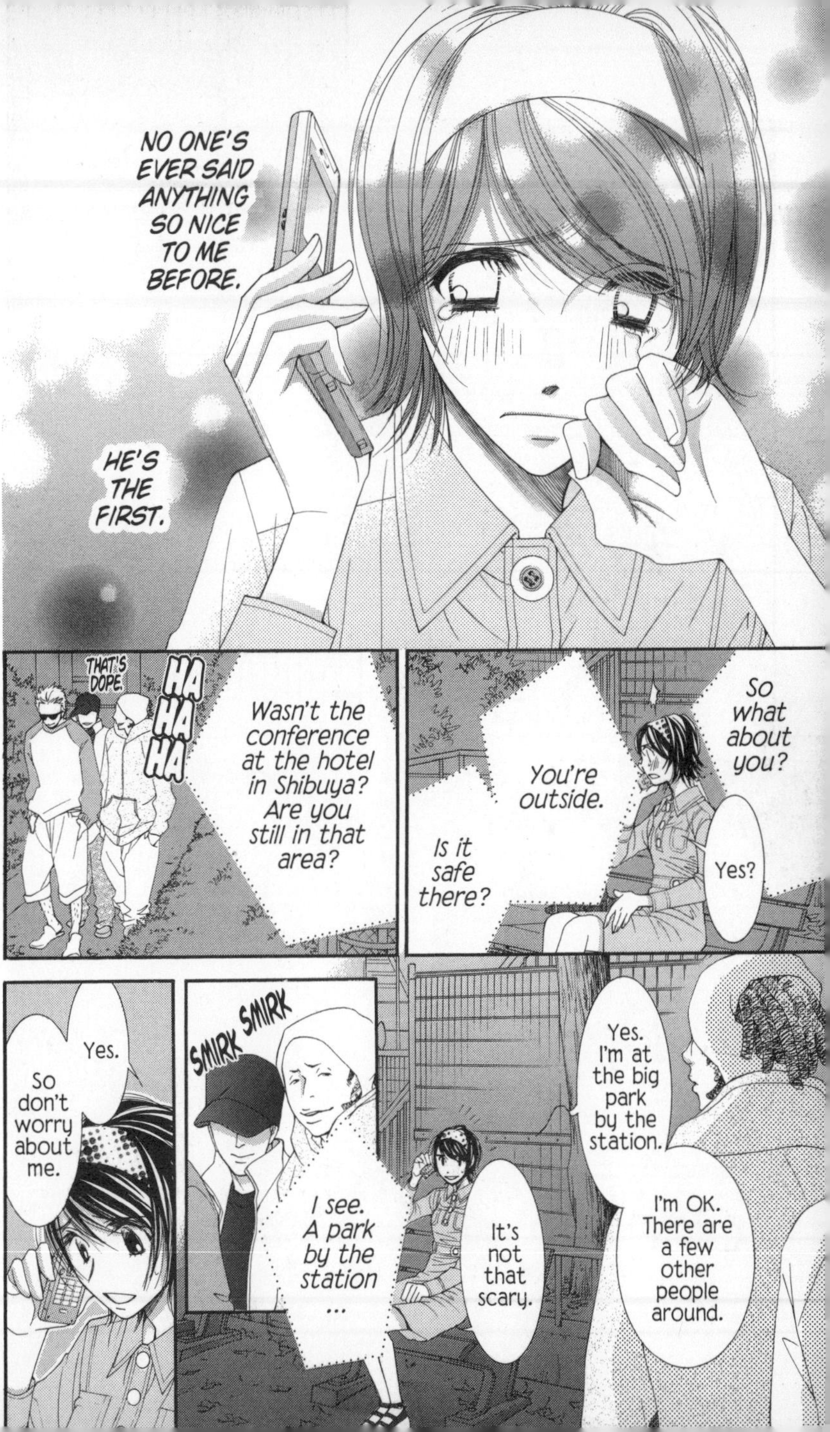
NO ONE'S EVER SAID ANYTHING SO NICE TO ME BEFORE.
HE'S THE FIRST.
So what about you?
Yes?
You're outside.
Is it safe there?
Wasn't the conference at the hotel in Shibuya? Are you still in that area?
HA HA HA
THAT'S DOPE.
Yes. I'm at the big park by the station.
I'm OK. There are a few other people around.
It's not that scary.
I see. A park by the station ...
SMIRK SMIRK
Yes.
So don't worry about me.

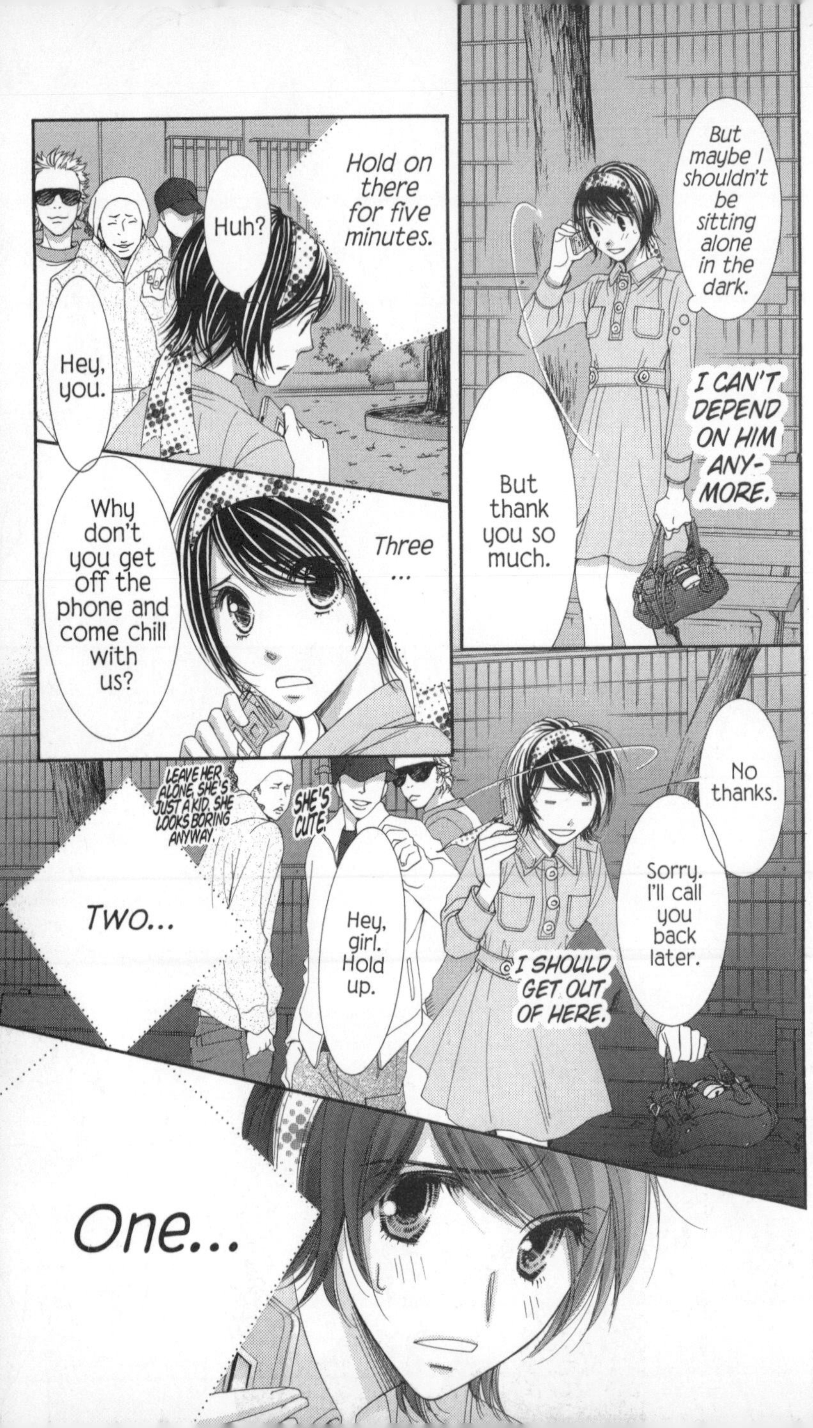

But maybe I shouldn't be sitting alone in the dark.
I CAN'T DEPEND ON HIM ANYMORE.
But thank you so much.
Hold on there for five minutes.
Huh?
Hey, you.
Three...
Why don't you get off the phone and come chill with us?
No thanks.
Sorry. I'll call you back later.
I SHOULD GET OUT OF HERE.
Hey, girl. Hold up.
SHE'S CUTE.
LEAVE HER ALONE, SHE'S JUST A KID. SHE LOOKS BORING ANYWAY.
Two...
One...

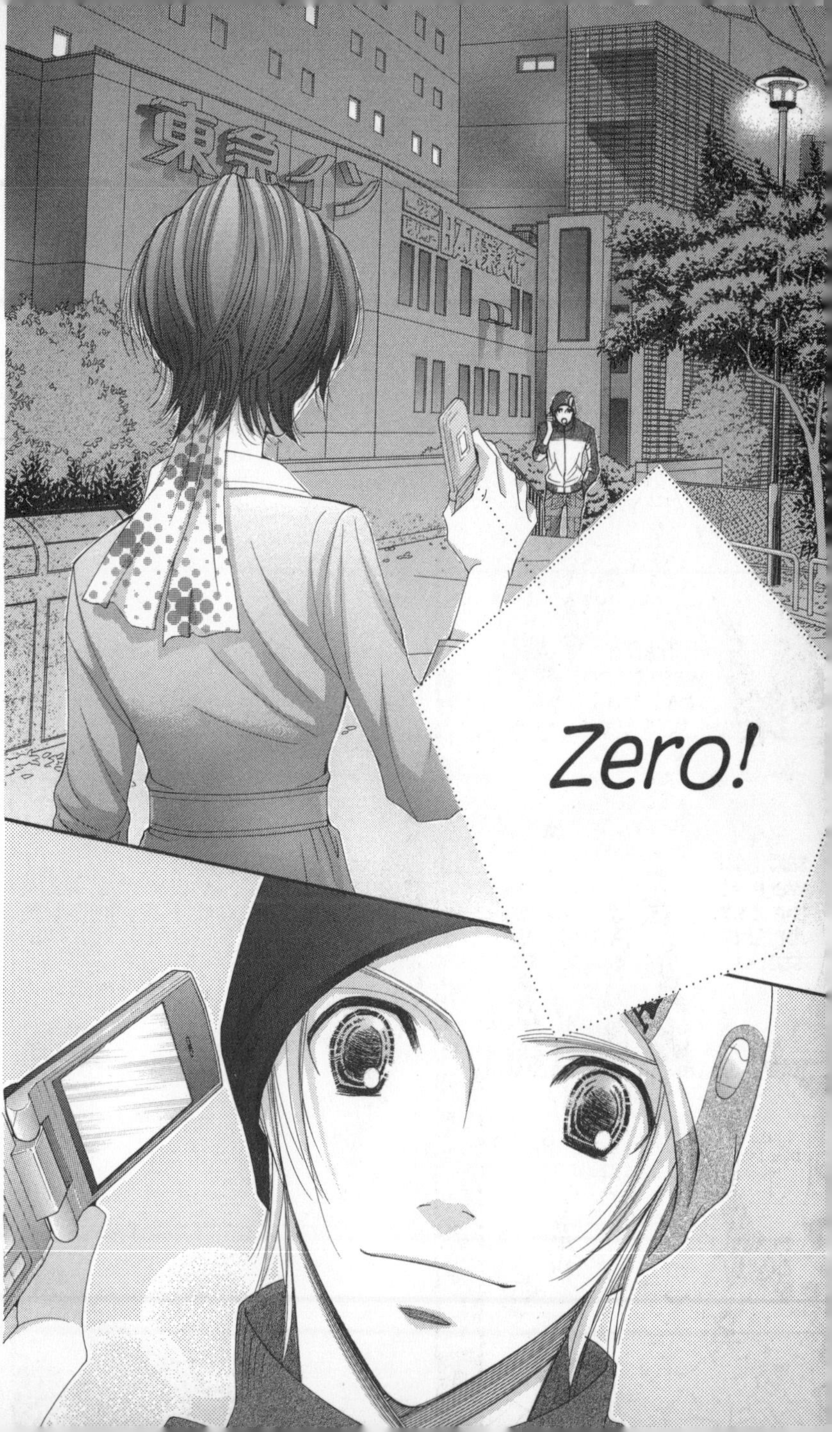
Zero!

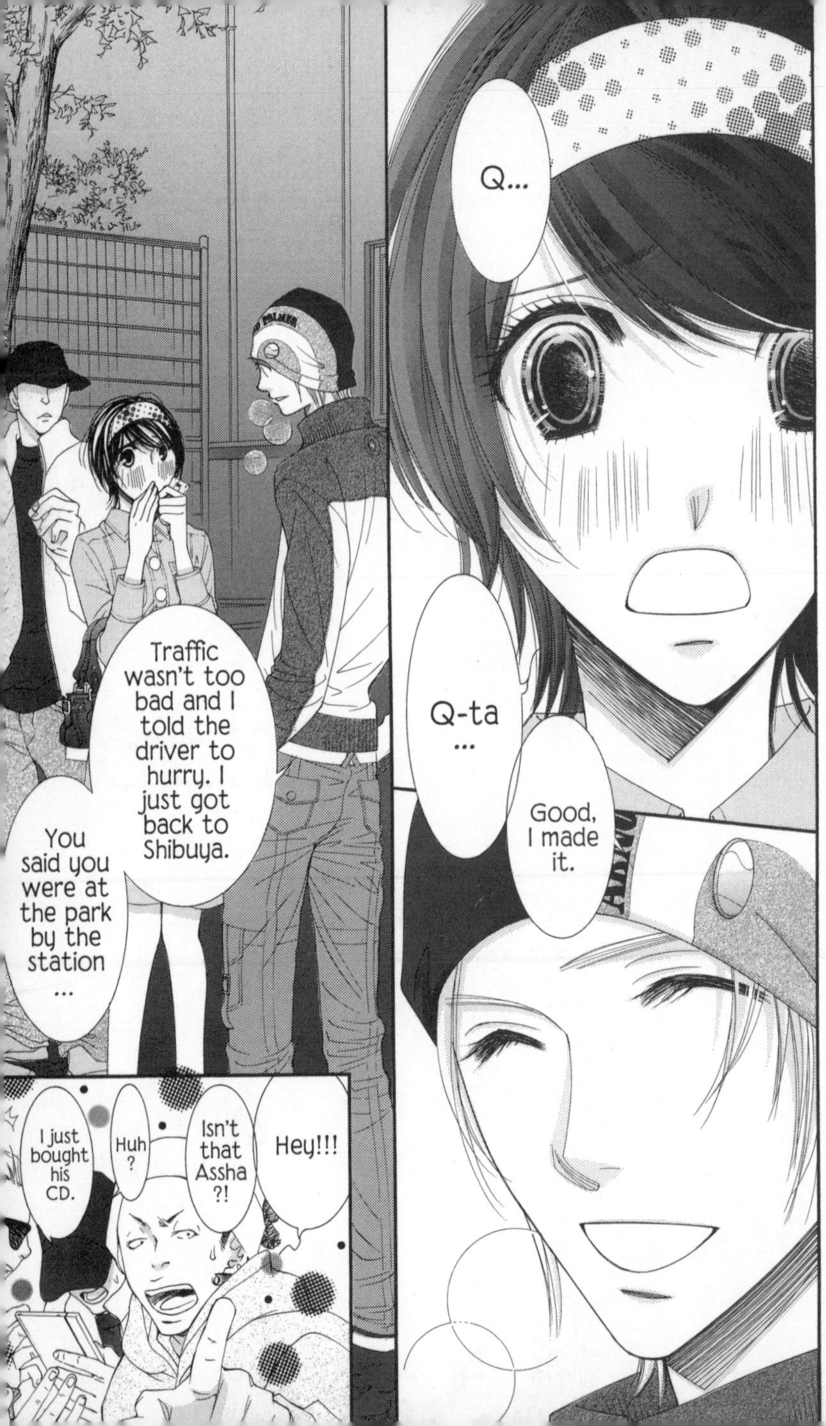
Q...
Q-ta ...
Good, I made it.
Traffic wasn't too bad and I told the driver to hurry. I just got back to Shibuya.
You said you were at the park by the station ...
Hey!!!
Isn't that Assha?!
Huh?
I just bought his CD.

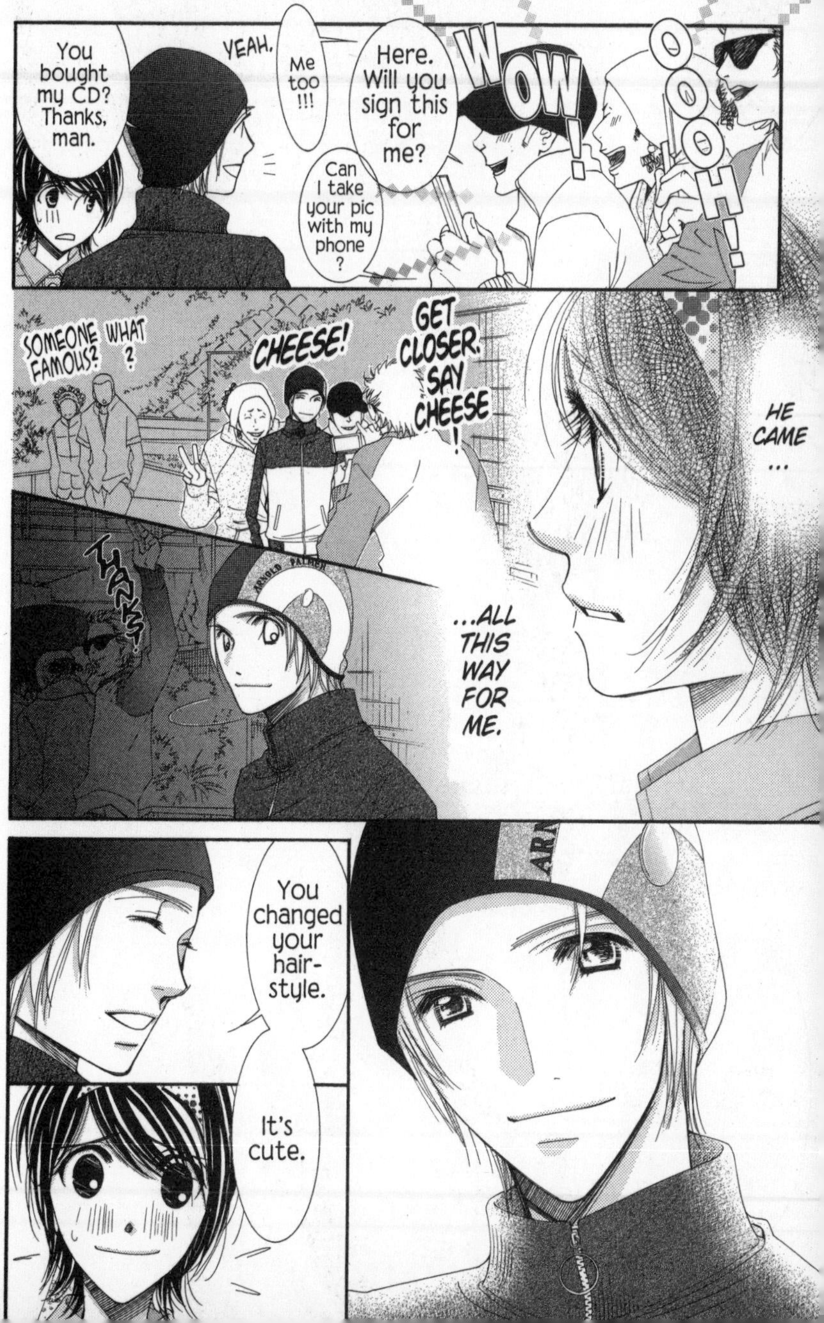
OOOOH!
WOW!
Here. Will you sign this for me?
Can I take your pic with my phone?
Me too!!!
YEAH.
You bought my CD? Thanks, man.
HE CAME...
...ALL THIS WAY FOR ME.
GET CLOSER. SAY CHEESE!
CHEESE!
WHAT?
SOMEONE FAMOUS?
THANKS!
You changed your hair-style.
It's cute.

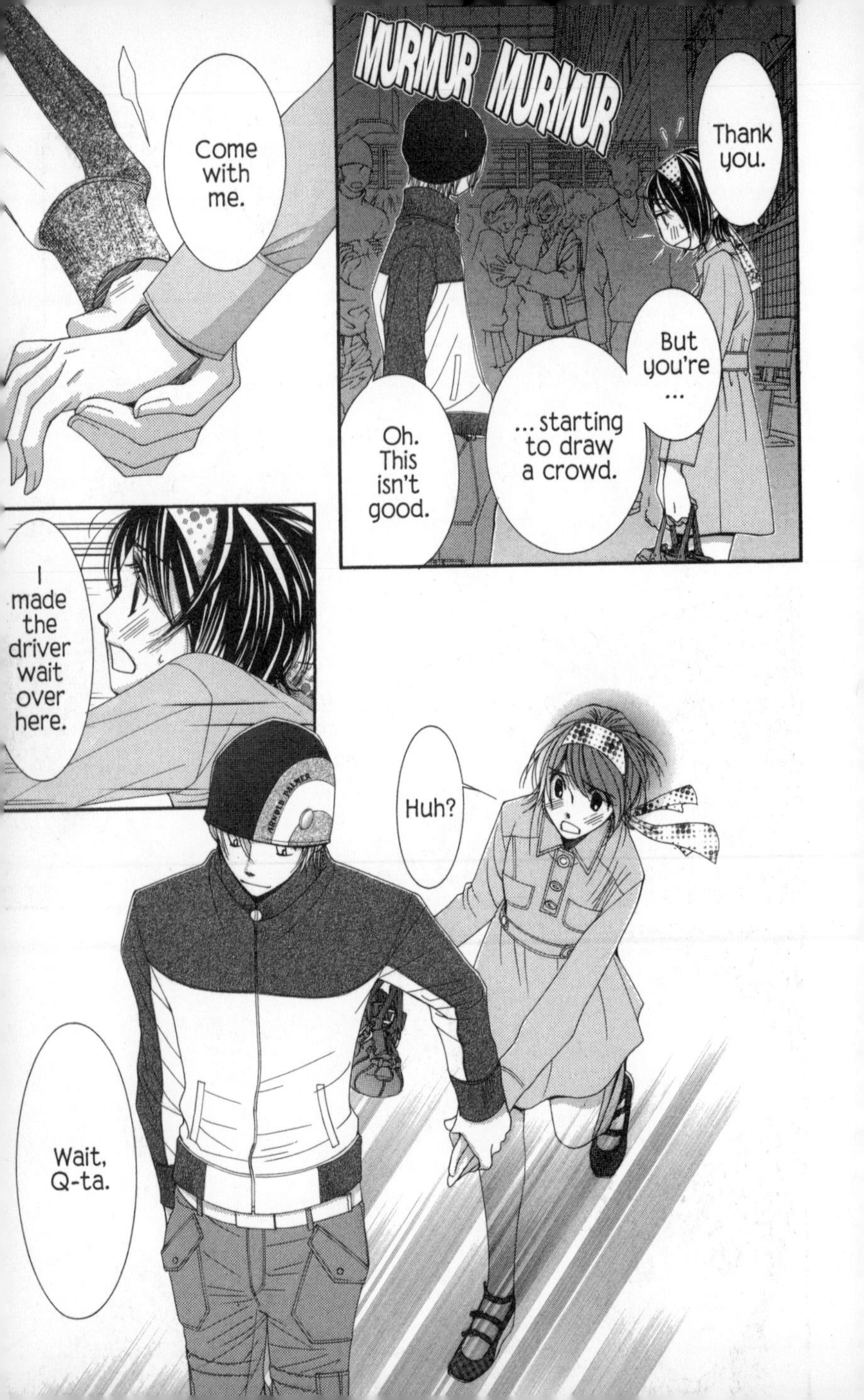
MURMUR MURMUR
Thank you.
But you're ...
... starting to draw a crowd.
Oh. This isn't good.
Come with me.
I made the driver wait over here.
Huh?
Wait, Q-ta.

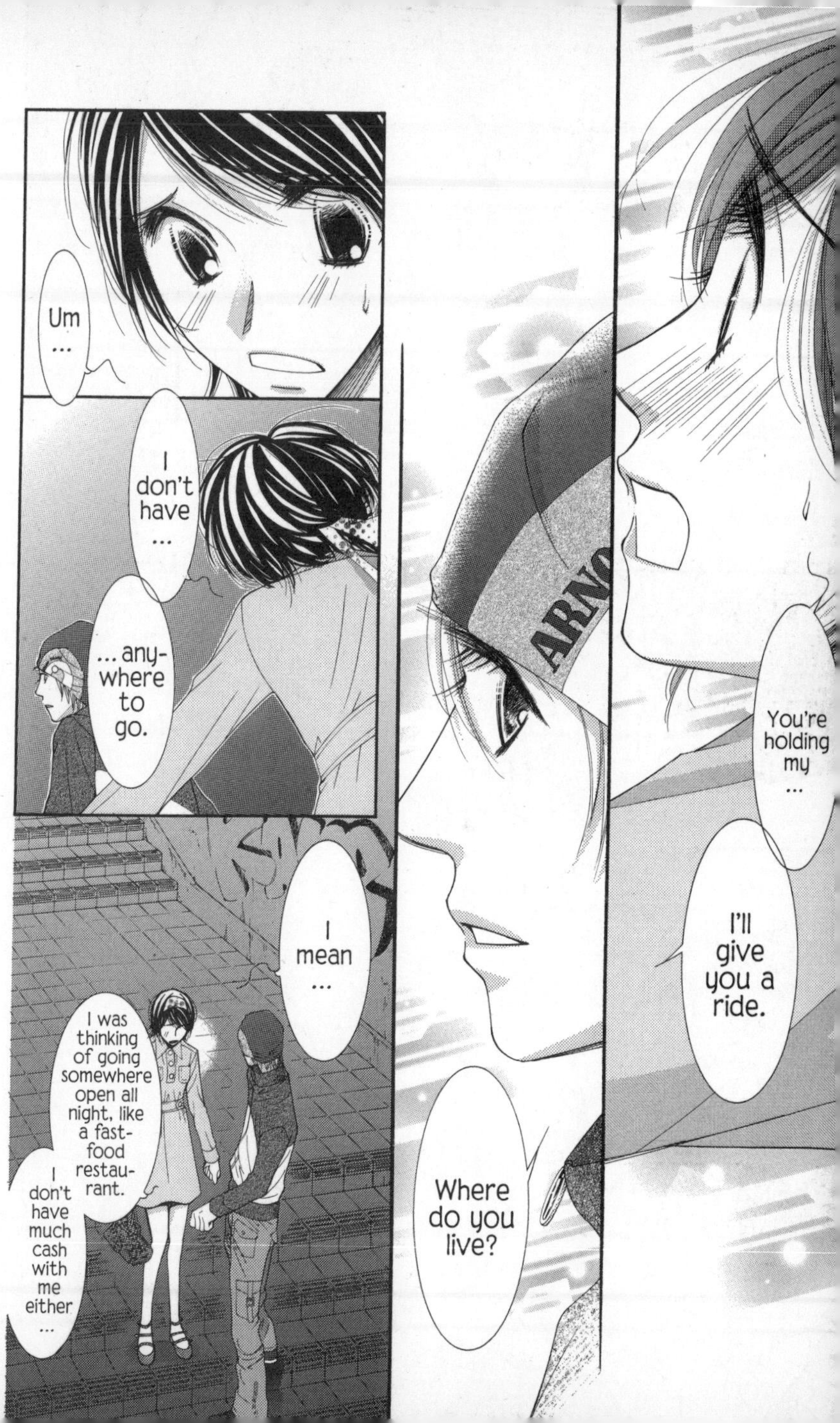
You're holding my ...
I'll give you a ride.
Where do you live?
ARNO
Um ...
I don't have ...
... anywhere to go.
I mean ...
I was thinking of going somewhere open all night, like a fast-food restaurant.
I don't have much cash with me either ...

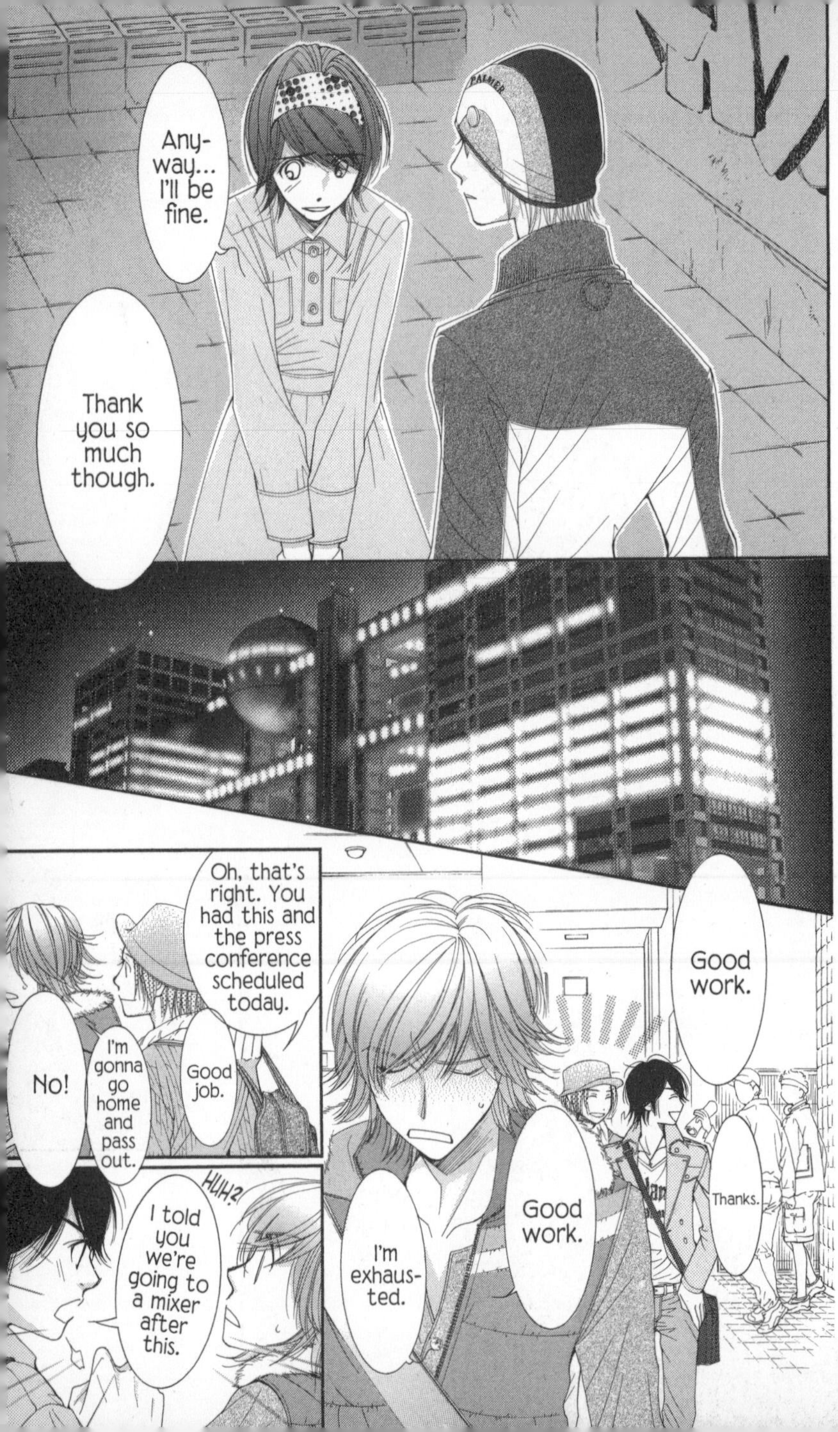
Any-way... I'll be fine.
Thank you so much though.
Good work.
Thanks.
Good work.
I'm exhaus-ted.
Oh, that's right. You had this and the press conference scheduled today.
Good job.
I'm gonna go home and pass out.
No!
HUH?
I told you we're going to a mixer after this.

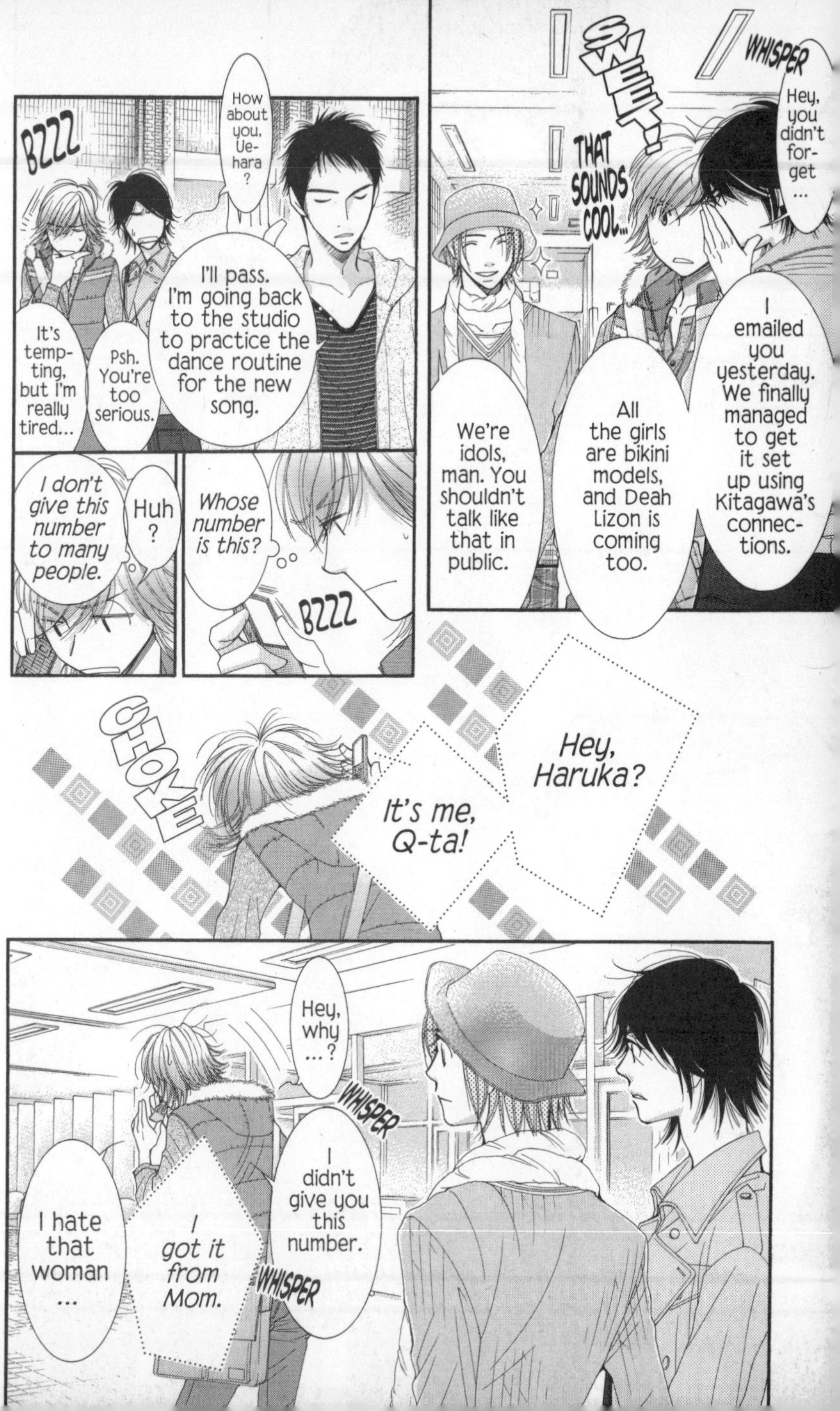
WHISPER
Hey, you didn't forget...
I emailed you yesterday. We finally managed to get it set up using Kitagawa's connections.
SWEET!
THAT SOUNDS COOL...
All the girls are bikini models, and Deah Lizon is coming too.
We're idols, man. You shouldn't talk like that in public.
How about you, Uehara?
BZZZ
I'll pass. I'm going back to the studio to practice the dance routine for the new song.
Psh. You're too serious.
It's tempting, but I'm really tired...
Whose number is this?
BZZZ
Huh?
I don't give this number to many people.
CHOKE
Hey, Haruka?
It's me, Q-ta!
Hey, why...?
WHISPER
I didn't give you this number.
WHISPER
I got it from Mom.
I hate that woman...

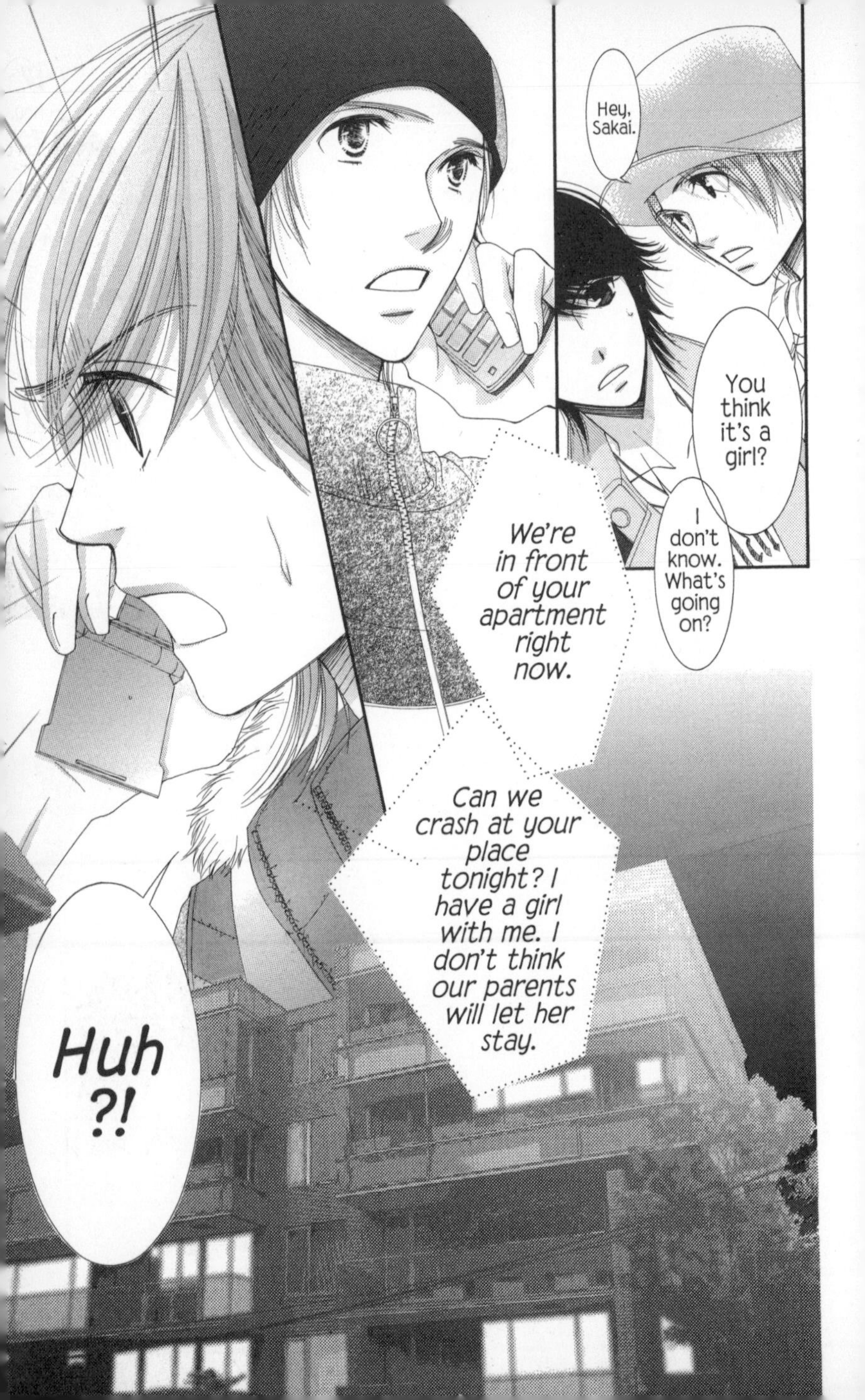
Hey, Sakai.
You think it's a girl?
I don't know. What's going on?
We're in front of your apartment right now.
Can we crash at your place tonight? I have a girl with me. I don't think our parents will let her stay.
Huh ?!

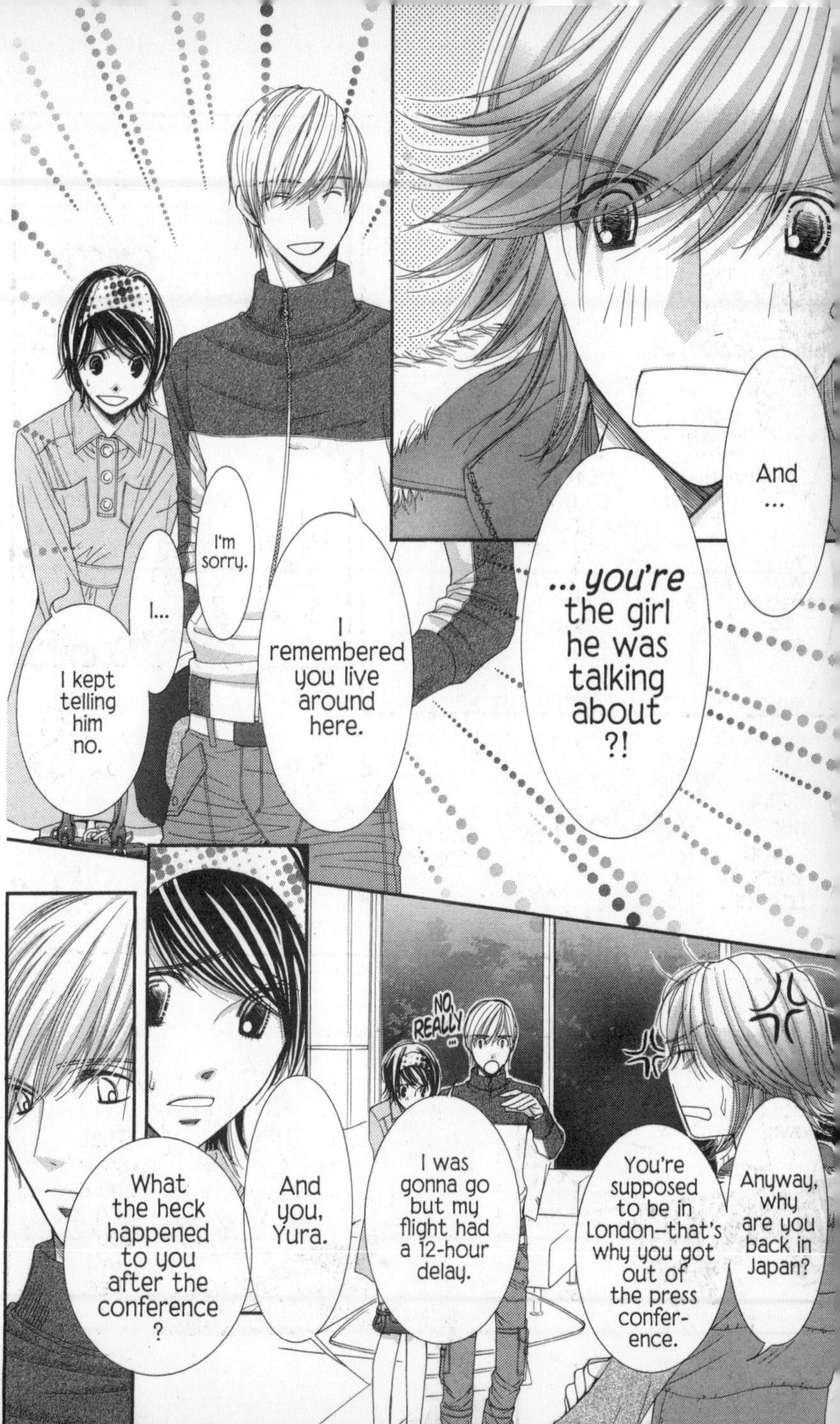
And ...
... you're the girl he was talking about ?!
I remembered you live around here.
I'm sorry.
I...
I kept telling him no.
Anyway, why are you back in Japan?
You're supposed to be in London—that's why you got out of the press conference.
NO, REALLY...
I was gonna go but my flight had a 12-hour delay.
And you, Yura.
What the heck happened to you after the conference ?

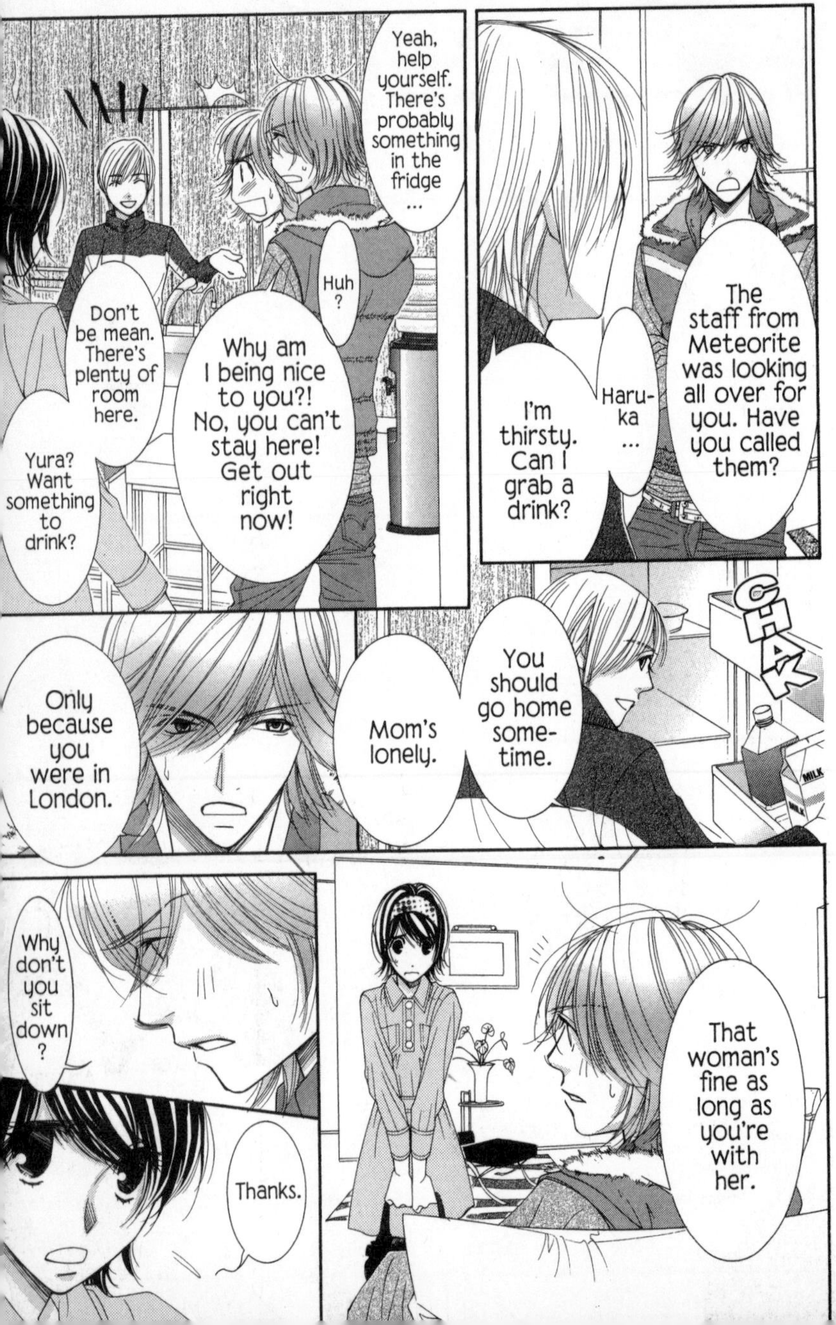
The staff from Meteorite was looking all over for you. Have you called them?
Haru-ka...
I'm thirsty. Can I grab a drink?
Yeah, help yourself. There's probably something in the fridge...
Huh?
Why am I being nice to you?! No, you can't stay here! Get out right now!
Don't be mean. There's plenty of room here.
Yura? Want something to drink?
CHAK
You should go home some-time.
Mom's lonely.
Only because you were in London.
That woman's fine as long as you're with her.
Why don't you sit down?
Thanks.

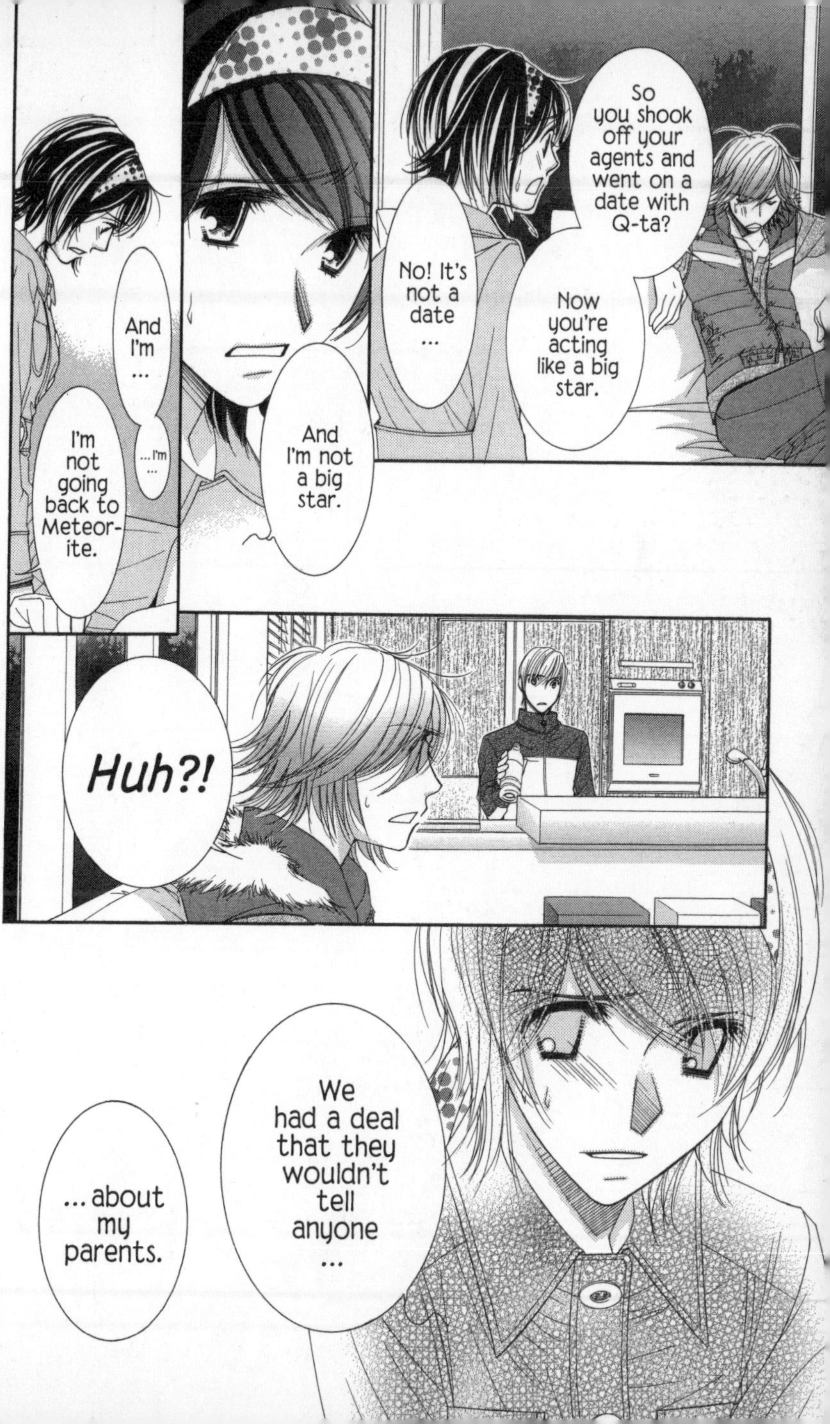
So you shook off your agents and went on a date with Q-ta?
Now you're acting like a big star.
No! It's not a date ...
And I'm not a big star.
And I'm ...
...I'm ...
I'm not going back to Meteor-ite.
Huh?!
We had a deal that they wouldn't tell anyone ...
... about my parents.

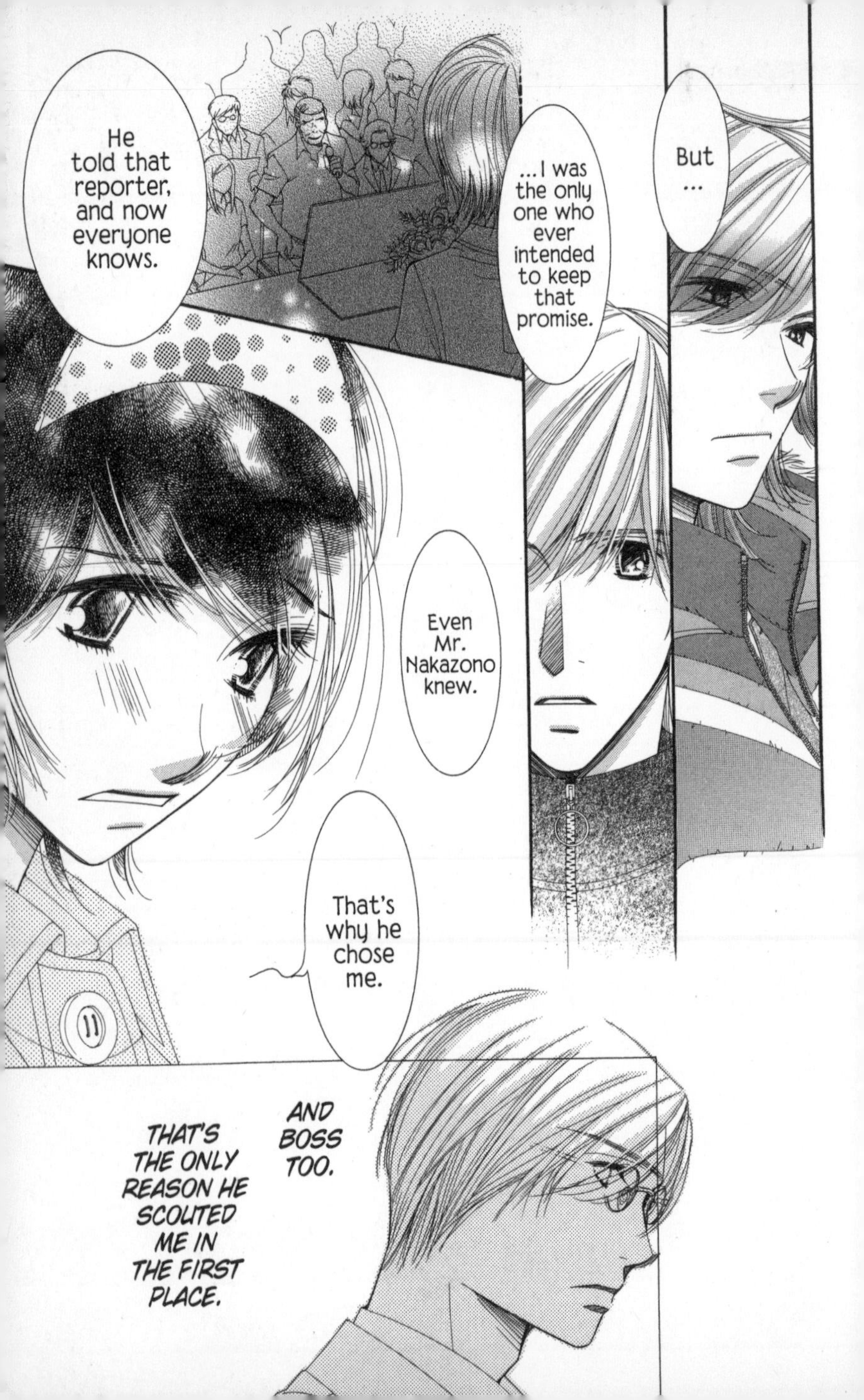
But ...
...I was the only one who ever intended to keep that promise.
He told that reporter, and now everyone knows.
Even Mr. Nakazono knew.
That's why he chose me.
AND BOSS TOO.
THAT'S THE ONLY REASON HE SCOUTED ME IN THE FIRST PLACE.

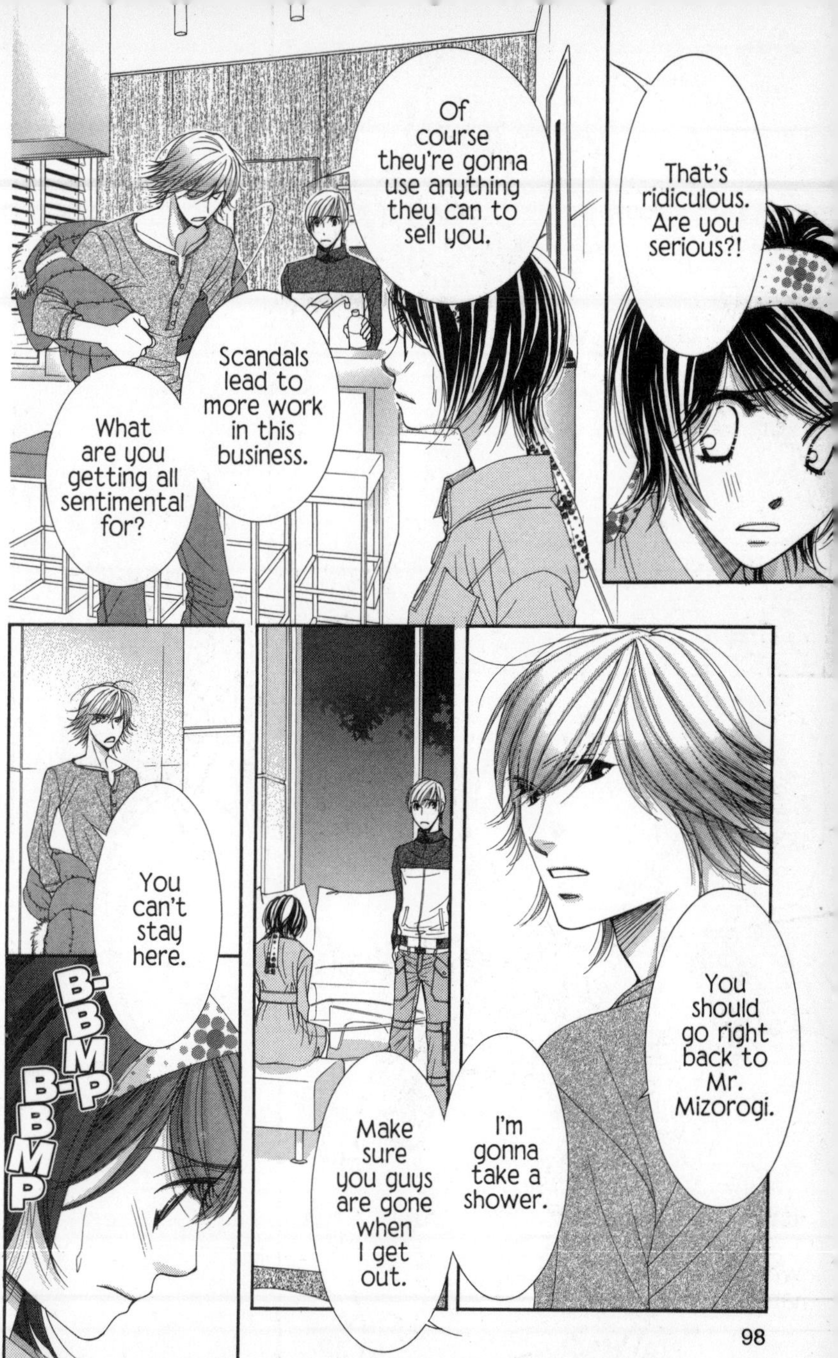
That's ridiculous. Are you serious?!
Of course they're gonna use anything they can to sell you.
Scandals lead to more work in this business.
What are you getting all sentimental for?
You should go right back to Mr. Mizorogi.
I'm gonna take a shower.
Make sure you guys are gone when I get out.
You can't stay here.
B-BMP B-BMP

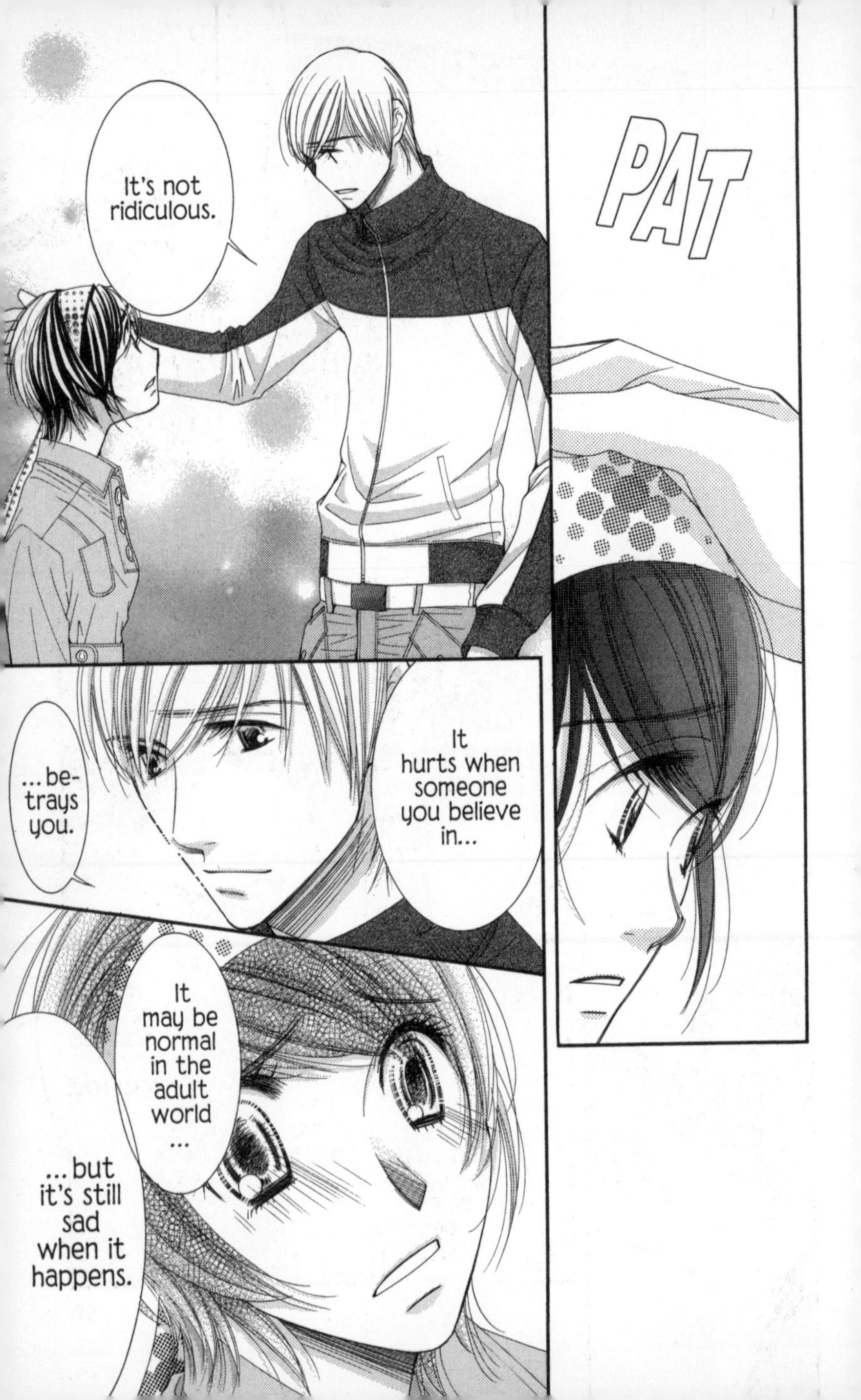
PAT
It's not ridiculous.
It hurts when someone you believe in...
...be-trays you.
It may be normal in the adult world...
...but it's still sad when it happens.

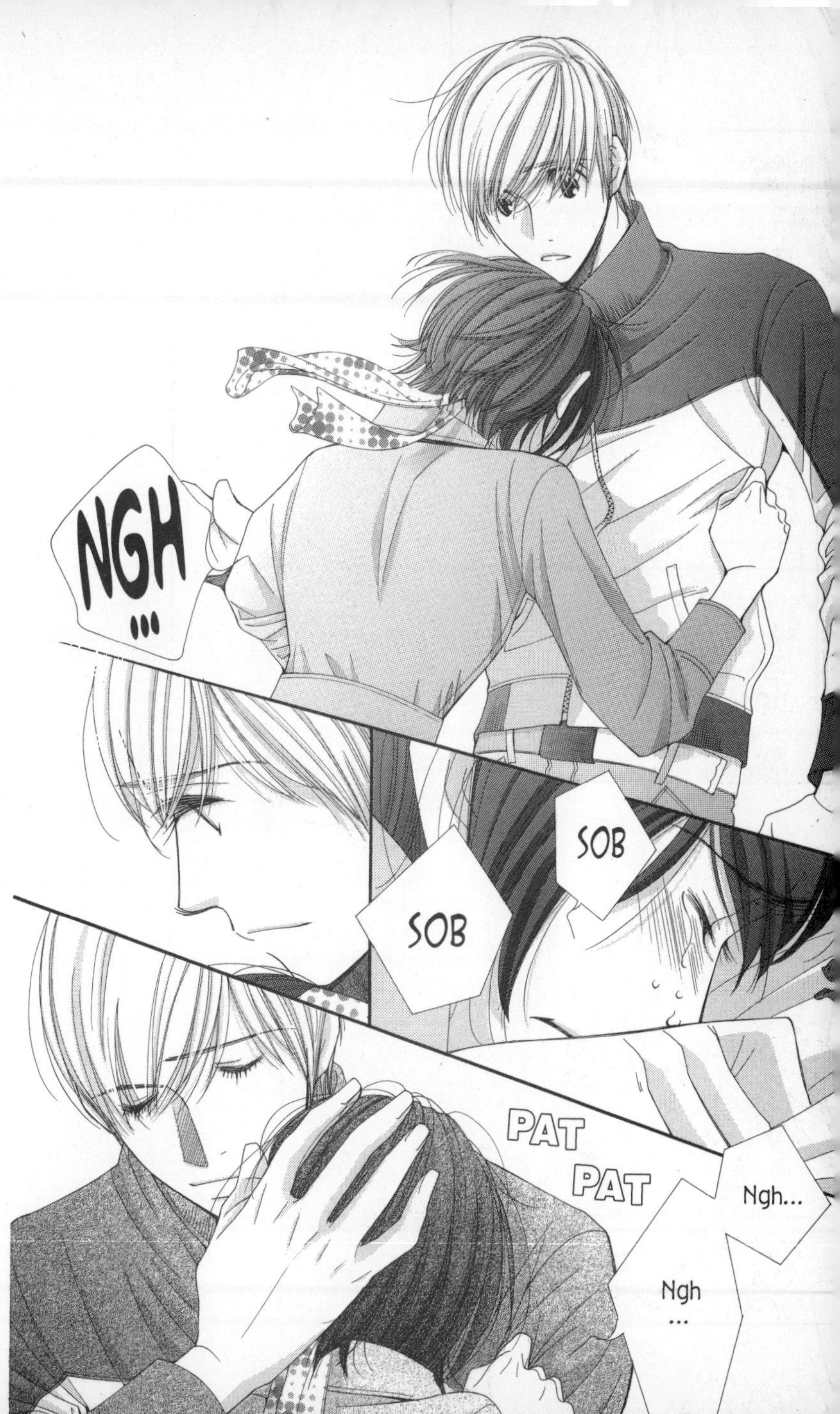
NGH...
SOB
SOB
PAT
PAT
Ngh...
Ngh
...

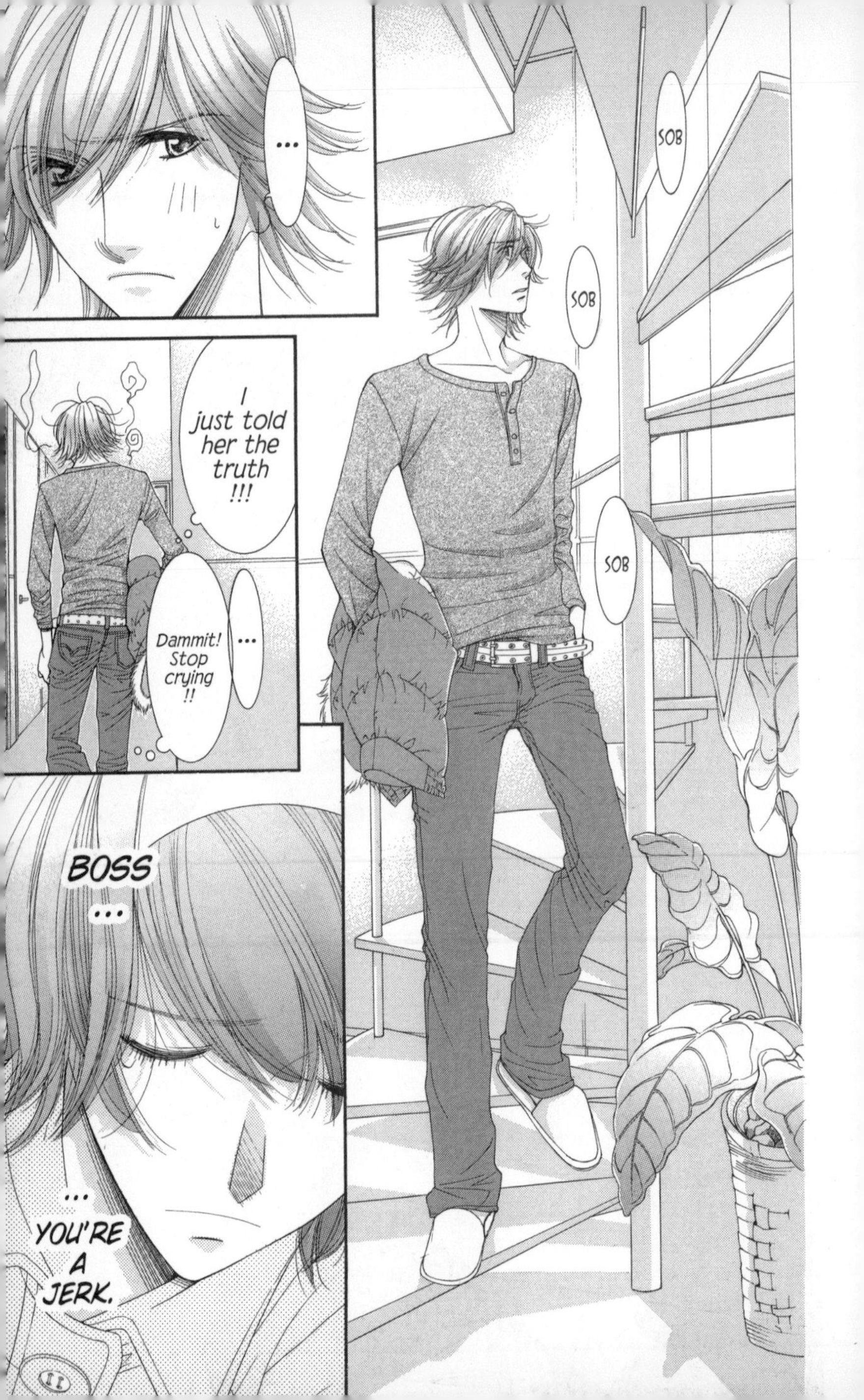
SOB
SOB
SOB
...
I just told her the truth !!!
...
Dammit! Stop crying !!
BOSS ...
... YOU'RE A JERK.

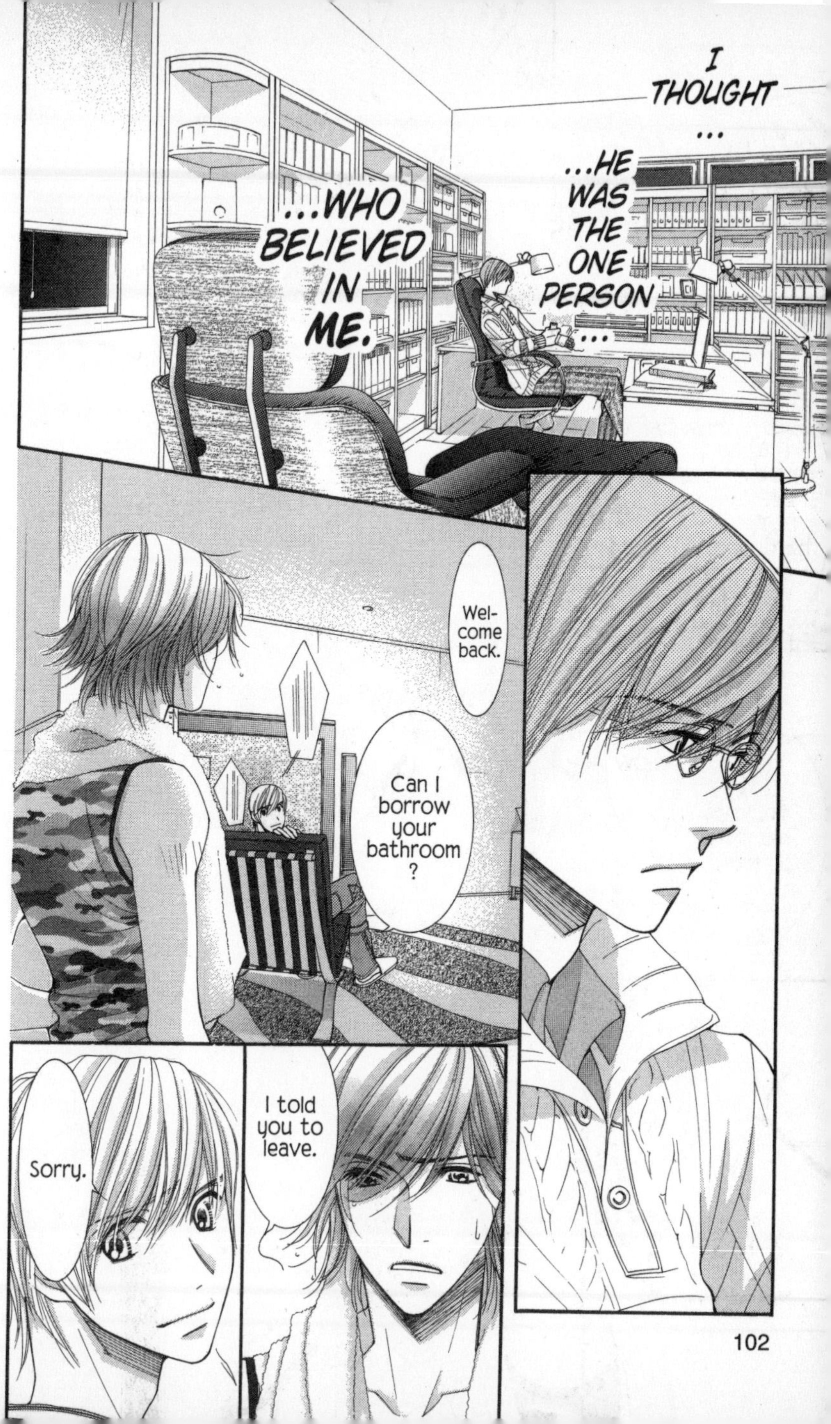
I THOUGHT ...
...HE WAS THE ONE PERSON ...
...WHO BELIEVED IN ME.
Wel-come back.
Can I borrow your bathroom ?
I told you to leave.
Sorry.

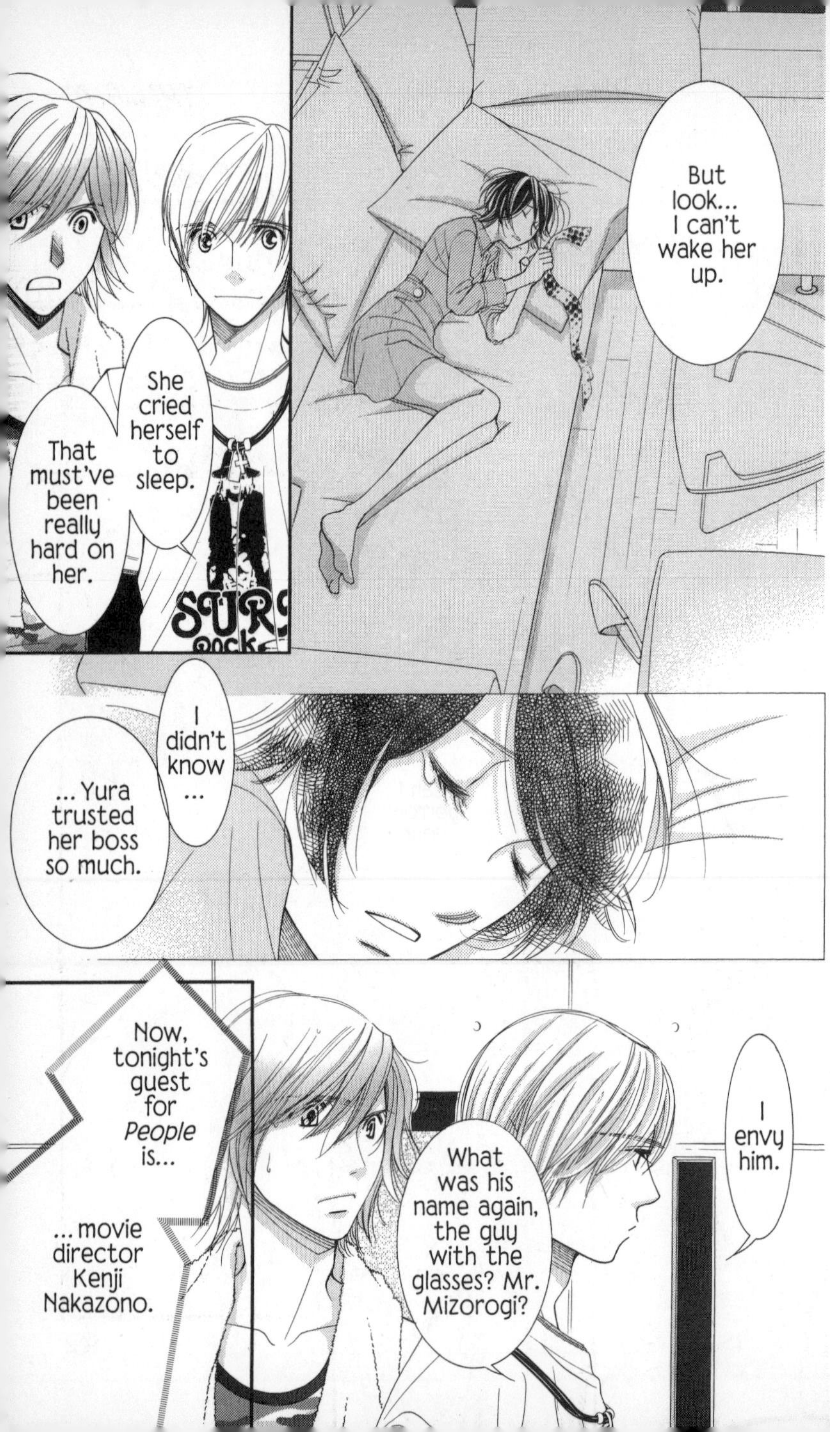
But look... I can't wake her up.
She cried herself to sleep.
That must've been really hard on her.
I didn't know ...
... Yura trusted her boss so much.
I envy him.
What was his name again, the guy with the glasses? Mr. Mizorogi?
Now, tonight's guest for *People* is...
... movie director Kenji Nakazono.

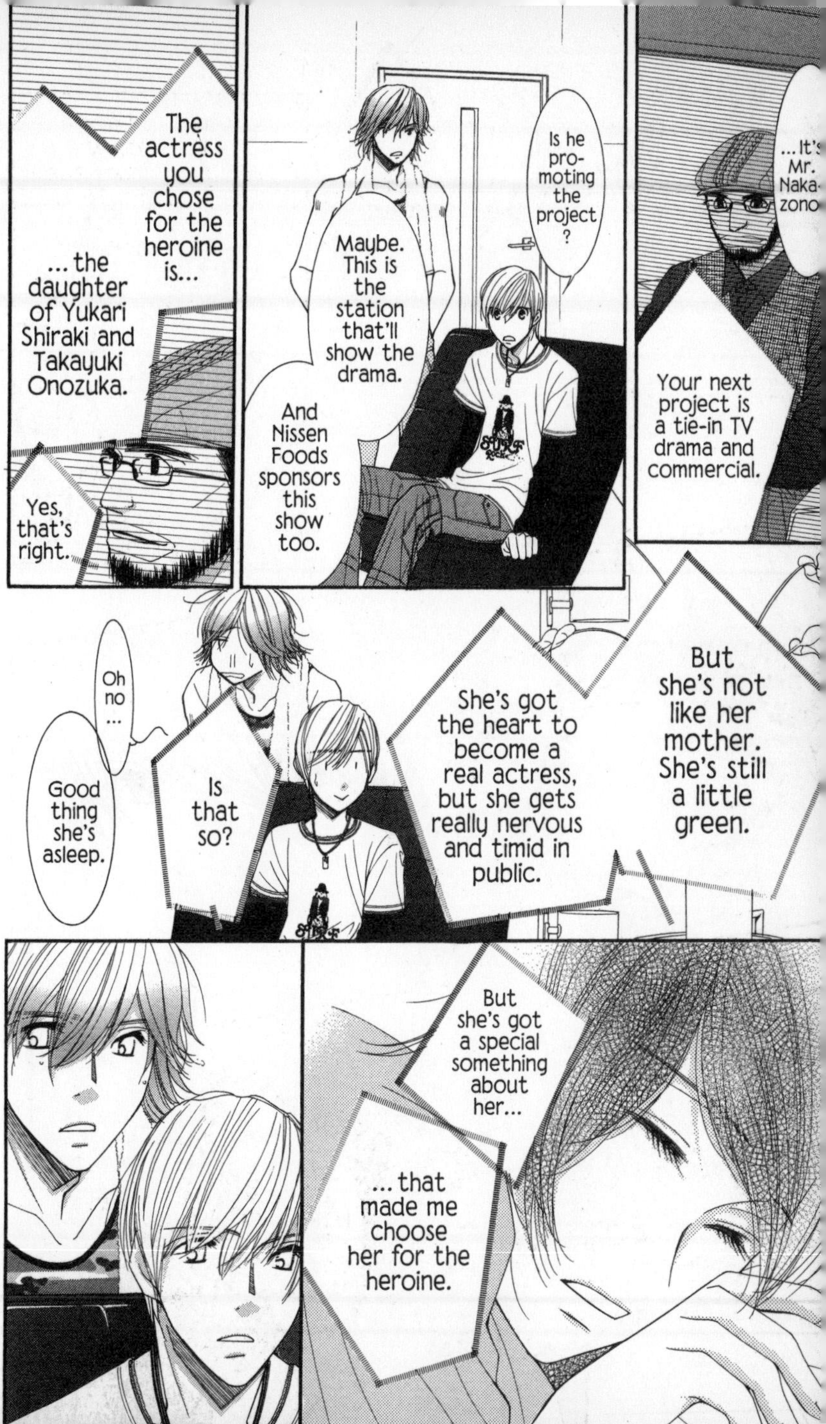
...It's Mr. Nakazono
Your next project is a tie-in TV drama and commercial.
Is he promoting the project?
Maybe. This is the station that'll show the drama.
And Nissen Foods sponsors this show too.
The actress you chose for the heroine is...
...the daughter of Yukari Shiraki and Takayuki Onozuka.
Yes, that's right.
But she's not like her mother. She's still a little green.
She's got the heart to become a real actress, but she gets really nervous and timid in public.
Is that so?
Oh no...
Good thing she's asleep.
But she's got a special something about her...
...that made me choose her for the heroine.

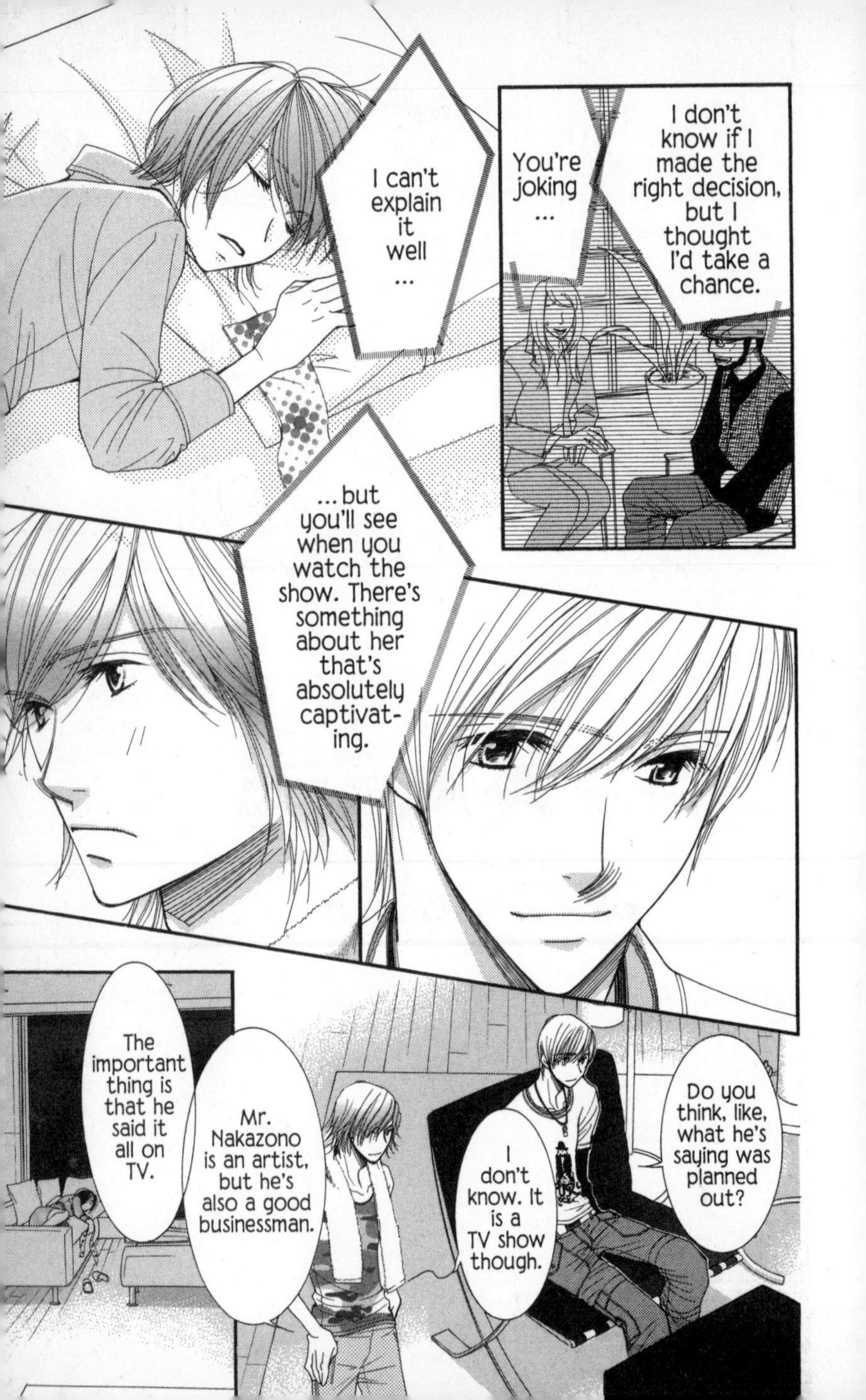
I don't know if I made the right decision, but I thought I'd take a chance.
You're joking ...
I can't explain it well ...
... but you'll see when you watch the show. There's something about her that's absolutely captivat-ing.
Do you think, like, what he's saying was planned out?
I don't know. It is a TV show though.
Mr. Nakazono is an artist, but he's also a good businessman.
The important thing is that he said it all on TV.

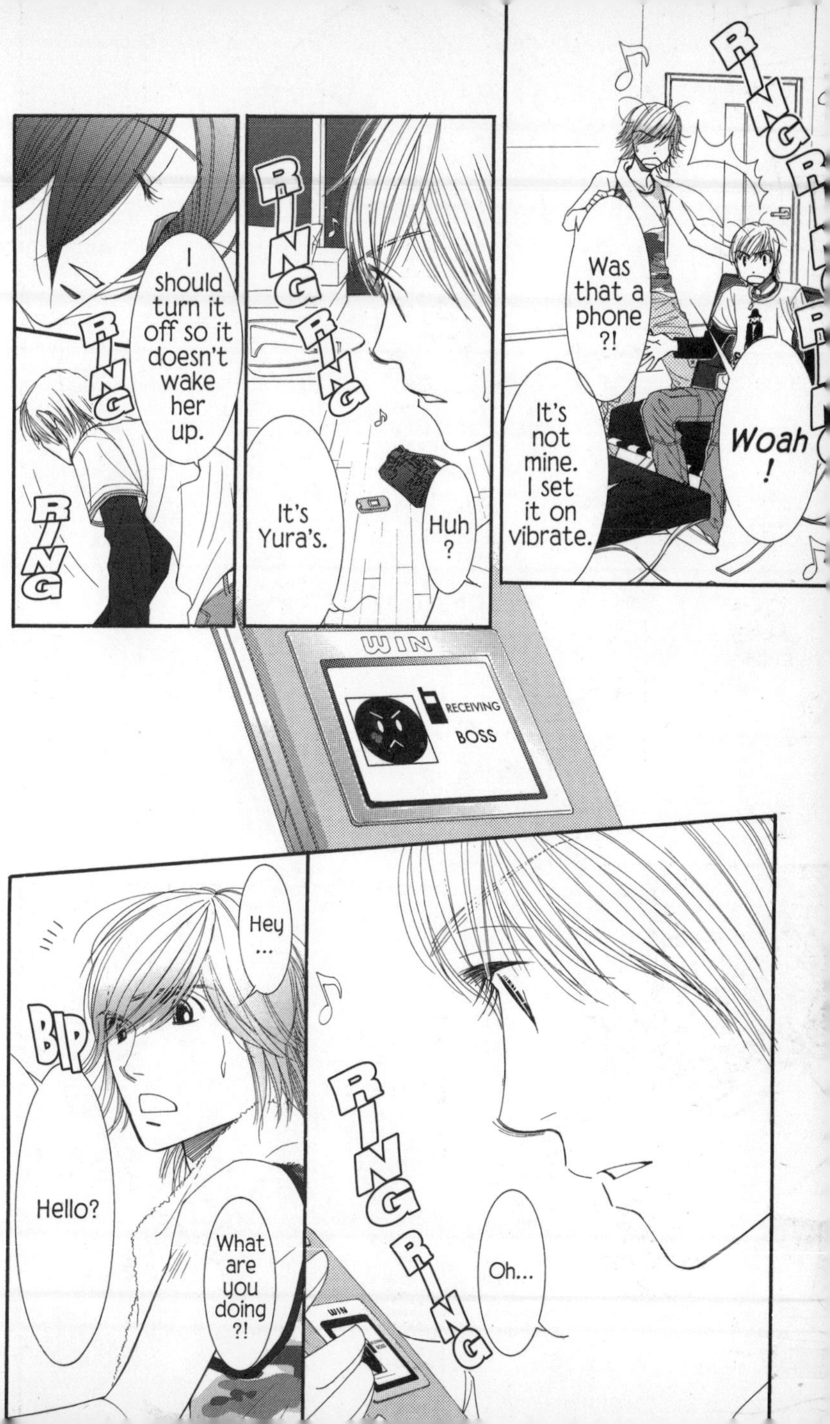
RING RING RING
Woah!
Was that a phone?!
It's not mine. I set it on vibrate.
RING RING
Huh?
It's Yura's.
I should turn it off so it doesn't wake her up.
RING RING
WIN
RECEIVING
BOSS
RING RING
Oh...
Hey...
BIP
What are you doing?!
Hello?

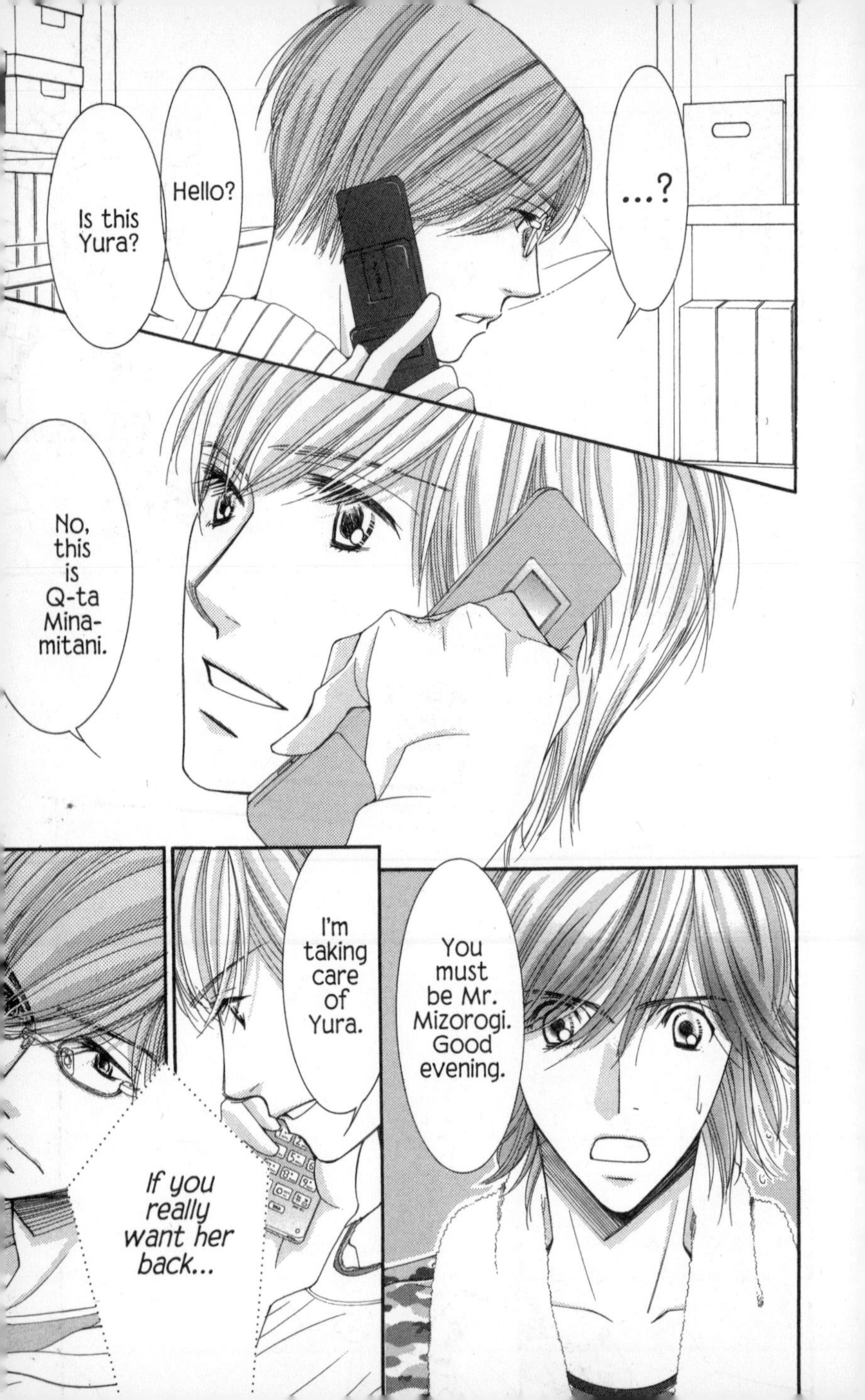
Hello?
Is this Yura?
...?
No, this is Q-ta Minamitani.
You must be Mr. Mizorogi. Good evening.
I'm taking care of Yura.
If you really want her back...

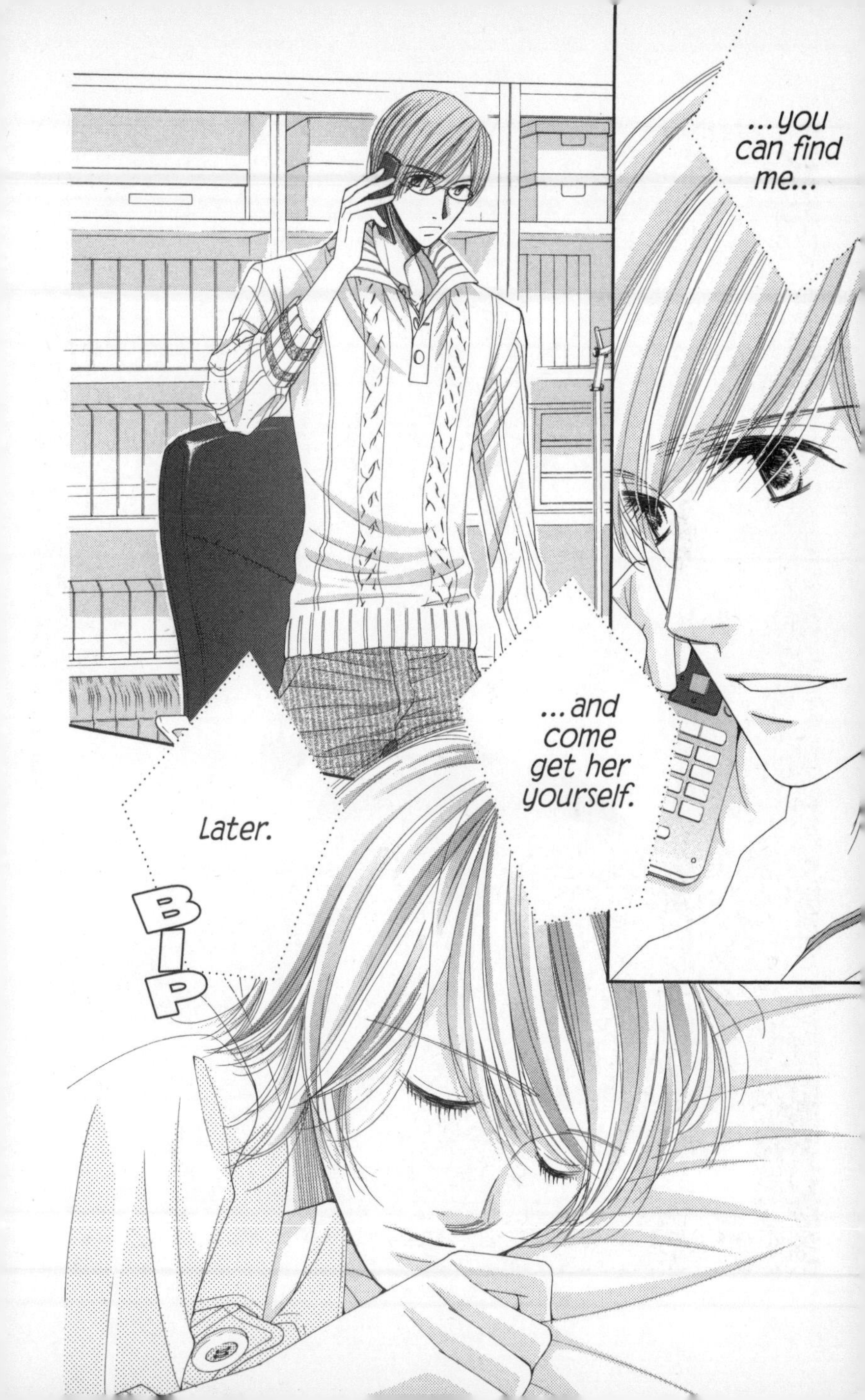
...you can find me...
...and come get her yourself.
Later.
BIP

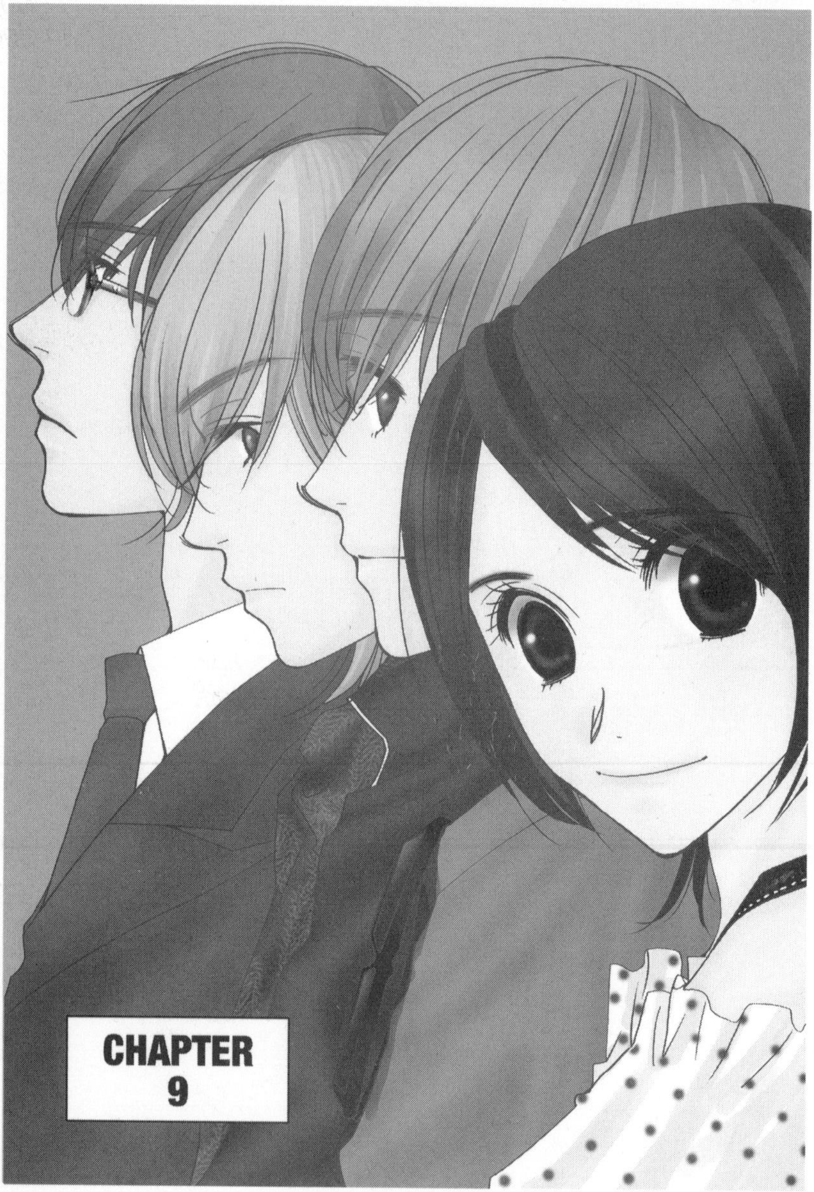
CHAPTER
9

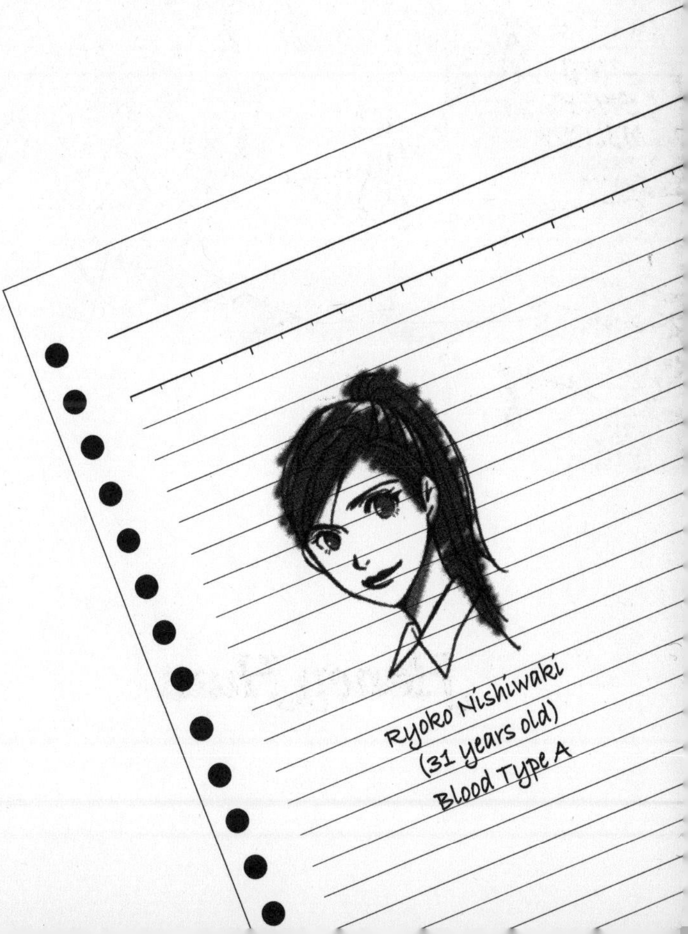
Ryoko Nishiwaki
(31 years old)
Blood Type A

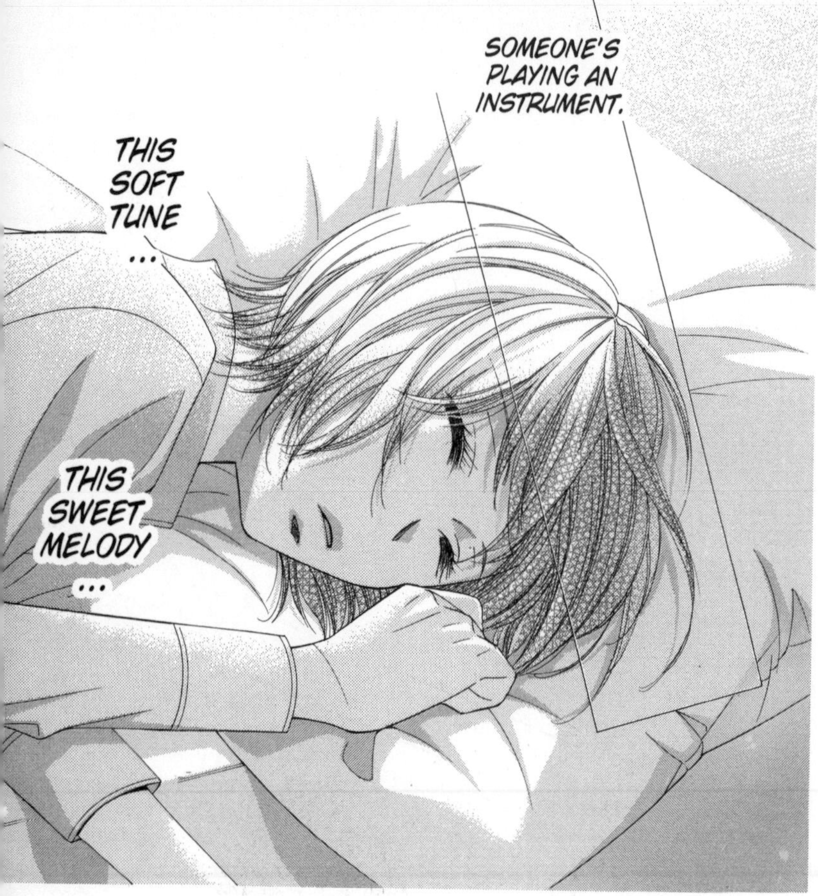
SOMEONE'S PLAYING AN INSTRUMENT.
THIS SOFT TUNE...
THIS SWEET MELODY...

Honey Hunt

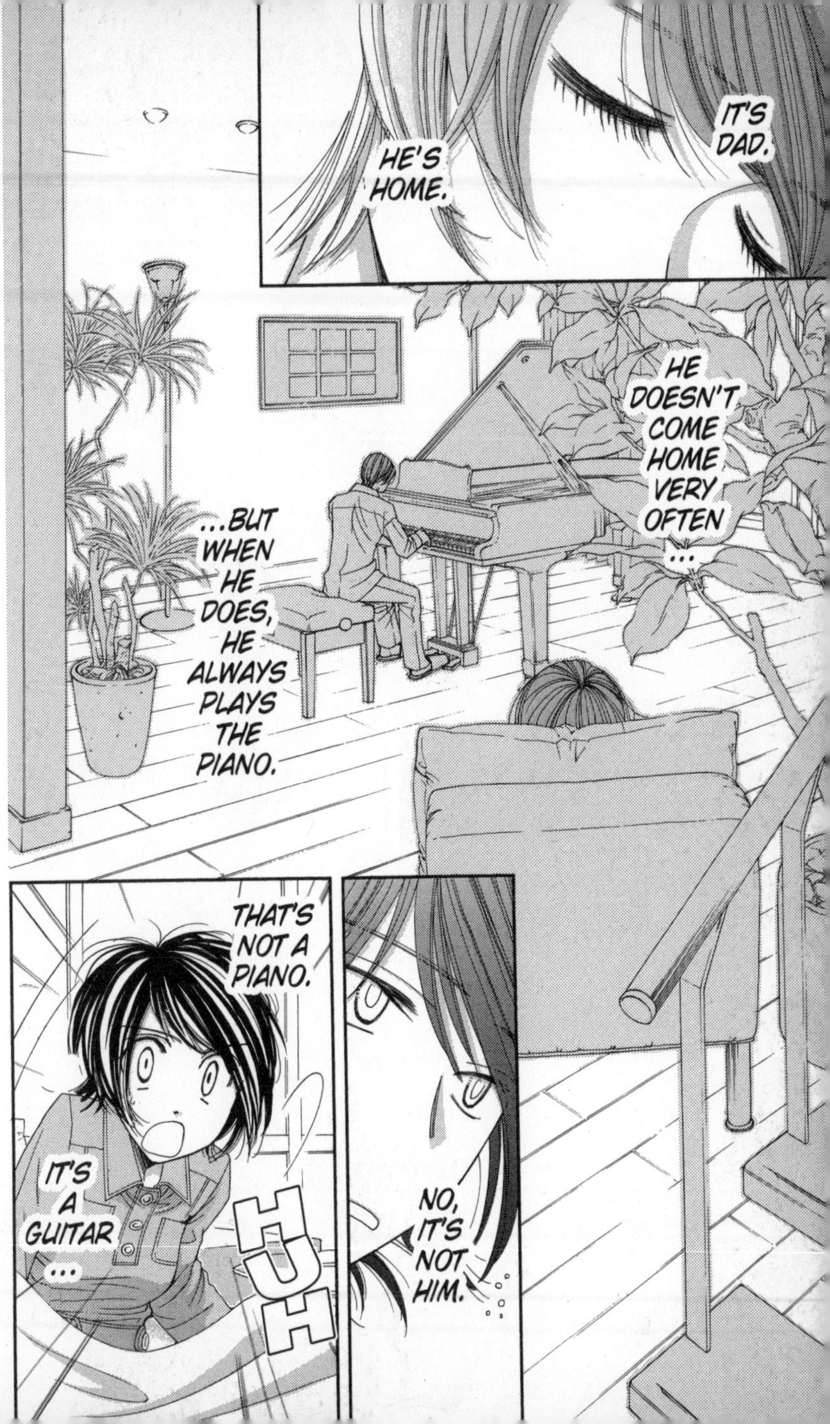
IT'S DAD.
HE'S HOME.
HE DOESN'T COME HOME VERY OFTEN...
...BUT WHEN HE DOES, HE ALWAYS PLAYS THE PIANO.
NO, IT'S NOT HIM.
THAT'S NOT A PIANO.
HUH
IT'S A GUITAR...

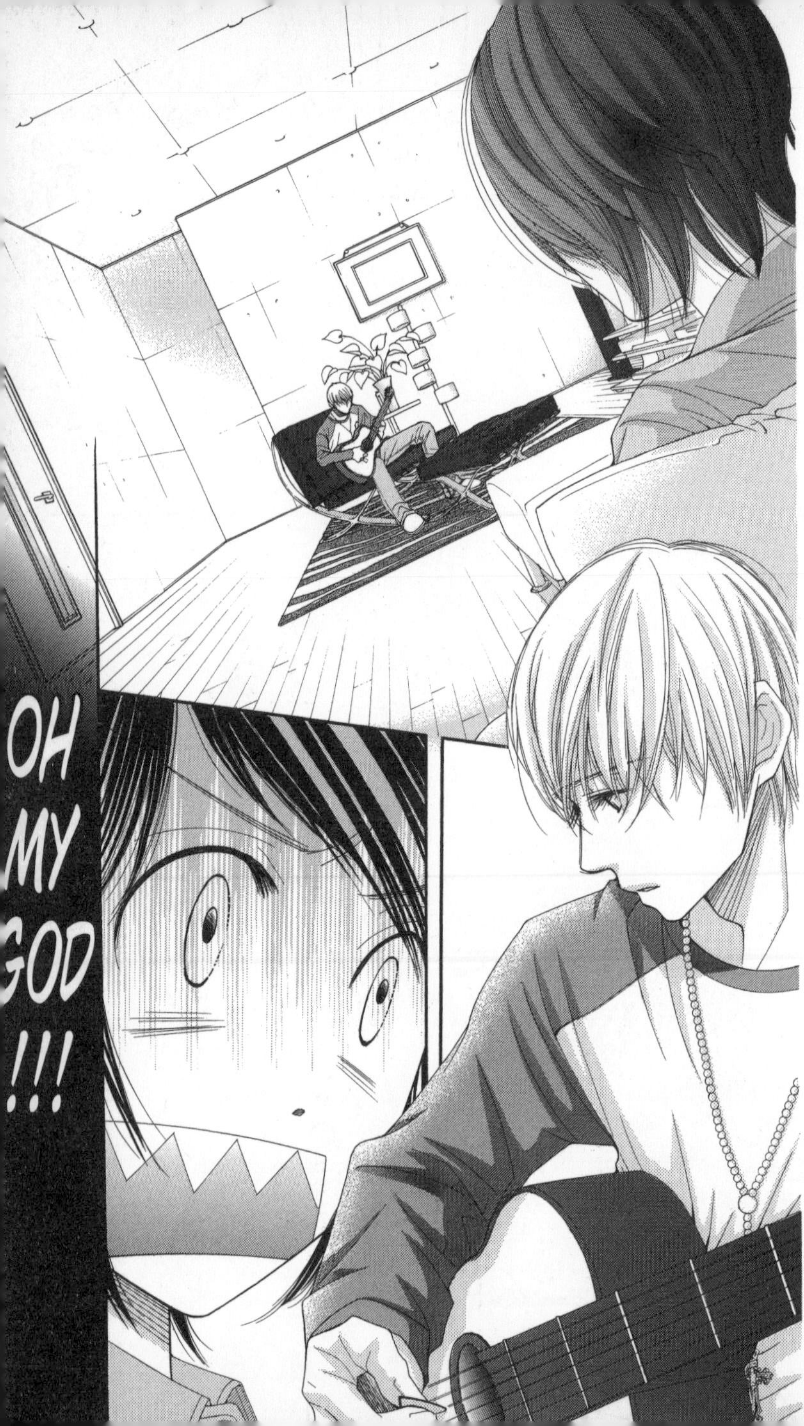
OH MY GOD !!!

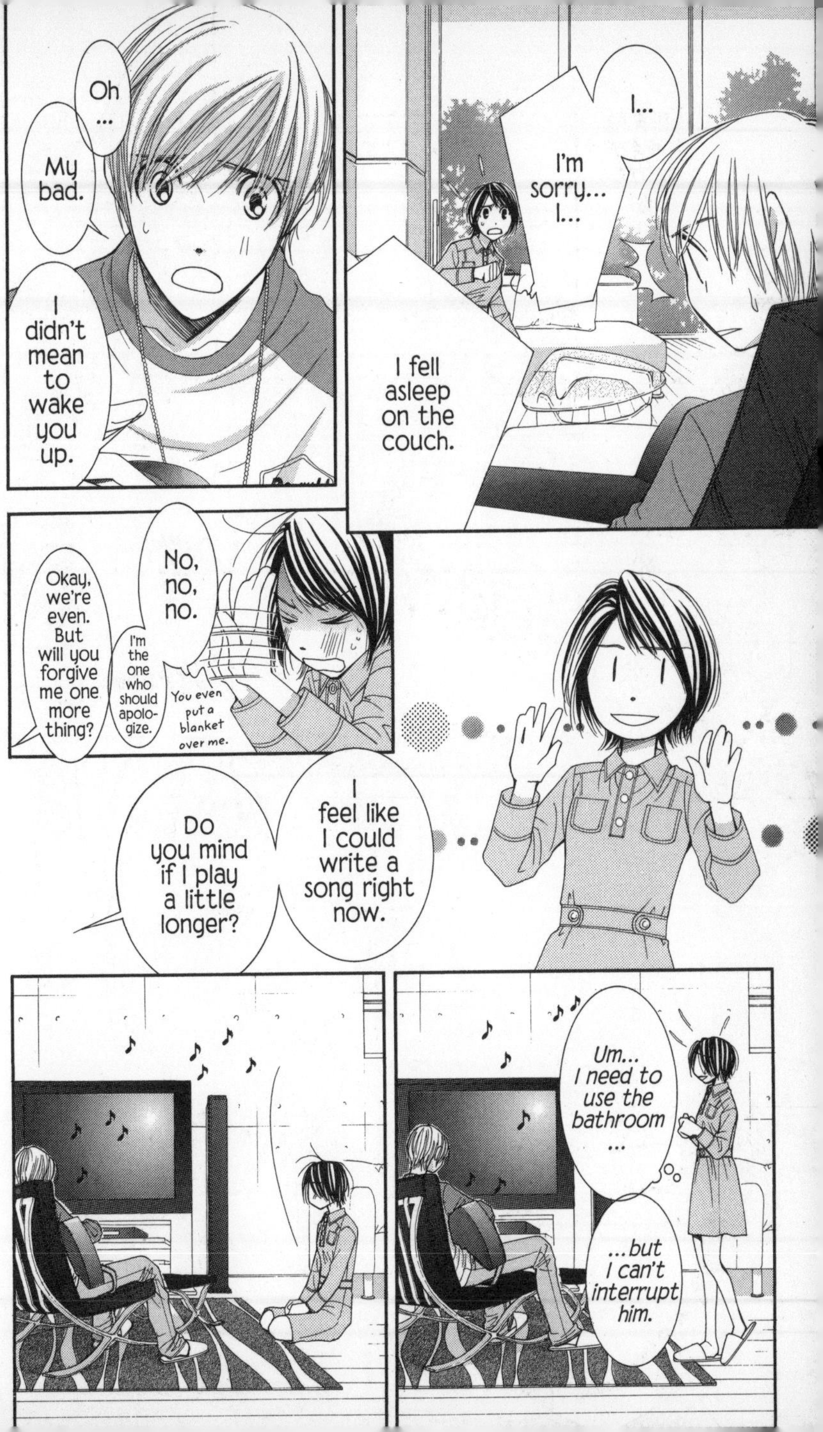
I...
I'm sorry... I...
I fell asleep on the couch.
Oh ...
My bad.
I didn't mean to wake you up.
No, no, no.
I'm the one who should apologize.
You even put a blanket over me.
Okay, we're even. But will you forgive me one more thing?
I feel like I could write a song right now.
Do you mind if I play a little longer?
Um... I need to use the bathroom ...
...but I can't interrupt him.

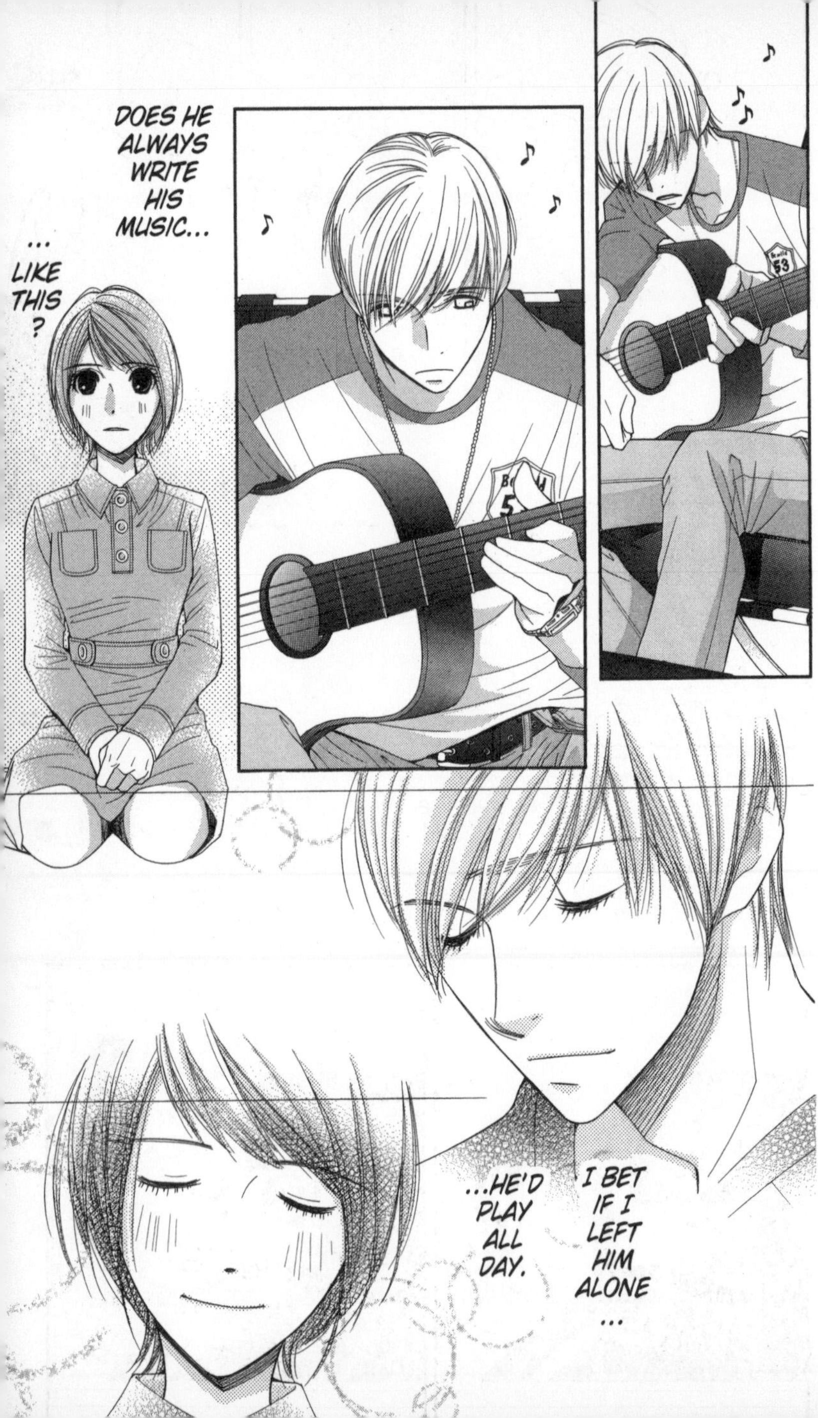
DOES HE ALWAYS WRITE HIS MUSIC...
...LIKE THIS?
I BET IF I LEFT HIM ALONE...
...HE'D PLAY ALL DAY.

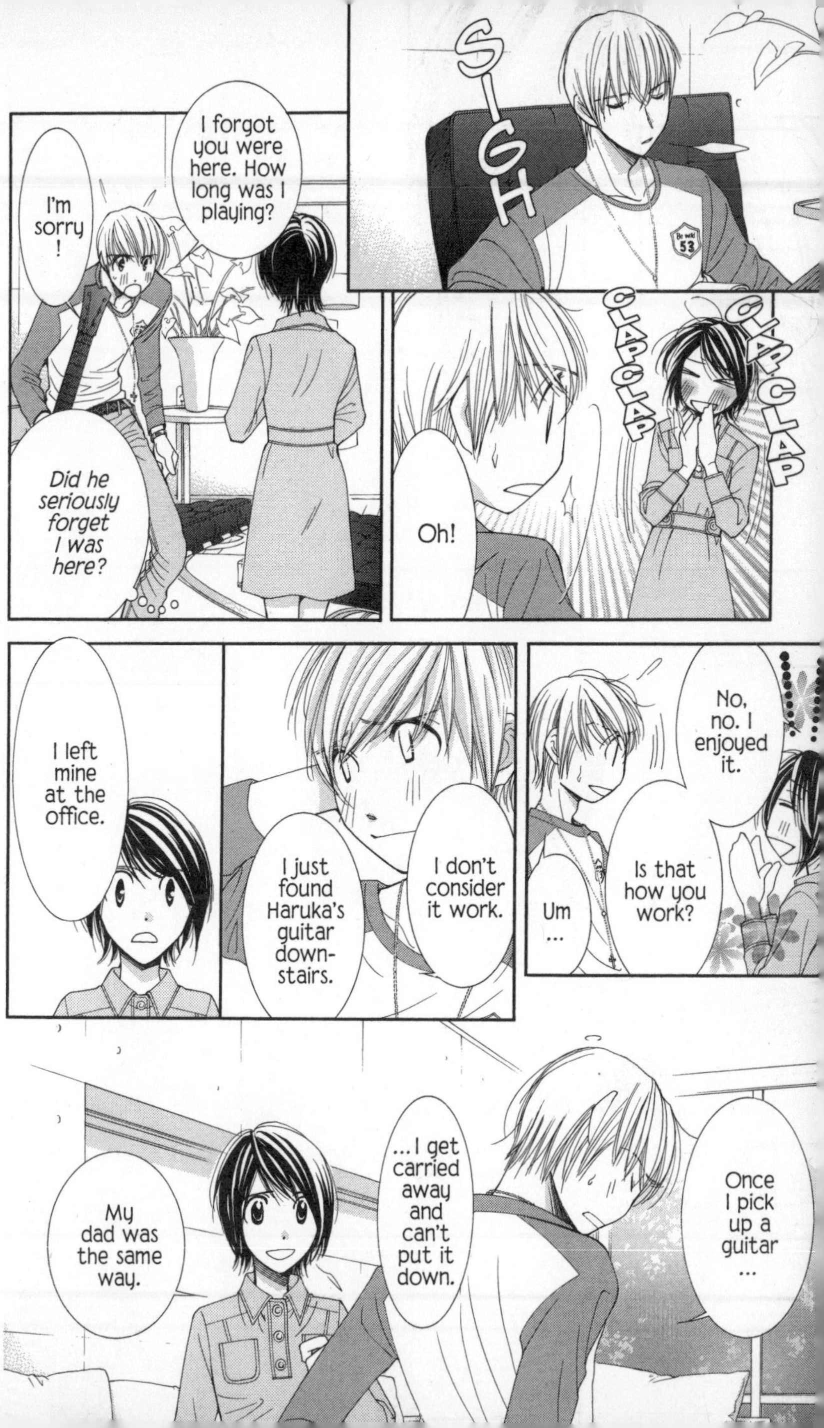
SIGH
CLAP CLAP
CLAP CLAP
Oh!
I forgot you were here. How long was I playing?
I'm sorry!
Did he seriously forget I was here?
No, no. I enjoyed it.
Is that how you work?
Um...
I don't consider it work.
I just found Haruka's guitar down-stairs.
I left mine at the office.
Once I pick up a guitar...
...I get carried away and can't put it down.
My dad was the same way.

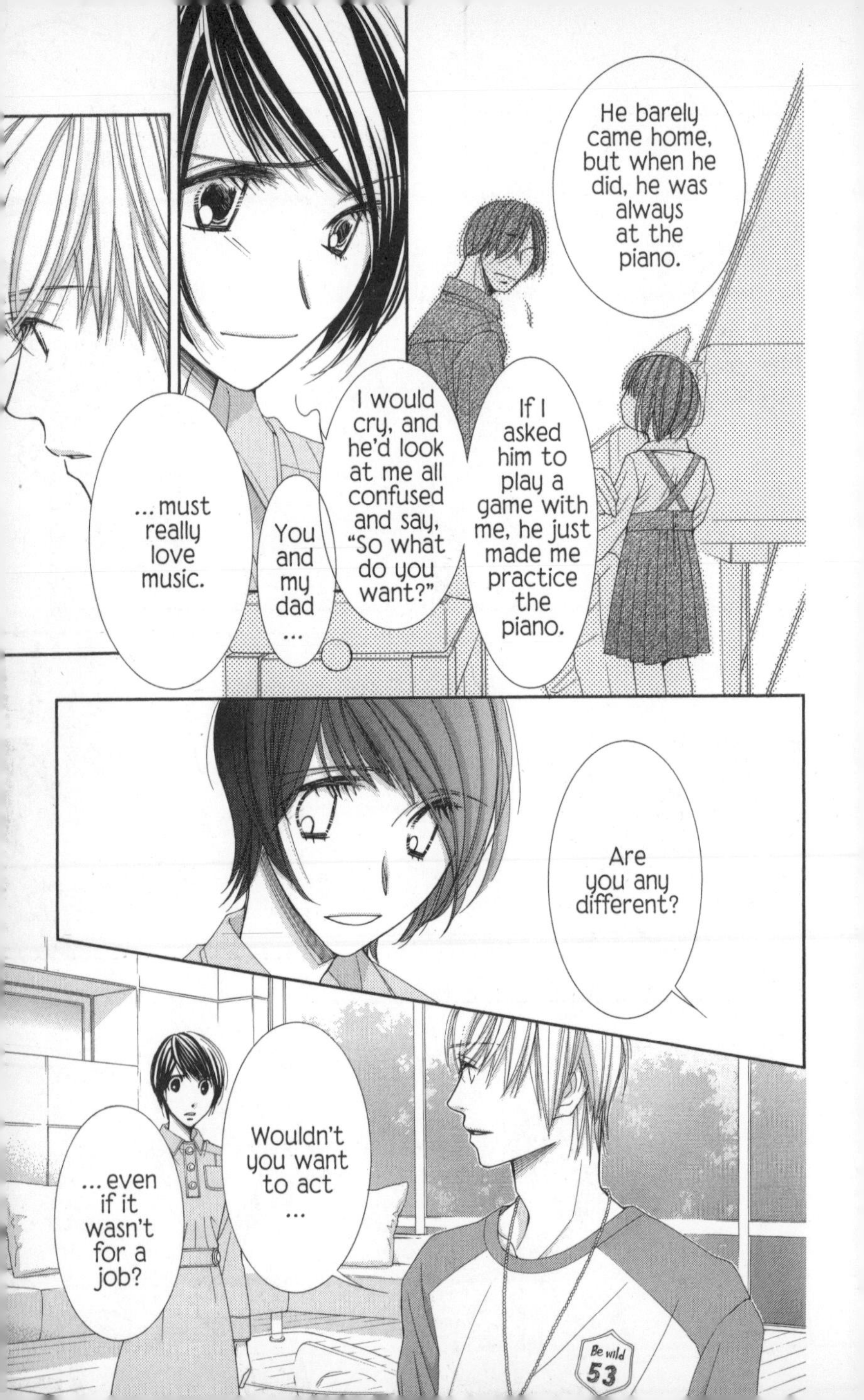
He barely came home, but when he did, he was always at the piano.
If I asked him to play a game with me, he just made me practice the piano.
I would cry, and he'd look at me all confused and say, "So what do you want?"
You and my dad...
...must really love music.
Are you any different?
Wouldn't you want to act...
...even if it wasn't for a job?
Be wild
53

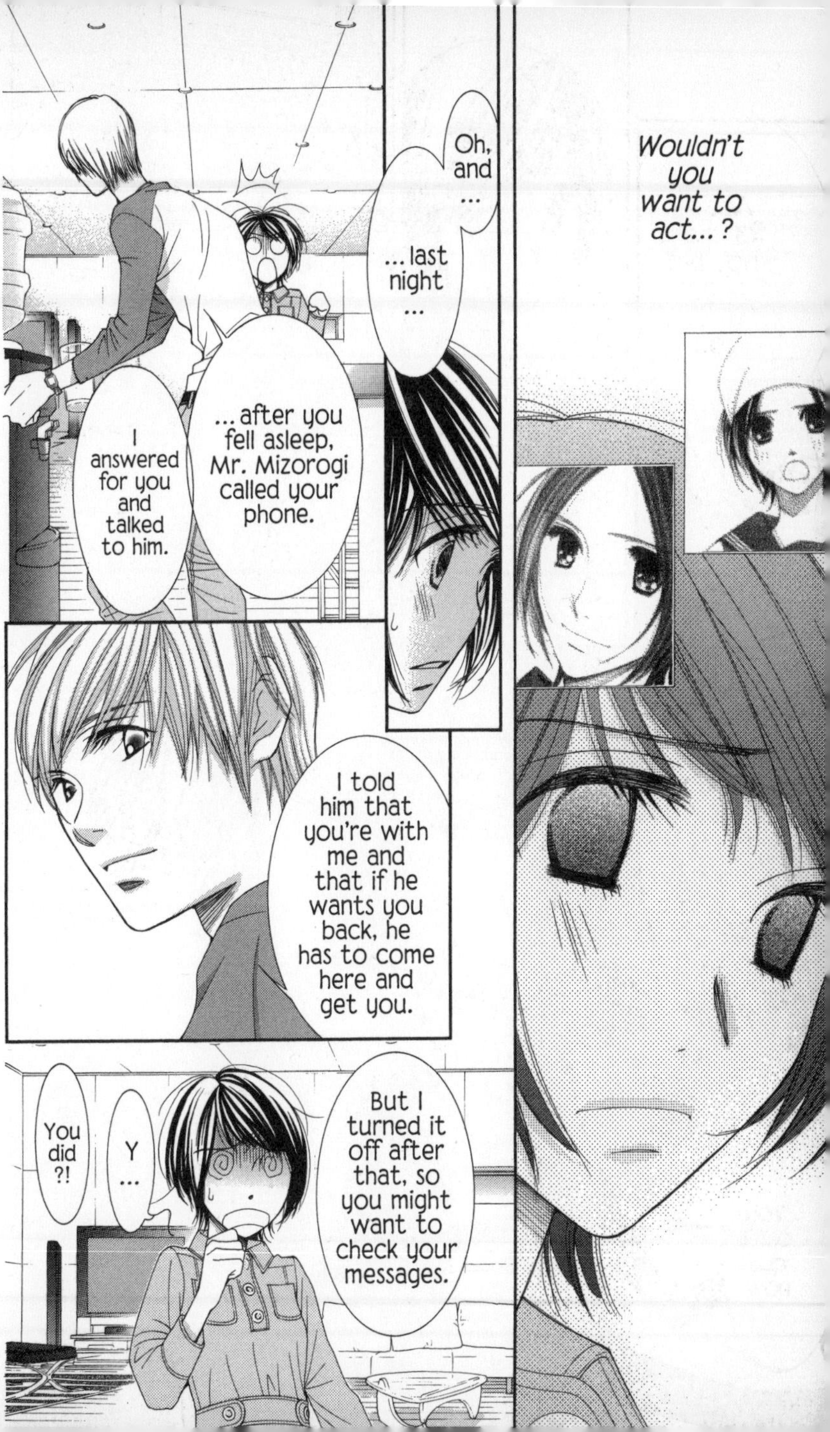

Wouldn't you want to act...?
Oh, and ...
... last night ...
... after you fell asleep, Mr. Mizorogi called your phone.
I answered for you and talked to him.
I told him that you're with me and that if he wants you back, he has to come here and get you.
But I turned it off after that, so you might want to check your messages.
Y ...
You did ?!

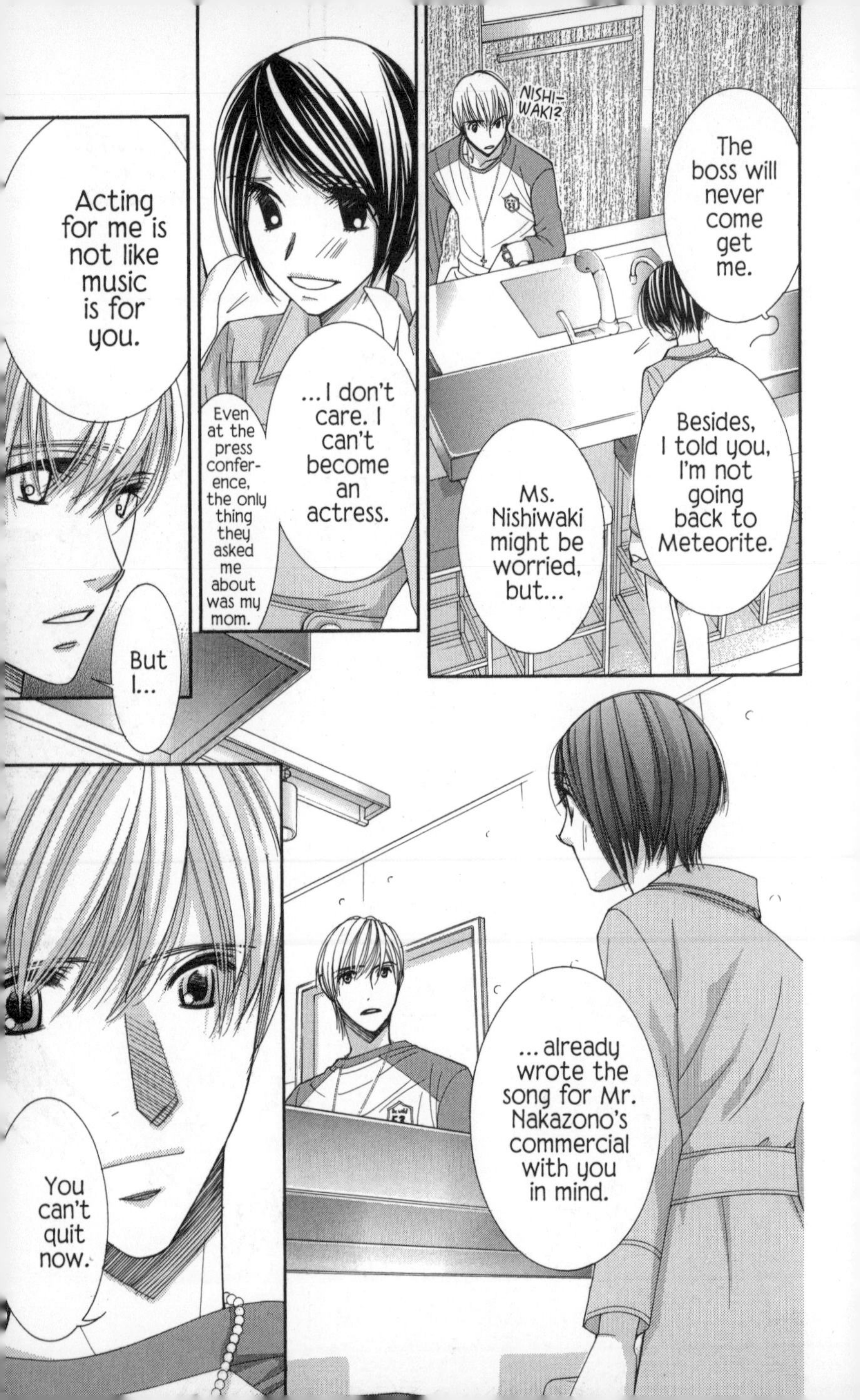
The boss will never come get me.
NISHI-WAKI?
Besides, I told you, I'm not going back to Meteorite.
Ms. Nishiwaki might be worried, but...
...I don't care. I can't become an actress.
Even at the press conference, the only thing they asked me about was my mom.
Acting for me is not like music is for you.
But I...
...already wrote the song for Mr. Nakazono's commercial with you in mind.
You can't quit now.

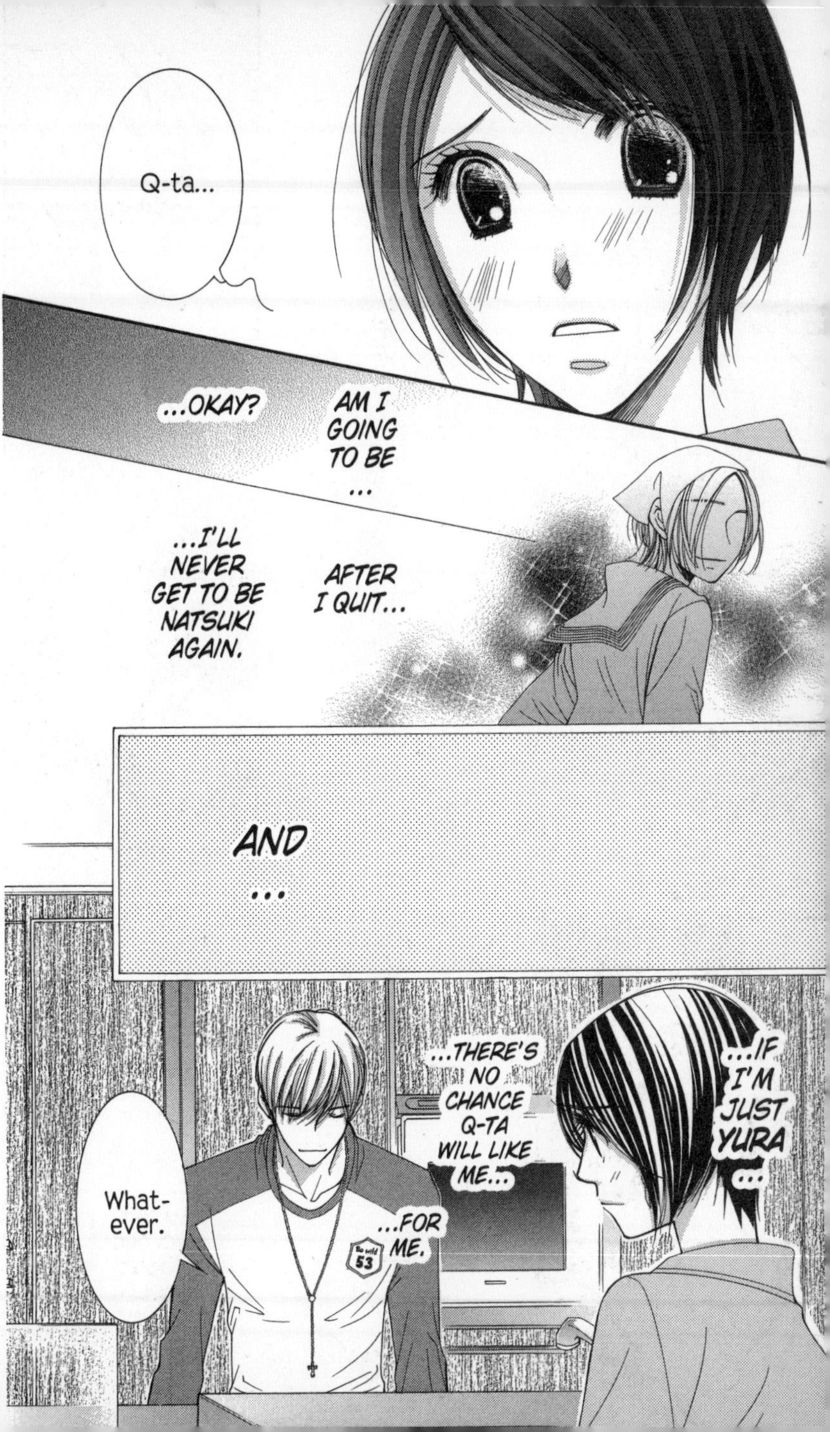

Q-ta...
AM I GOING TO BE ...
...OKAY?
AFTER I QUIT...
...I'LL NEVER GET TO BE NATSUKI AGAIN.
AND ...
...IF I'M JUST YURA ...
...THERE'S NO CHANCE Q-TA WILL LIKE ME...
...FOR ME.
What-ever.

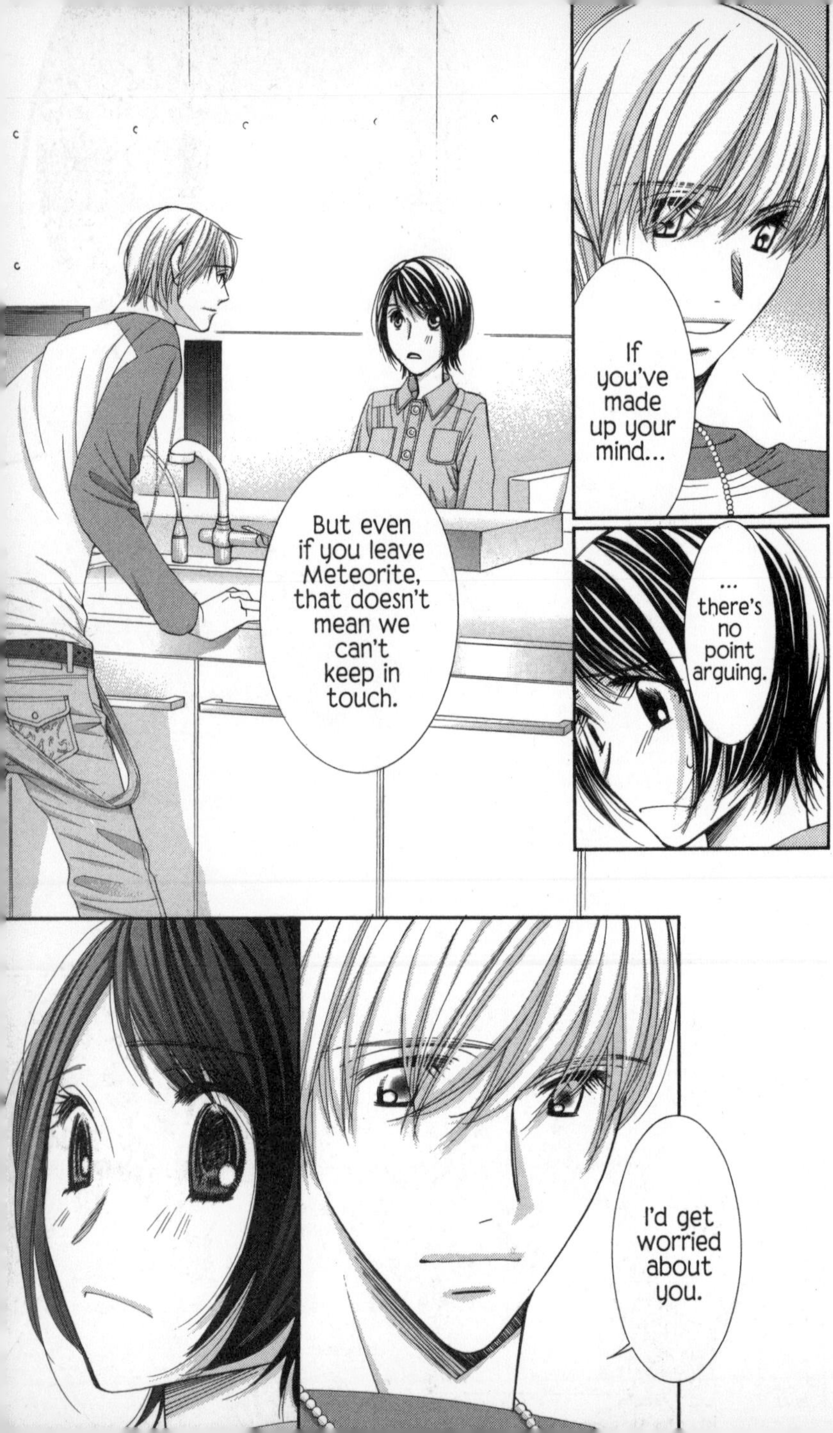
If you've made up your mind...
... there's no point arguing.
But even if you leave Meteorite, that doesn't mean we can't keep in touch.
I'd get worried about you.

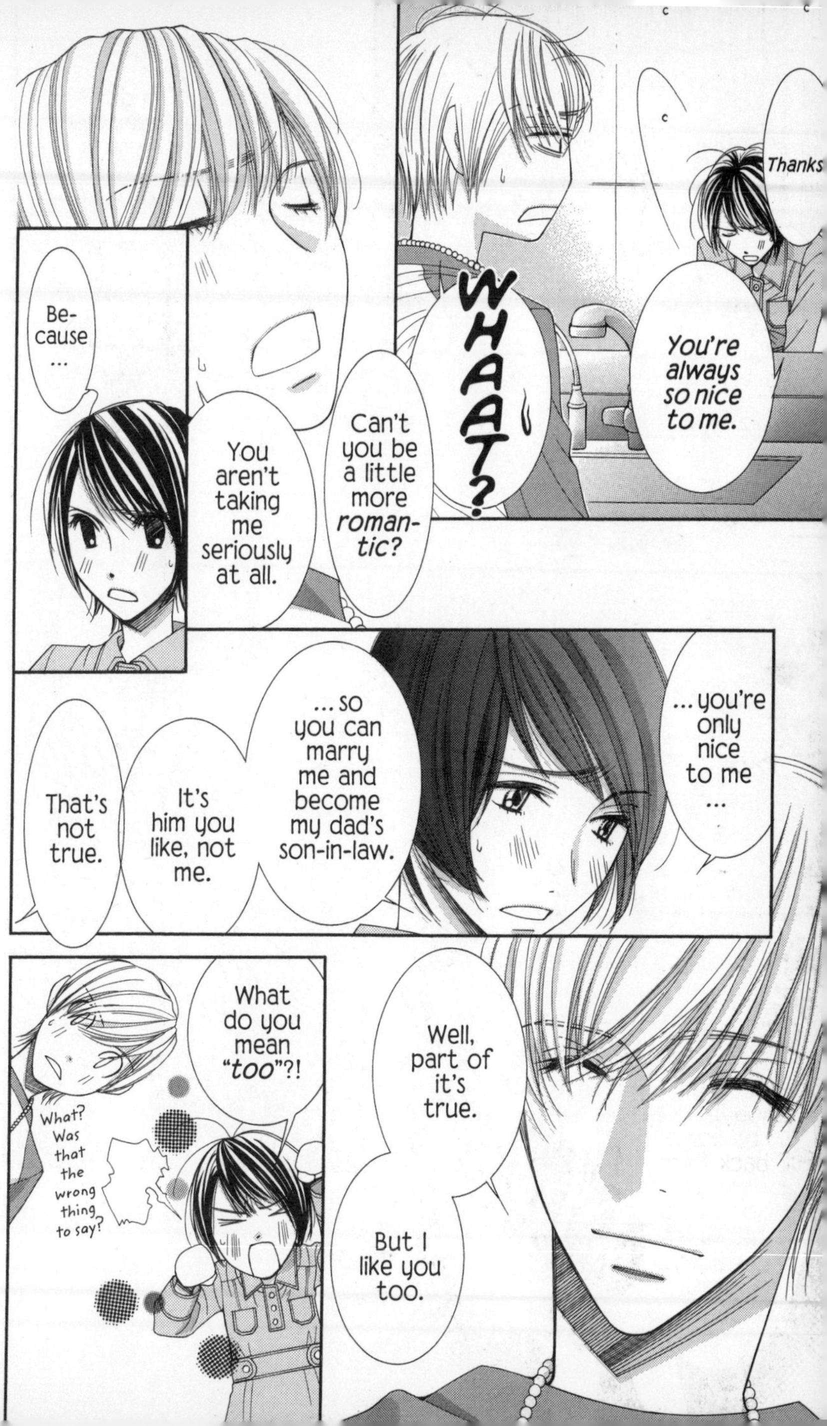
Thanks
You're always so nice to me.
WHAAT?
Can't you be a little more romantic?
You aren't taking me seriously at all.
Be-cause ...
... you're only nice to me ...
... so you can marry me and become my dad's son-in-law.
It's him you like, not me.
That's not true.
Well, part of it's true.
But I like you too.
What do you mean "too"?!
What? Was that the wrong thing to say?

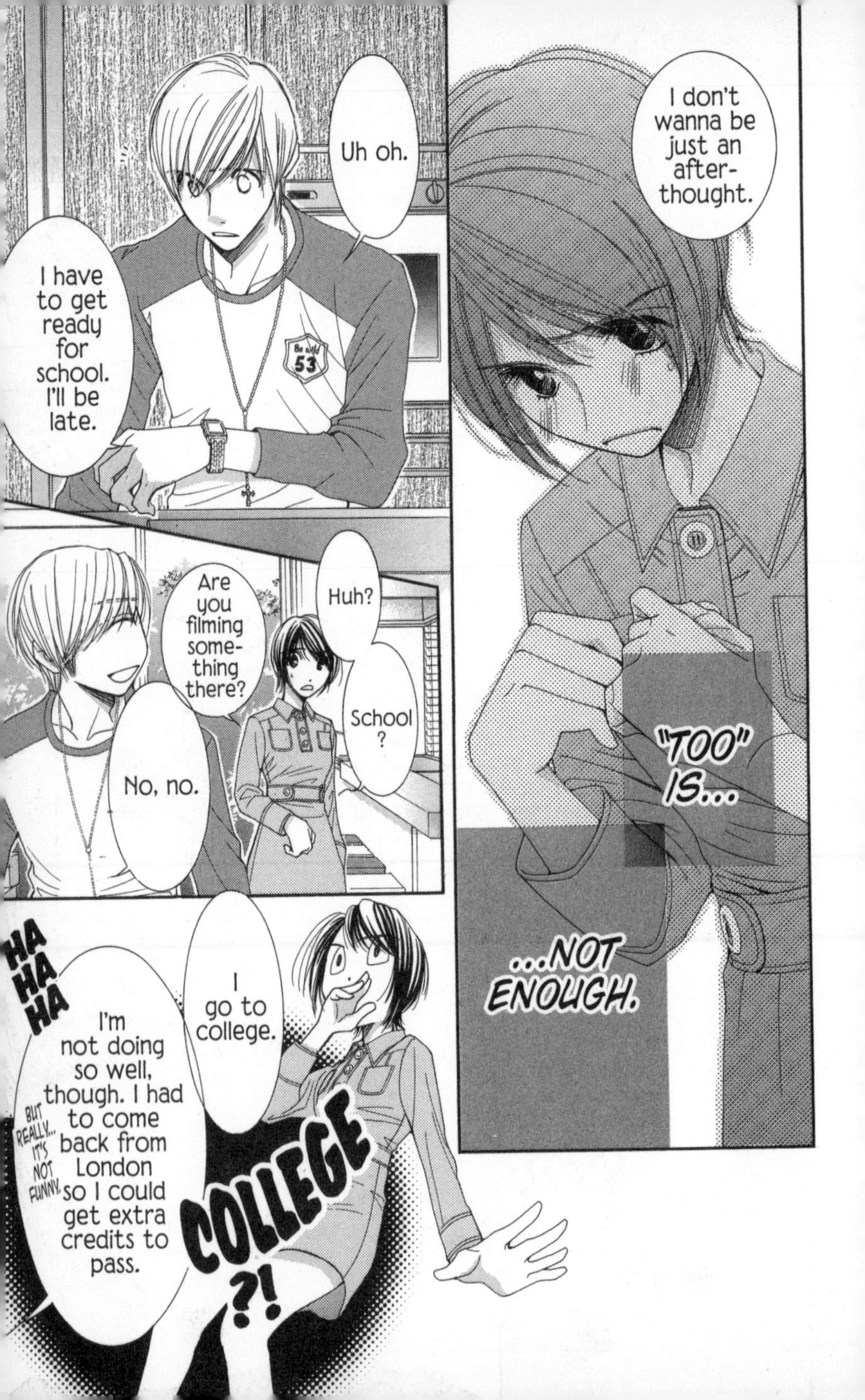
I don't wanna be just an after-thought.
"TOO" IS...
...NOT ENOUGH.
Uh oh.
I have to get ready for school. I'll be late.
Huh?
School?
Are you filming something there?
No, no.
COLLEGE ?!
I go to college.
I'm not doing so well, though. I had to come back from London so I could get extra credits to pass.
BUT REALLY... IT'S NOT FUNNY.
HA HA HA

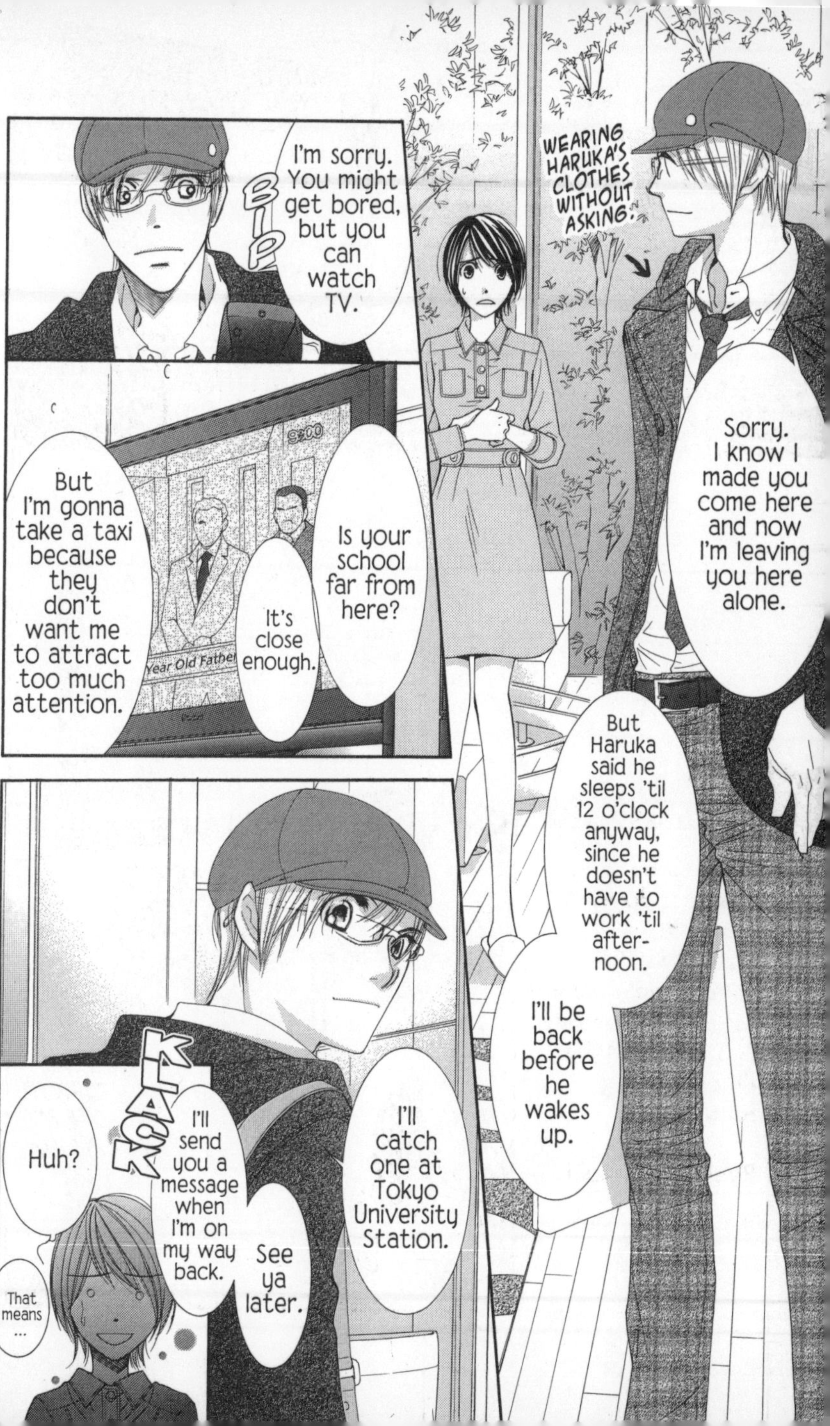
WEARING HARUKA'S CLOTHES WITHOUT ASKING.
Sorry. I know I made you come here and now I'm leaving you here alone.
But Haruka said he sleeps 'til 12 o'clock anyway, since he doesn't have to work 'til after-noon.
I'll be back before he wakes up.
I'm sorry. You might get bored, but you can watch TV.
BIP
Is your school far from here?
It's close enough.
But I'm gonna take a taxi because they don't want me to attract too much attention.
Year Old Father
I'll catch one at Tokyo University Station.
I'll send you a message when I'm on my way back.
See ya later.
KLACK
Huh?
That means...

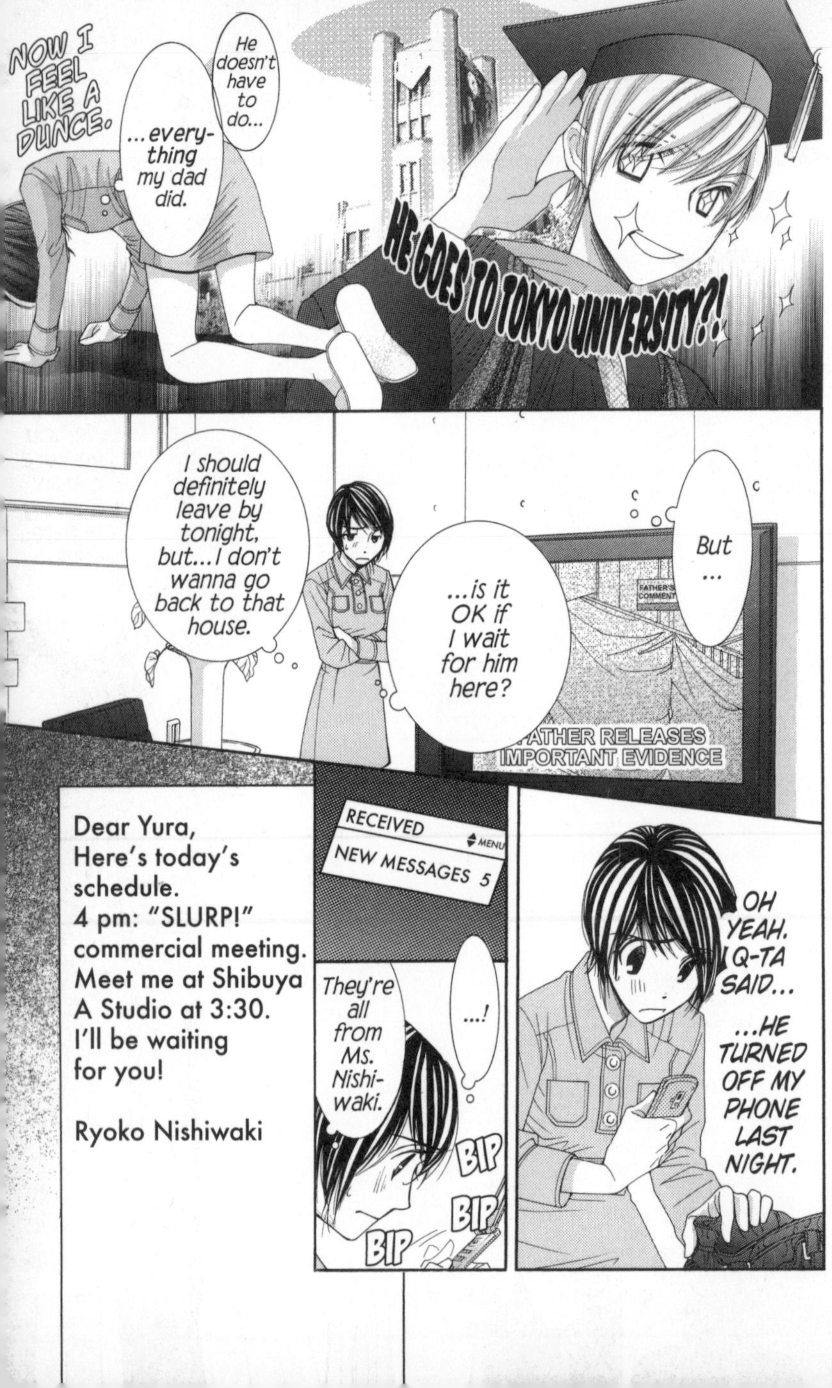
HE GOES TO TOKYO UNIVERSITY?!
He doesn't have to do...
...every-thing my dad did.
NOW I FEEL LIKE A DUNCE.
But...
...is it OK if I wait for him here?
FATHER'S COMMENT
FATHER RELEASES IMPORTANT EVIDENCE
I should definitely leave by tonight, but...I don't wanna go back to that house.
OH YEAH. Q-TA SAID...
...HE TURNED OFF MY PHONE LAST NIGHT.
RECEIVED
MENU
NEW MESSAGES 5
...!
They're all from Ms. Nishi-waki.
BIP
BIP
BIP
Dear Yura,
Here's today's schedule.
4 pm: "SLURP!" commercial meeting.
Meet me at Shibuya A Studio at 3:30.
I'll be waiting for you!
Ryoko Nishiwaki

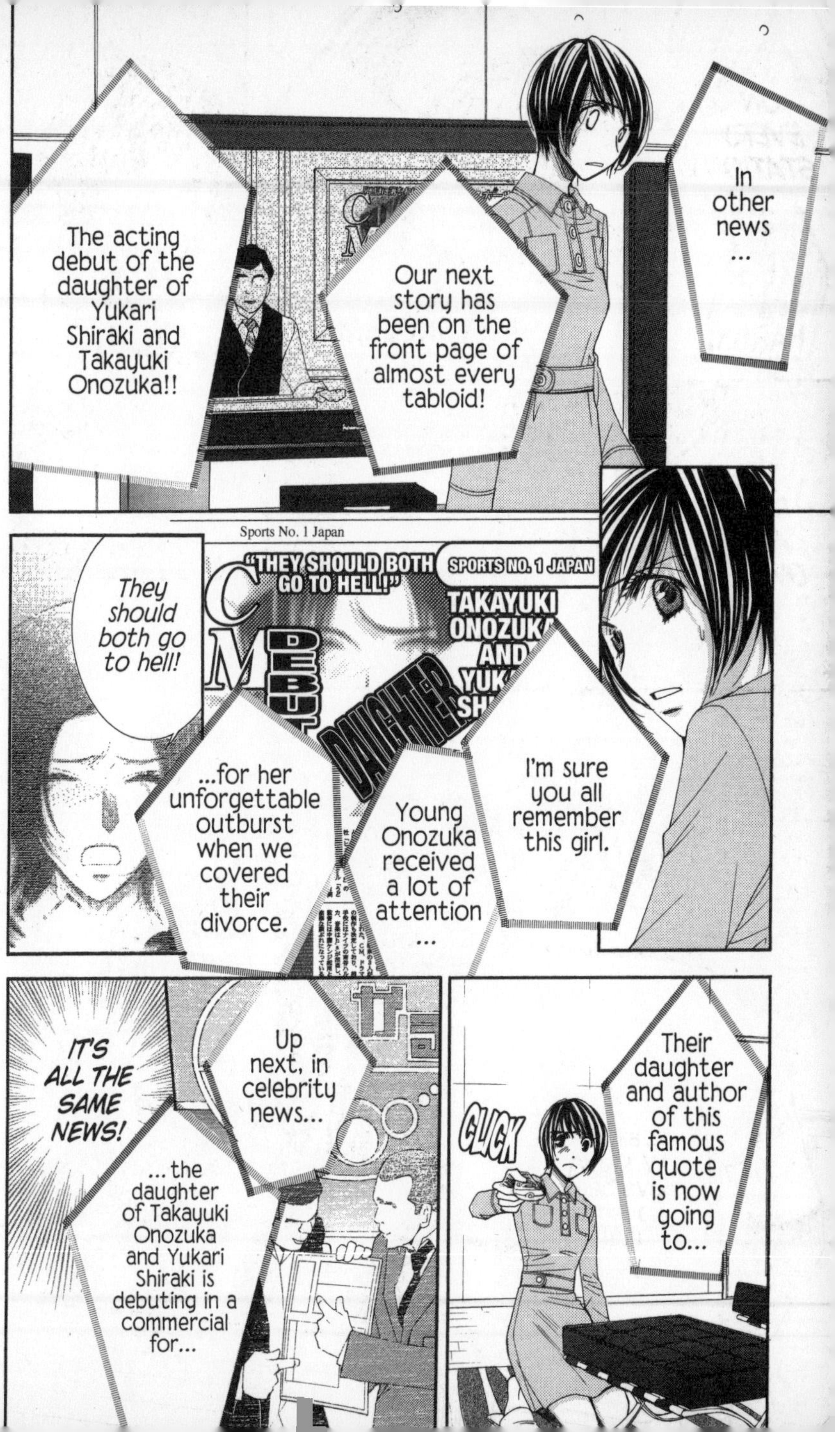
In other news...
Our next story has been on the front page of almost every tabloid!
The acting debut of the daughter of Yukari Shiraki and Takayuki Onozuka!!
I'm sure you all remember this girl.
Young Onozuka received a lot of attention...
Sports No. 1 Japan
SPORTS NO. 1 JAPAN
"THEY SHOULD BOTH GO TO HELL!"
DEBUT
DAUGHTER
...for her unforgettable outburst when we covered their divorce.
They should both go to hell!
Their daughter and author of this famous quote is now going to...
CLICK
Up next, in celebrity news...
...the daughter of Takayuki Onozuka and Yukari Shiraki is debuting in a commercial for...
IT'S ALL THE SAME NEWS!

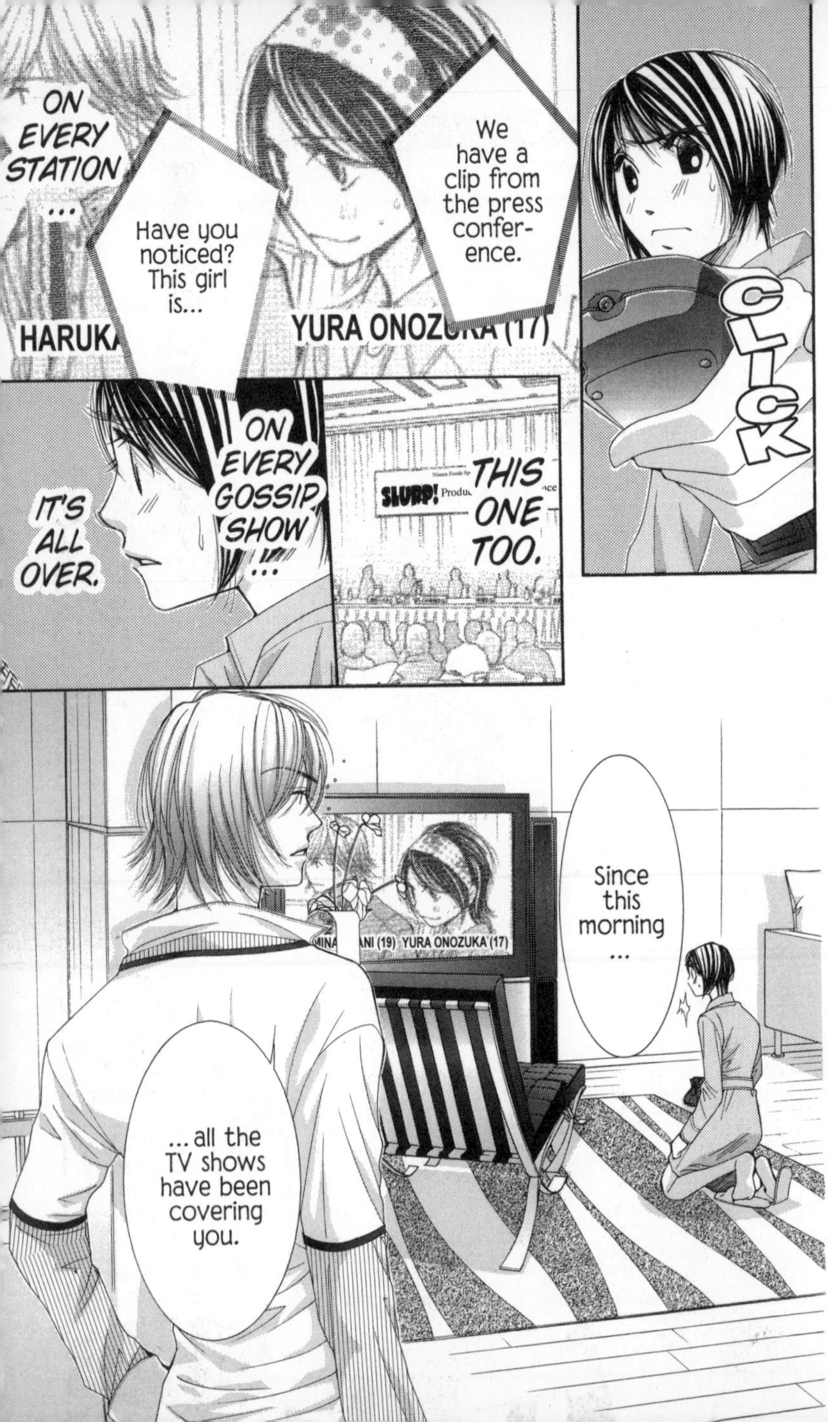
CLICK
We have a clip from the press conference.
Have you noticed? This girl is...
ON EVERY STATION...
YURA ONOZUKA (17)
HARUKA
SLURP!
THIS ONE TOO.
ON EVERY GOSSIP SHOW...
IT'S ALL OVER.
Since this morning...
YURA ONOZUKA (17)
...all the TV shows have been covering you.

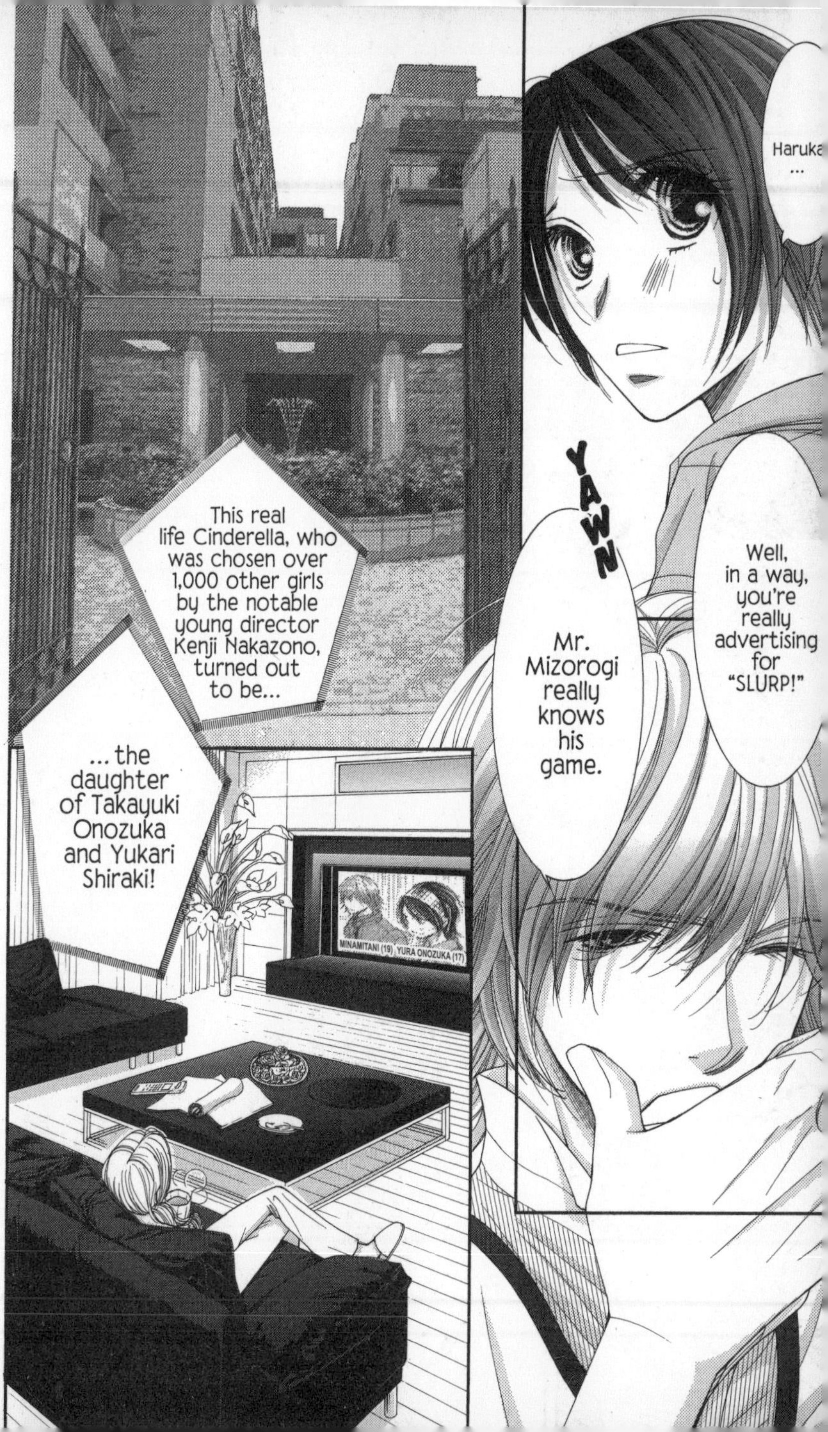
Haruka ...
Well, in a way, you're really advertising for "SLURP!"
YAWN
Mr. Mizorogi really knows his game.
This real life Cinderella, who was chosen over 1,000 other girls by the notable young director Kenji Nakazono, turned out to be...
... the daughter of Takayuki Onozuka and Yukari Shiraki!
MINAMITANI (19) YURA ONOZUKA (17)

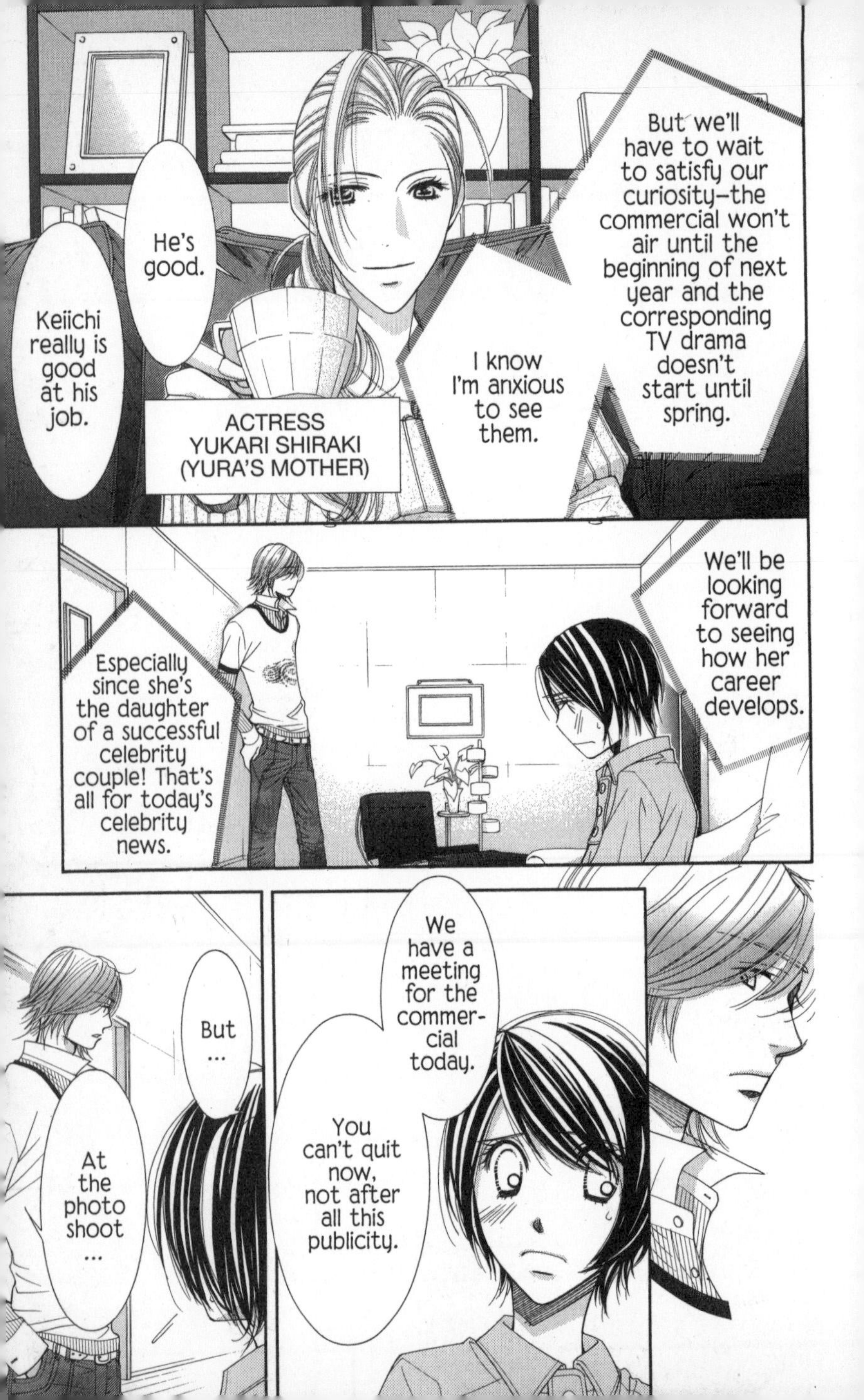
But we'll have to wait to satisfy our curiosity—the commercial won't air until the beginning of next year and the corresponding TV drama doesn't start until spring.
I know I'm anxious to see them.
He's good.
ACTRESS YUKARI SHIRAKI (YURA'S MOTHER)
Keiichi really is good at his job.
We'll be looking forward to seeing how her career develops.
Especially since she's the daughter of a successful celebrity couple! That's all for today's celebrity news.
We have a meeting for the commercial today.
You can't quit now, not after all this publicity.
But ...
At the photo shoot ...

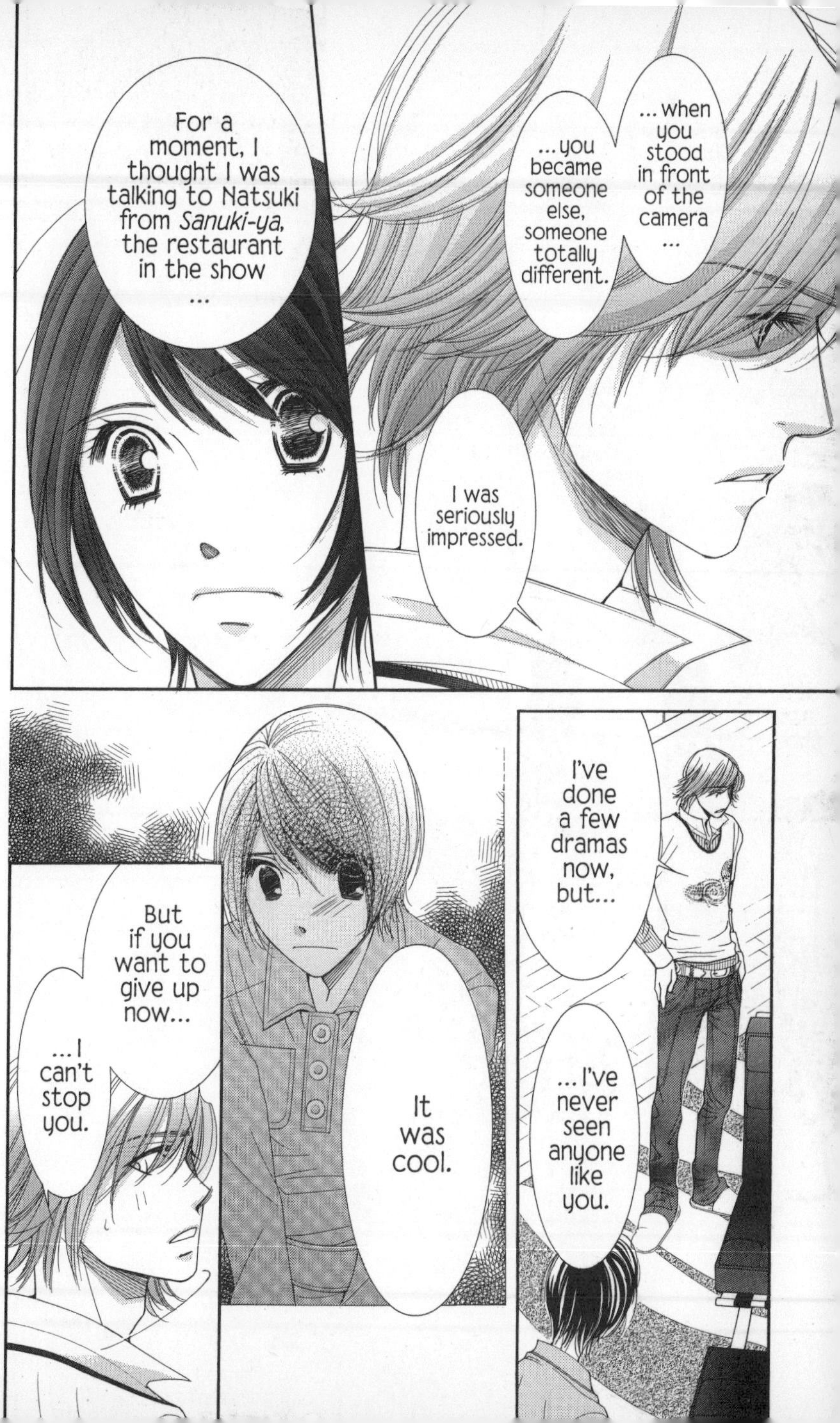

... when you stood in front of the camera ...
... you became someone else, someone totally different.
For a moment, I thought I was talking to Natsuki from *Sanuki-ya*, the restaurant in the show ...
I was seriously impressed.
I've done a few dramas now, but...
... I've never seen anyone like you.
It was cool.
But if you want to give up now...
... I can't stop you.

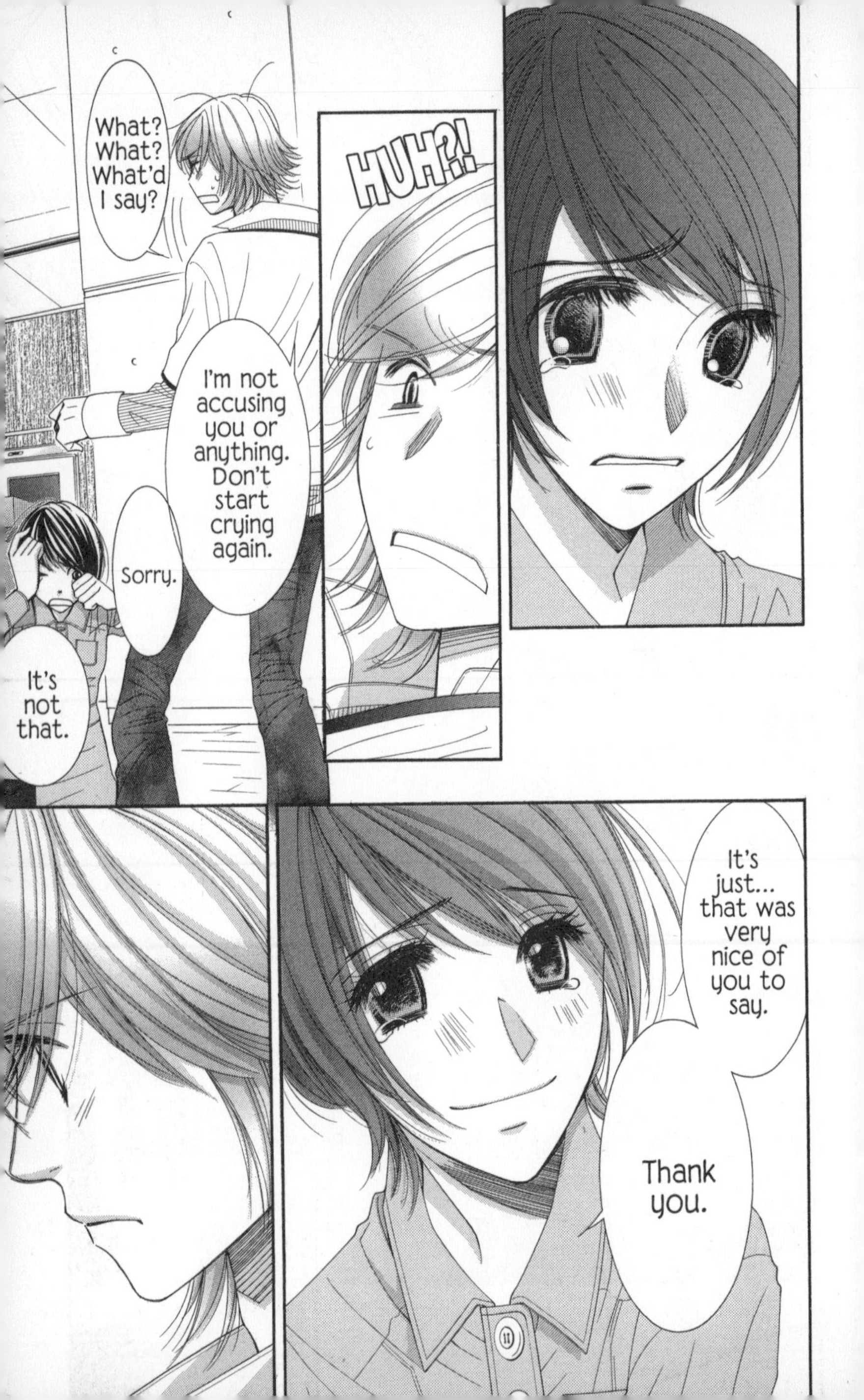
HUH?!
What? What? What'd I say?
I'm not accusing you or anything. Don't start crying again.
Sorry.
It's not that.
It's just... that was very nice of you to say.
Thank you.

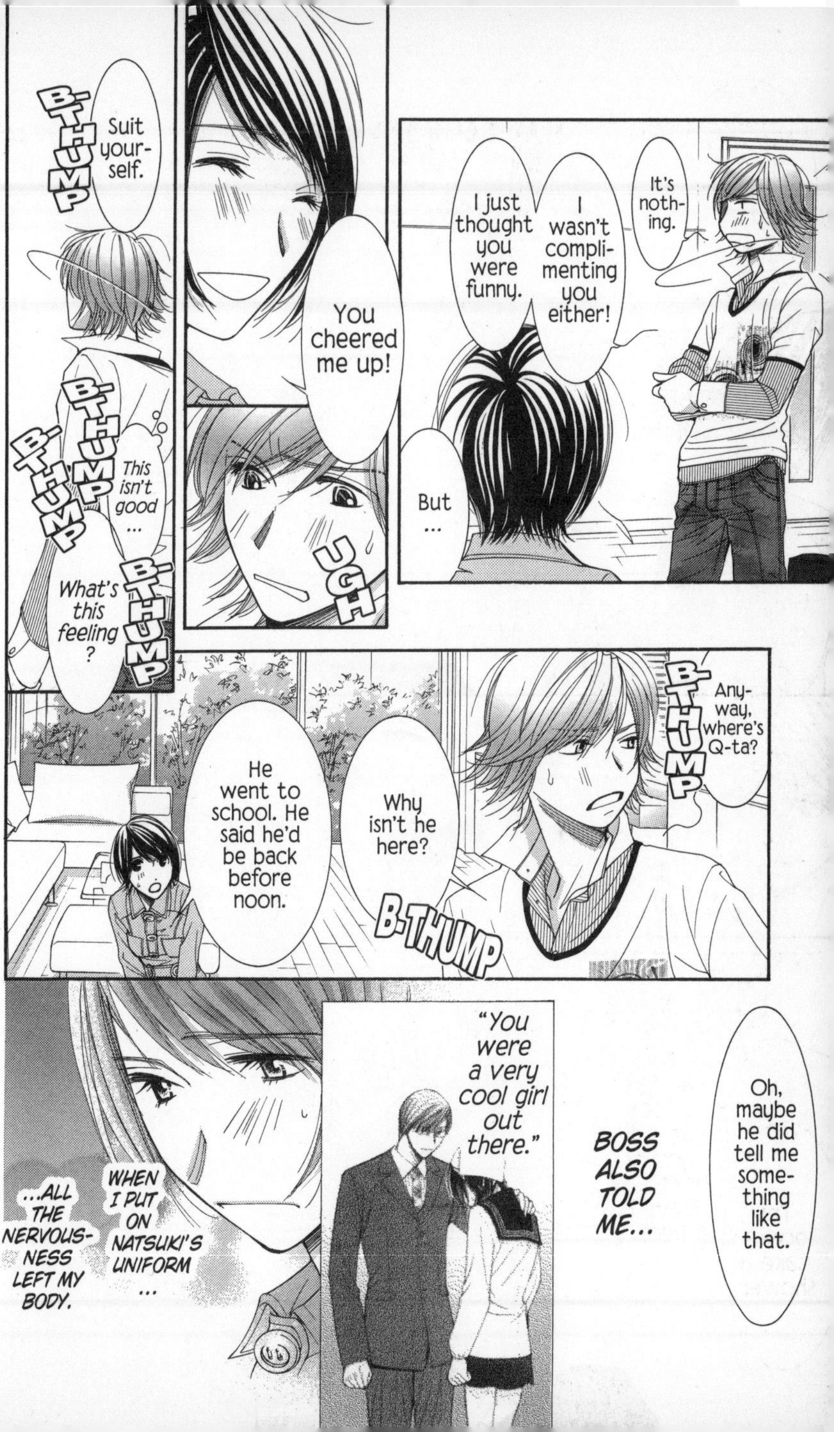

It's nothing.
I wasn't complimenting you either!
I just thought you were funny.
But...
You cheered me up!
UGH
Suit yourself.
B-THUMP
B-THUMP
B-THUMP
This isn't good...
What's this feeling?
B-THUMP
B-THUMP
Anyway, where's Q-ta?
Why isn't he here?
B-THUMP
He went to school. He said he'd be back before noon.
Oh, maybe he did tell me something like that.
BOSS ALSO TOLD ME...
"You were a very cool girl out there."
WHEN I PUT ON NATSUKI'S UNIFORM...
...ALL THE NERVOUSNESS LEFT MY BODY.

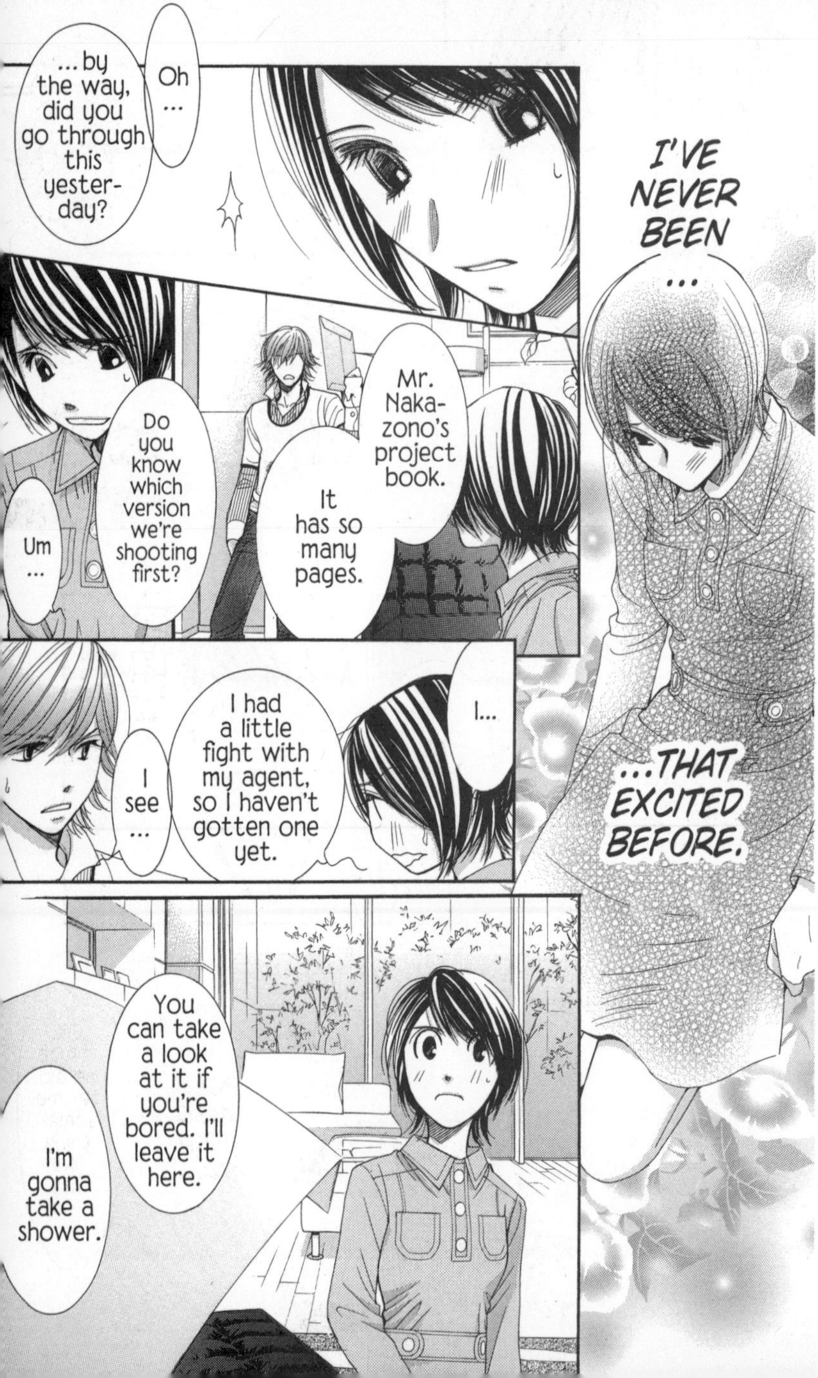
I'VE NEVER BEEN ...
...THAT EXCITED BEFORE.
Oh ...
... by the way, did you go through this yesterday?
Mr. Nakazono's project book.
It has so many pages.
Do you know which version we're shooting first?
Um ...
I...
I had a little fight with my agent, so I haven't gotten one yet.
I see ...
You can take a look at it if you're bored. I'll leave it here.
I'm gonna take a shower.

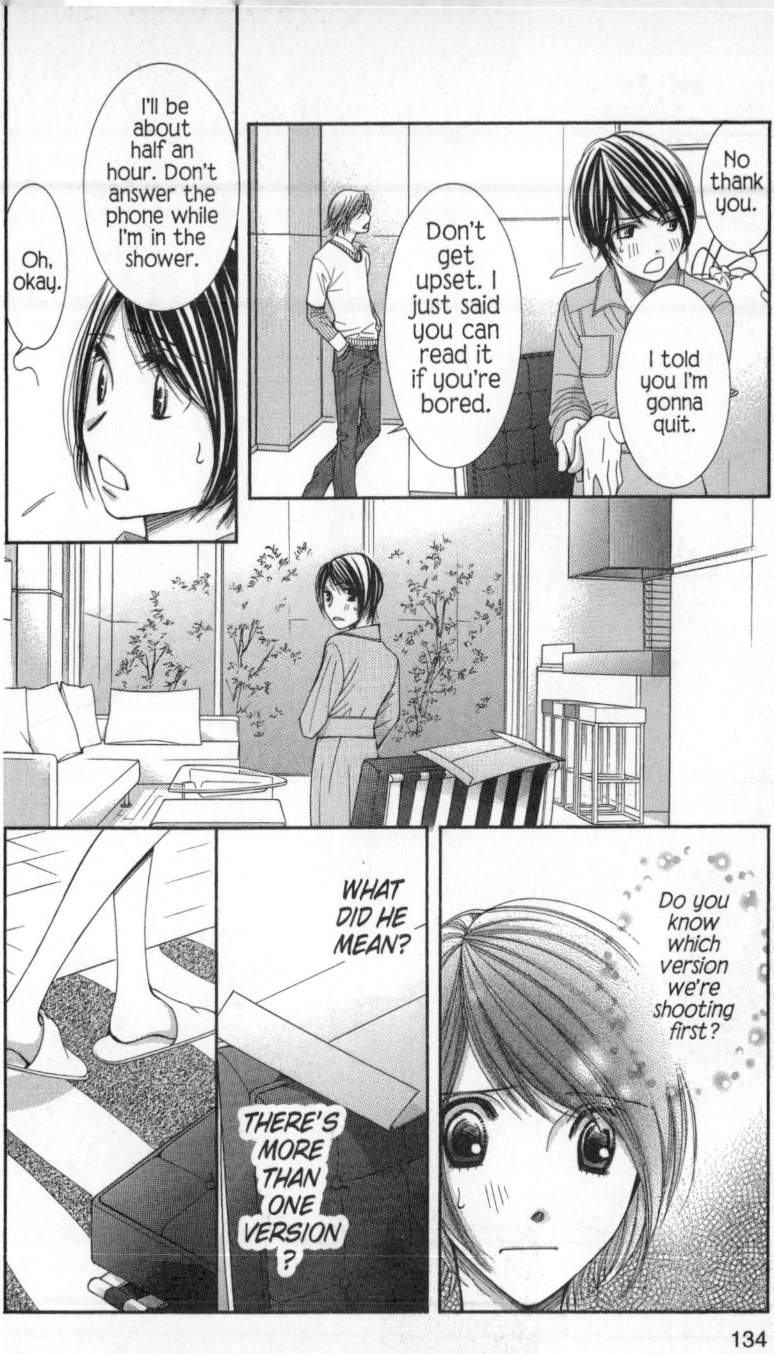
No thank you.
I told you I'm gonna quit.
Don't get upset. I just said you can read it if you're bored.
I'll be about half an hour. Don't answer the phone while I'm in the shower.
Oh, okay.
Do you know which version we're shooting first?
WHAT DID HE MEAN?
THERE'S MORE THAN ONE VERSION?

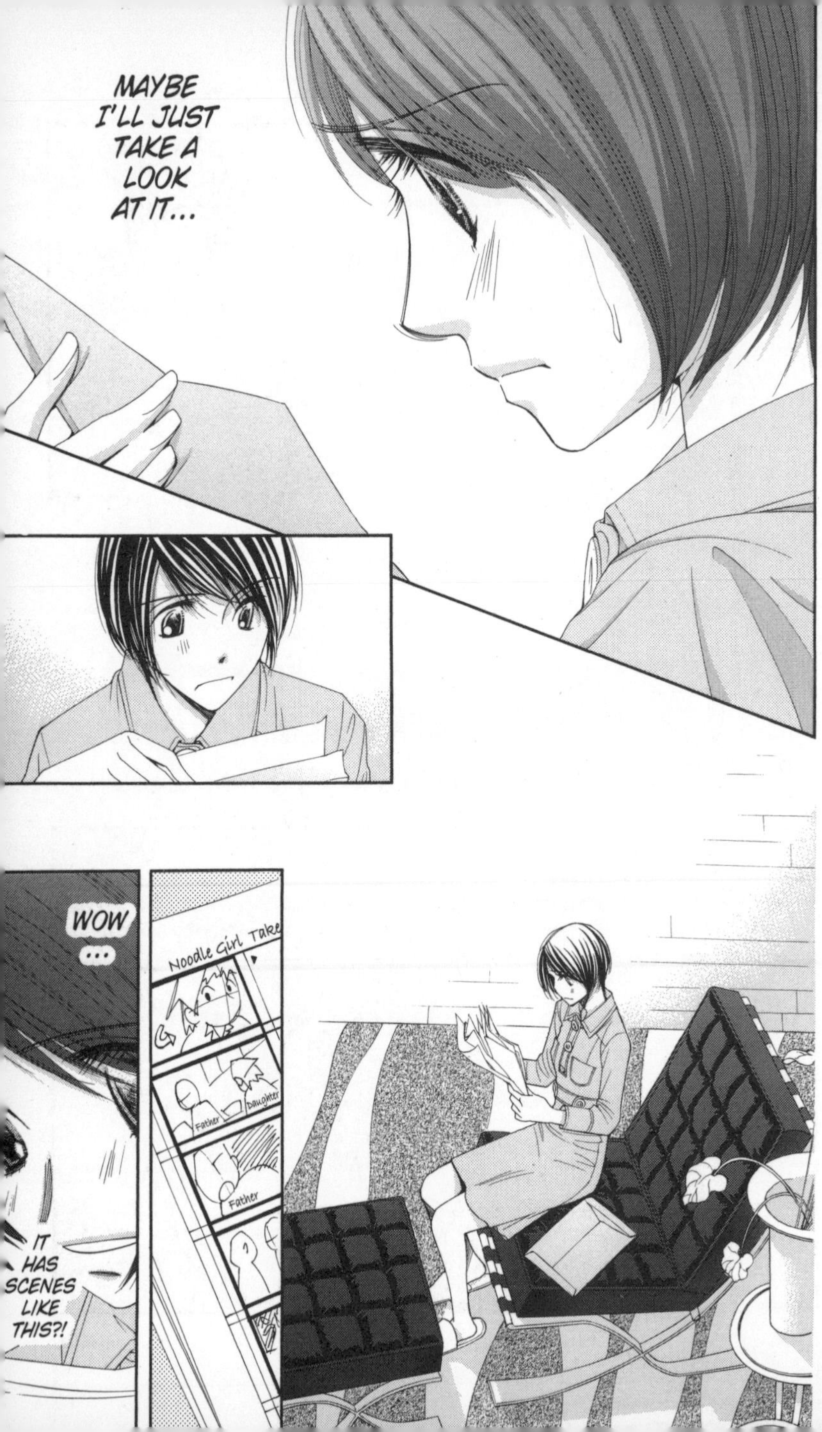
MAYBE I'LL JUST TAKE A LOOK AT IT...
Noodle Girl Take
Father
Daughter
Father
WOW ...
IT HAS SCENES LIKE THIS?!

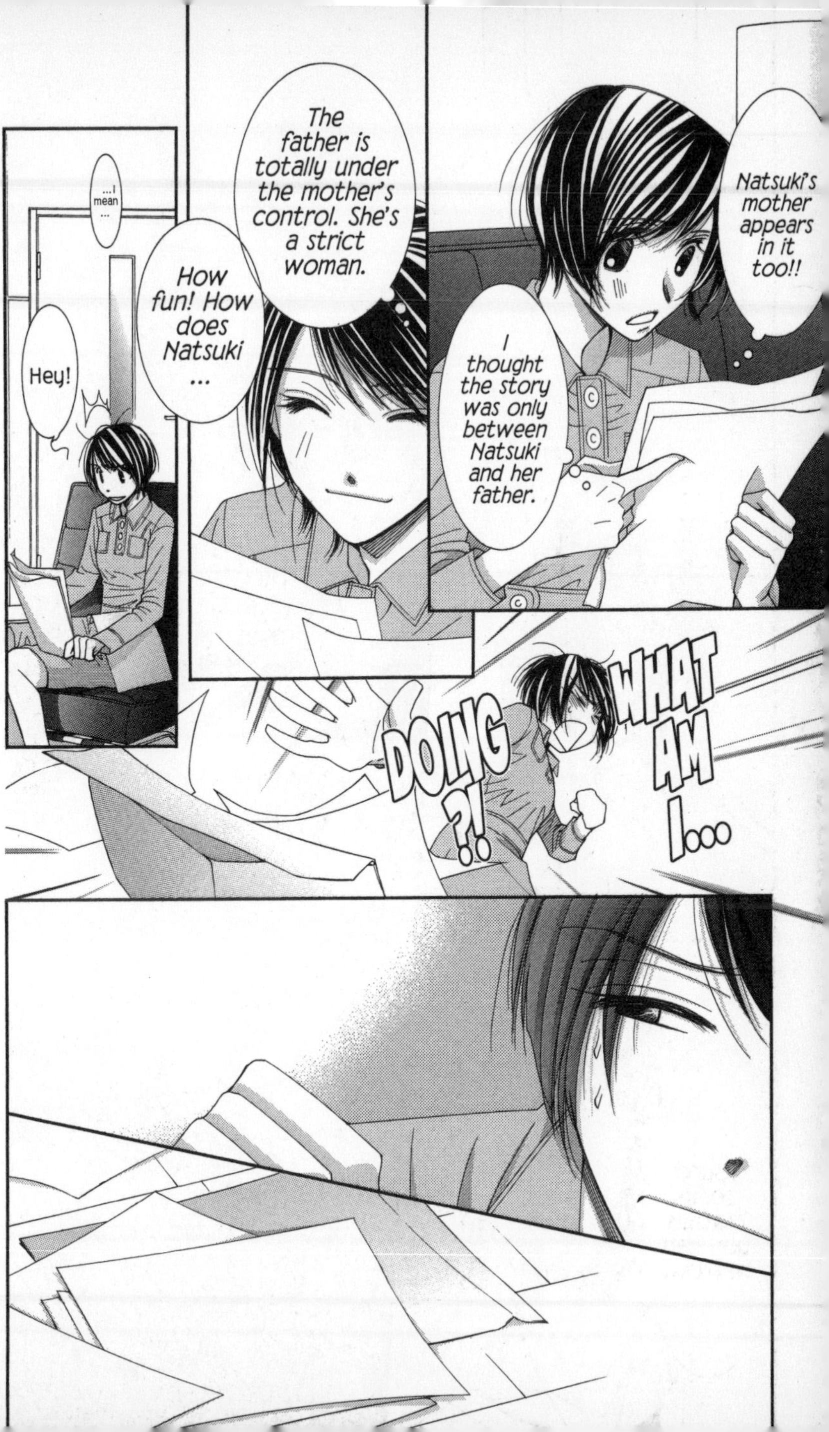
Natsuki's mother appears in it too!!
I thought the story was only between Natsuki and her father.
The father is totally under the mother's control. She's a strict woman.
How fun! How does Natsuki ...
...I mean ...
Hey!
WHAT AM I... DOING?!

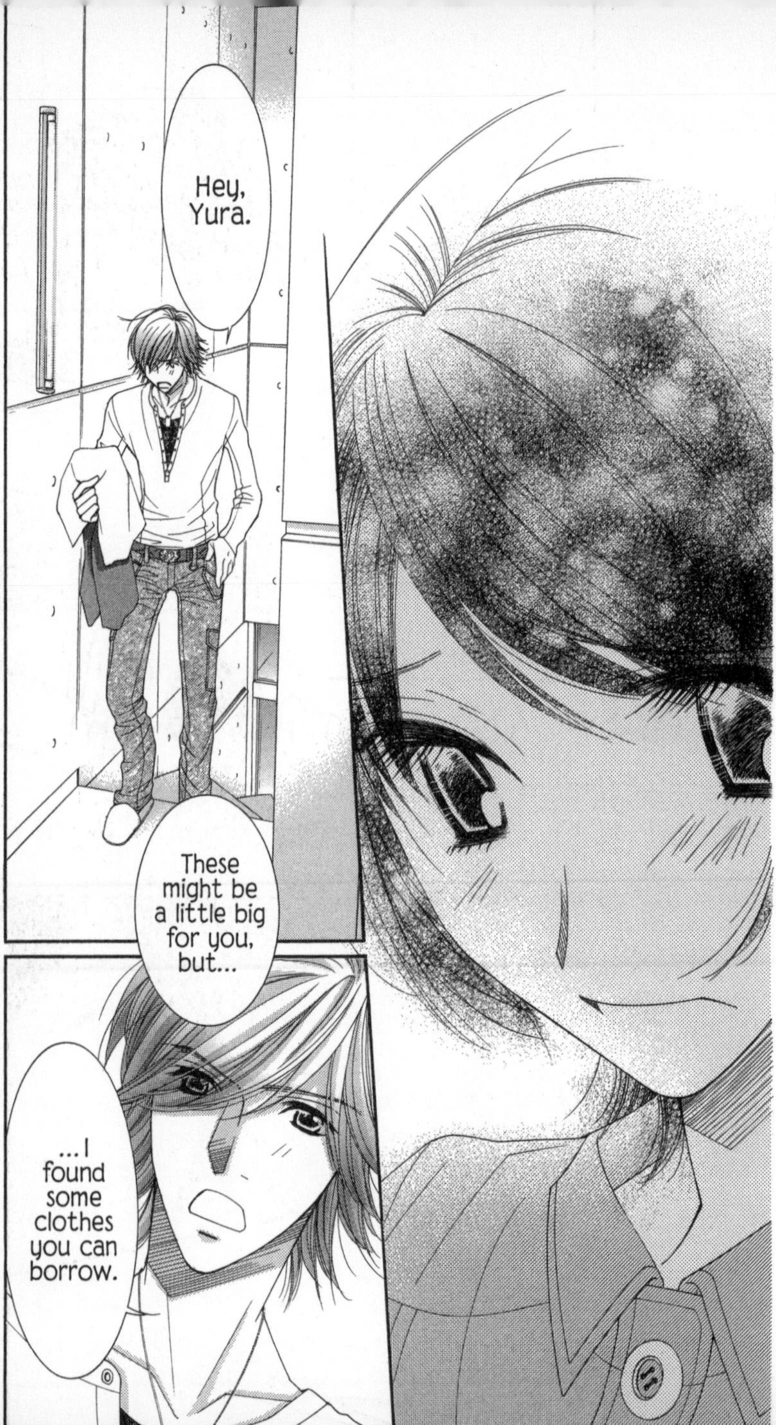
Hey, Yura.
These might be a little big for you, but...
...I found some clothes you can borrow.

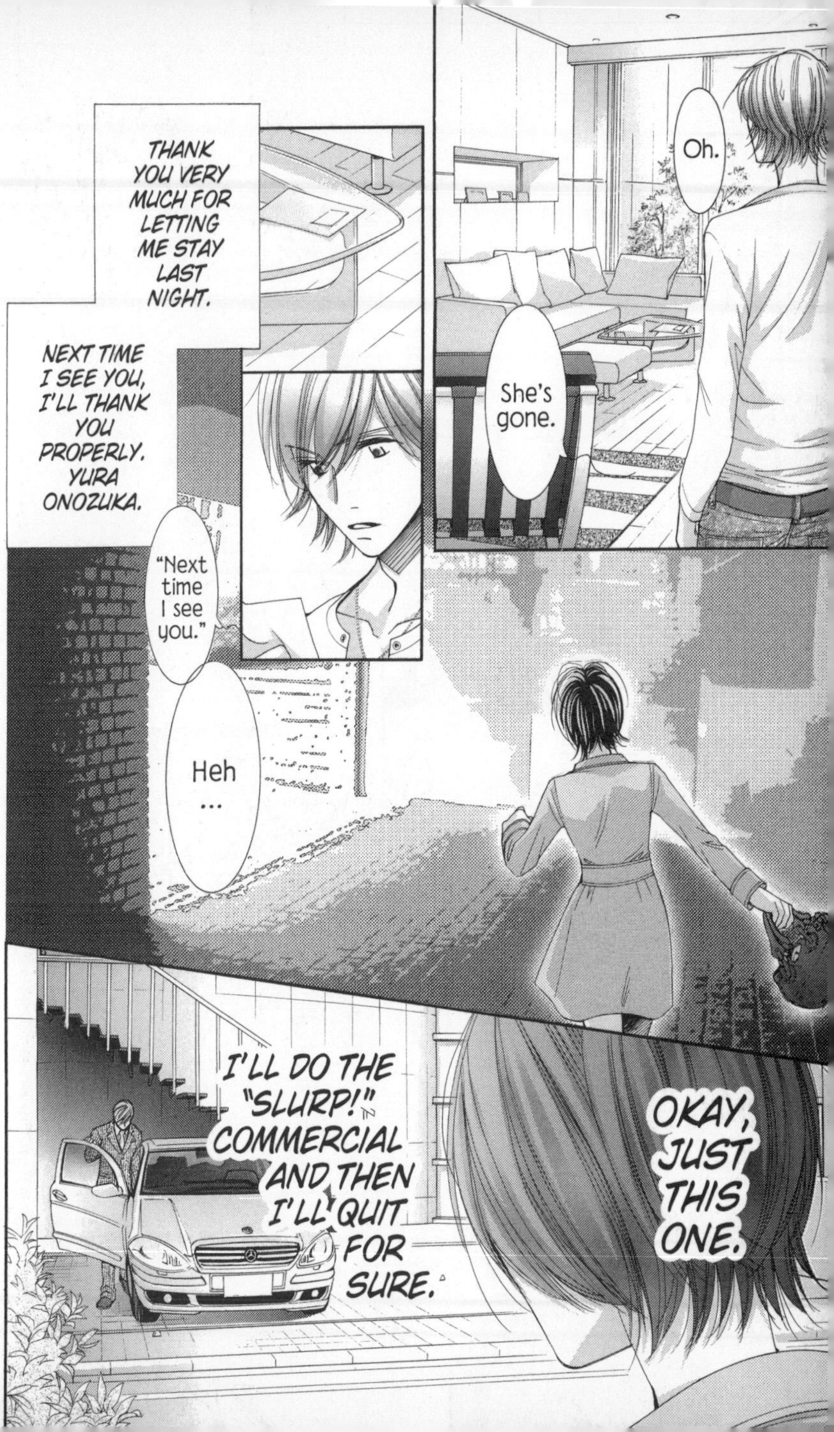
Oh.
She's gone.
THANK YOU VERY MUCH FOR LETTING ME STAY LAST NIGHT.
NEXT TIME I SEE YOU, I'LL THANK YOU PROPERLY. YURA ONOZUKA.
"Next time I see you."
Heh ...
OKAY, JUST THIS ONE.
I'LL DO THE "SLURP!"™ COMMERCIAL AND THEN I'LL QUIT FOR SURE.

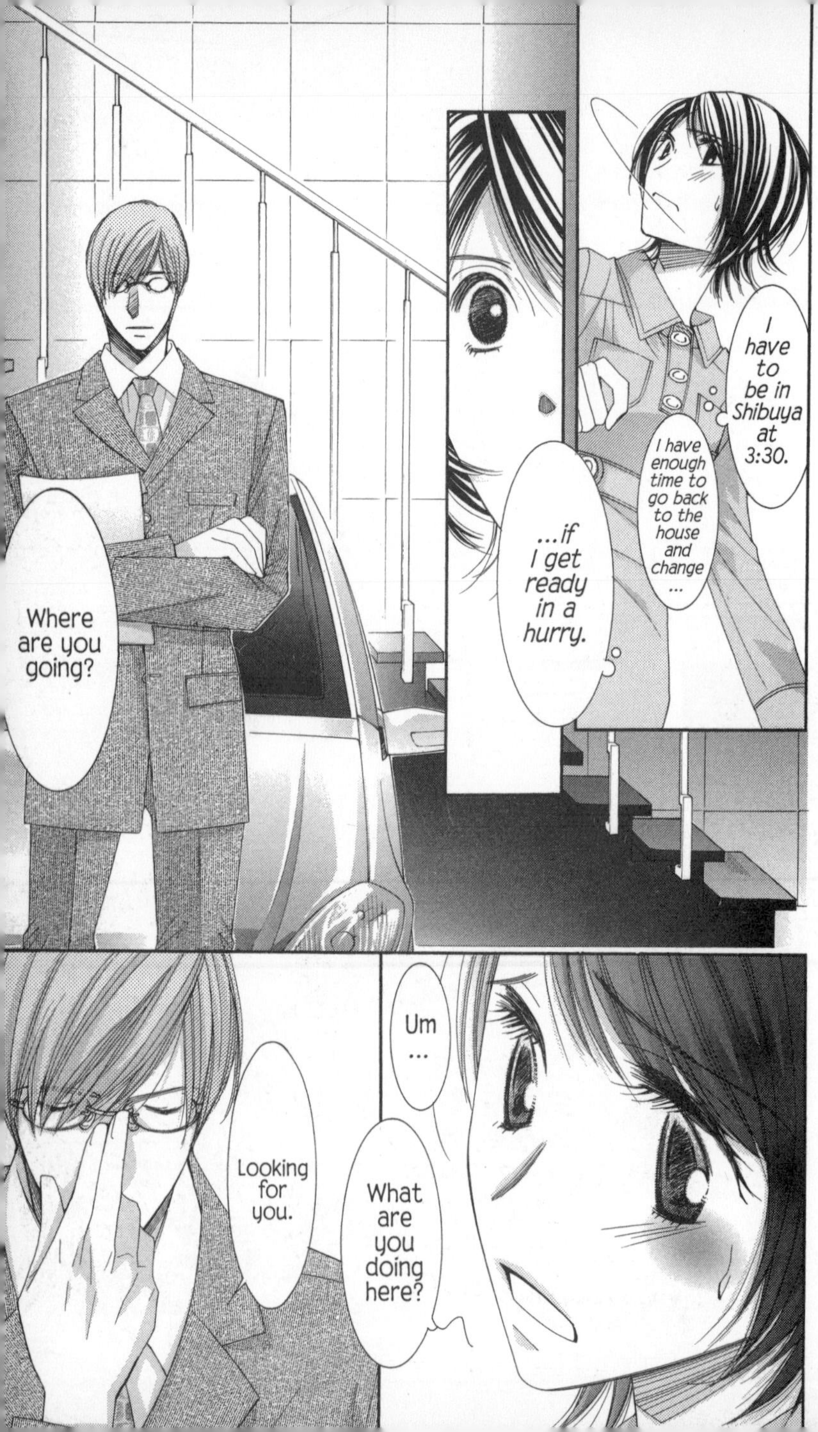
I have to be in Shibuya at 3:30.
I have enough time to go back to the house and change ...
...if I get ready in a hurry.
Where are you going?
Um ...
What are you doing here?
Looking for you.

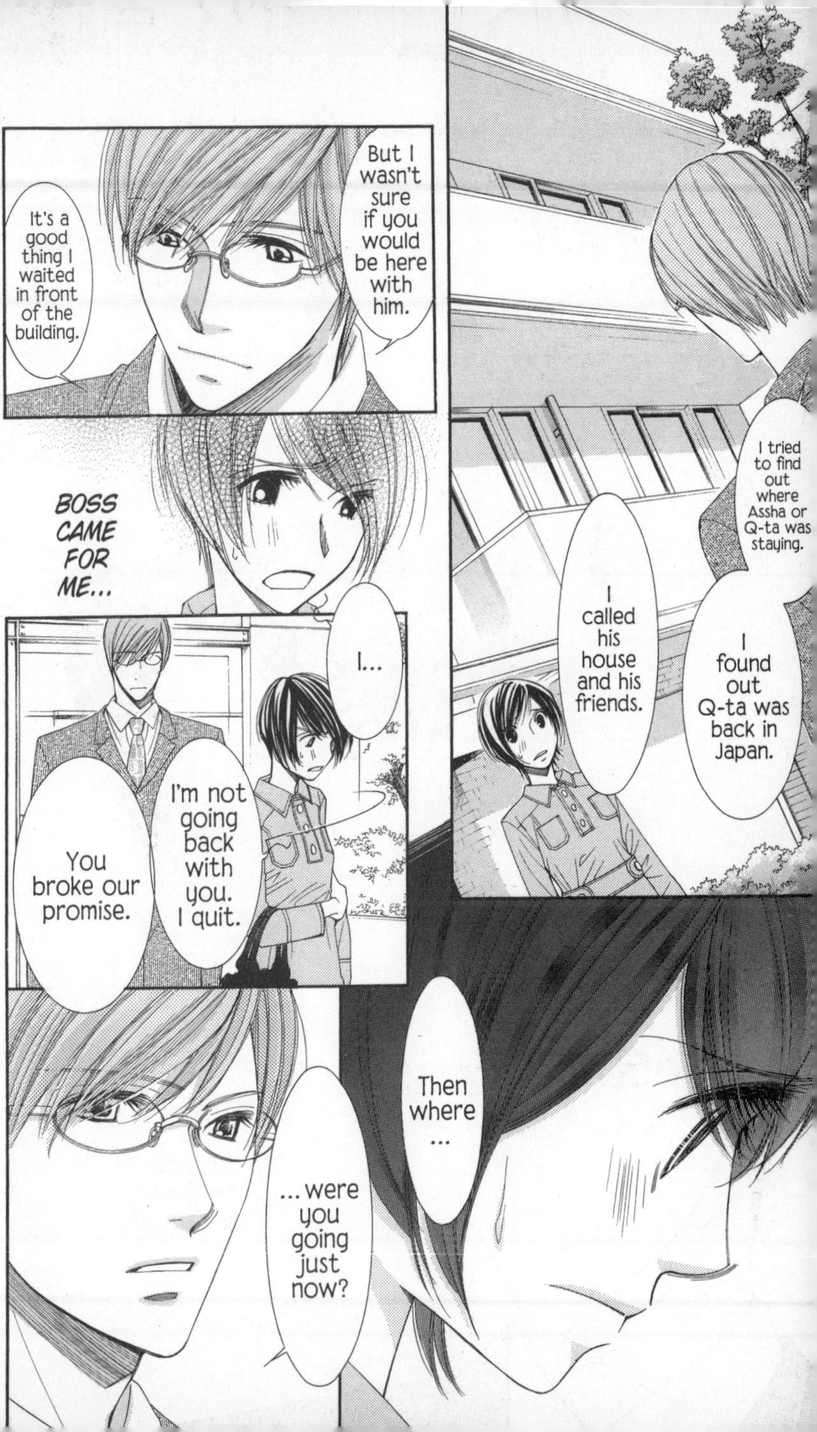
I tried to find out where Assha or Q-ta was staying.
I found out Q-ta was back in Japan.
I called his house and his friends.
But I wasn't sure if you would be here with him.
It's a good thing I waited in front of the building.
BOSS CAME FOR ME...
I...
I'm not going back with you. I quit.
You broke our promise.
Then where...
...were you going just now?

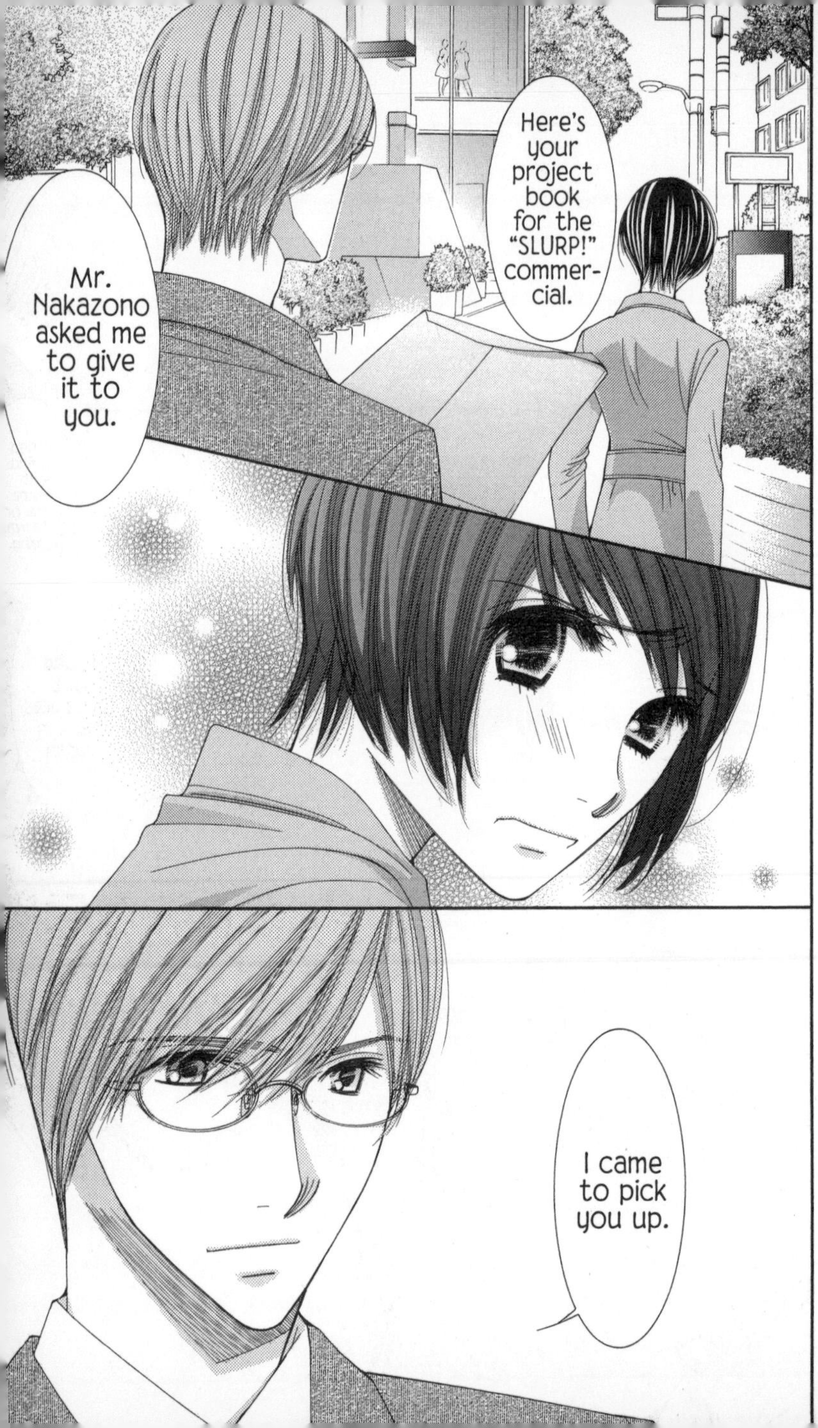
Here's your project book for the "SLURP!" commercial.
Mr. Nakazono asked me to give it to you.
I came to pick you up.

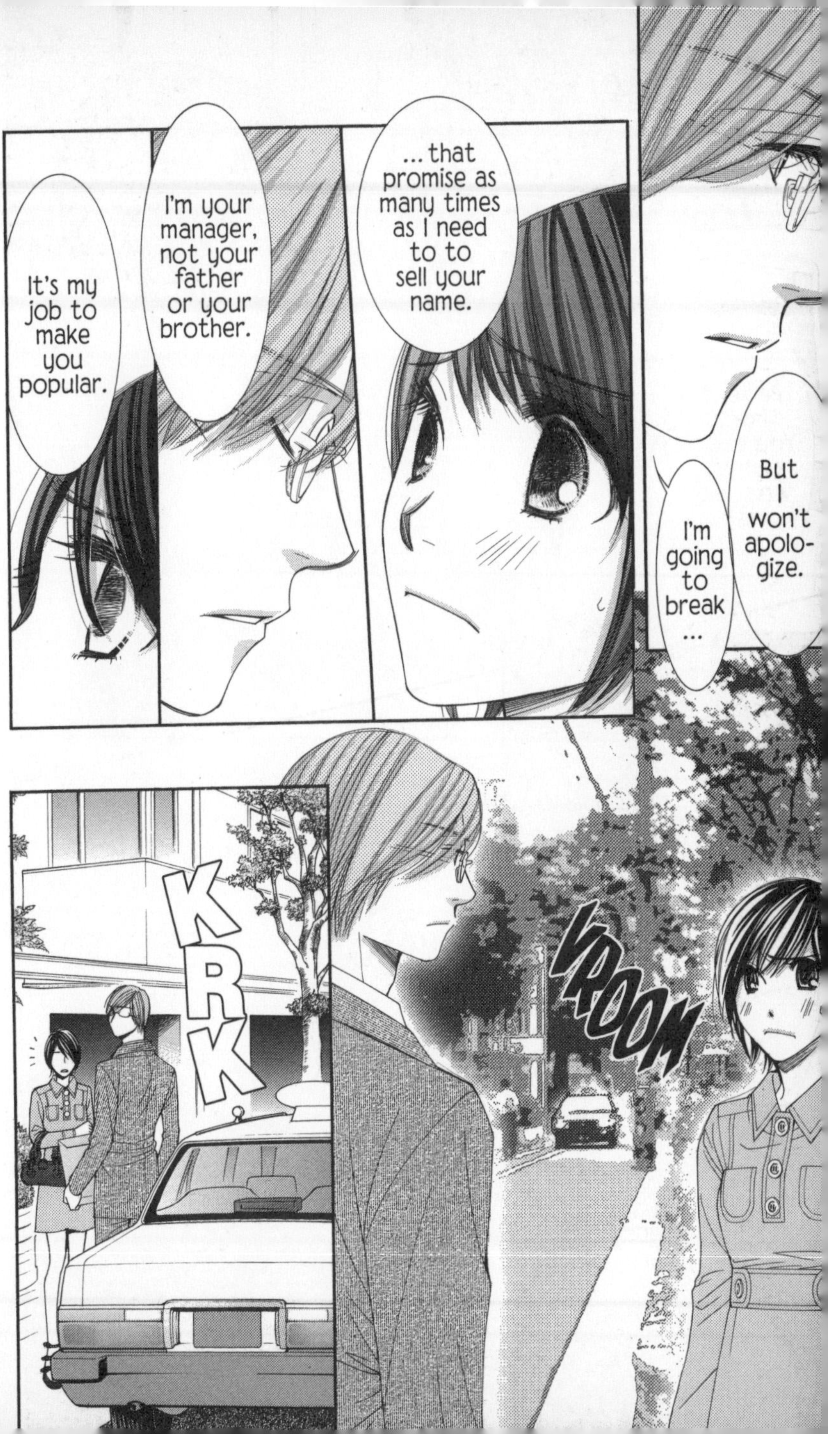
But I won't apologize.
I'm going to break...
...that promise as many times as I need to to sell your name.
I'm your manager, not your father or your brother.
It's my job to make you popular.
VROOM
KRK

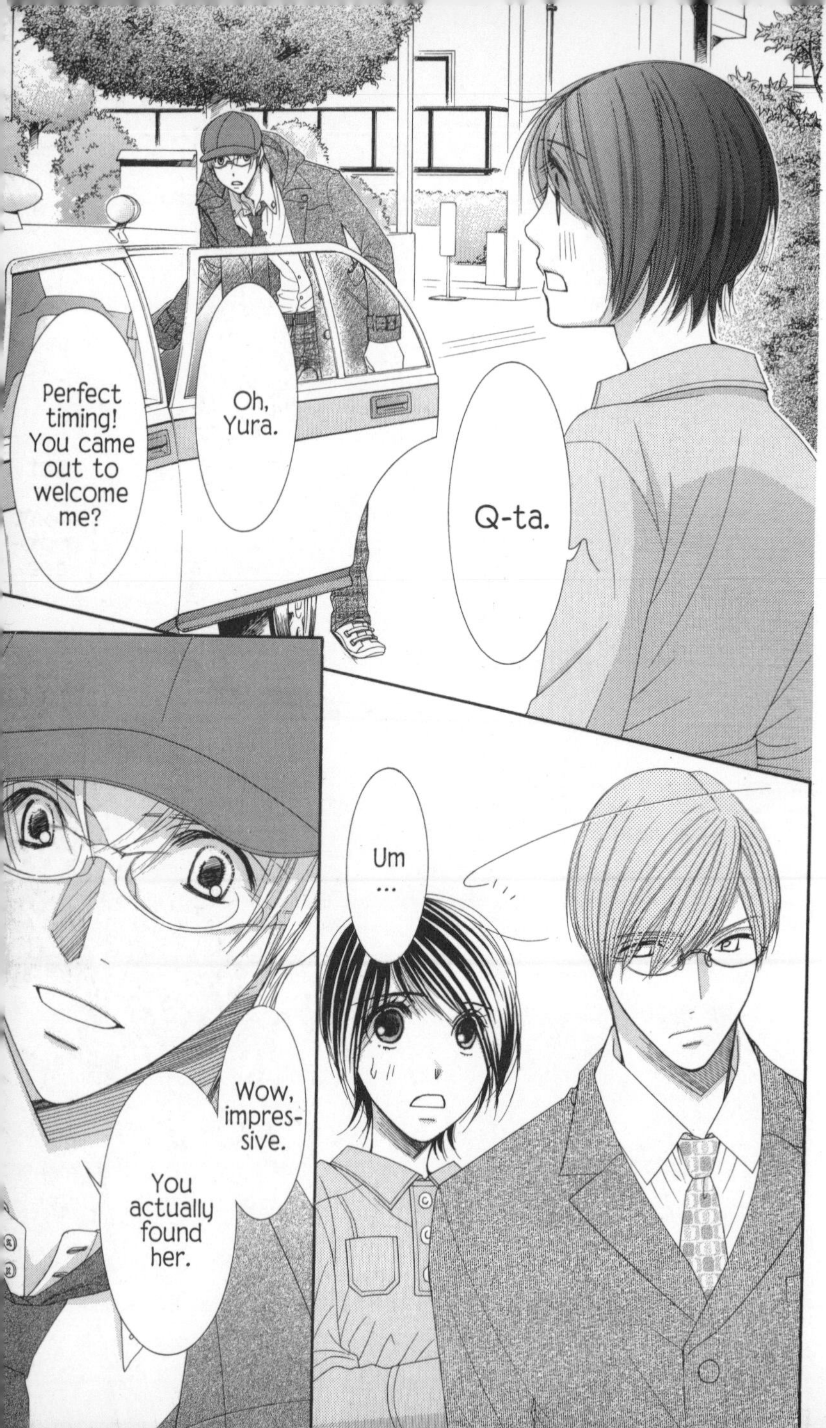
Q-ta.
Oh, Yura.
Perfect timing! You came out to welcome me?
Um ...
Wow, impressive.
You actually found her.

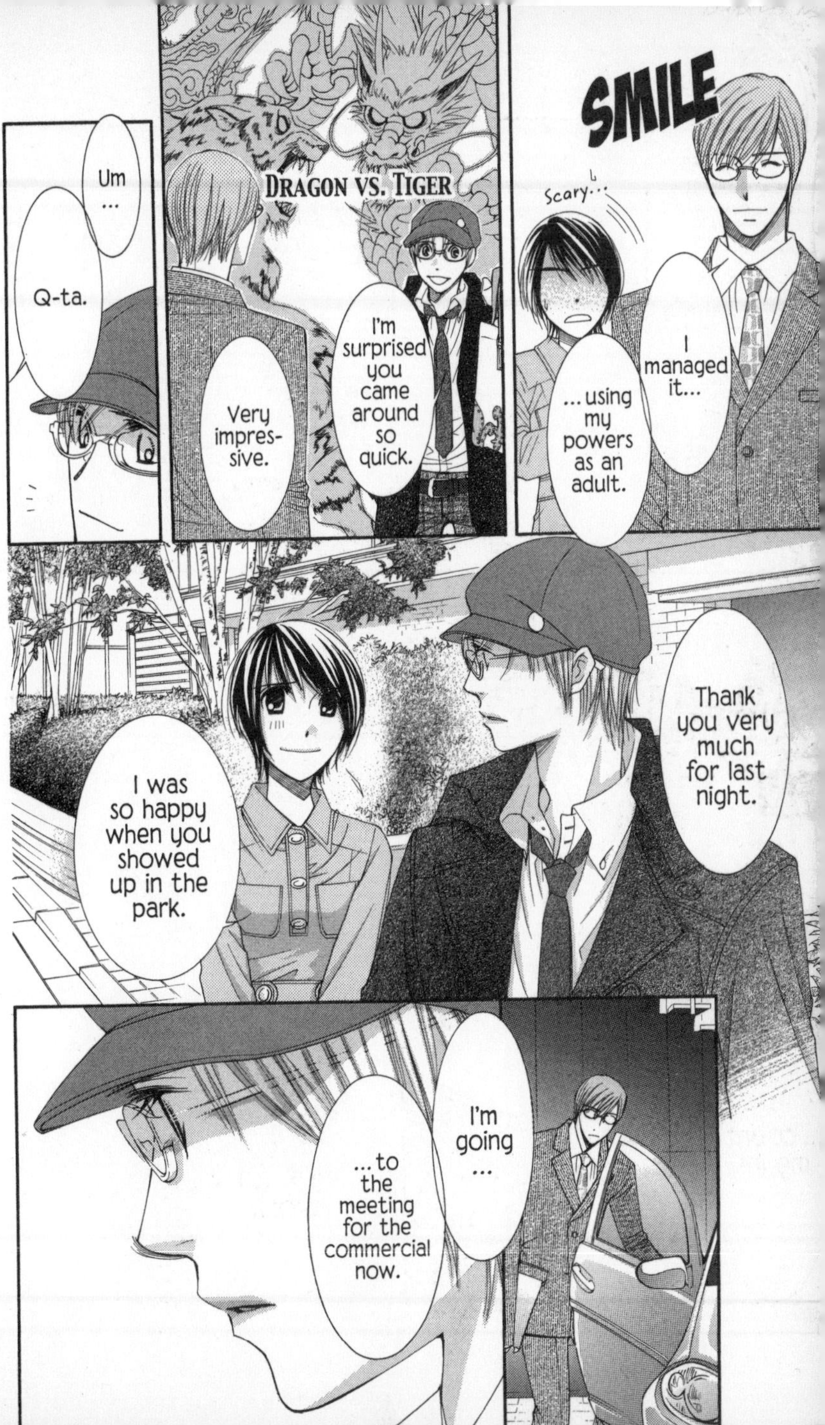
SMILE
Scary...
I managed it...
...using my powers as an adult.
DRAGON VS. TIGER
I'm surprised you came around so quick.
Very impressive.
Um...
Q-ta.
Thank you very much for last night.
I was so happy when you showed up in the park.
I'm going...
...to the meeting for the commercial now.

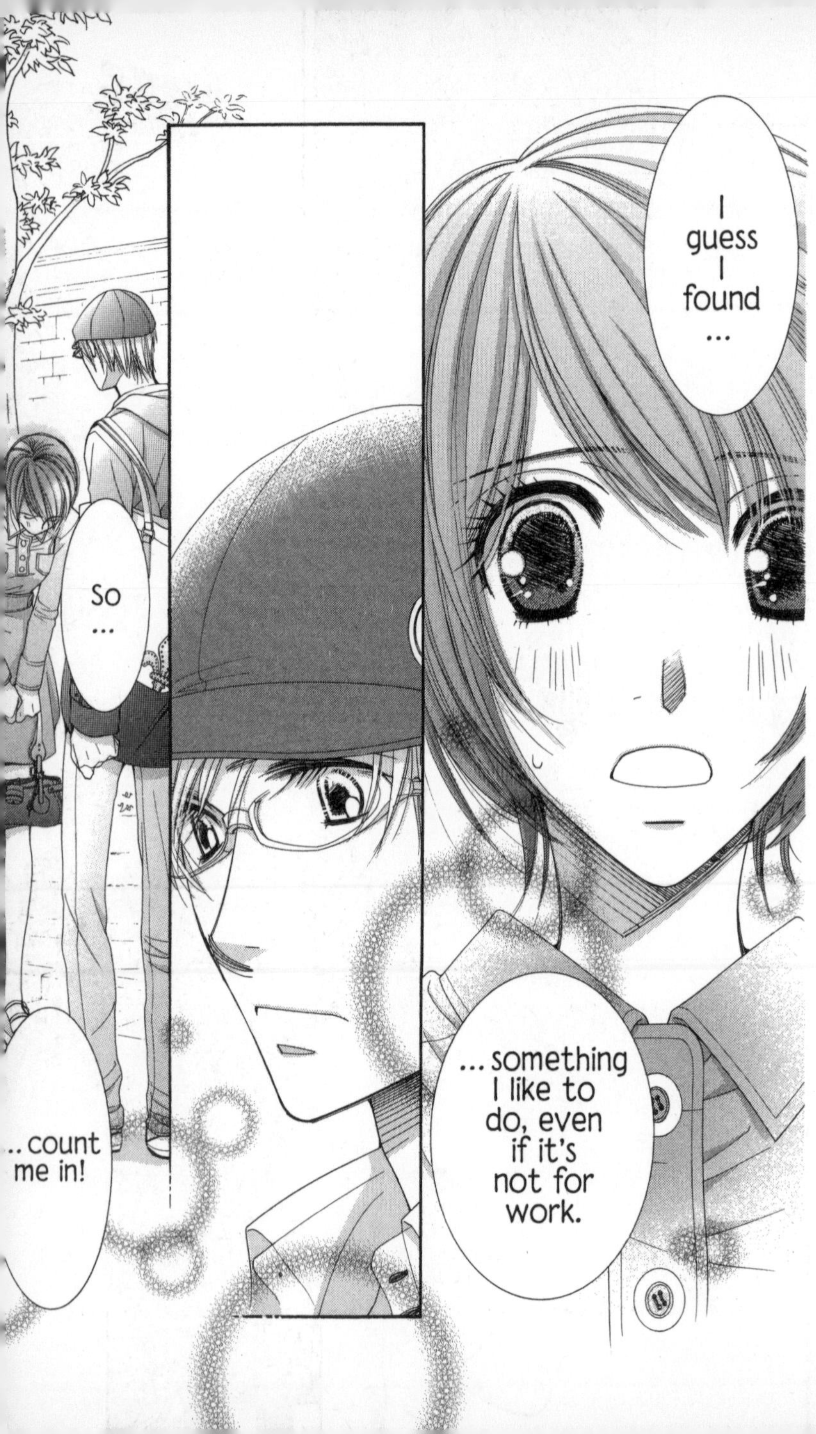
I guess I found...
...something I like to do, even if it's not for work.
So...
...count me in!

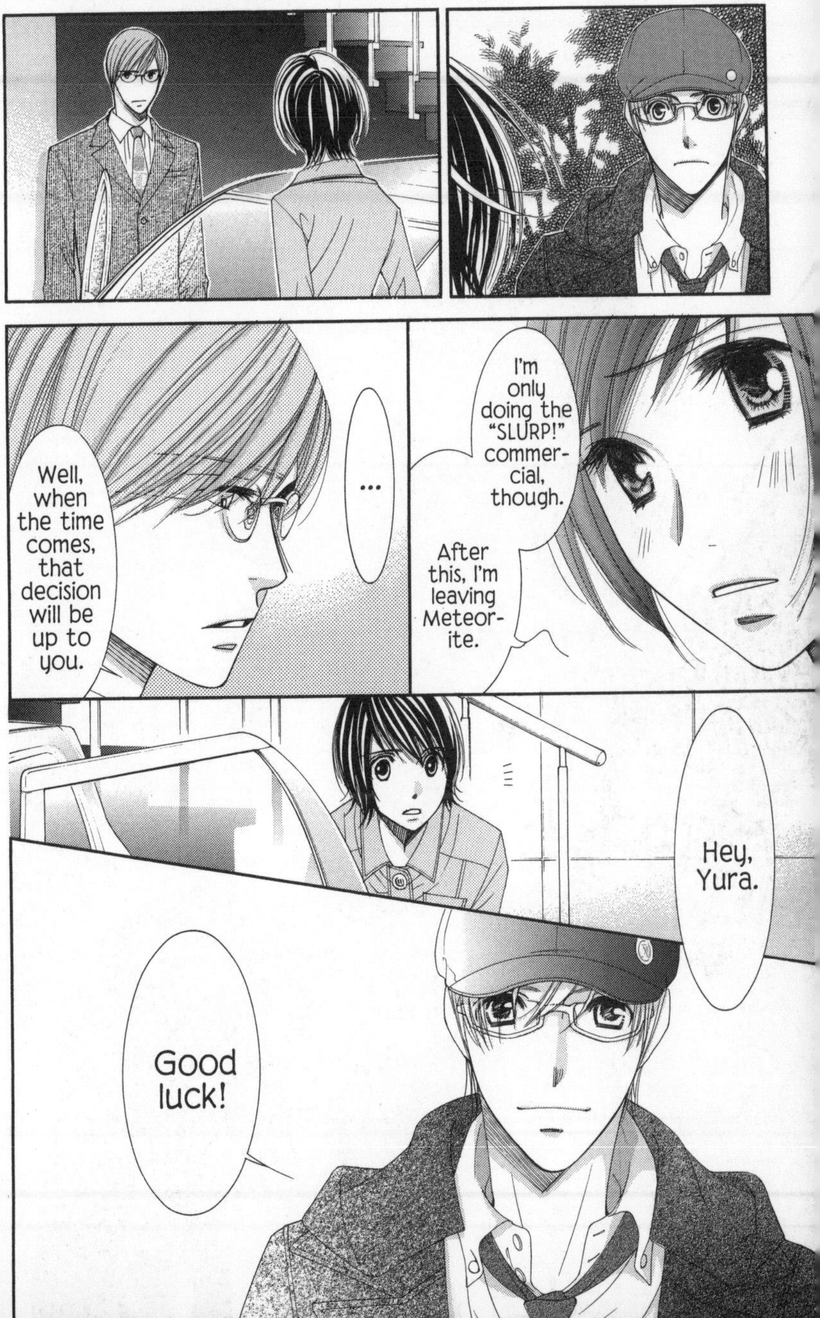
I'm only doing the "SLURP!" commercial, though.
After this, I'm leaving Meteor-ite.
...
Well, when the time comes, that decision will be up to you.
Hey, Yura.
Good luck!

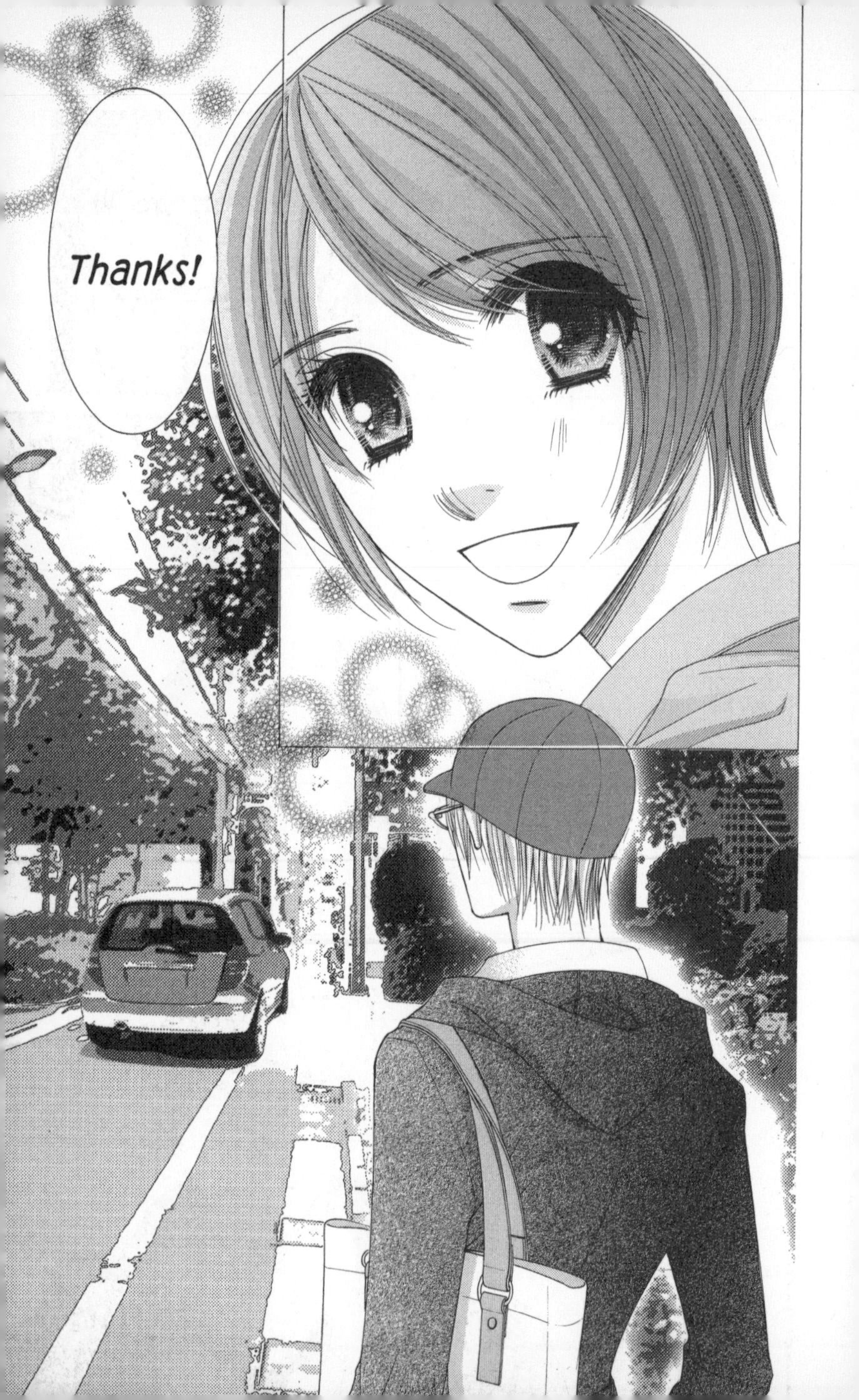
Thanks!

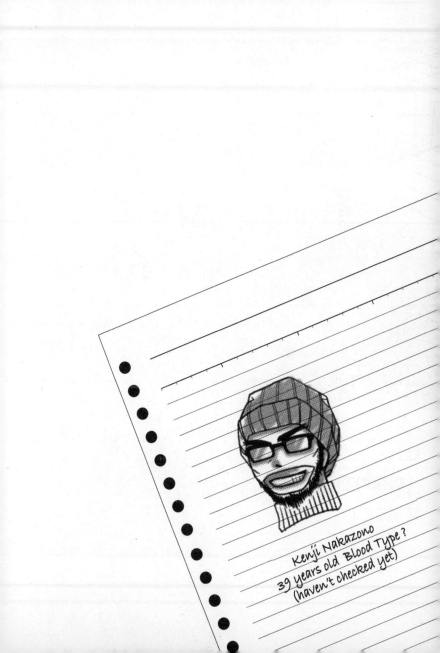

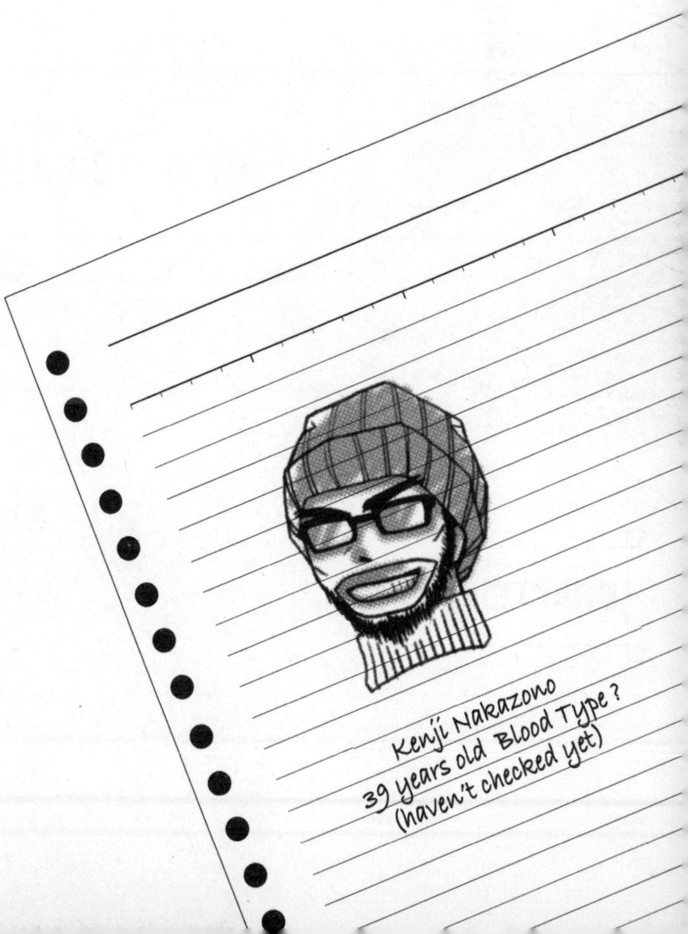
Kenji Nakazono
39 years old Blood Type ?
(haven't checked yet)

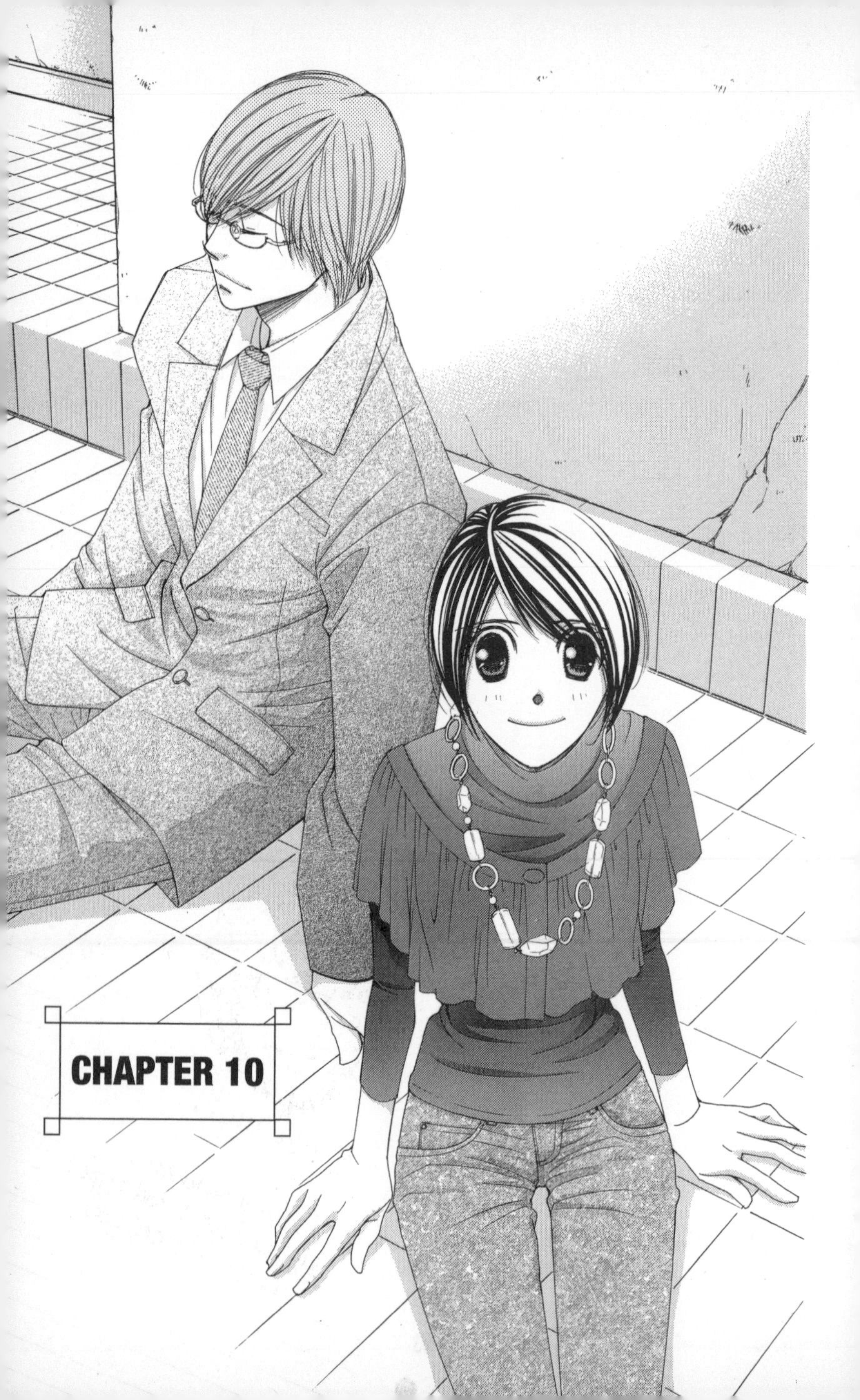
CHAPTER 10

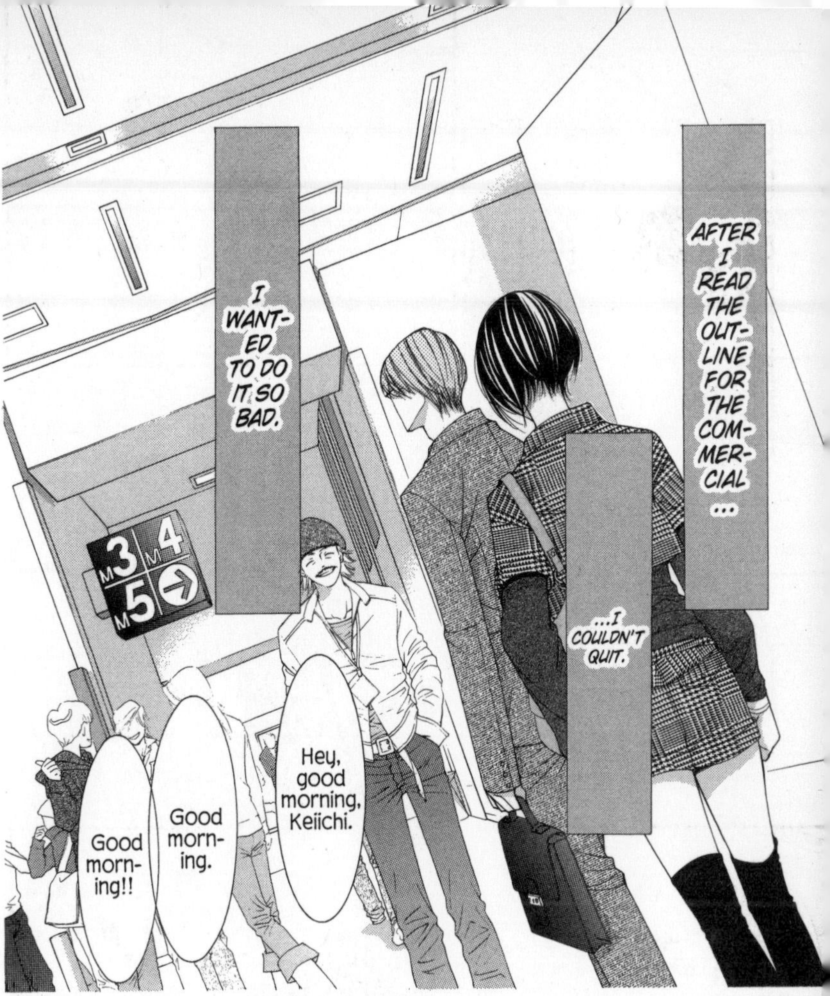
AFTER I READ THE OUTLINE FOR THE COMMERCIAL...
...I COULDN'T QUIT.
I WANTED TO DO IT SO BAD.
Hey, good morning, Keiichi.
Good morning.
Good morning!!

Honey Hunt

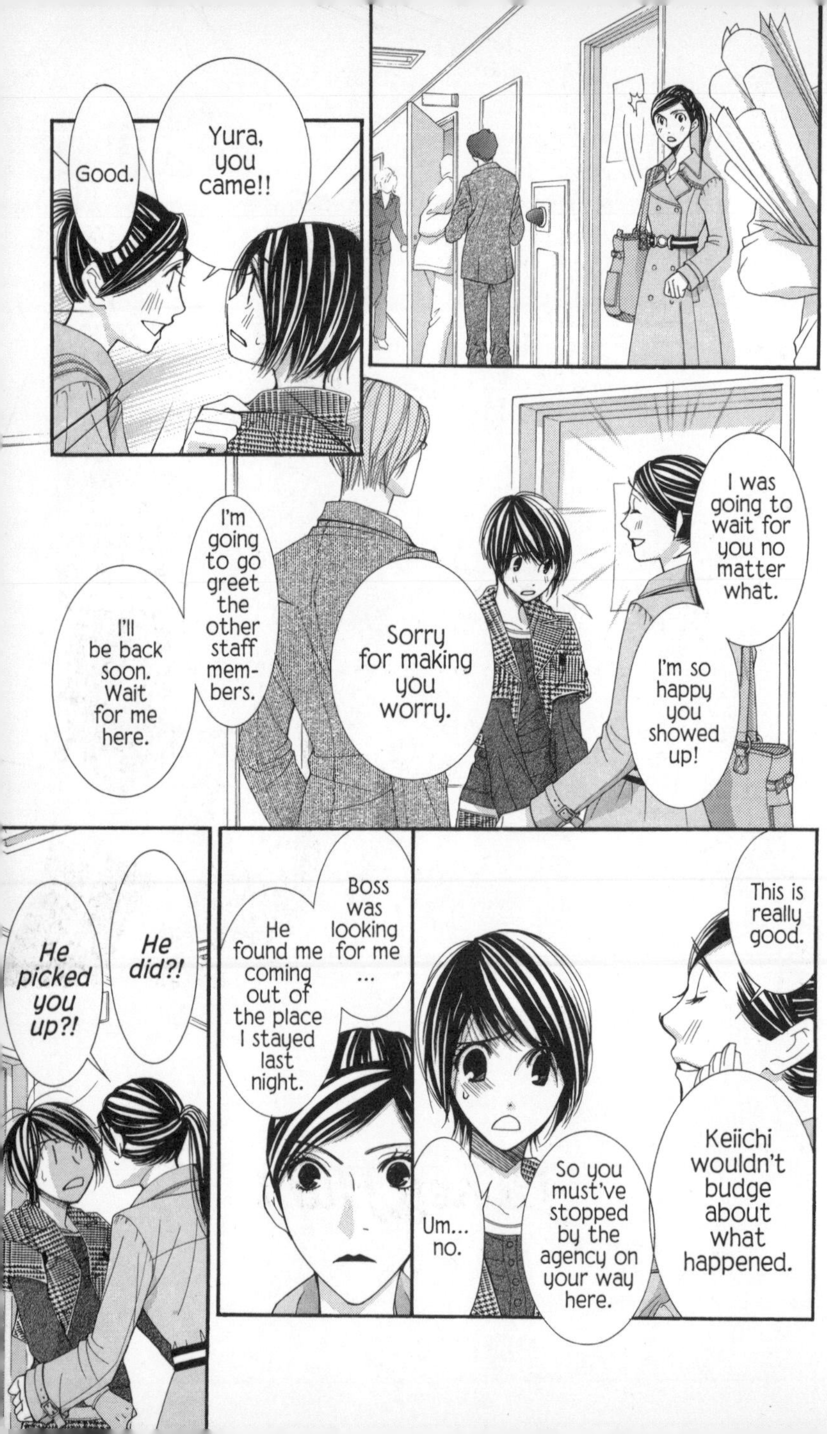
Yura, you came!!
Good.
I was going to wait for you no matter what.
I'm so happy you showed up!
Sorry for making you worry.
I'm going to go greet the other staff members.
I'll be back soon. Wait for me here.
This is really good.
Keiichi wouldn't budge about what happened.
So you must've stopped by the agency on your way here.
Um... no.
Boss was looking for me...
He found me coming out of the place I stayed last night.
He did?!
He picked you up?!

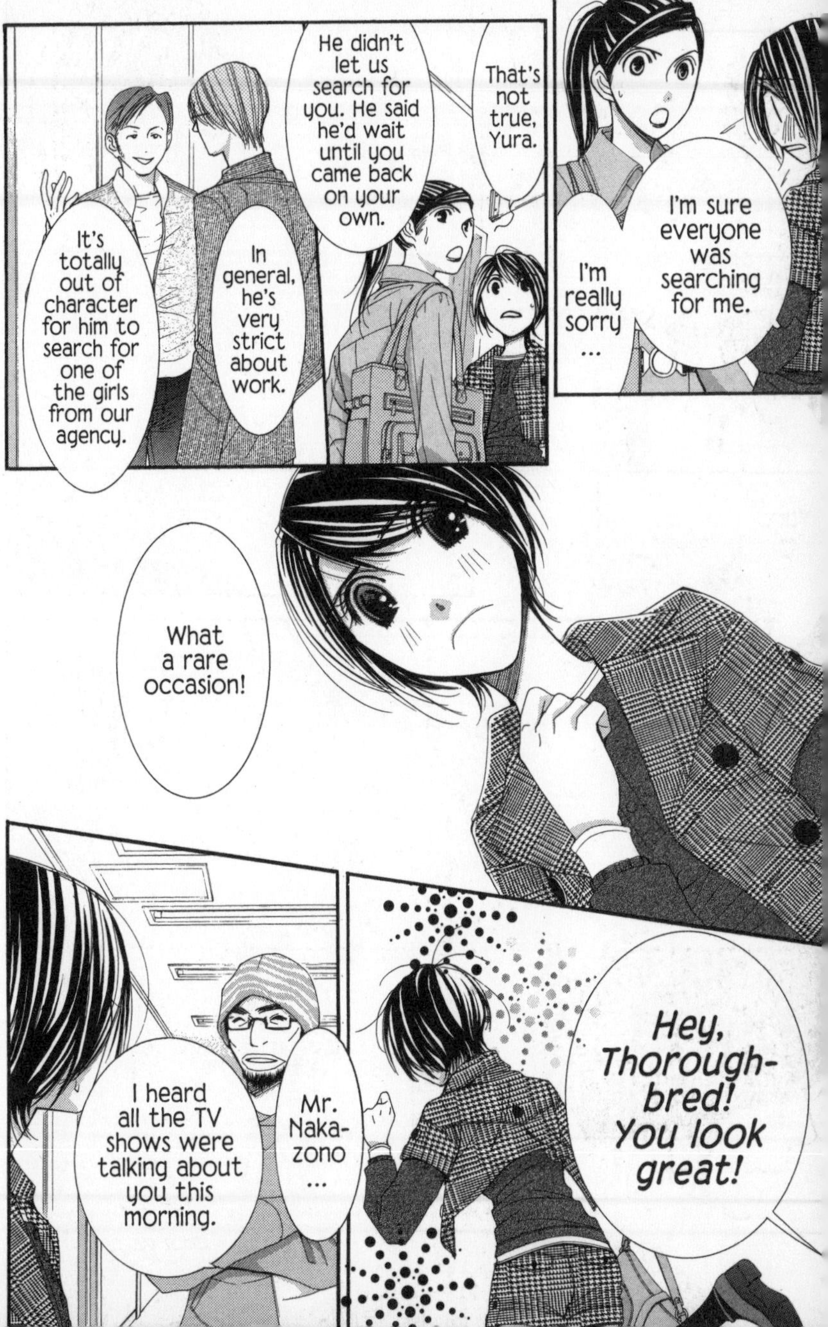
I'm sure everyone was searching for me.
I'm really sorry ...
That's not true, Yura.
He didn't let us search for you. He said he'd wait until you came back on your own.
In general, he's very strict about work.
It's totally out of character for him to search for one of the girls from our agency.
What a rare occasion!
Hey, Thoroughbred! You look great!
Mr. Nakazono ...
I heard all the TV shows were talking about you this morning.

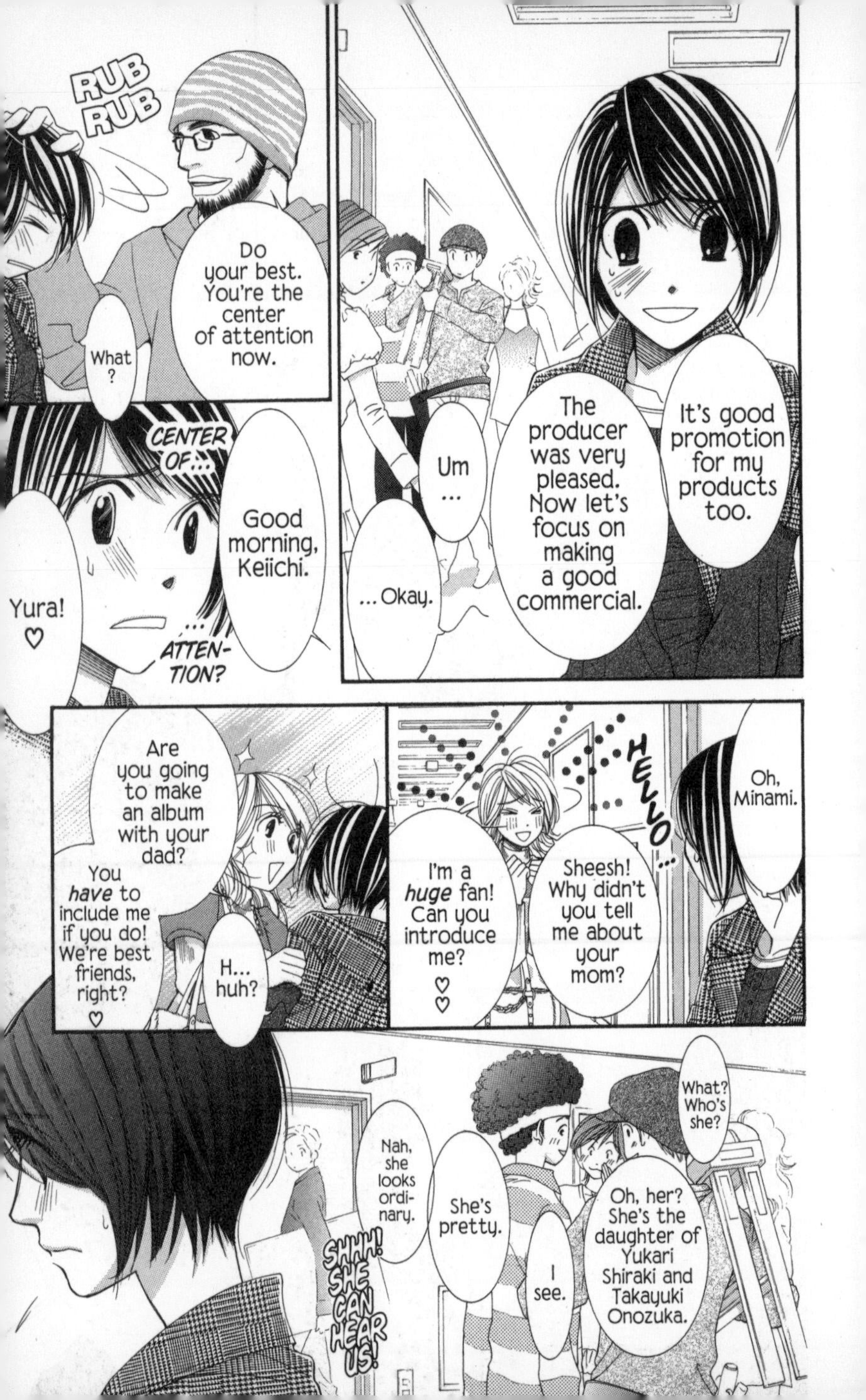
It's good promotion for my products too.
The producer was very pleased. Now let's focus on making a good commercial.
Um ...
... Okay.
RUB RUB
Do your best. You're the center of attention now.
What?
Good morning, Keiichi.
CENTER OF...
... ATTENTION?
Yura! ♡
Oh, Minami.
HELLO...
Sheesh! Why didn't you tell me about your mom?
I'm a *huge* fan! Can you introduce me? ♡♡
Are you going to make an album with your dad?
You *have* to include me if you do! We're best friends, right? ♡
H... huh?
What? Who's she?
Oh, her? She's the daughter of Yukari Shiraki and Takayuki Onozuka.
I see.
She's pretty.
Nah, she looks ordinary.
SHHH! SHE CAN HEAR US!

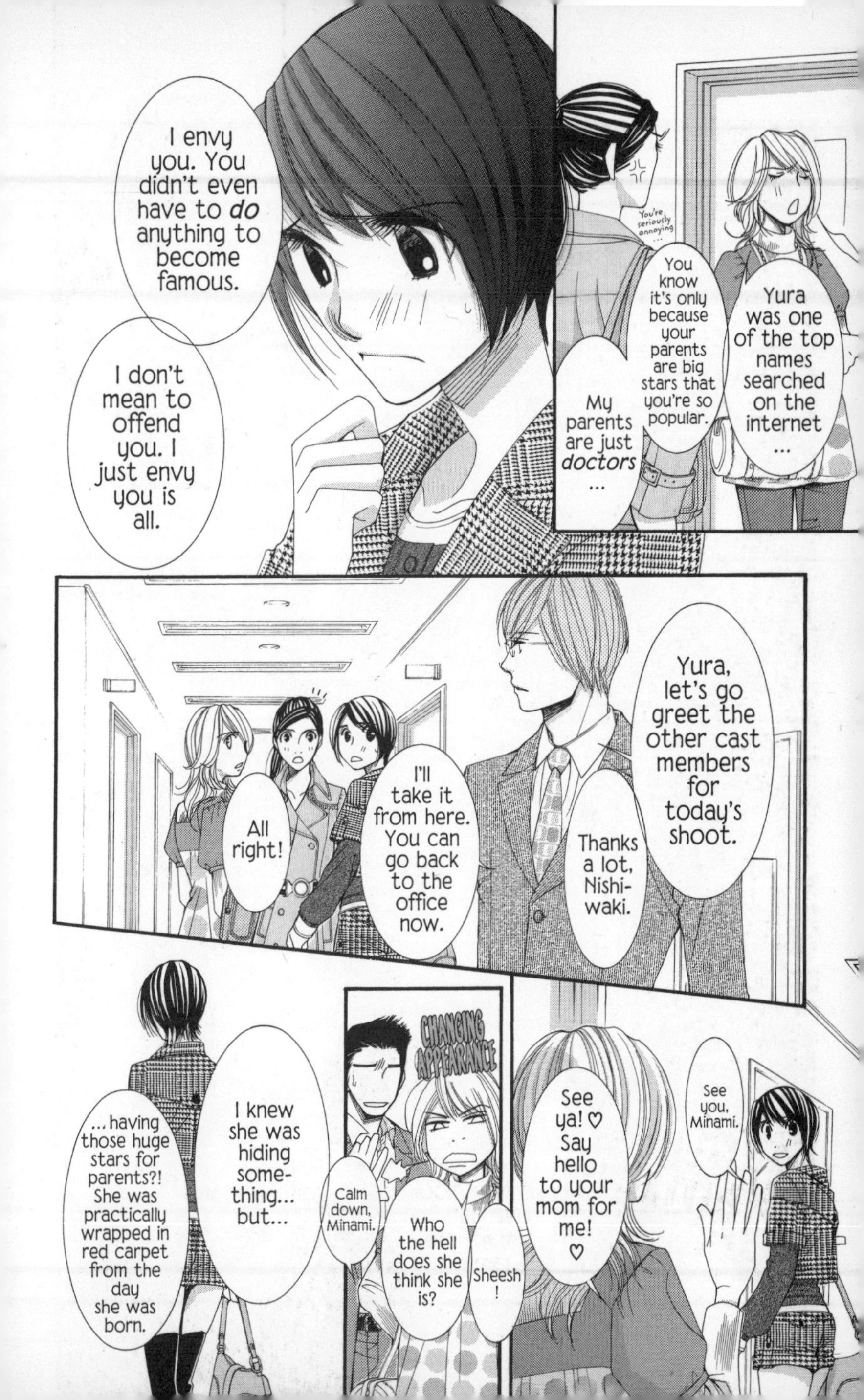

Yura was one of the top names searched on the internet...
You know it's only because your parents are big stars that you're so popular.
You're seriously annoying...
My parents are just *doctors*...
I envy you. You didn't even have to *do* anything to become famous.
I don't mean to offend you. I just envy you is all.
Yura, let's go greet the other cast members for today's shoot.
Thanks a lot, Nishi-waki.
I'll take it from here. You can go back to the office now.
All right!
See you, Minami.
See ya! ♡ Say hello to your mom for me! ♡
Sheesh!
CHANGING APPEARANCE
Who the hell does she think she is?
Calm down, Minami.
I knew she was hiding some-thing... but...
...having those huge stars for parents?! She was practically wrapped in red carpet from the day she was born.

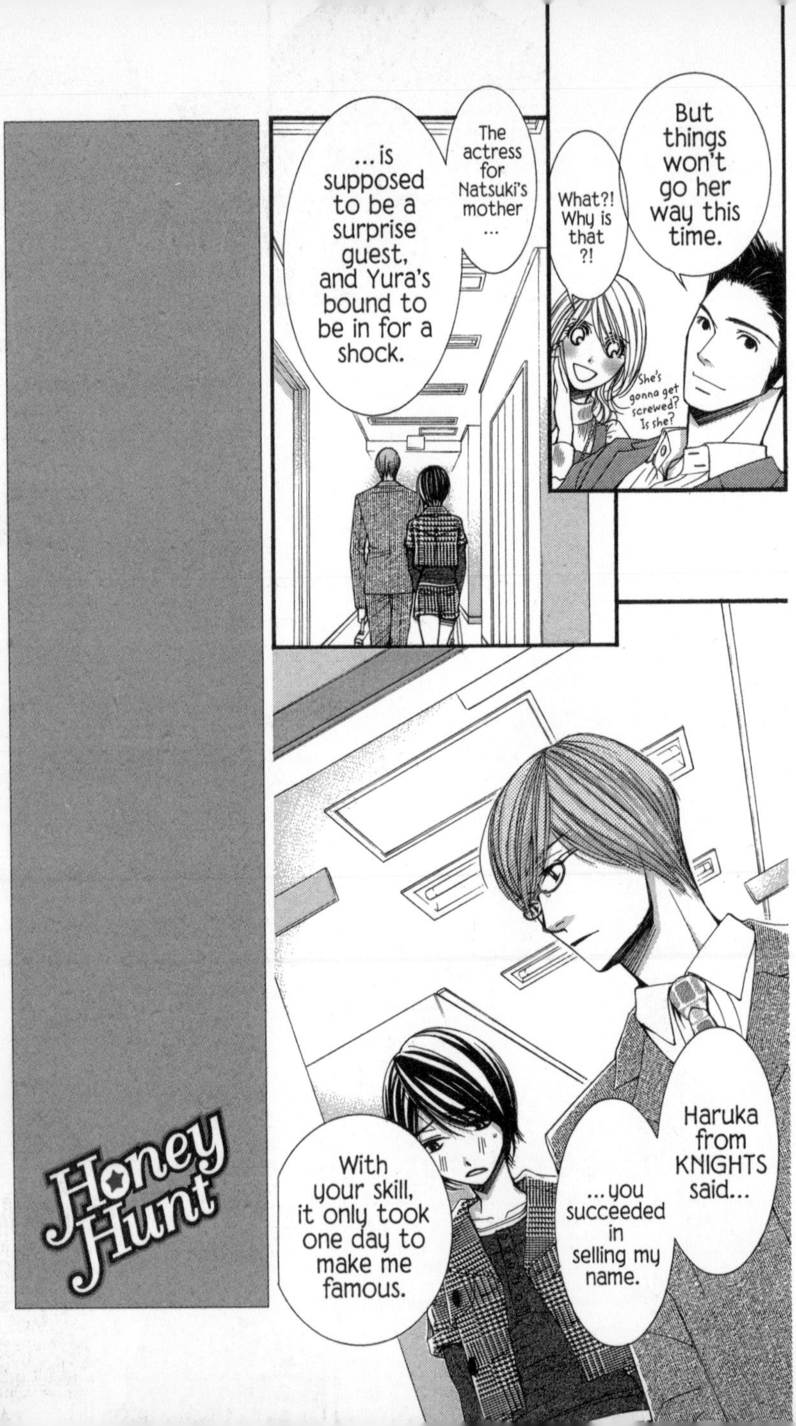
But things won't go her way this time.
What?! Why is that ?!
She's gonna get screwed? Is she?
The actress for Natsuki's mother ...
... is supposed to be a surprise guest, and Yura's bound to be in for a shock.
Haruka from KNIGHTS said...
...you succeeded in selling my name.
With your skill, it only took one day to make me famous.

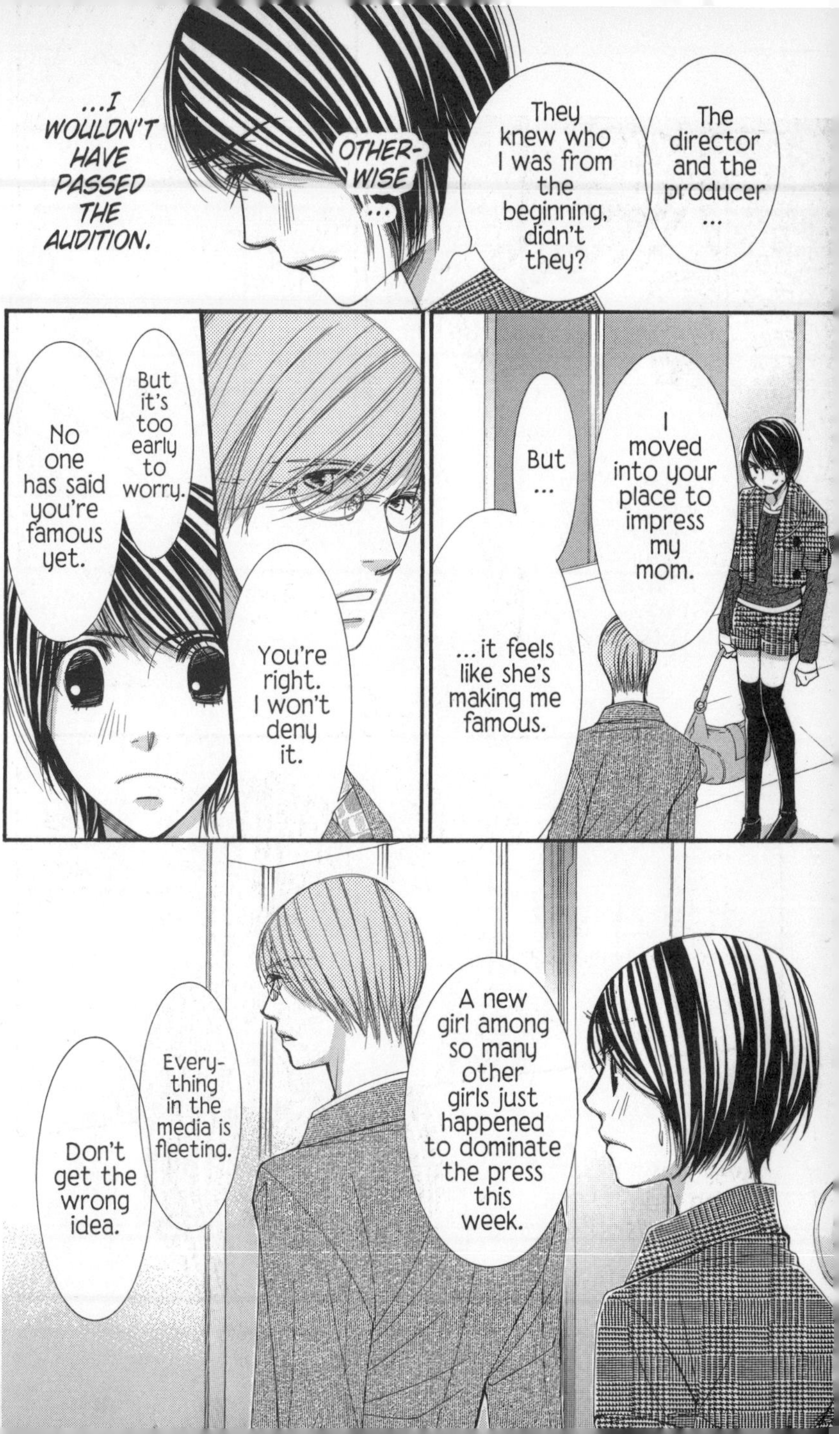
The director and the producer ...
They knew who I was from the beginning, didn't they?
OTHER-WISE ...
...I WOULDN'T HAVE PASSED THE AUDITION.
I moved into your place to impress my mom.
But ...
...it feels like she's making me famous.
You're right. I won't deny it.
But it's too early to worry.
No one has said you're famous yet.
A new girl among so many other girls just happened to dominate the press this week.
Every-thing in the media is fleeting.
Don't get the wrong idea.

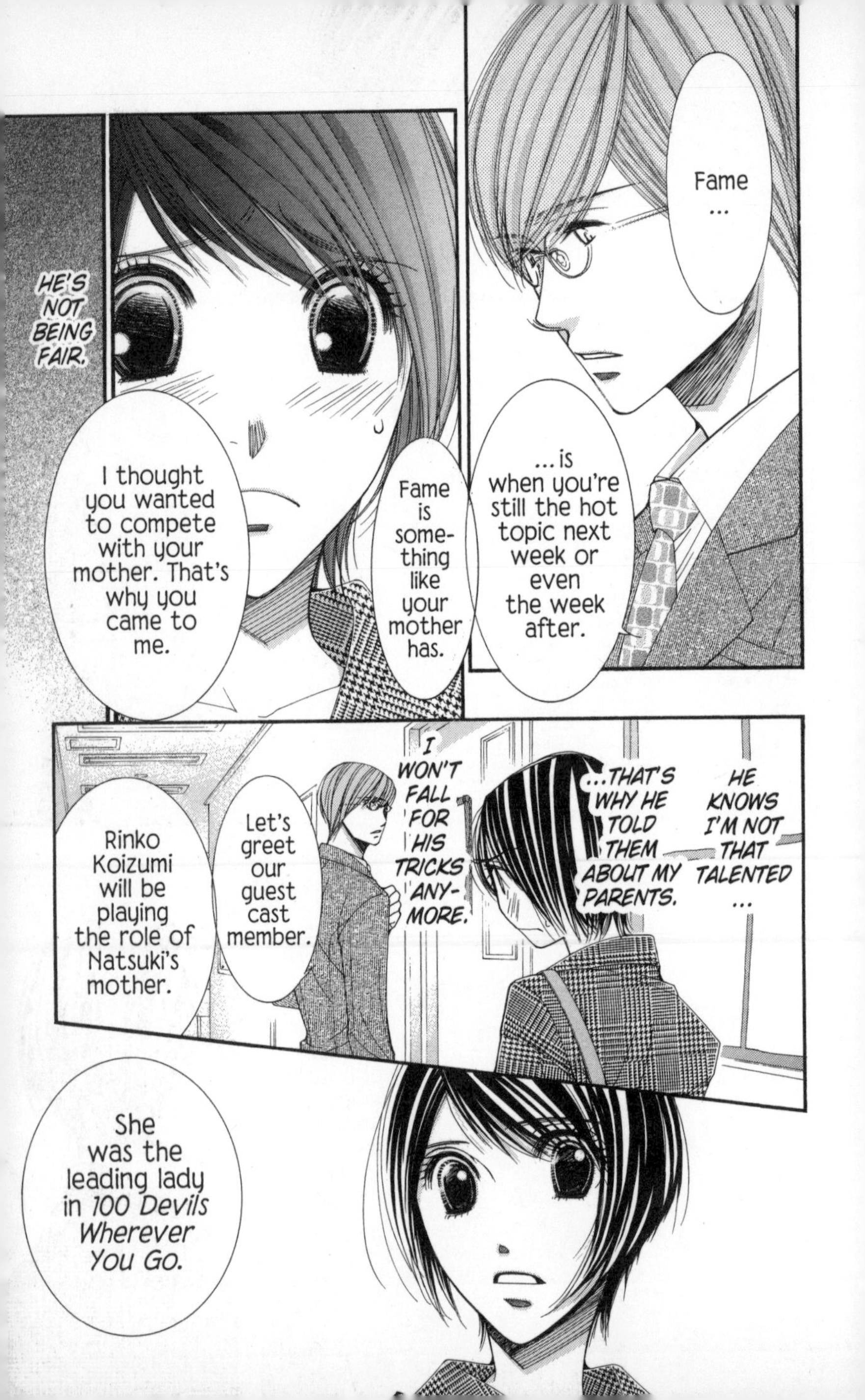
Fame ...
... is when you're still the hot topic next week or even the week after.
Fame is some-thing like your mother has.
I thought you wanted to compete with your mother. That's why you came to me.
HE'S NOT BEING FAIR.
HE KNOWS I'M NOT THAT TALENTED ...
...THAT'S WHY HE TOLD THEM ABOUT MY PARENTS.
I WON'T FALL FOR HIS TRICKS ANY-MORE.
Let's greet our guest cast member.
Rinko Koizumi will be playing the role of Natsuki's mother.
She was the leading lady in *100 Devils Wherever You Go.*

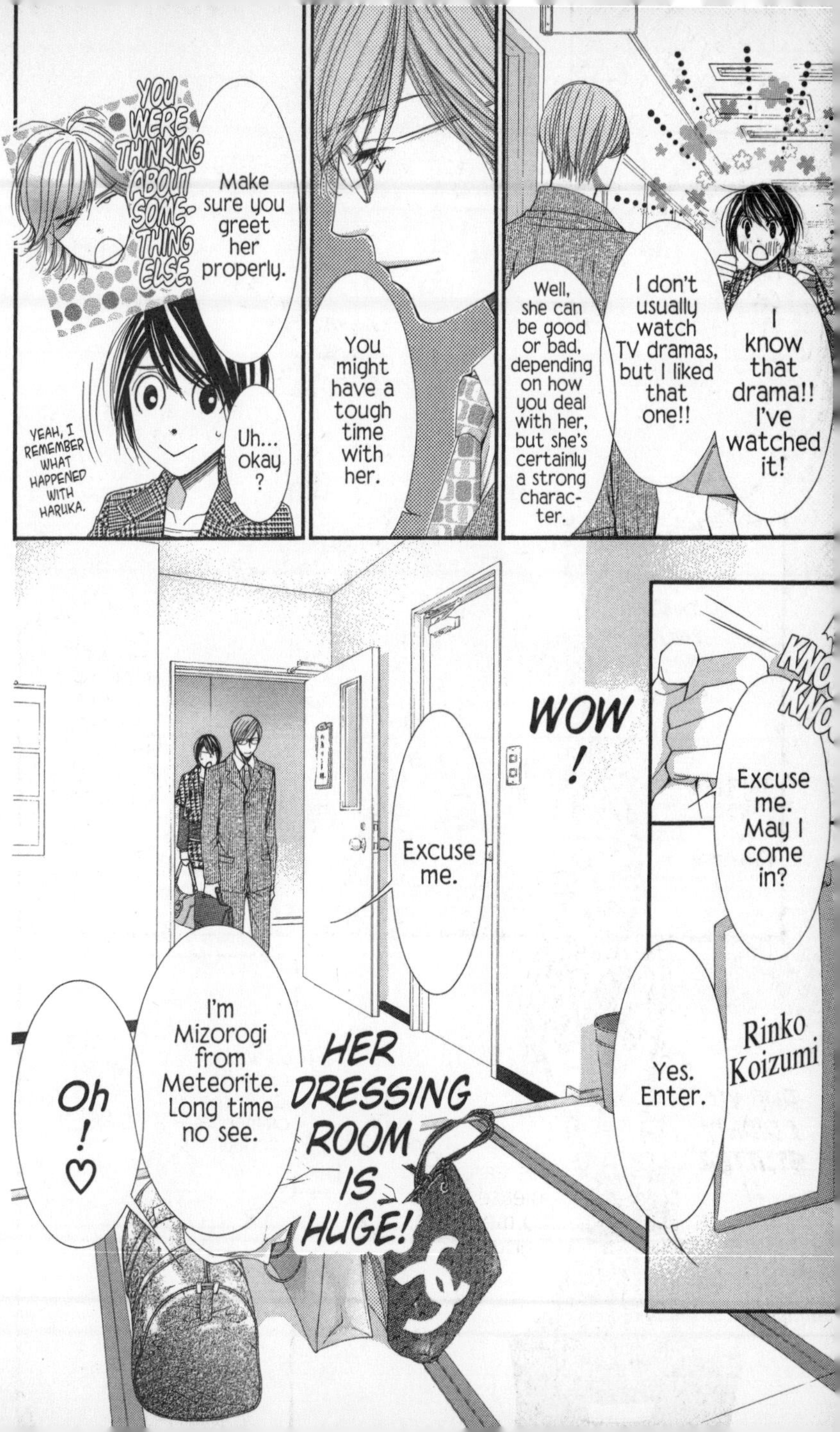
I know that drama!! I've watched it!
I don't usually watch TV dramas, but I liked that one!!
Well, she can be good or bad, depending on how you deal with her, but she's certainly a strong charac-ter.
You might have a tough time with her.
Make sure you greet her properly.
YOU WERE THINKING ABOUT SOME-THING ELSE.
Uh... okay?
YEAH, I REMEMBER WHAT HAPPENED WITH HARUKA.
KNO KNO
Excuse me. May I come in?
Rinko Koizumi
Yes. Enter.
WOW!
Excuse me.
HER DRESSING ROOM IS HUGE!
I'm Mizorogi from Meteorite. Long time no see.
Oh! ♡

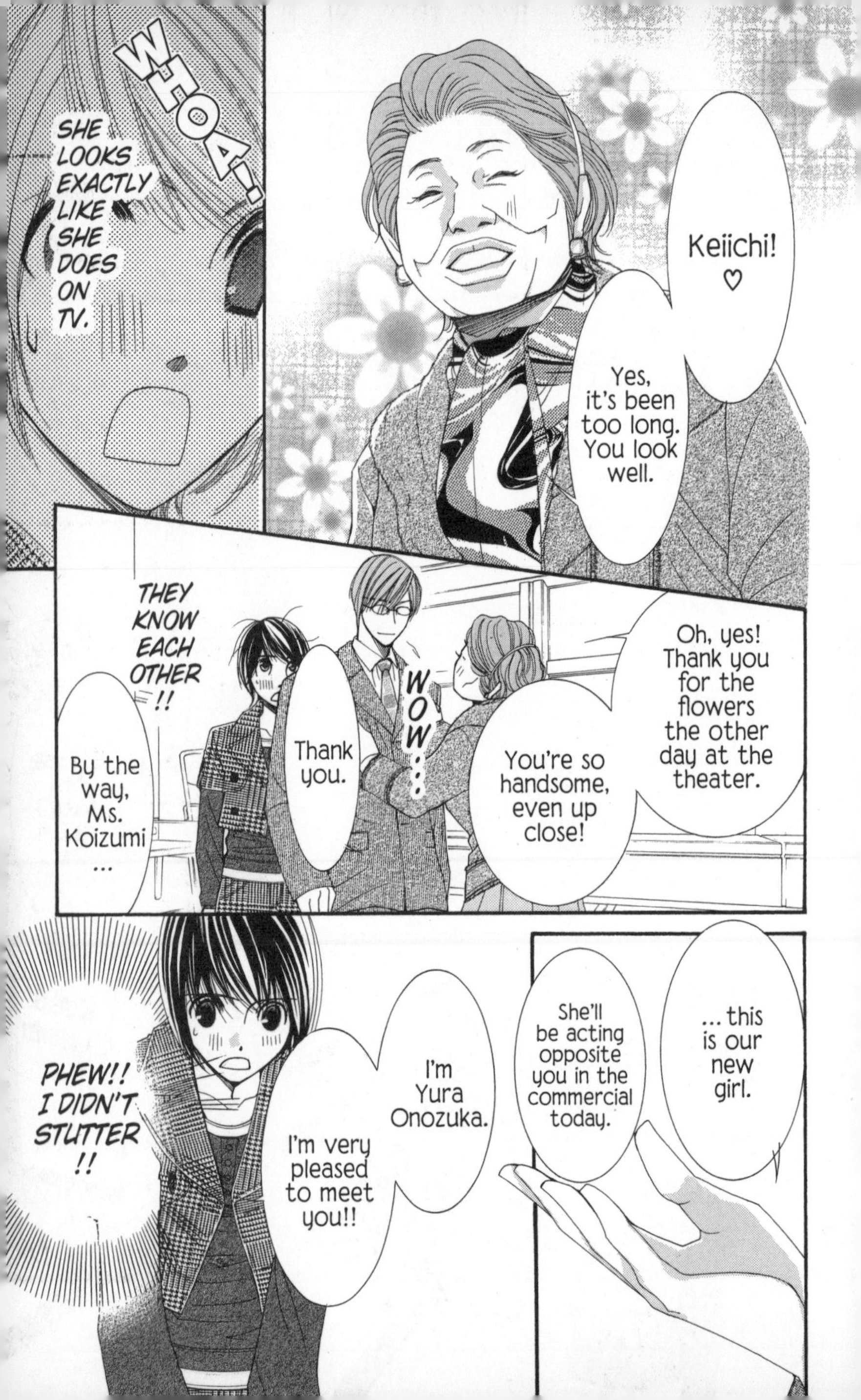
Keiichi! ♡
Yes, it's been too long. You look well.
WHOA-!!
SHE LOOKS EXACTLY LIKE SHE DOES ON TV.
Oh, yes! Thank you for the flowers the other day at the theater.
You're so handsome, even up close!
WOW...
Thank you.
THEY KNOW EACH OTHER!!
By the way, Ms. Koizumi...
... this is our new girl.
She'll be acting opposite you in the commercial today.
I'm Yura Onozuka.
I'm very pleased to meet you!!
PHEW!! I DIDN'T STUTTER!!

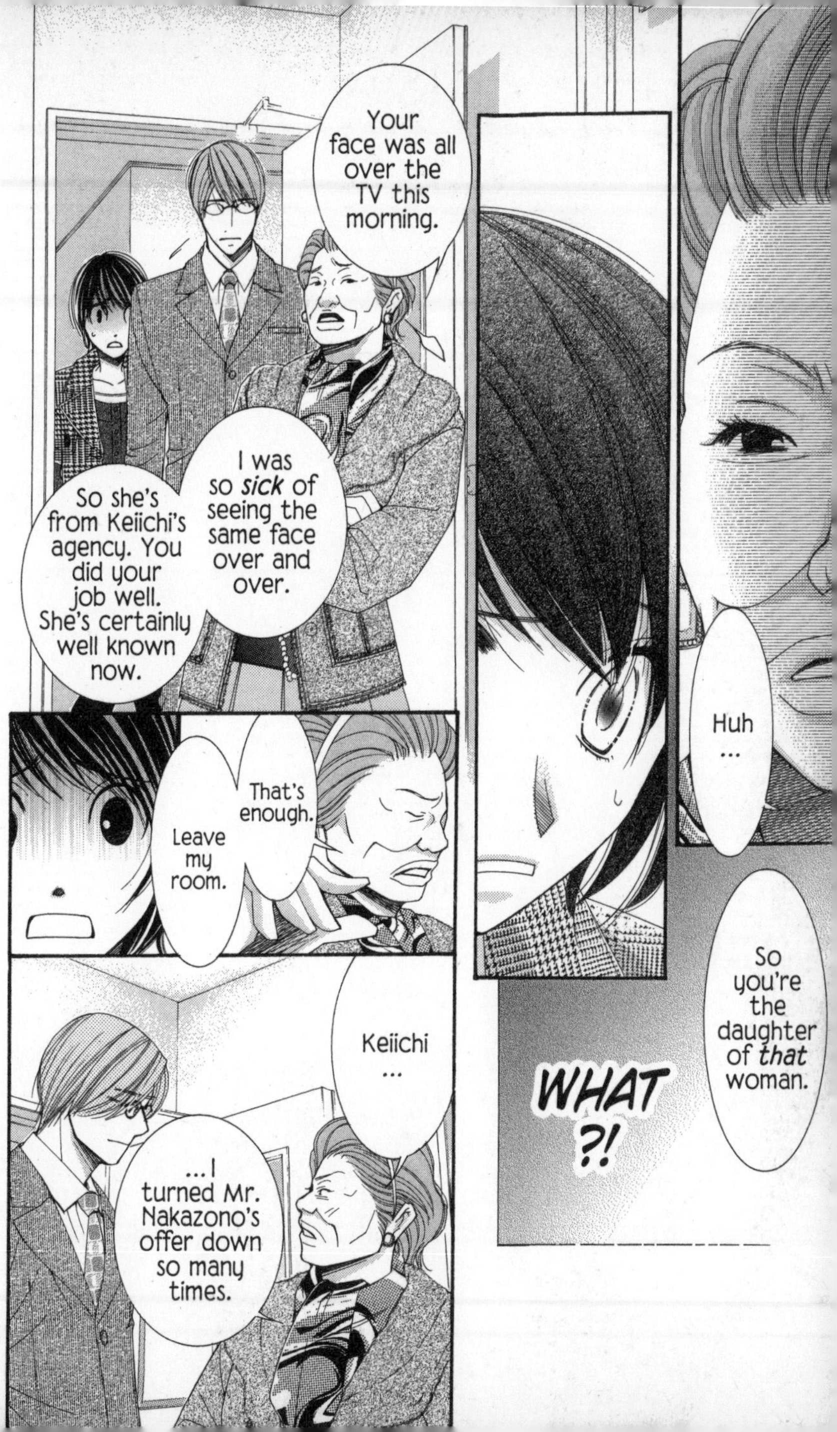
Huh ...
So you're the daughter of *that* woman.
WHAT ?!
Your face was all over the TV this morning.
I was so *sick* of seeing the same face over and over.
So she's from Keiichi's agency. You did your job well. She's certainly well known now.
That's enough.
Leave my room.
Keiichi ...
...I turned Mr. Nakazono's offer down so many times.

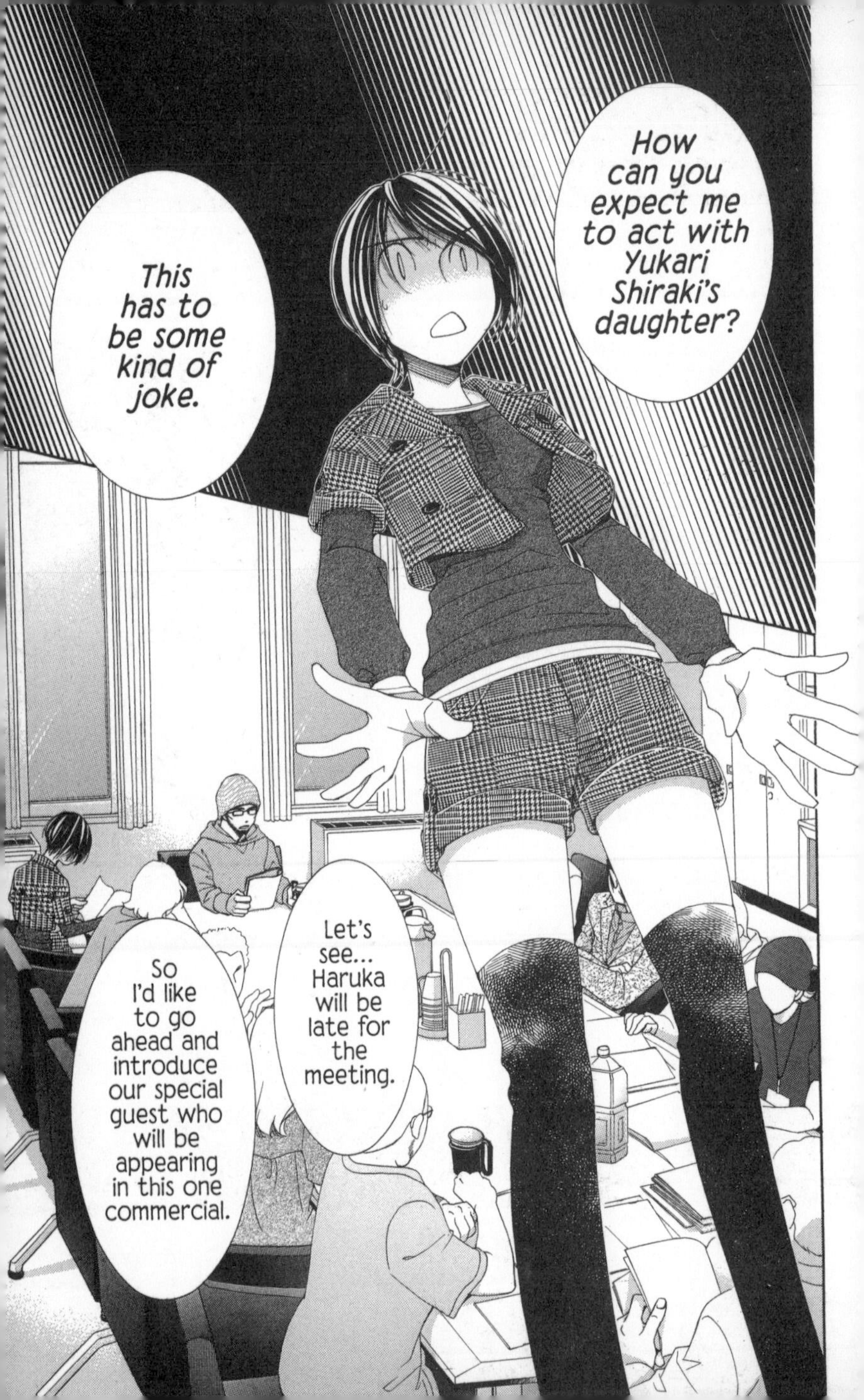
How can you expect me to act with Yukari Shiraki's daughter?
This has to be some kind of joke.
Let's see... Haruka will be late for the meeting.
So I'd like to go ahead and introduce our special guest who will be appearing in this one commercial.

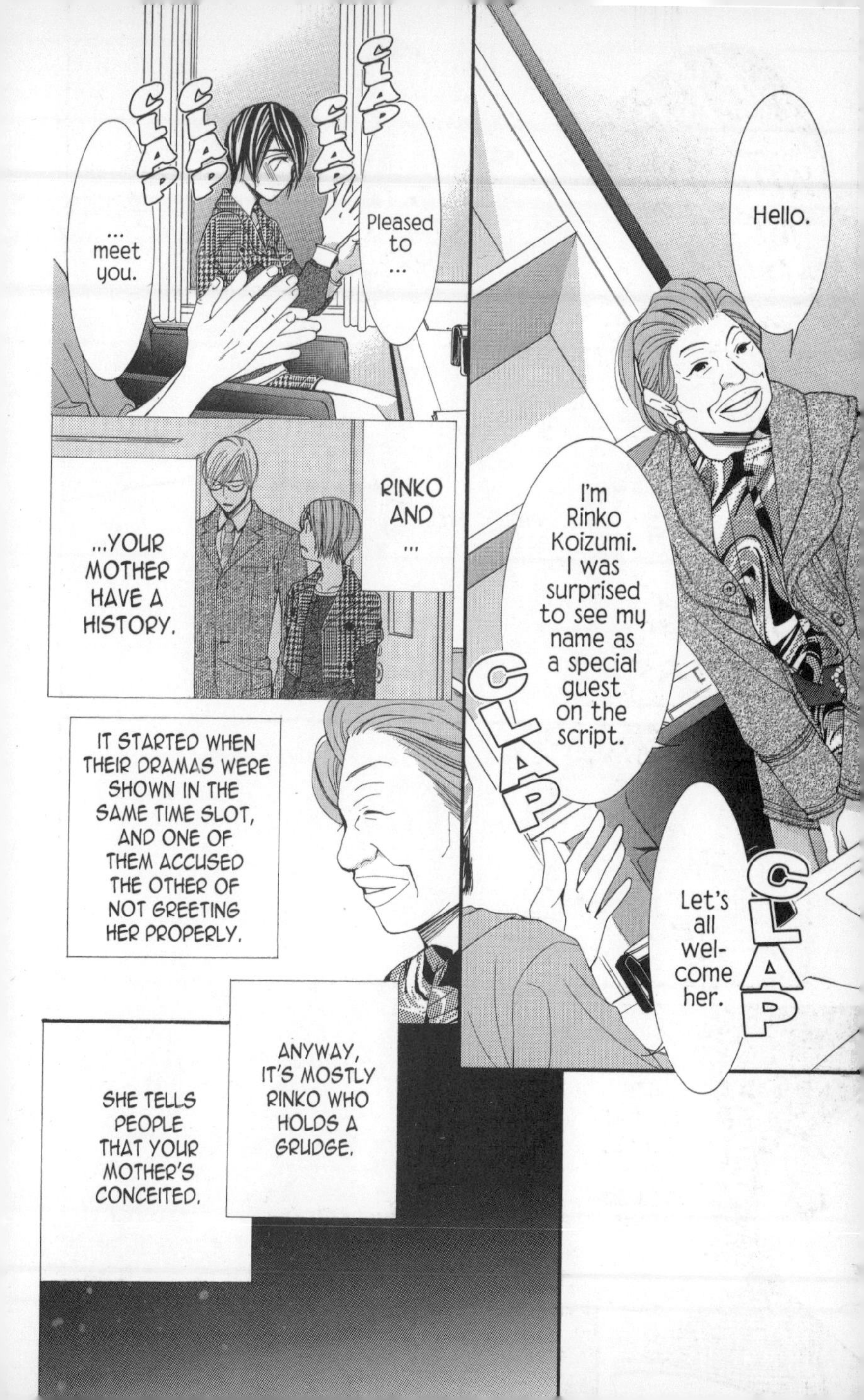
Hello.
I'm Rinko Koizumi. I was surprised to see my name as a special guest on the script.
CLAP
Let's all wel-come her.
CLAP
CLAP
CLAP
Pleased to ...
CLAP
CLAP
... meet you.
RINKO AND ...
...YOUR MOTHER HAVE A HISTORY.
IT STARTED WHEN THEIR DRAMAS WERE SHOWN IN THE SAME TIME SLOT, AND ONE OF THEM ACCUSED THE OTHER OF NOT GREETING HER PROPERLY.
ANYWAY, IT'S MOSTLY RINKO WHO HOLDS A GRUDGE.
SHE TELLS PEOPLE THAT YOUR MOTHER'S CONCEITED.

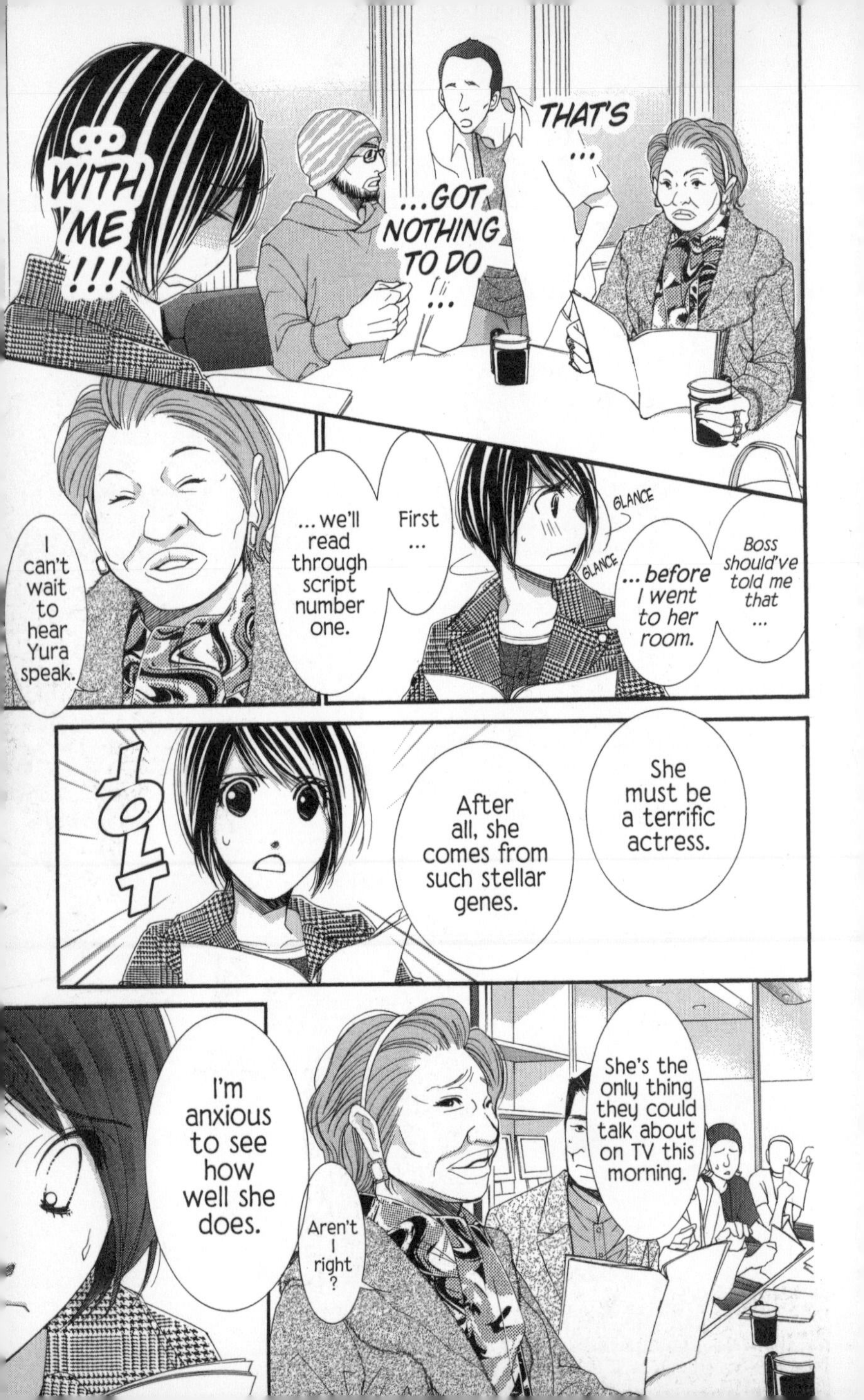
THAT'S ...
...GOT NOTHING TO DO ...
... WITH ME !!!
GLANCE
GLANCE
Boss should've told me that ...
... before I went to her room.
First ...
... we'll read through script number one.
I can't wait to hear Yura speak.
She must be a terrific actress.
After all, she comes from such stellar genes.
JOLT
She's the only thing they could talk about on TV this morning.
Aren't I right?
I'm anxious to see how well she does.

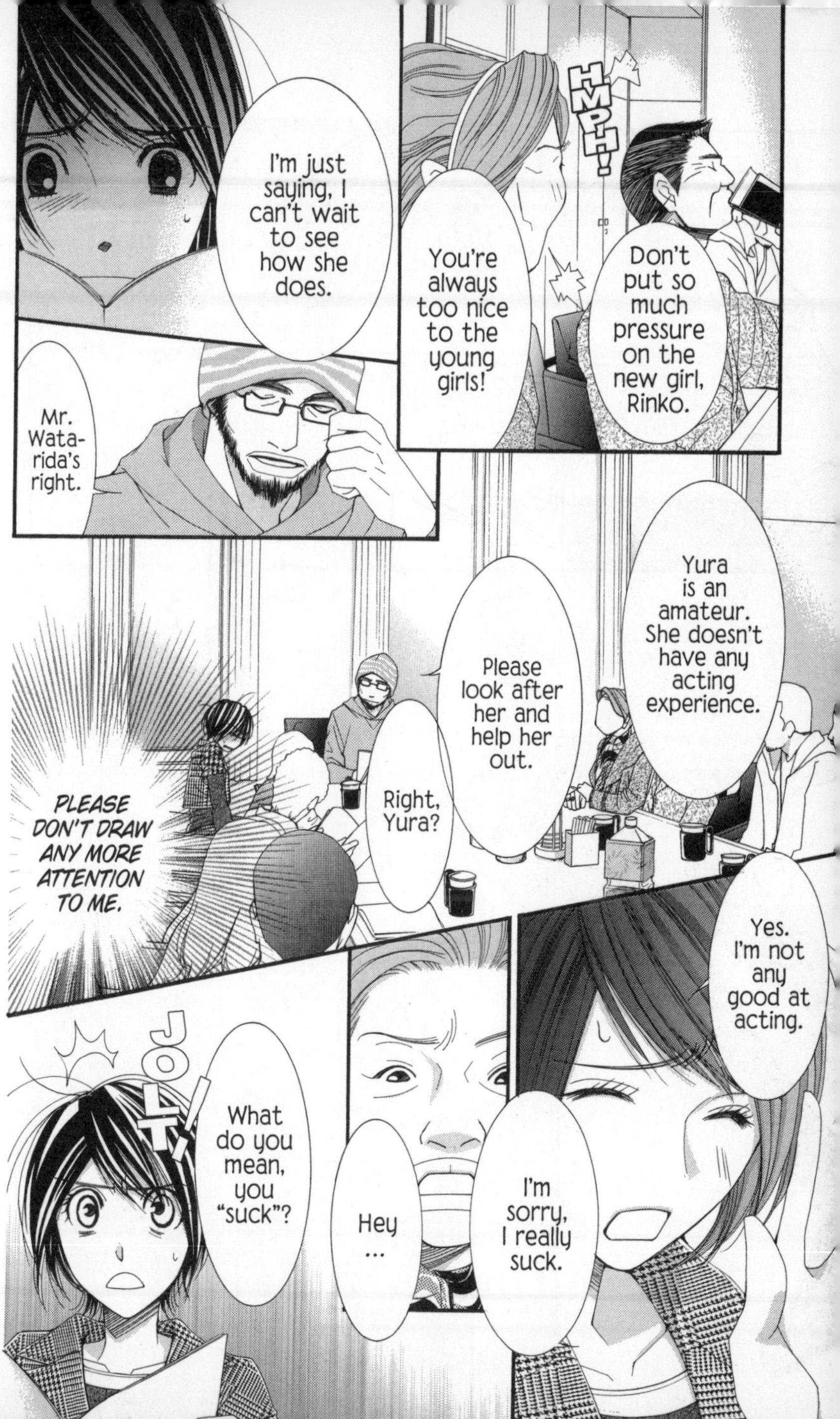
HMPH!
Don't put so much pressure on the new girl, Rinko.
You're always too nice to the young girls!
I'm just saying, I can't wait to see how she does.
Mr. Watarida's right.
Yura is an amateur. She doesn't have any acting experience.
Please look after her and help her out.
Right, Yura?
PLEASE DON'T DRAW ANY MORE ATTENTION TO ME.
Yes. I'm not any good at acting.
I'm sorry, I really suck.
Hey ...
JOLT!
What do you mean, you "suck"?

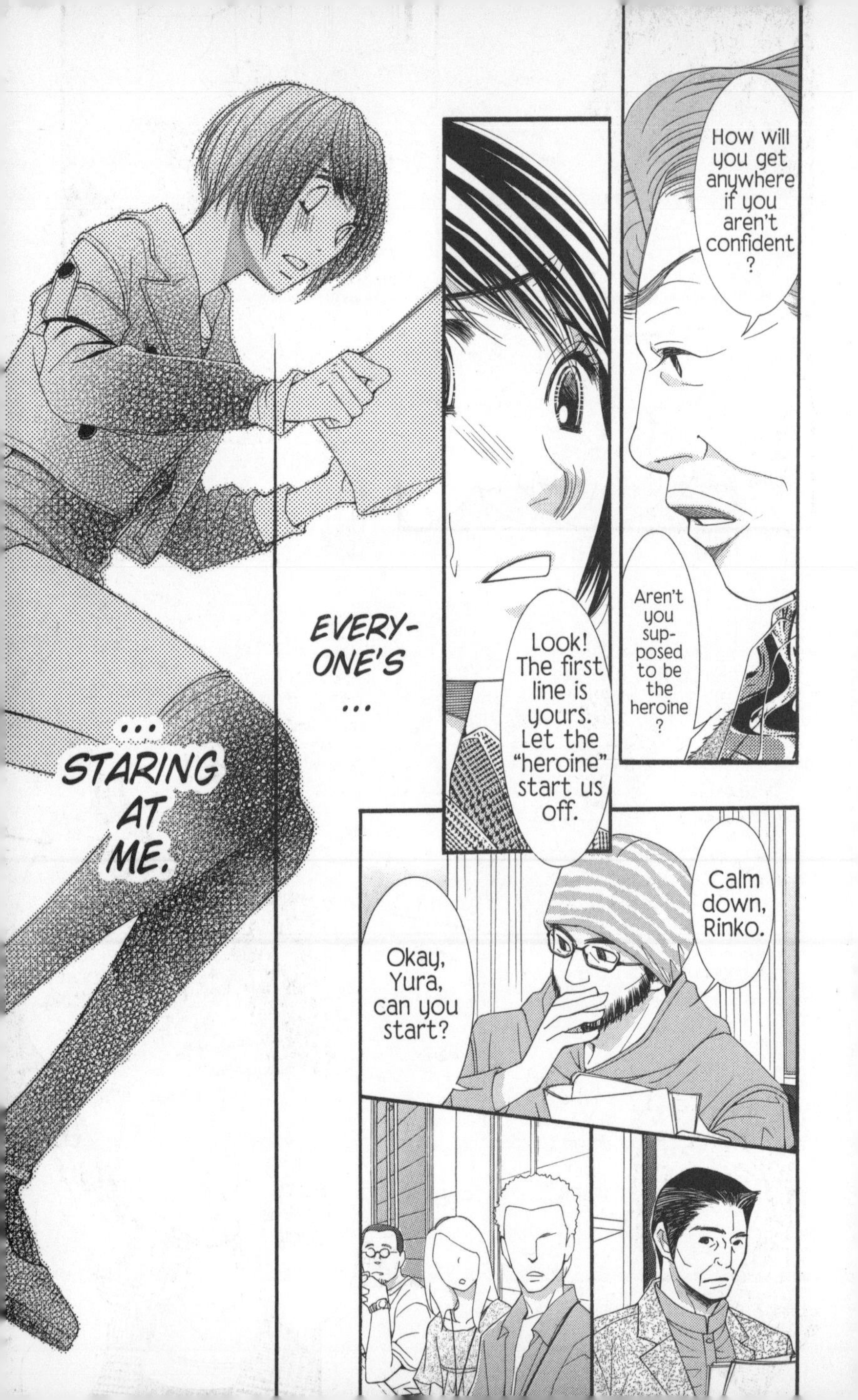
How will you get anywhere if you aren't confident?
Aren't you sup-posed to be the heroine?
Look! The first line is yours. Let the "heroine" start us off.
Calm down, Rinko.
Okay, Yura, can you start?
EVERY-ONE'S ...
... STARING AT ME.

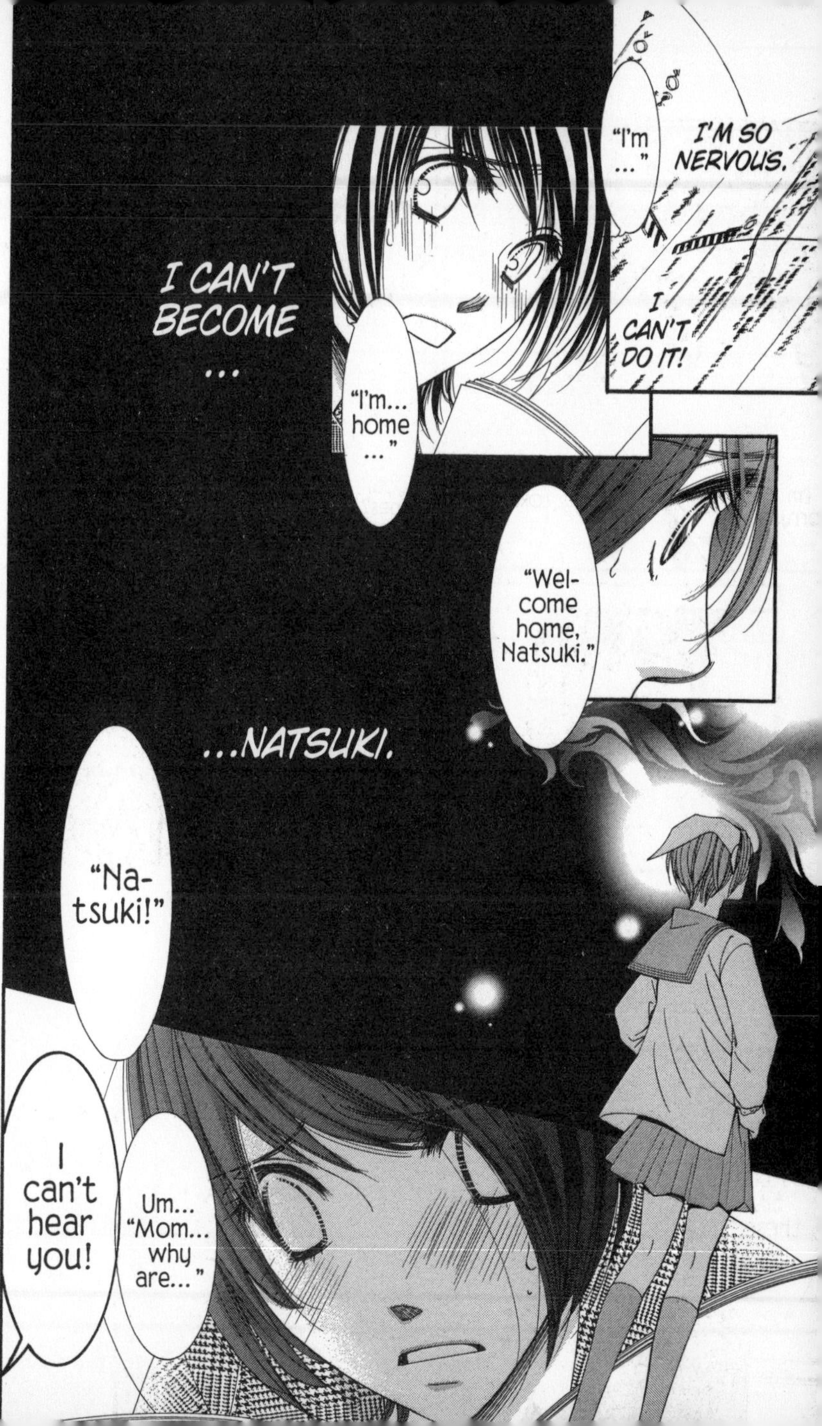
I'M SO NERVOUS.
"I'm ..."
I CAN'T DO IT!
"I'm... home ..."
I CAN'T BECOME ...
"Wel-come home, Natsuki."
...NATSUKI.
"Na-tsuki!"
Um... "Mom... why are..."
I can't hear you!

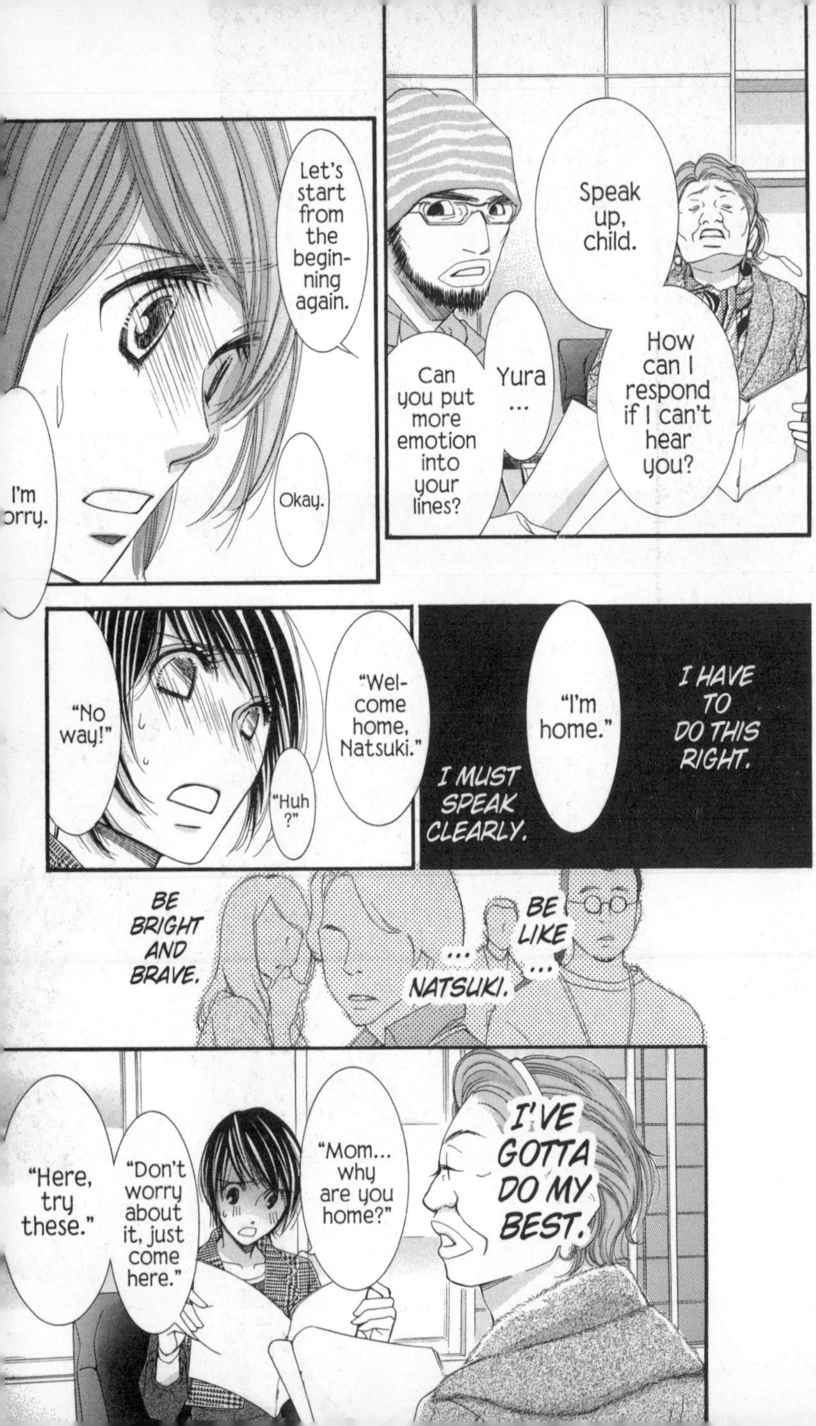
Speak up, child.
How can I respond if I can't hear you?
Yura ...
Can you put more emotion into your lines?
Let's start from the begin-ning again.
Okay.
I'm orry.
I HAVE TO DO THIS RIGHT.
"I'm home."
I MUST SPEAK CLEARLY.
"Wel-come home, Natsuki."
"Huh?"
"No way!"
BE LIKE ... NATSUKI.
... BE BRIGHT AND BRAVE.
I'VE GOTTA DO MY BEST.
"Mom... why are you home?"
"Don't worry about it, just come here."
"Here, try these."

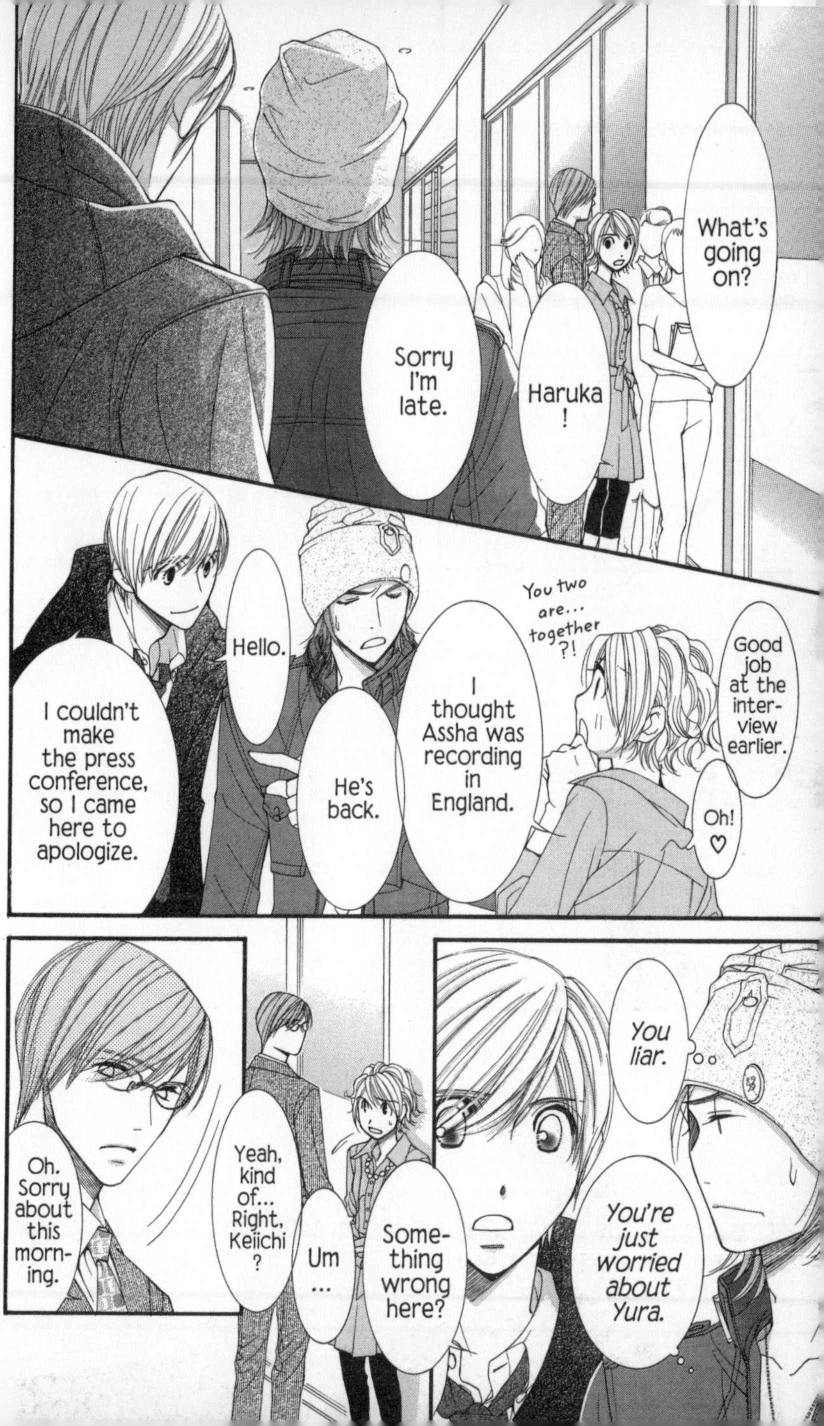
What's going on?
Haruka!
Sorry I'm late.
Good job at the inter-view earlier.
Oh! ♡
You two are... together?!
I thought Assha was recording in England.
Hello.
He's back.
I couldn't make the press conference, so I came here to apologize.
You liar.
You're just worried about Yura.
Some-thing wrong here?
Um...
Yeah, kind of... Right, Keiichi?
Oh. Sorry about this morn-ing.

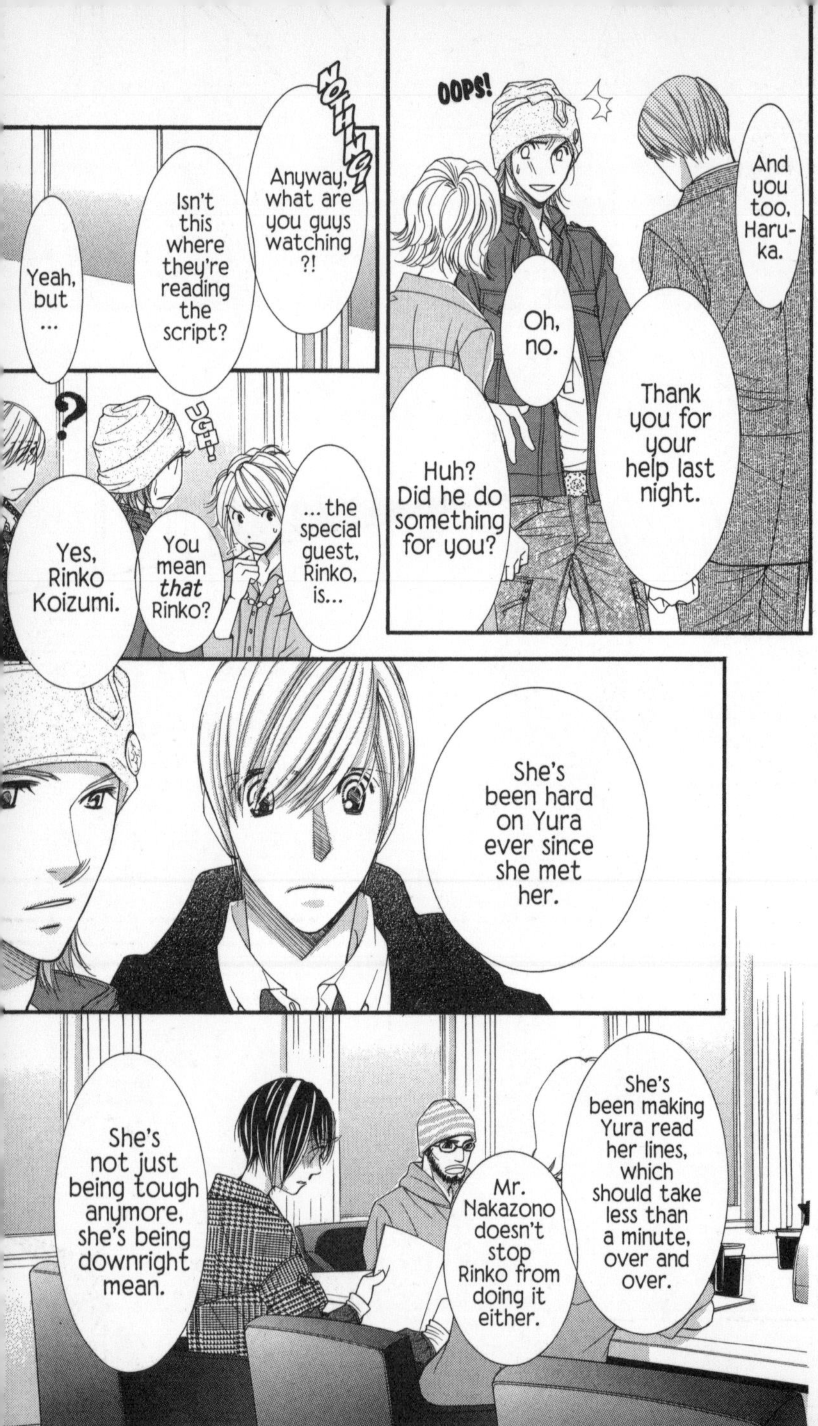

And you too, Haru-ka.
OOPS!
Thank you for your help last night.
Oh, no.
Huh? Did he do something for you?
NOTHING!
Anyway, what are you guys watching?!
Isn't this where they're reading the script?
Yeah, but ...
... the special guest, Rinko, is...
UGH!
You mean *that* Rinko?
?
Yes, Rinko Koizumi.
She's been hard on Yura ever since she met her.
She's been making Yura read her lines, which should take less than a minute, over and over.
Mr. Nakazono doesn't stop Rinko from doing it either.
She's not just being tough anymore, she's being downright mean.

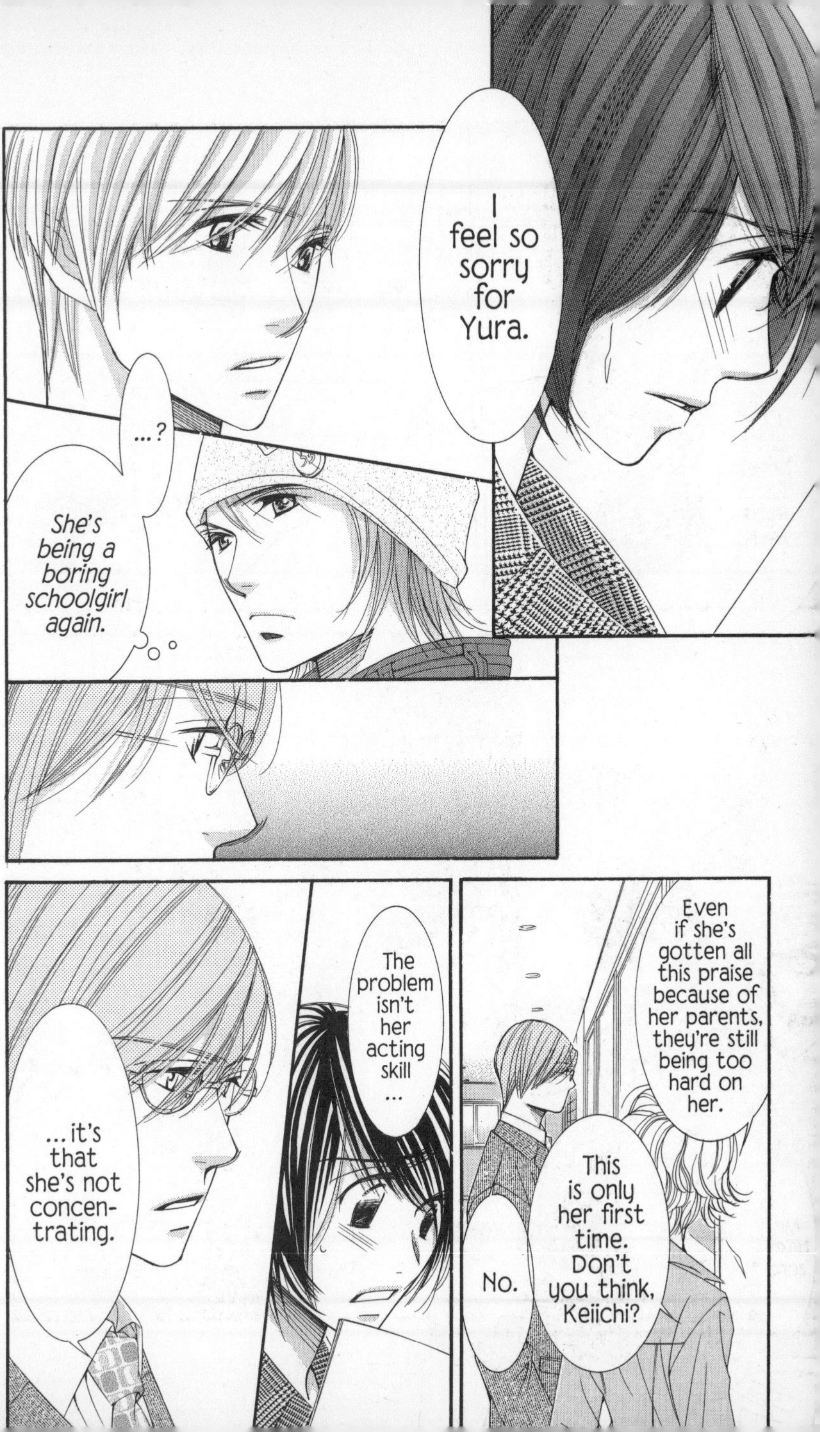
I feel so sorry for Yura.
...?
She's being a boring schoolgirl again.
Even if she's gotten all this praise because of her parents, they're still being too hard on her.
This is only her first time. Don't you think, Keiichi?
No.
The problem isn't her acting skill...
...it's that she's not concentrating.

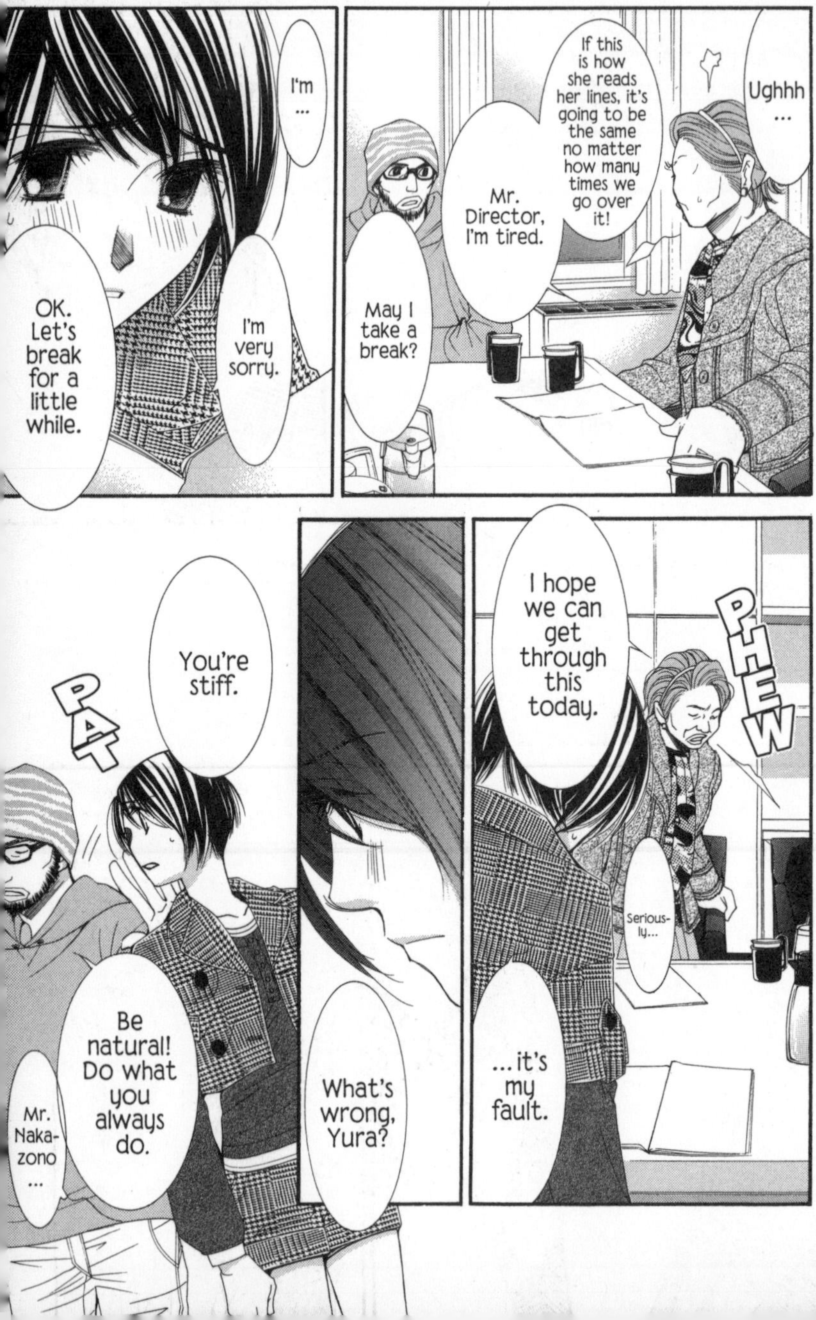
Ughhh...
If this is how she reads her lines, it's going to be the same no matter how many times we go over it!
Mr. Director, I'm tired.
May I take a break?
I'm...
I'm very sorry.
OK. Let's break for a little while.
I hope we can get through this today.
PHEW
Seriously...
...it's my fault.
What's wrong, Yura?
You're stiff.
PAT
Be natural! Do what you always do.
Mr. Nakazono...

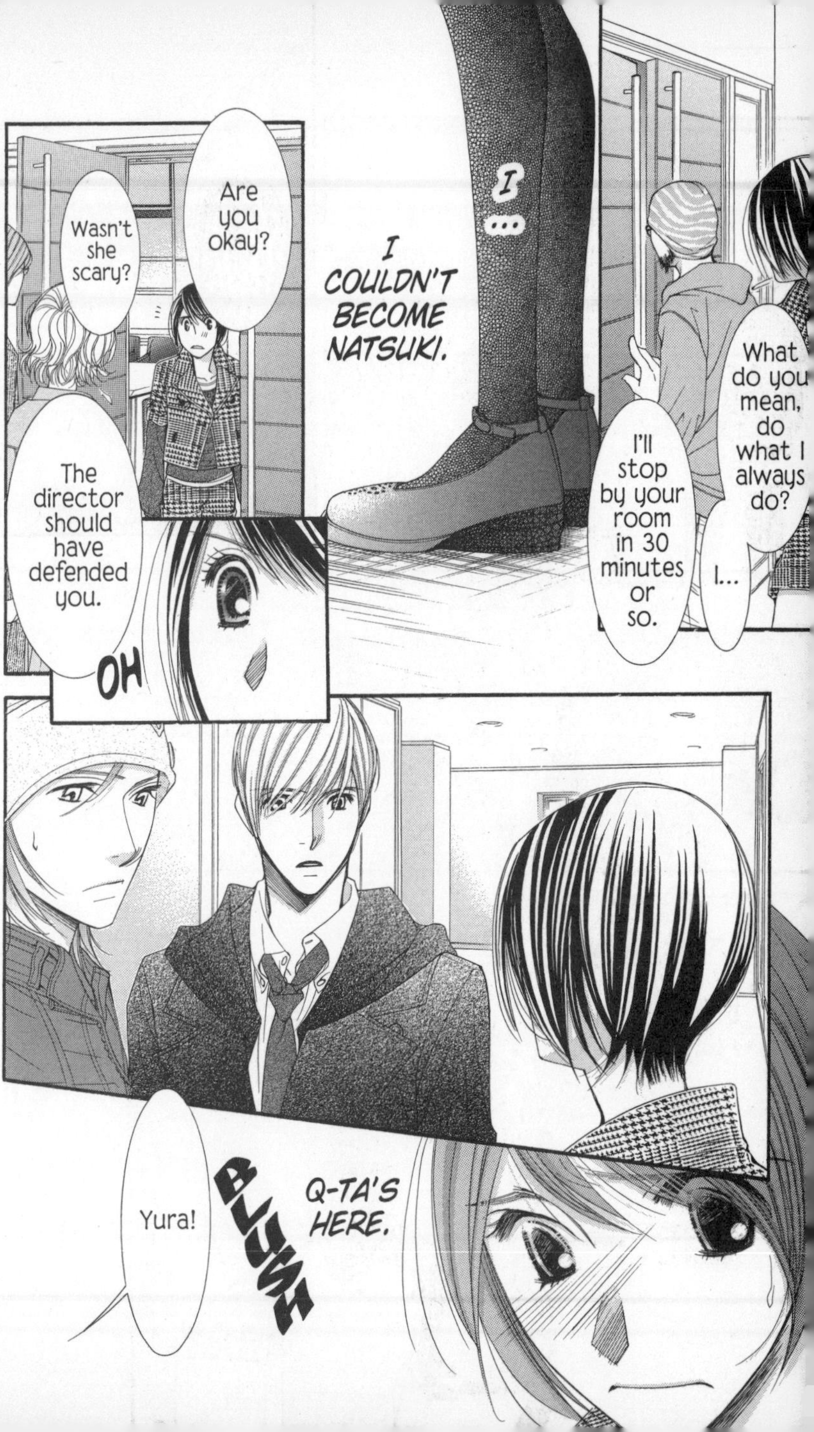
What do you mean, do what I always do?
I...
I'll stop by your room in 30 minutes or so.
I ...
I COULDN'T BECOME NATSUKI.
Are you okay?
Wasn't she scary?
The director should have defended you.
OH
Q-TA'S HERE.
BLUSH
Yura!

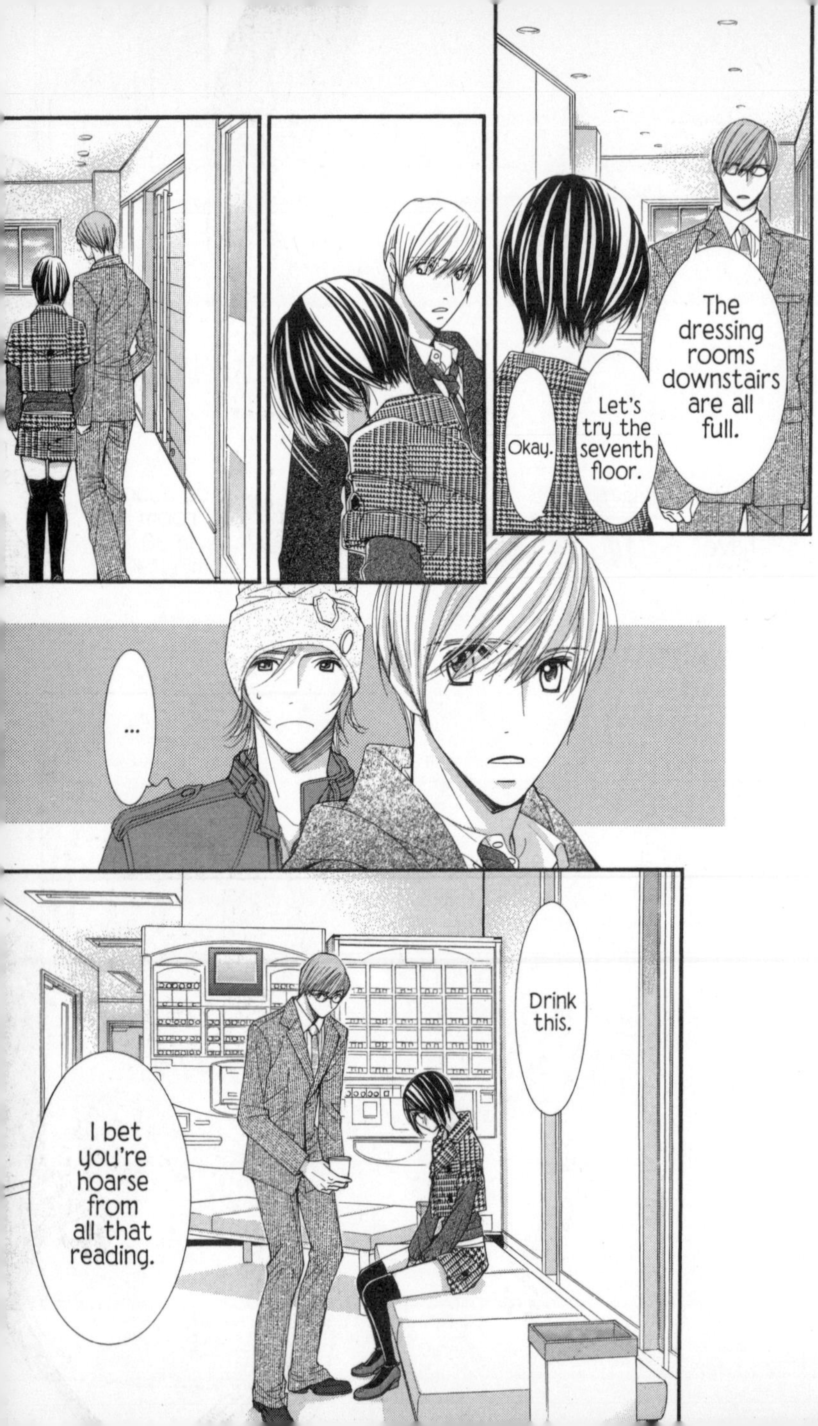
The dressing rooms downstairs are all full.
Let's try the seventh floor.
Okay.
...
Drink this.
I bet you're hoarse from all that reading.

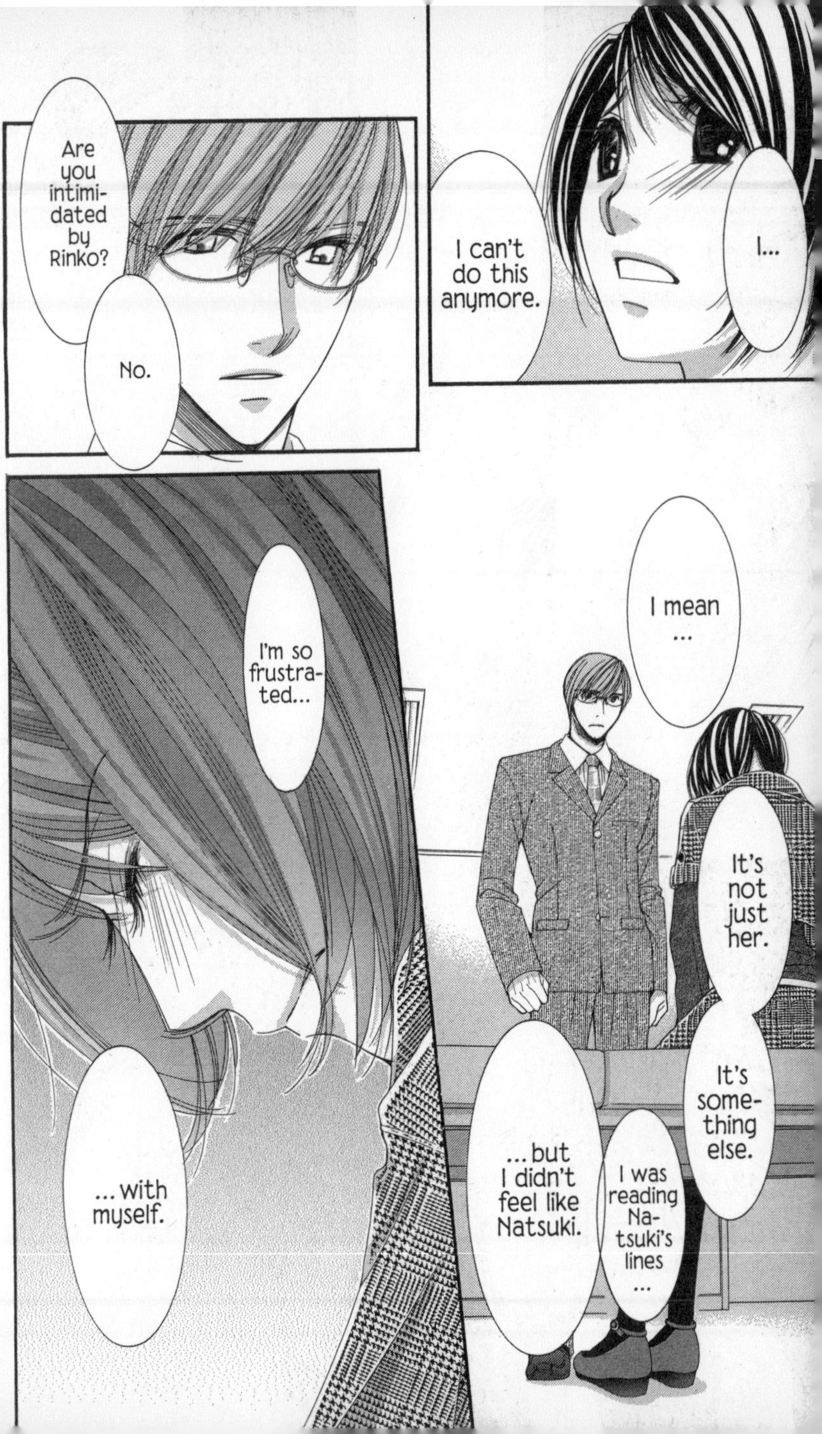
I...
I can't do this anymore.
Are you intimidated by Rinko?
No.
I mean ...
It's not just her.
It's something else.
I was reading Natsuki's lines ...
... but I didn't feel like Natsuki.
I'm so frustrated...
... with myself.

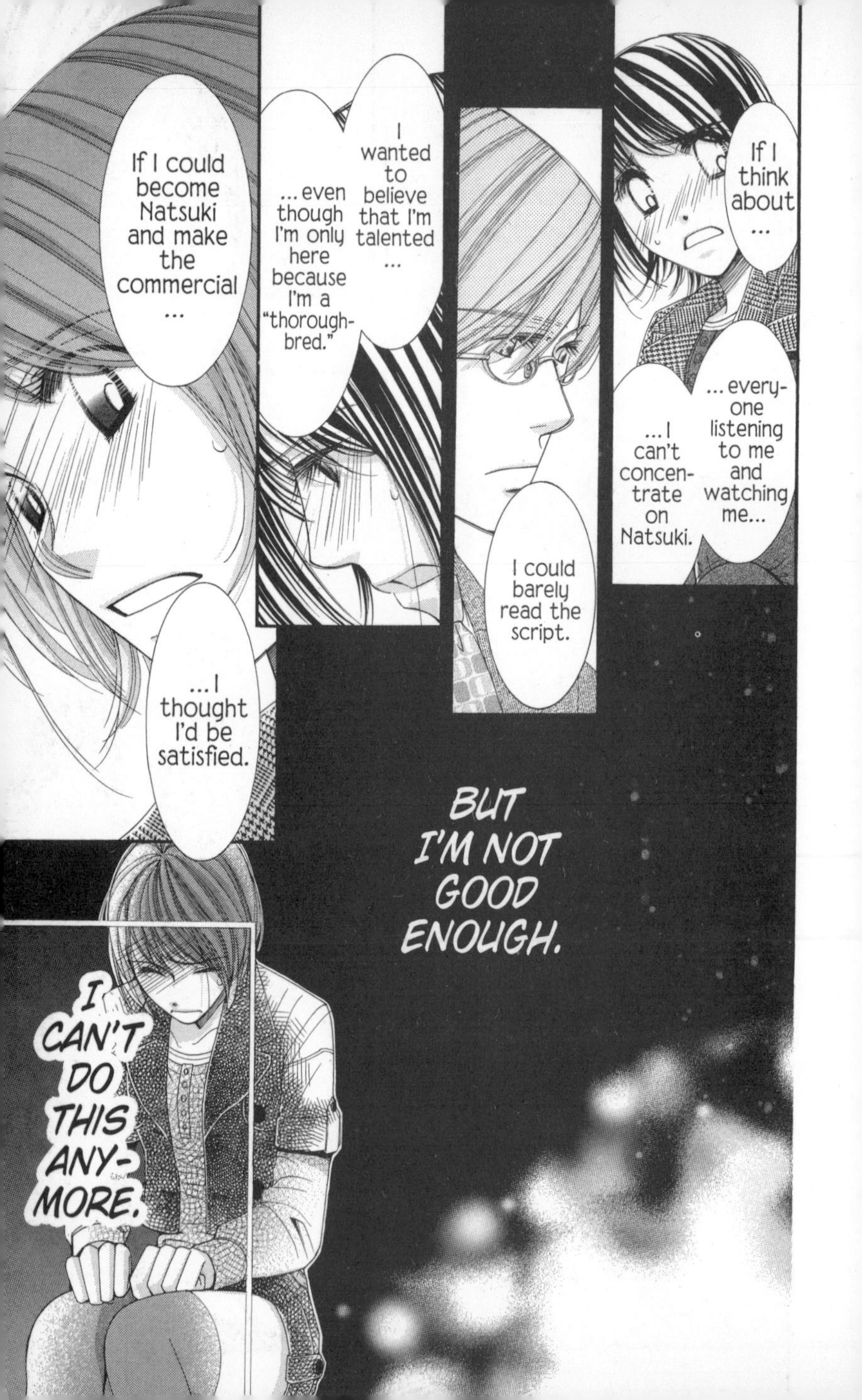
If I think about...
...every-one listening to me and watching me...
...I can't concen-trate on Natsuki.
I could barely read the script.
I wanted to believe that I'm talented...
...even though I'm only here because I'm a "thorough-bred."
If I could become Natsuki and make the commercial...
...I thought I'd be satisfied.
BUT I'M NOT GOOD ENOUGH.
I CAN'T DO THIS ANY-MORE.

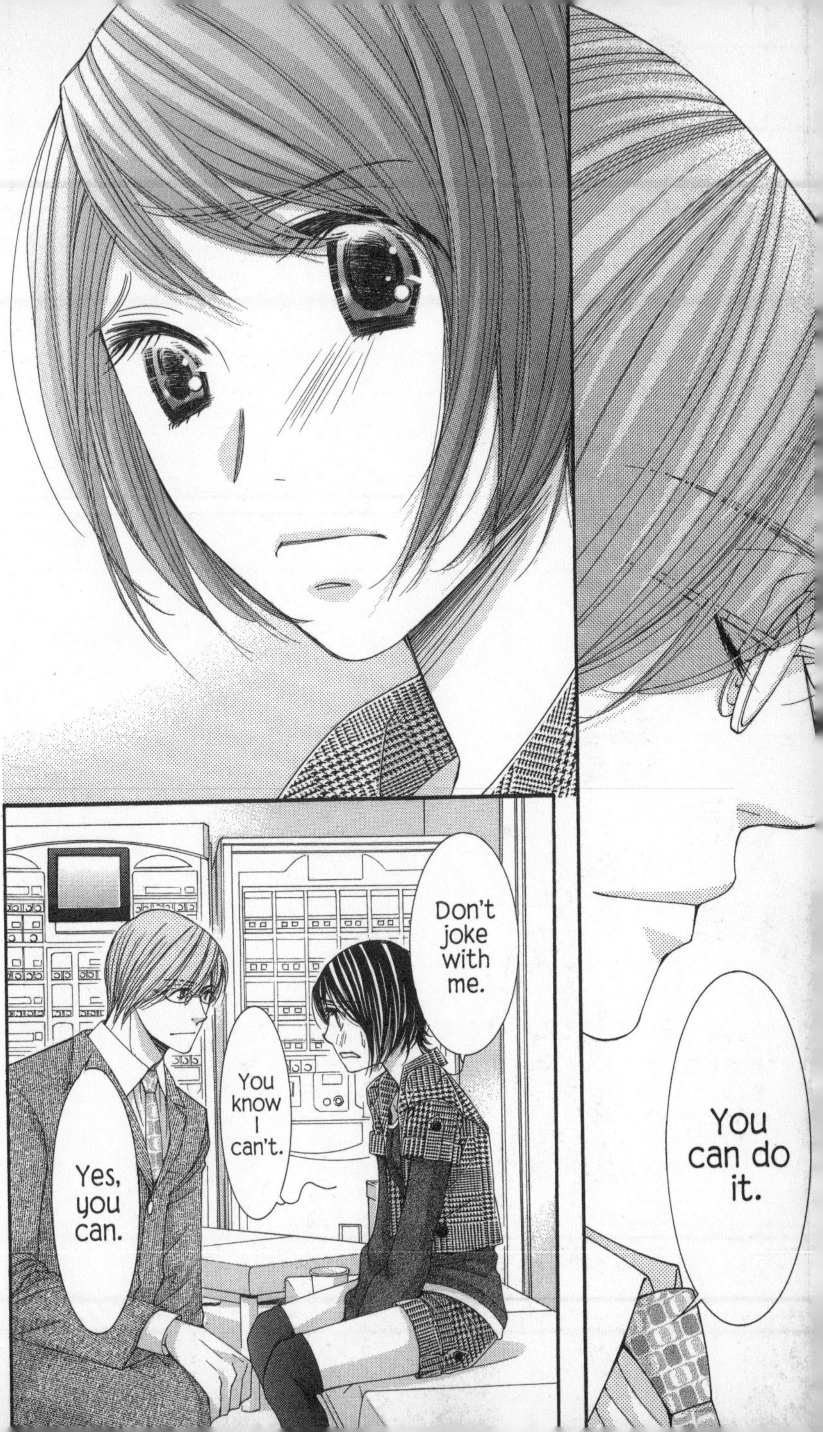
You can do it.
Don't joke with me.
You know I can't.
Yes, you can.

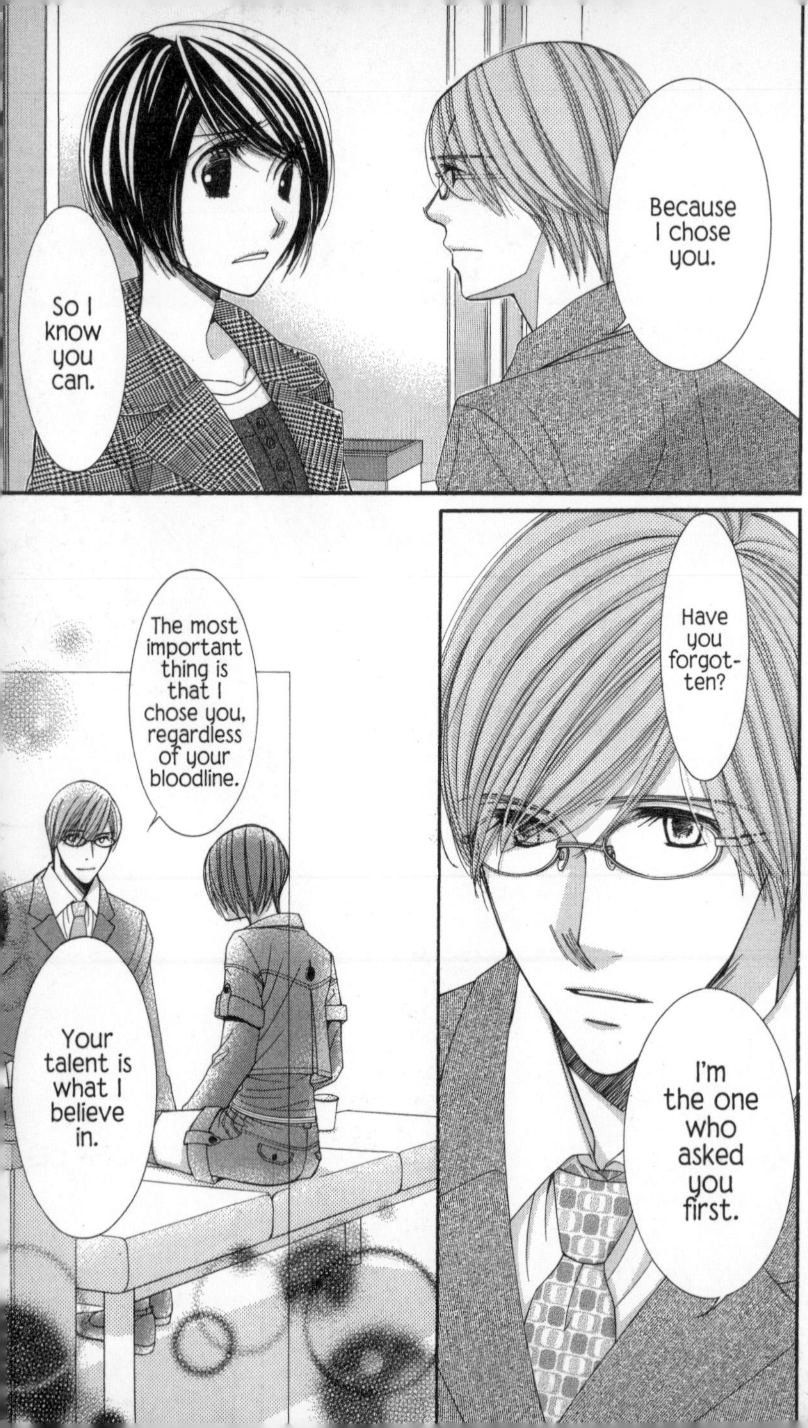
Because I chose you.
So I know you can.
Have you forgot-ten?
I'm the one who asked you first.
The most important thing is that I chose you, regardless of your bloodline.
Your talent is what I believe in.

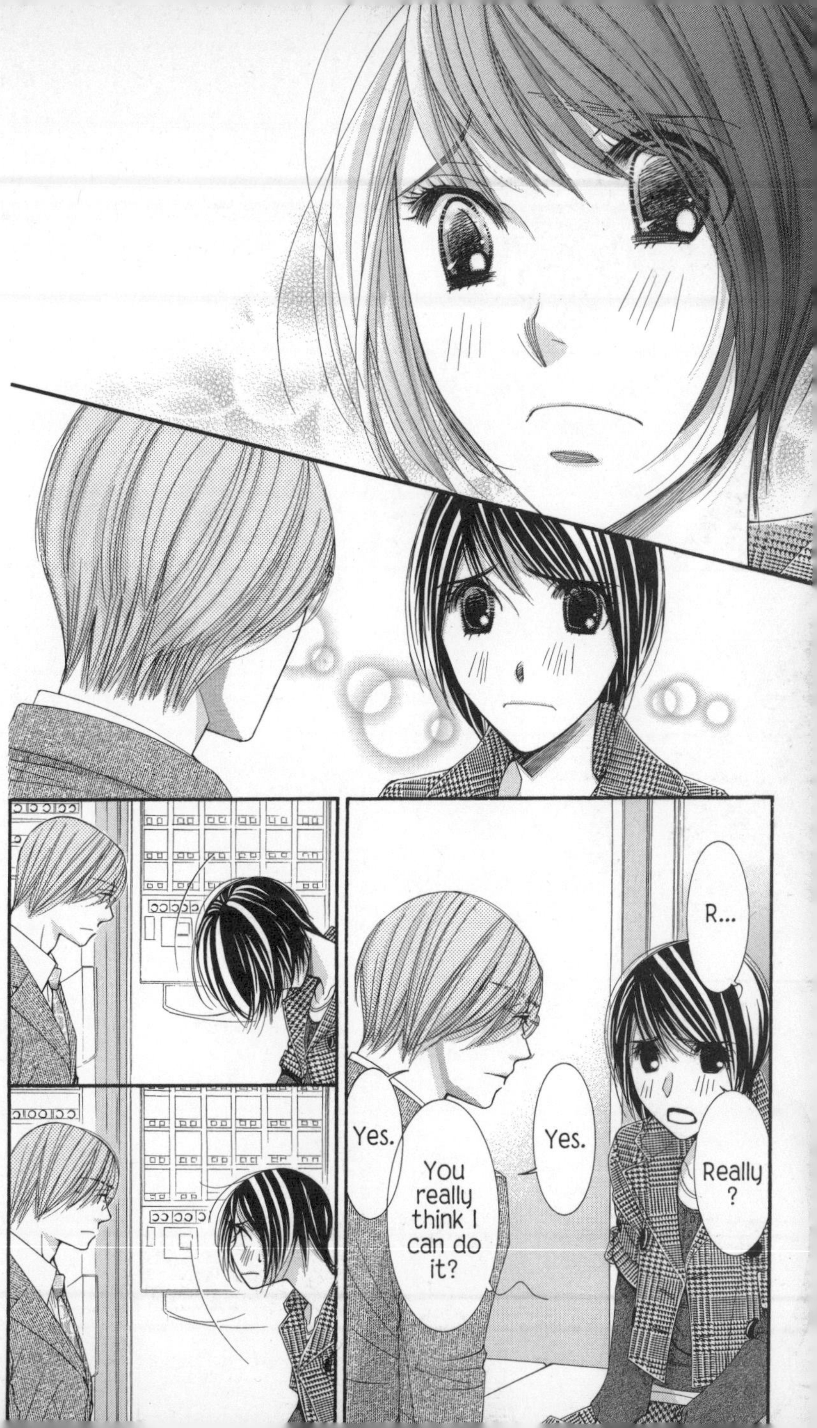
R...
Really?
Yes.
You really think I can do it?
Yes.

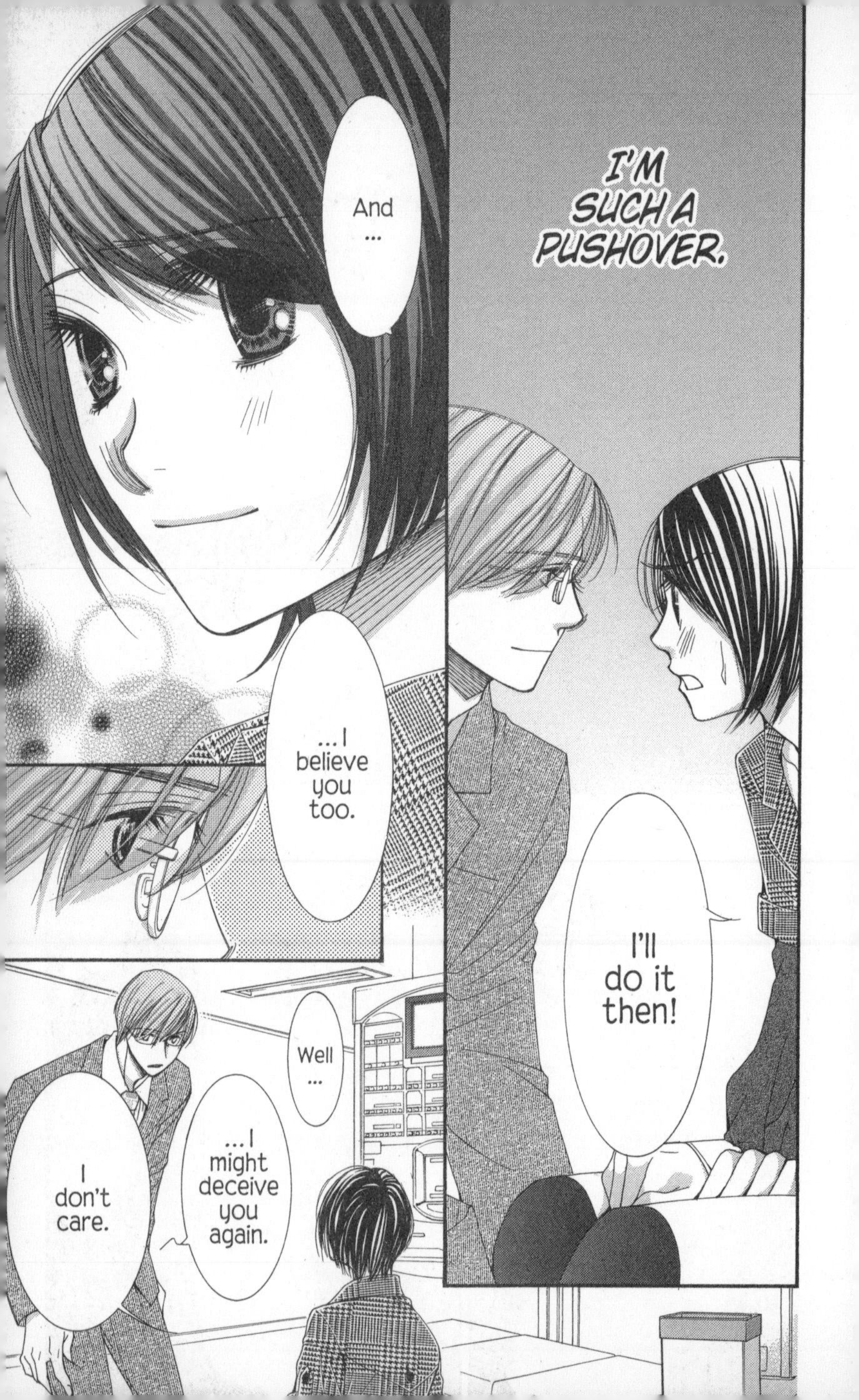
I'M SUCH A PUSHOVER.
I'll do it then!
And ...
...I believe you too.
Well ...
...I might deceive you again.
I don't care.

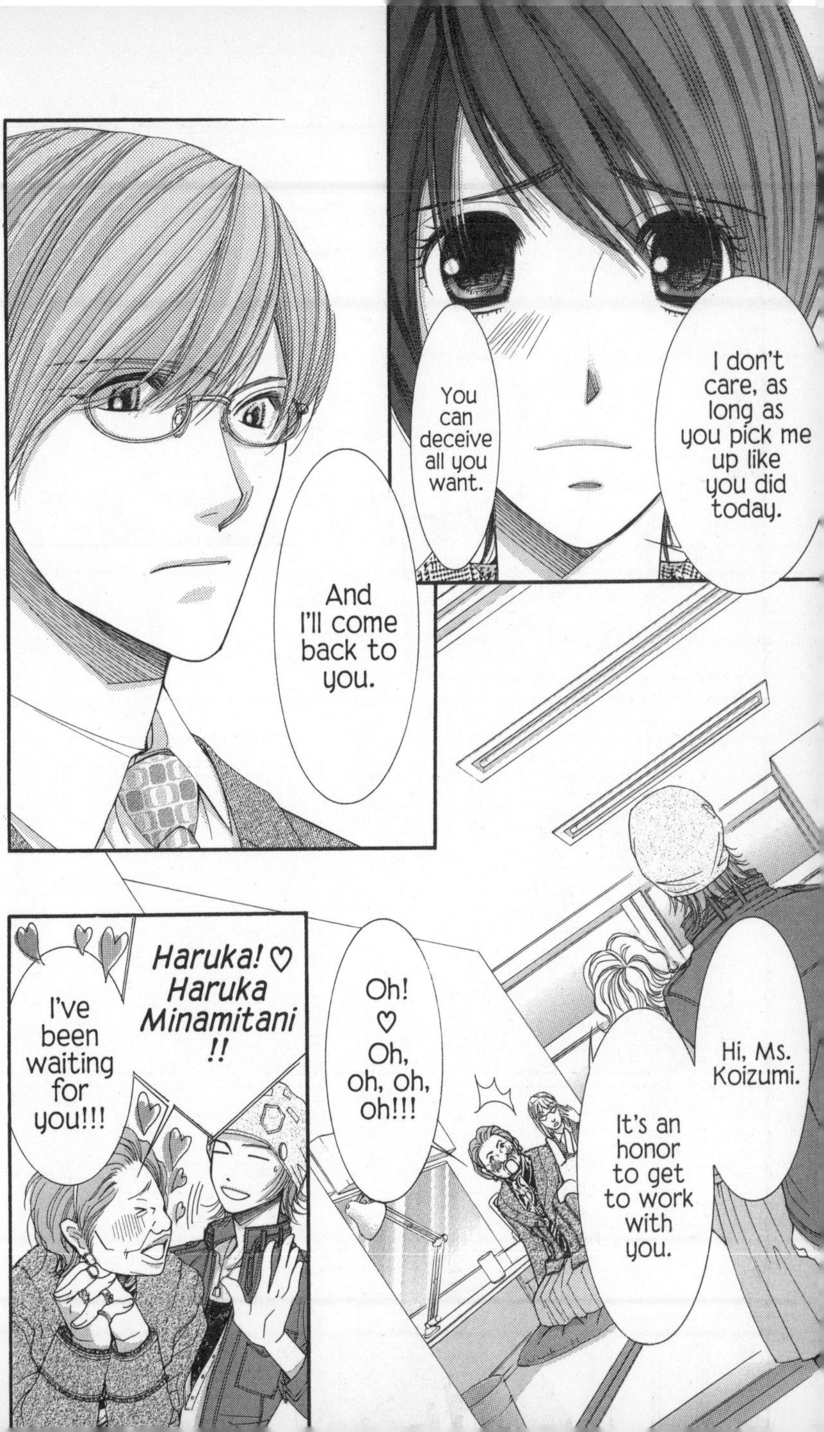
I don't care, as long as you pick me up like you did today.
You can deceive all you want.
And I'll come back to you.
Hi, Ms. Koizumi.
It's an honor to get to work with you.
Oh! ♡ Oh, oh, oh, oh!!!
Haruka! ♡ Haruka Minamitani !!
I've been waiting for you!!!

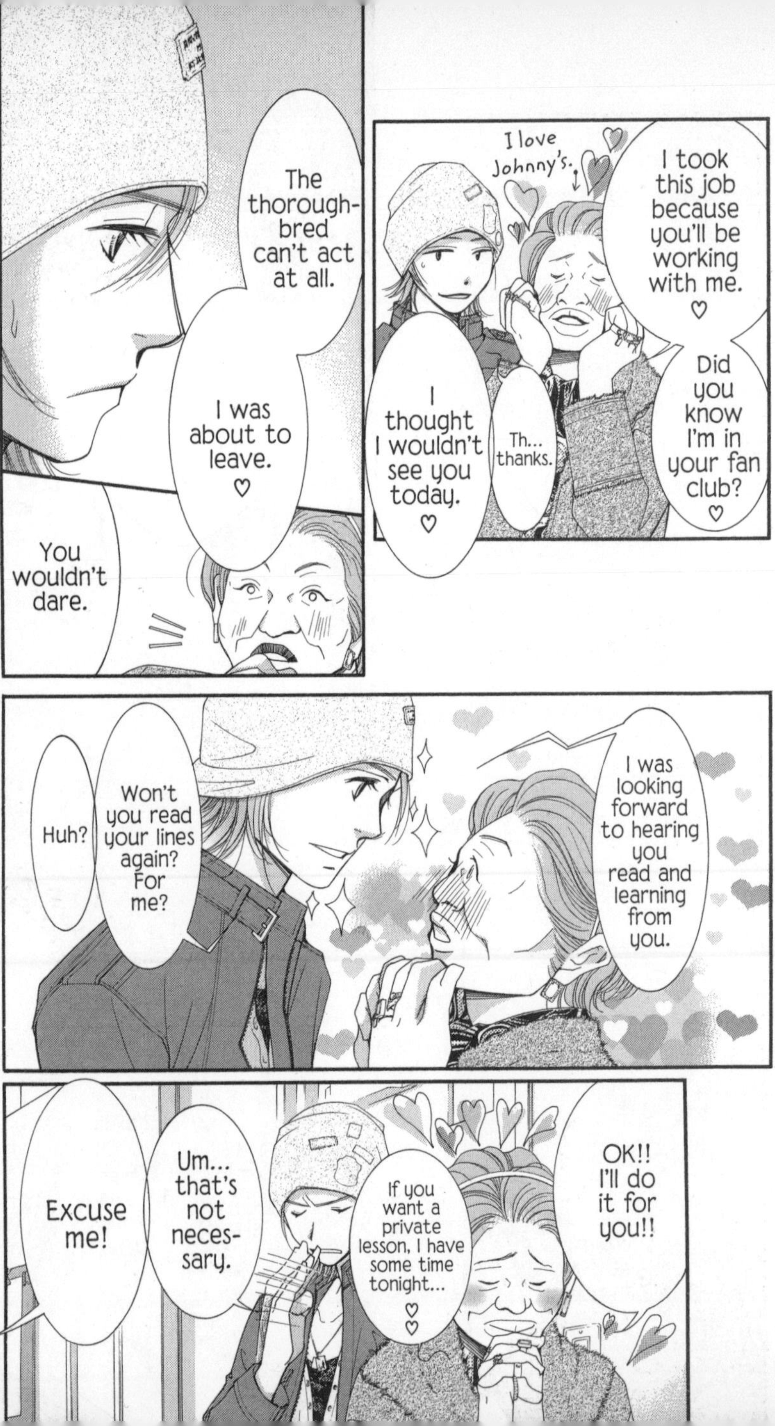
I love Johnny's.
I took this job because you'll be working with me. ♡
Did you know I'm in your fan club? ♡
Th... thanks.
I thought I wouldn't see you today. ♡
The thorough-bred can't act at all.
I was about to leave. ♡
You wouldn't dare.
I was looking forward to hearing you read and learning from you.
Won't you read your lines again? For me?
Huh?
OK!! I'll do it for you!!
If you want a private lesson, I have some time tonight... ♡ ♡
Um... that's not neces-sary.
Excuse me!

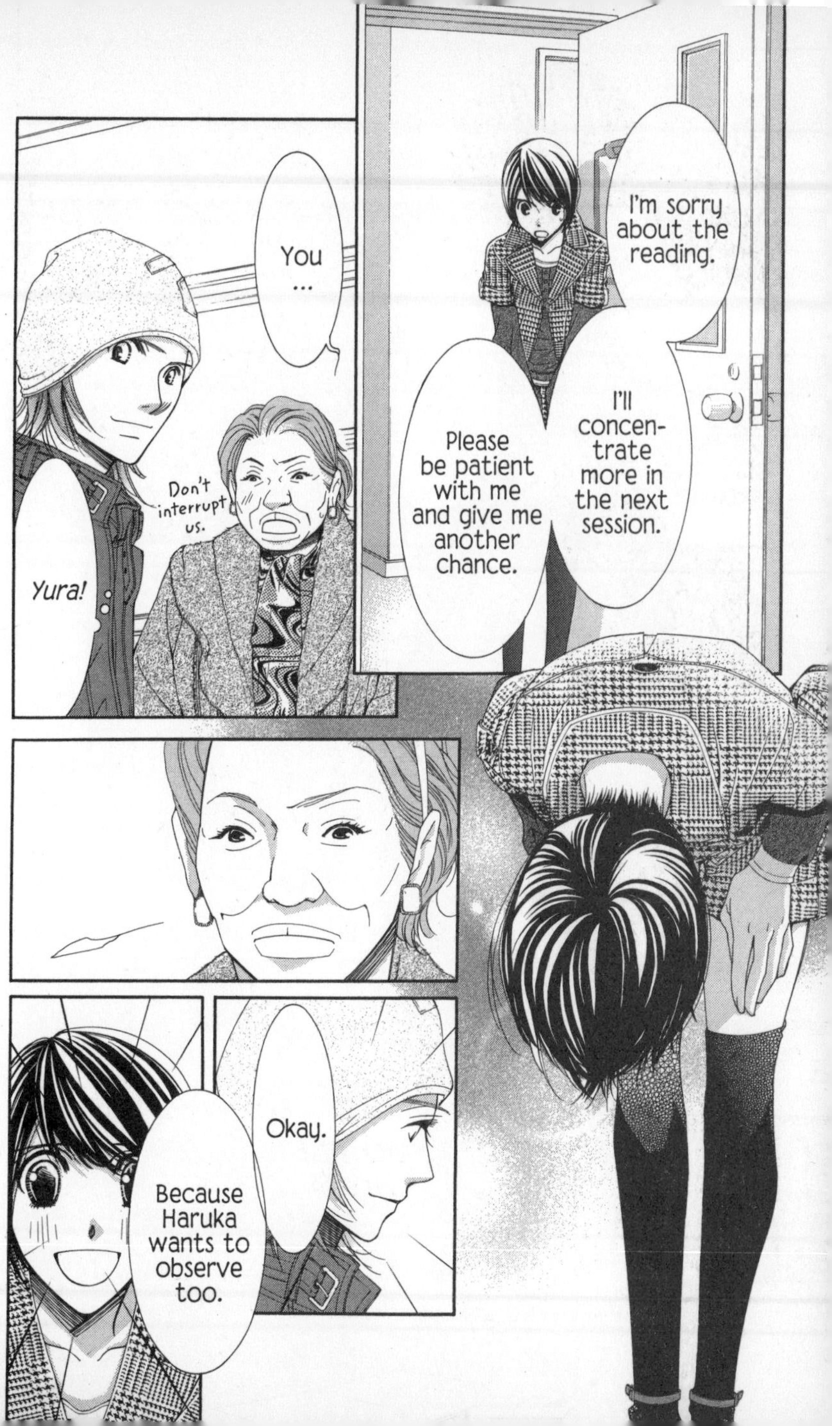
I'm sorry about the reading.
I'll concen-trate more in the next session.
Please be patient with me and give me another chance.
You ...
Don't interrupt us.
Yura!
Okay.
Because Haruka wants to observe too.

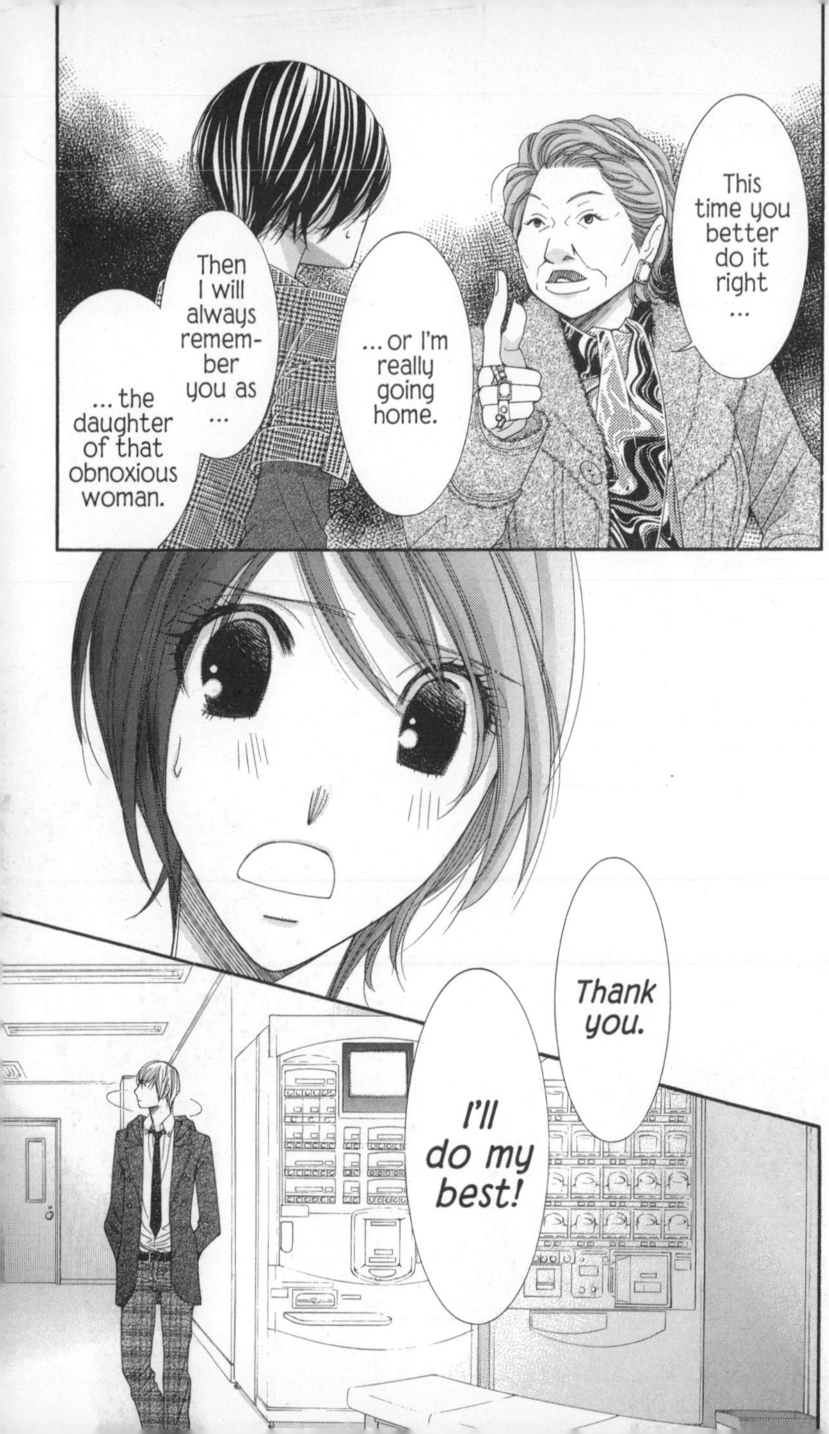

This time you better do it right ...
... or I'm really going home.
Then I will always remem-ber you as ...
... the daughter of that obnoxious woman.
Thank you.
I'll do my best!

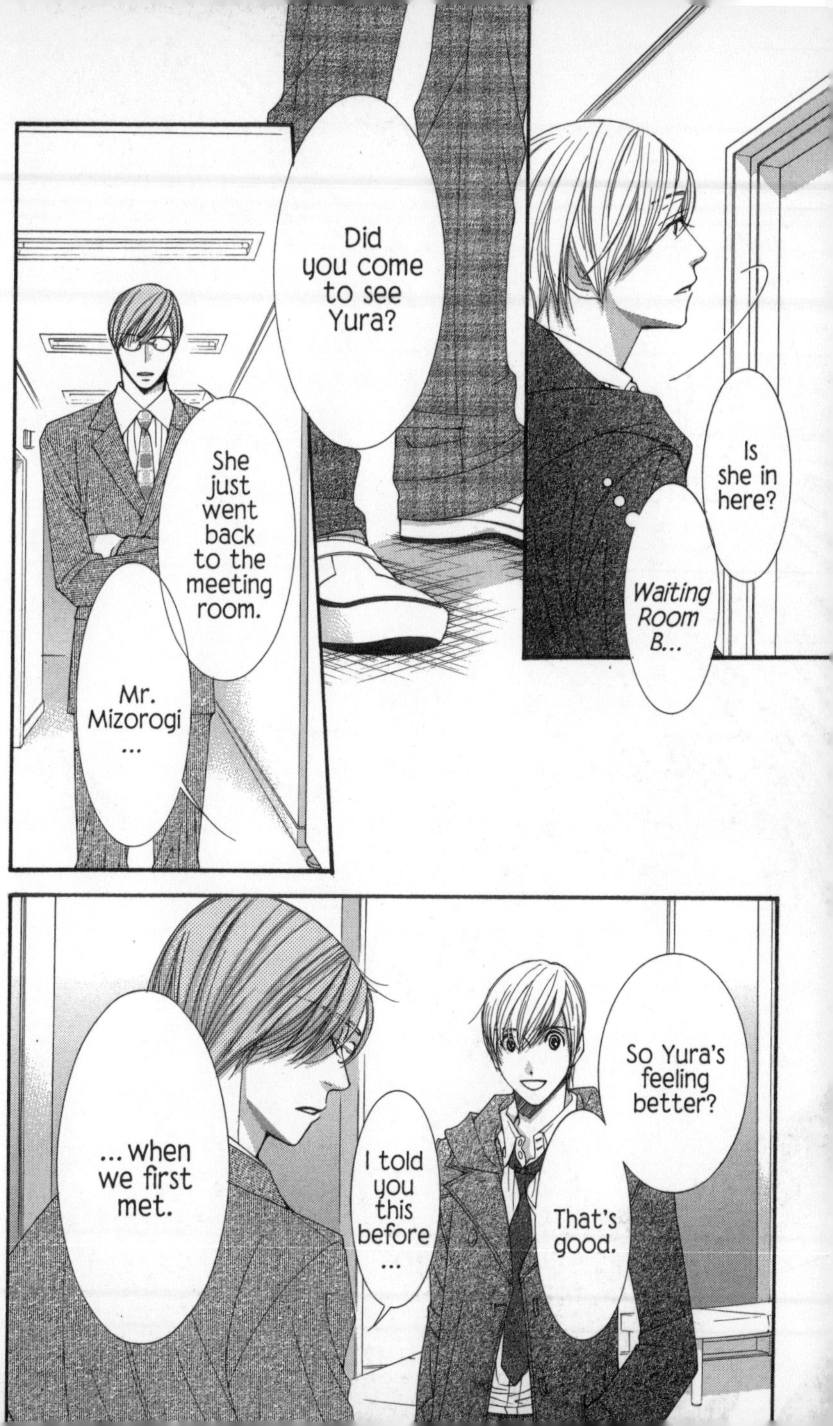
Is she in here?
Waiting Room B...
Did you come to see Yura?
She just went back to the meeting room.
Mr. Mizorogi...
So Yura's feeling better?
That's good.
I told you this before...
...when we first met.

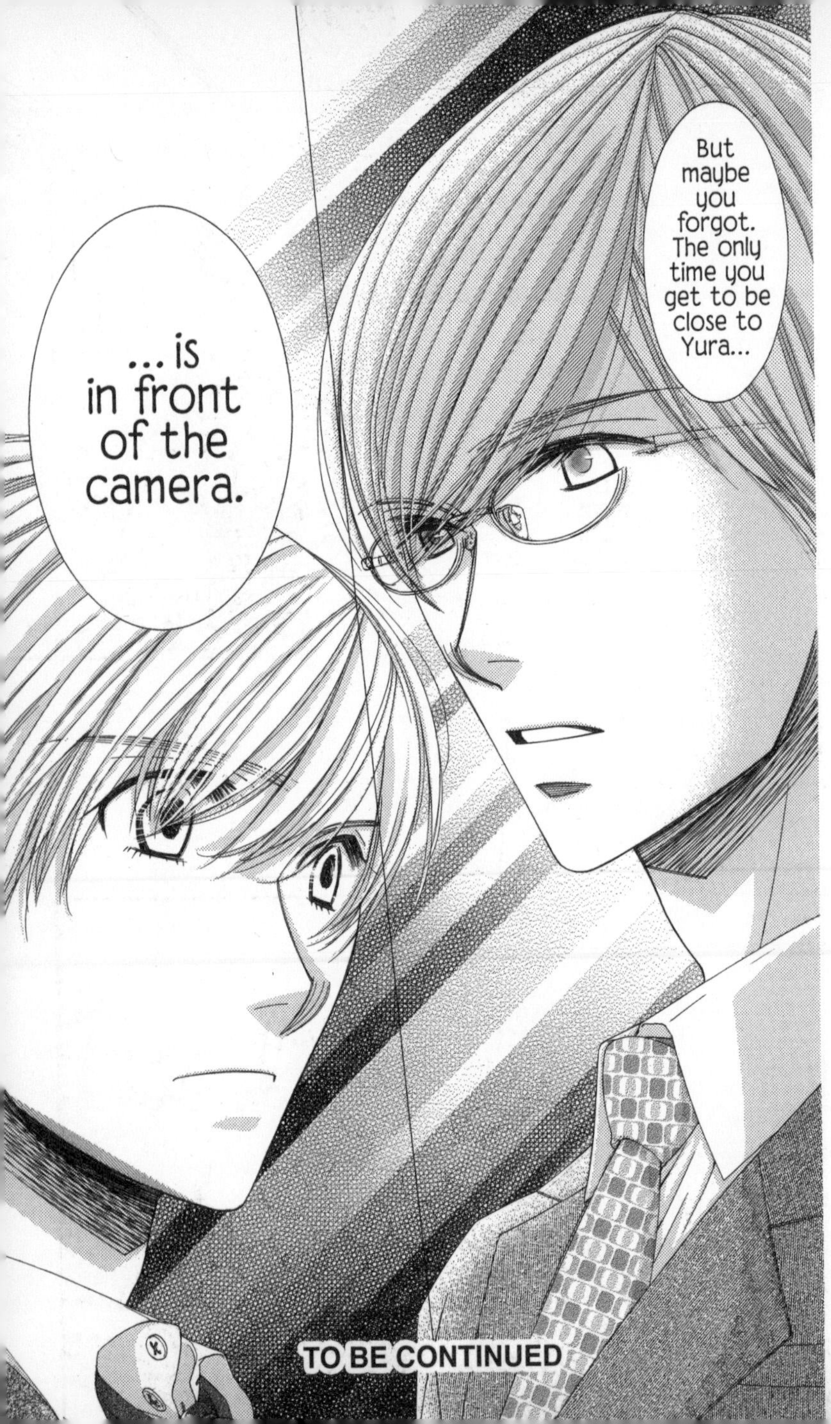
But maybe you forgot. The only time you get to be close to Yura...
...is in front of the camera.
TO BE CONTINUED

MIKI AIHARA

Here we go with the second volume.
I continue to put effort into the magazine series as
well, with the help of many people. I've also been
keeping up with my blog, which I started when the
first volume came out. At that time, I was thinking
about writing for only three months...but these
days I wonder if I should continue a little longer.

Miki Aihara, from Shizuoka Prefecture, is the creator
of the manga series *Hot Gimmick*. She began her
career with *Lip Conscious!*, which ran in *Bessatsu
Shojo Comic*. Her other work includes *Seiten Taisei*
(The Clear, Wide Blue Sky), *So Bad!*, and *Tokyo Boys
& Girls*. She's a Gemini whose hobbies include movies
and shopping.

Honey Hunt
VOL. 2

The Shojo Beat Manga Edition

This manga volume contains material that was originally published in English in *Shojo Beat* magazine, February 2009–June 2009 issues. Artwork in the magazine may have been altered slightly from what is presented in this volume.

STORY AND ART BY MIKI AIHARA

English Adaptation/Liz Forbes
Translation/Ari Yasuda, HC Language Solutions, Inc.
Touch-up Art & Lettering/Rina Mapa
Design/Ronnie Casson
Editor/Kit Fox

Editor in Chief, Books/Alvin Lu
Editor in Chief, Magazines/Marc Weidenbaum
VP, Publishing Licensing/Rika Inouye
VP, Sales & Product Marketing/Gonzalo Ferreyra
VP, Creative/Linda Espinosa
Publisher/Hyoe Narita

Printed in Canada

Published by VIZ Media, LLC
P.O. Box 77010
San Francisco, CA 94107

Shojo Beat Manga Edition
10 9 8 7 6 5 4 3 2 1
First printing, July 2009

store.viz.com

PARENTAL ADVISORY
HONEY HUNT is rated T+ for Older Teen and is recommended for ages 16 and up. This volume contains suggestive themes and adult situations.

RATED T+ FOR OLDER TEEN

ratings.viz.com

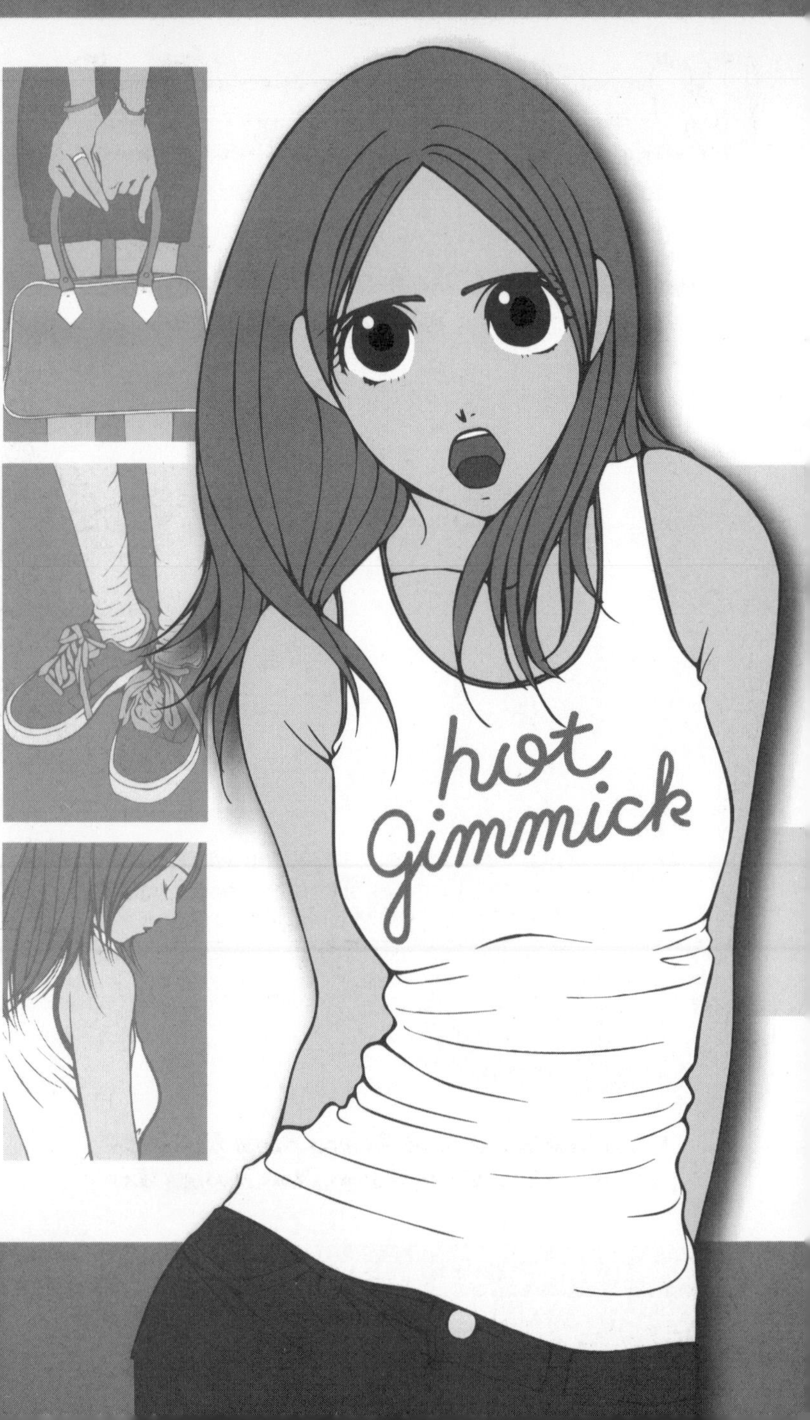
hot
Gimmick